JACKSON & POWELL ON
PROFESSIONAL LIABILITY

VOLUMES IN THE COMMON LAW LIBRARY

Arlidge, Eady & Smith on Contempt
Benjamin's Sale of Goods
Bowstead & Reynolds on Agency
Bullen & Leake & Jacob's Precedents of Pleadings
Charlesworth & Percy on Negligence
Chitty on Contracts
Clerk & Lindsell on Torts
Gatley on Libel and Slander
Goff & Jones, The Law of Restitution
Jackson & Powell on Professional Negligence
McGregor on Damages
Phipson on Evidence

The Common Law Library

JACKSON & POWELL ON PROFESSIONAL LIABILITY

FOURTH SUPPLEMENT TO THE EIGHTH EDITION

Law stated as at 28 September 2020

SWEET & MAXWELL

THOMSON REUTERS

Published in 2021 by Thomson Reuters,
trading as Sweet & Maxwell. Thomson Reuters is registered in England &
Wales, Company No. 1679046.
Registered office and address for service: 5 Canada Square, Canary Wharf,
London E14 5AQ.

For further information on our products and services, visit *http://
www.sweetandmaxwell.co.uk.*

Computerset by Sweet & Maxwell.
Printed and bound by CPI Group (UK) Ltd, Croydon, CR0 4YY.
A CIP catalogue record of this book is available from the British Library.

Main Work: 978-0-414-05752-4

Fourth Supplement (print): 978-0-414-08287-8

Fourth Supplement (ebook): 978-0-414-08289-2

Fourth Supplement (print and ebook): 978-0-414-08288-5

FSC
www.fsc.org
MIX
Paper from
responsible sources
FSC® C013604

BEN PATTEN QC, BA
Of the Middle Temple

AMANDA SAVAGE QC, LLB, BCL
Of the Middle Temple, Barrister

BEN SMILEY, MA
Of the Middle Temple, Barrister

JAMIE SMITH QC, MA
Of Lincoln's Inn

GEORGE SPALTON, MA, LLM
Of Lincoln's Inn, Barrister

DAVID TURNER QC, MA
Of Gray's Inn

CAN YEGINSU, MA, LLB, LLM
Of the Inner Temple, Barrister

CONSULTANT EDITORS

THE RT. HON. SIR RUPERT JACKSON, MA, LLB
Formerly one of Her Majesty's Lord Justices of Appeal
Of the Middle Temple

JOHN L. POWELL QC, MA, LLB
Of the Middle Temple

HOW TO USE THIS SUPPLEMENT

This is the Fourth Supplement to the Eighth Edition of *Jackson & Powell on Professional Liability* and has been compiled according to the structure of the main volume.

At the beginning of each chapter of this Supplement, a mini table of contents of the sections in the main volume has been included. Where a heading in this table of contents has been marked with a square pointer, this indicates that there is relevant information in this Supplement to which the reader should refer. Material that is new to the Cumulative Supplement is indicated by the symbol ■. Material that has been included from the previous supplement is indicated by the symbol □.

Within each chapter, updating information is referenced to the relevant paragraph in the main volume.

TABLE OF CONTENTS

TABLE OF CASES

TABLE OF STATUTES

References in bold indicate where legislation is reproduced in full.

NEW ZEALAND

TABLE OF STATUTORY INSTRUMENTS

TABLE OF PRACTICE DIRECTIONS

CHAPTER 2

DUTIES AND OBLIGATIONS

1. PROFESSIONAL LIABILITY

(a) Positive Duties

Replace footnote 10 with:

2-003   [10] *Montgomery v Lanarkshire Health Board* [2015] UKSC 11; [2015] A.C. 1430 (departing from *Sidaway v Friern Hospital Management Committee* [1957] 1 W.L.R. 582 HL). Per Lords Kerr and Reed at [87]:

"The doctor is … under a duty to take reasonable care to ensure that the patient is aware of any material risks involved in any recommended treatment, and of any reasonable alternative or variant treatments. The test of materiality is whether, in the circumstances of the particular case, a reasonable person in the patient's position would be likely to attach significance to the risk, or the doctor is or should reasonably be aware that the particular patient would be likely to attach significance to it."

See further paras 13-014 to 13-020 below.

Kerr J in *O'Hare v Coutts & Co* [2016] EWHC 2224 (QB) similarly held that the *Bolam* test did not apply to "the required extent of communication between financial adviser and client to ensure the client understands the advice and the risks attendant on a recommended investment" (at [204]): see further para.15-023 below. In a case concerning negligent advice on conveyancing issues, the Court of Appeal of Northern Ireland, having referred to *Montgomery*, stated

"a solicitor is bound to take reasonable care to ensure that the client understands the material legal risks that arise in any transaction which the client has asked the solicitor to handle on his behalf … the test of materiality is whether a reasonable client would be likely to attach significance to the risks arising which should be reasonably foreseeable to the competent solicitor."

See *Baird v Hastings* [2015] NICA 22 at [34] per Girvan LJ.

See too *Thomas v Triodos Bank NV* [2017] EWHC 314 (QB); [2018] 1 B.C.L.C. 530 where HH Judge Havelock-Allan QC considered whether "the Montgomery formulation" applied to the defendant bank's duty to give information to its customers regarding their desire to fix interest rates under a commercial lending arrangement. He stated that, if there were doubt as to how far the defendant should go in informing the customers, he would resort to that formulation; but the need to do so was much reduced (compared to *O'Hare v Coutts & Co* [2016] EWHC 2224 (QB)) by the factors that: (a) the bank's duty was to give information and not advice; and (b) there was a broad consensus between the parties' banking experts as to the scope of the information to be given—see [87] and [88].

In *Barker v Baxendale Walker Solicitors* [2017] EWCA Civ 2056; [2018] 1 W.L.R. 1905 the Court of Appeal held that the *Bolam* test applied to a solicitor advising on the efficacy of a tax avoidance scheme. *Montgomery* was distinguished on the basis that in *Barker* "legal advice was the very service which was being provided and which was being relied upon. There can be no separation between the advice and any appropriate caveats as to risk" (per Asplin LJ at [64]). The Court left open whether Kerr J's approach in *O'Hare* was correct (per Asplin LJ at [64]).

(c) Regulation and Professional Standards

Replace footnote 18 with:

[18] See *Clerk & Lindsell on Torts*, 22nd edn, Ch.9.   **2-010**

2. CONTRACTUAL LIABILITY

(a) The Position at Common Law

Replace footnote 29 with:

[29] See the analysis of Jackson LJ in *Minkin v Landsberg* [2015] EWCA Civ 1152; [2016] 1 W.L.R. 1489   **2-014** at [38] as to the vexed question of what work may be said to be "reasonably incidental" to the agreed engagement. Jackson LJ expressed himself in "more cautious" terms as to whether the professional person carries a burden to document a narrower than "normal" retainer—see [39]. cf. *Hurlingham Estates Ltd v Wilde & Partners* [1997] 1 Lloyd's Rep. 525 at 526 per Lightman J. In determining what is "reasonably incidental", regard may be had to the level of the defendant's fees: see *Thomas v Hugh James Ford Simey Solicitors* [2017] EWCA Civ 1303; [2018] P.N.L.R. 5 per Jackson LJ at [43]; and *Bank of Ireland v Watts Group Plc* [2017] EWHC 1667 (TCC); 173 Con. L.R. 240 per Coulson J at [61]. In *Lyons v Fox Williams LLP* [2018] EWCA Civ 2347; [2019] P.N.L.R. 9, Patten LJ stated that *Minkin* is not authority "for the proposition that the solicitor is required to carry out investigative tasks in areas he has not been asked to deal with however beneficial to the client that might in fact have turned out to be" (at [42]).

3. TORTIOUS LIABILITY

(a) The Tort of Negligence

Replace footnote 65 with:

[65] For a general discussion of the tort of negligence, which is beyond the scope of this book, see   **2-024** *Charlesworth & Percy on Negligence*, 14th edn.

(b) Theoretical Basis for the Duty of Care

(iv)   The Threefold Test

Analysis

Replace footnote 114 with:

[114] [1990] 2 A.C. 605. Discussed in paras 17-054 to 17-063, below. Paragraphs 2–042 to 2–046 were   **2-042** referred to with apparent approval by the Court of Appeal in *CGL Group Ltd v Royal Bank of Scotland Plc* [2017] EWCA Civ 1073; [2018] 1 W.L.R. 2137 per Beatson LJ at [59] (footnote 7).

Summary

After paragraph 2-046, add new paragraph 2-046A:

2-046A   However, the practical limitations of this approach had been underlined from the start.[122A]

[122A] See further paras 2-064A to 2-064G, below.

(v)   The Exclusive Approach

Replace paragraph 2-048 (to incorporate amendment to footnote 124) with:

2-048   Lord Oliver grappled with these problems in *Caparo Industries Plc v Dickman*[123] in the passage quoted in para.2-044, above. He recognised that it was impossible to state "some general principle which will determine liability in an infinite variety of circumstances".[124] He went on to commend the incremental approach stated by Brennan J in *Sutherland Shire Council v Heyman*.[125]

[123] [1990] 2 A.C. 605.

[124] See further the later decisions of the Supreme Court in *Michael v Chief Constable of South Wales* [2015] UKSC 2; [2015] A.C. 1732, *Robinson v Chief Constable of West Yorkshire Police* [2018] UKSC 4; [2018] A.C. 736, *NRAM Ltd v Steel* [2018] UKSC 13; [2018] 1 W.L.R. 1190, *James-Bowen v Commissioner of Police of the Metropolis* [2018] UKSC 40; [2018] 1 W.L.R. 4021, and *Playboy Club London Ltd v Banca Nazionale del Lavoro SpA* [2018] UKSC 43; [2018] 1 W.L.R. 4041 discussed in paras 2-064A to 2-064G below.

[125] (1984–1985) 157 C.L.R. 424.

Relationship between the incremental approach and the threefold test

Replace paragraph 2-051 with:

2-051   Despite the words of caution sounded by Lord Bridge and Lord Oliver in *Caparo Industries Plc v Dickman*,[138] the threefold test described in paras 2-041 to 2-046A, above was not supplanted by an incremental approach. Rather the incremental approach was seen as providing guidance to the application of the threefold test and a warning of the potential danger of deciding whether a particular duty of care is owed simply by reference to general statements of principle.[139] It can also be analysed as providing an alternative approach which should lead to the same answer in any given case.[139A]

[138] [1995] 2 A.C. 605. See paras 2-043, 2-044 and 2-048, above.

[139] "The incremental approach also has been the subject of criticism but in the absence of some guiding principle of universal application, this approach ensures that developments in the law will take place in measured steps": *Bank of Credit and Commerce International (Overseas) Ltd v Price Waterhouse (No.2)* [1998] P.N.L.R. 564 at 586 per Sir Brian Neill. In *Reeman v Department of Transport* [1997] P.N.L.R. 618, Phillips LJ, having said that the threefold test was the correct approach, said at 625A–625C:

> "When confronted with a novel situation the court does not, however, consider these matters in isolation. It does so by comparison with established categories of negligence to see whether the facts amount to no more than a small extension of a situation already covered by authority, or whether a finding of the existence of a duty of care would effect a significant extension of the law of negligence. Only in exceptional cases will the court accept that the interests of justice justify such an extension of the law."

[139A] See para.2-060, below.

(vi) Extensions of Hedley Byrne

Application of *Hedley Byrne* to parties in contractual relationship

Replace paragraph 2-057 with:

This question arose for decision in *Henderson v Merrett Syndicates Ltd*.[158] The names on a number of syndicates at Lloyd's brought actions against both their members' agents and managing agents in respect of massive losses which they had suffered. Saville J, the Court of Appeal and the House of Lords all held that, in addition to their various contractual duties, managing agents owed a duty of care in tort both to direct and indirect names to carry out their functions with reasonable skill and care. The principal speech was given by Lord Goff, with whom Lord Keith, Lord Mustill, Lord Nolan and Lord Browne-Wilkinson agreed. Lord Goff stated that the governing principle was that contained in *Hedley Byrne*. This established liability for words as well as deeds, and for pure economic loss as well as physical damage. The assumption of responsibility, although it had been criticised,[159] was "at least in cases such as the present" a crucial feature for establishing *Hedley Byrne* liability.[160] Towards the end of his discussion of general principle Lord Goff stated:

> "It follows that, once the case is identified as falling within the *Hedley Byrne* principle, there should be no need to embark upon any further enquiry whether it is 'fair, just and reasonable' to impose liability for economic loss—a point which is, I consider, of some importance in the present case."[161]

On that basis if a case can be brought within the *Hedley Byrne* principle by means of the incremental approach, it is not necessary to embark upon any other test. Only in a truly novel situation is there a need to consider whether it is "fair, just and reasonable" to impose liability.[162]

2-057

[158] [1995] 2 A.C. 145. Discussed in Ch.19. Further discussed by Powell in "Professional and client: the duty of care", published in Birks (ed), *Wrongs and Remedies in the Twenty-First Century* (Clarendon Press, 1996), pp.58–61.

[159] *Smith v Eric S Bush* [1990] 1 A.C. 831 at 862B–862F and 864H per Lord Griffiths; *Caparo Industries Plc v Dickman* [1990] 2 A.C. 605 at 628G per Lord Roskill. See also *Phelps v Hillingdon BC* [2001] 2 A.C. 619 at 654E per Lord Slynn: "The phrase means simply that the law recognises that there is a duty of care. It is not so much that responsibility is assumed as that it recognised or imposed by law." References to recent academic criticism are listed in the speech of Lord Steyn in *Williams v Natural Health Life Foods Ltd* [1998] 1 W.L.R. 830 at 837C–837D.

[160] *Henderson v Merrett* [1995] 2 A.C. 145 at 180–181.

[161] ibid. at 181.

[162] See paras 2-064A to 2-064G, below.

(vii) The Co-existence of Different Approaches

Three routes to the same destination

Replace footnote 181 with:

[181] 22nd edn, para.8–029.

2-063

After paragraph 2-064, add new sub-section (viiA) and new paragraphs 2-064A to 2-064G:

(viiA) Rejection of the Threefold Test as a Practical Guide

2-064A   By a series of recent cases the Supreme Court has rejected the proposition that *Caparo* is authority for a threefold approach of general application. First, in *Michael v Chief Constable of South Wales Police*[188A] Lord Toulson, with whom Lord Neuberger, Lord Mance, Lord Reed and Lord Hodge agreed, noted that Lord Bridge in *Caparo Industries Plc v Dickman*[188B] had added that the concepts of proximity and fairness "were not susceptible of any definition which would make them useful as practical tests, but were little more than labels to attach to features of situations which the law recognised as giving rise to a duty of care".[188C] Lord Toulson went on to state: "Paradoxically, [that part of Lord Bridge's speech set out at para.2-043, above] has sometimes come to be treated as a blueprint for deciding cases, despite the pains which the author took to make clear that it was not intended to be any such thing".[188D]

2-064B   Secondly, in *Robinson v Chief Constable of West Yorkshire Police*,[188E] the Supreme Court held that two police officers owed a duty of care to a passer-by who was injured when a scuffle broke out as the officers were seeking to arrest a suspect in a busy shopping street. Lord Reed, with whom Baroness Hale and Lord Hodge agreed, stated that "[t]he proposition that there is a *Caparo* test which applies to all claims in the modern law of negligence, and that in consequence the court will only impose a duty of care where it considers it fair, just and reasonable to do so on the particular facts, is mistaken".[188F] Lord Reed considered that Lord Bridge had applied the incremental approach in *Caparo Industries Plc v Dickman*,[188G] "and not a supposed tripartite test".[188H] As such, the role played by a consideration of what is "fair, just and reasonable" is confined to the exercise of the court's judgment when deciding whether a duty of care should be recognised in a novel type of case. Lord Reed explained the correct approach in this way:

> "Where the existence or non-existence of a duty of care has been established, a consideration of justice and reasonableness forms part of the basis on which the law has arrived at the relevant principles. It is therefore unnecessary and inappropriate to reconsider whether the existence of the duty is fair, just and reasonable (subject to the possibility that this court may be invited to depart from an established line of authority). Nor, a fortiori, can justice and reasonableness constitute a basis for discarding established principles and deciding each case according to what the court may regard as its broader merits. Such an approach would be a recipe for inconsistency and uncertainty ...
>
> It is normally only in a novel type of case, where established principles do not provide an answer, that the courts need to go beyond those principles in order to decide whether a duty of care should be recognised. Following the *Caparo* case, the characteristic approach of the common law in such situations is to develop incrementally and by analogy with established authority. The drawing of any analogy depends on identifying the legally significant features of the situations with which the earlier authorities were concerned. The courts also have to exercise judgment when deciding whether a duty of care should be recognised in a novel type of case. It is the exercise of judgment in those circumstances that involves consideration of what is 'fair, just and reasonable'."[188I]

2-064C   Thirdly, in *NRAM Ltd v Steel*,[188J] the Supreme Court decided that a mortgage lender was not owed a duty of care by its borrower's solicitor, who had sent an email to the lender wrongly confirming that the entirety of the secured indebtedness was to be paid off by a sale of commercial property. Referring both to *Michael v Chief Constable of South Wales Police*[188K] and to *Robinson v Chief Constable of*

West Yorkshire Police,[188L] the Court reaffirmed that "the House in the *Caparo Industries* case did not endorse the threefold test".[188M]

In the light of these decisions it is clear, if it was not before, that the threefold **2-064D** test referred to in *Caparo Industries Plc v Dickman*[188N] is not to be adopted as a practical means of deciding whether a duty of care is owed. Instead, the Supreme Court has identified the voluntary assumption of responsibility test as the "foundation" for determining whether a duty of care is owed. It was described as such by the Supreme Court in both *NRAM v Steel*[188O] and in *Playboy Club London Ltd v Banca Nazionale del Lavoro SpA*.[188P] In most professional negligence cases, the extended *Hedley Byrne* principle should therefore be capable of yielding the principled answer to whether a duty of care is owed. However, the *Hedley Byrne* approach will not be apposite in all situations. Certain fact-patterns will be more suitable to the incremental approach.

In cases having fact-patterns that are the same or substantially the same as exist- **2-064E** ing cases where a duty has been recognised, the extended *Hedley Byrne* principle and the incremental approach may be viewed as two discrete approaches. In truly novel situations, the two approaches share common characteristics. Once it has been determined that there is no relevant category of existing case, both approaches require the courts to exercise a judgment whether an extra step in the law is justified. So, in *NRAM v Steel*,[188Q] the Court stated, as to the extended *Hedley Byrne* principle, that "it may require cautious incremental development in order to fit cases to which it does not readily apply."[188R]

As regards the incremental approach, this by definition involves a close **2-064F** consideration of the justifiability of imposing a duty of care in a novel category of case. In *Robinson v Chief Constable of West Yorkshire Police*,[188S] Lord Reed stated:

> "Properly understood, the *Caparo* case thus achieves a balance between legal certainty and justice. In the ordinary run of cases, courts consider what has been decided previously and follow the precedents (unless it is necessary to consider whether the precedents should be departed from). In cases where the question whether a duty of care arises has not previously been decided, the courts will consider the closest analogies in the existing law, with a view to maintaining the coherence of the law and the avoidance of inappropriate distinctions. They will also weigh up the reasons for and against imposing liability, in order to decide whether the existence of a duty of care would be just and reasonable."[188T]

As part of its examination of the appropriateness of taking the incremental step, **2-064G** whether applying the extended *Hedley Byrne* approach or the incremental test, the courts will give consideration to what is fair, just and reasonable. This approach was adopted by the Supreme Court in *James-Bowen v Commissioner of Police of the Metropolis*.[188U] There, the Court held that no duty of care was owed by the Commissioner to serving officers in respect of the terms of settlement of a civil claim brought by a suspected terrorist who alleged assault by the officers. The case was considered by the Supreme Court to be "very clearly one in which it is sought to extend a duty of care to a new situation".[188V] As such, the Court's approach was (1) to gauge how closely the facts were to a case in which a duty has been held to exist and (2) to test the proposed duty "against considerations of legal policy and judgment will have to be exercised with particular regard to both the achievement of justice in the particular case and the coherent development of the law".[188W]

[188A] [2015] UKSC 2; [2015] A.C. 1732. For the facts and further analysis see para.2-092, below.

[188B] [1990] 2 A.C. 605.

[188C] ibid. at [103].

188D ibid. at [103].

188E [2018] UKSC 4; [2018] A.C. 736.

188F ibid. at [21].

188G [1990] 2 A.C. 605.

188H [2018] UKSC 4; [2018] A.C. 736 at [25].

188I ibid. at [26]-[27].

188J [2018] UKSC 13; [2018] 1 W.L.R. 1190.

188K [2015] UKSC 2; [2015] A.C. 1732.

188L [2018] UKSC 4; [2018] A.C. 736.

188M ibid. at [22] per Lord Wilson (with whom the other members of the Court agreed).

188N [1990] 2 A.C. 605.

188O [2018] UKSC 13; [2018] 1 W.L.R. 1190 at [24] per Lord Wilson.

188P [2018] UKSC 43; [2018] 1 W.L.R. 4041 at [7] per Lord Sumption (with whom all the other members of the Court agreed). The Court declined to impose a duty of care upon a bank giving a reference as to a customer's financial good standing.

188Q [2018] UKSC 13; [2018] 1 W.L.R. 1190.

188R ibid. at [24] per Lord Wilson.

188S [2018] UKSC 4; [2018] A.C. 736.

188T Ibid. at [29].

188U [2018] UKSC 40; [2018] 1 W.L.R. 4021.

188V ibid. at [23] per Lord Lloyd-Jones (with whom the other members of the Court agreed).

188W ibid. at [23]. See too the judgment of Lord Reed in *N v Poole BC* [2019] UKSC 25; [2020] A.C. 780 at [64].

(viii) *Commonwealth Approaches to Duty of Care Issues*

New Zealand

Replace footnote 198 with:

2-068

198 *North Shore City Council v Body Corporate 188529* [2010] NZSC 158; [2011] 2 N.Z.L.R. 289 at [26] per Tipping J, giving the judgment of Blanchard, Tipping, McGrath and Anderson JJ. Elias J gave a concurring judgment. See also *North Shore City Council v Att-Gen* [2012] NZSC 49; [2012] N.Z.L.R. 341 and *Body Corporate No.207624* [2012] NZSC 83; [2013] 3 N.Z.L.R. 341 and, in particular, the judgment of Blanchard, McGrath and William Young JJ at [147]–[161] for a helpful review of the approach adopted to deciding whether a duty of care is owed in a novel situation. In *Invercargill City Council v Southland Indoor Leisure Centre Charitable Trust* [2017] NZSC 190; [2018] 1 N.Z.L.R. 278 the New Zealand Supreme Court disagreed with the conclusion of the Court of Appeal in that case that the rationale identified in earlier cases for imposing a duty of care on the certifying council "does not extend to protecting the economic interests of a commissioning owner which has chosen to protect itself against physical damage and economic loss by engaging professional advisers and contractors" per Harrison and Cooper JJ at [190]. The Supreme Court considered the issue of vulnerability fell to be looked at not in relation to the claimant in the case at hand but in relation to likely claimants as a class. See the judgment of the Court at [86].

Canada

After paragraph 2-075, add new paragraph 2-075A:

2-075A
    The modified *Anns* approach was endorsed by the Supreme Court of Canada in *Deloitte & Touche LLP v Livent Inc.*220A By a majority of 4:3 the Court upheld part of the trial judge's ruling that auditors owed a duty of care to a company the subject of a statutory audit and losses arising from the auditors' failure to identify the fraudulent operation of the company fell within the scope of the duty. The analysis of the majority placed emphasis on the following aspects of the modified *Anns* test:

(1) as regards the first stage, proximity is more usefully to be considered before foreseeability[220B]; (2) the fact of and nature of the defendant's undertaking of responsibility to the claimant and the reliance by the claimant are the determinative factors in the proximity analysis[220C]; (3) in the event that proximity is found on the basis of an established category, the second stage does not fall for consideration[220D]; and (4) only in rare cases should liability be denied at the second stage, once the first stage indicates that a duty of care should be recognised.[220E]

[220A] [2017] SCC 63; [2017] 2 S.C.R. 855. See further Ch.17, below.

[220B] ibid. at [24] per Gascon and Brown JJ (delivering the judgment also of Karakatsanis and Rowe JJ).

[220C] ibid. at [30].

[220D] ibid. at [28].

[220E] ibid. at [41].

Australia

Replace footnote 237 with:

[237] ibid. at [201]–[202]. Gummow J's reference to "salient features" was taken from the judgment of Stephen J in *Caltex Oil (Australia) Pty Ltd v The Dredge Willemstad* (1976) 136 C.L.R. 529 at 576–577. Recent Australian cases show a tendency to examine the applicability, on the facts of each case, of 17 "salient features" identified by Allsop P in *Caltex Refineries (QLD) Pty Ltd v Stavar* [2009] NSWCA 258; (2009) 75 N.S.W.L.R. 649 at [103]. However, the *Stavar* features must not be treated as a "shopping list"—see *Strategic Formwork Pty Ltd v Hitchen* [2018] NSWCA 54 per Basten JA at [62].

2-078

Replace paragraph 2-079 (to incorporate new text following "identify guiding principles." at the end of the paragraph and an amendment to footnote 244) with:

In *Sullivan v Moody*,[238] the High Court of Australia held that medical practitioners and others investigating allegations of child abuse did not owe a duty of care in tort to the relations of the children. They also held that the threefold test did not apply in Australia.[239] It is now clear that "proximity" has ceased to be the test in Australia.[240] More recently, in *Woolcock Street Investments Pty Ltd v CDG Pty Ltd*[241] the High Court of Australia has identified "vulnerability" as an important requirement, its significance having emerged from the decisions in *Caltex Oil (Australia) Pty Ltd v The Dredge Willemstad*[242] and *Perre v Apand Pty Ltd*.[243] "Vulnerability" refers to the injured party's inability to protect himself from the defendant's carelessness, either entirely or so that any resulting loss would fall on the defendant.[244] However, this is not put forward as a universal test. Australia appears to have abandoned any single, simple "test" and to be applying an incremental approach while still seeking to identify guiding principles. An incremental duty of care is unlikely to be recognised if it results in a lack of coherence in the law, considered as a whole.[244A]

2-079

[238] [2001] HCA 59; (2001) 183 A.L.R. 404.

[239] Although Kirby J supported it in *Graham Barclay Oysters Pty Ltd v Ryan* [2002] HCA 54 at [229]–[244].

[240] See also *Woolcock Street Investments Pty Ltd v CDG Pty Ltd* [2004] HCA 16; (2004) 216 C.L.R. 515 at [18] in the judgment of Gleeson CJ, Gummow, Hayne and Heydon JJ. Indeed, so firm is the rejection of "proximity" that in *Imbree v McNeilly* [2008] HCA 40 the High Court of Australia overturned its earlier decision in *Cook v Cook* [1986] HCA 73; (1986) 162 C.L.R. 376, which has been based upon "proximity", observing that it was based upon "reasoning that does not accord with subsequent decisions of this Court denying the utility of that concept as a determinant of duty".

[241] [2004] HCA 16; [2005] B.L.R. 92.

[242] (1976) 136 C.L.R. 529.

[243] [1999] HCA 36; (1999) 198 C.L.R. 180.

[244] [2004] HCA 16 at [23] in the judgment of Gleeson CJ, Gummow, Hayne and Heydon JJ, [80] in the judgment of McHugh J, [168] in the judgment of Kirby J and [222] in the judgment of Callinan J. The issue of "vulnerability" was taken into account by the Supreme Court of the Australian Capital Territory in *Monaghan v Australian Capital Territory (No 2)* [2016] ACTSC 352, as one of the 17 "salient features" referred to by Allsop P in *Caltex Refineries (Qld) Pty Ltd v Stavar* [2009] NSWCA 258; (2009) 75 N.S.W.L.R. 649 (New South Wales Court of Appeal)—see Mossop AsJ at [85]–[107].

[244A] See the summary in the judgment of Refshauge J in *Corkhill v Commonwealth of Australia (No.3)* [2018] ACTSC 87 (Supreme Court of the Australian Capital Territory) at [416]–[423].

(ix)   Analysis

Limited role of statements of general principle

After "closely analogous decision." at the end of the paragraph, add new footnote 252A:

2-081   [252A] See the recent approach of the Supreme Court discussed at paras 2-064A to 2-064G, above.

The underlying principles

Replace footnote 275 with:

2-086   [275] *Dorset Yacht Co Ltd v Home Office* [1970] A.C. 1004 at 1058 per Lord Diplock. Lord Diplock was discussing the judicial approach to questions of public policy when deciding whether a duty of care was owed, but the principle is the same.

See also *D v East Berkshire Community NHS Trust* [2005] UKHL 23; [2005] 2 A.C. 373 at [100] per Lord Rodger and the discussion of the recent Supreme Court cases at paras 2-064A to 2-064G, above.

The "just and reasonable" question

After "purely pragmatic considerations." at the end of the paragraph, add new footnote 289A:

2-090   [289A] See the recent approach of the Supreme Court discussed at paras 2-064A to 2-064G, above.

Assumption of responsibility and the extended *Hedley Byrne* principle

After "taken so far." at the end of the paragraph, add new footnote 309A:

2-092   [309A] Albeit the Supreme Court has stated in recent cases that the assumption of responsibility test is the foundation for determining whether a duty of care is owed. It has also rejected the threefold test as a practical means of deciding whether a duty of care is owed. See paras 2-064A to 2-064G, above.

After paragraph 2-092, add new paragraph 2-092A:

2-092A   In *Customs and Excise Commissioners v Barclays Bank Plc*,[309B] Lord Mance identified at [93] "two core categories of case" where the assumption of responsibility test was particularly useful, namely: where there was a fiduciary relationship; and where the defendant has voluntarily answered a question or tenders skilled advice or services in circumstances where he knows or ought to know that an identified claimant will rely on his answers or advice. In *Burgess v Lejonvarn*,[309C] the Court of Appeal applied this rationalisation when endorsing the trial judge's use of the assumption of responsibility test to determine whether an architect, who had not been retained by her clients, nonetheless owed to them a duty of care in relation to garden landscaping works (he held she did)—see Hamblen LJ at [59]–[61].

[309B] [2006] UKHL 28; [2007] 1 A.C. 181.

[309C] [2017] EWCA Civ 254; [2017] P.N.L.R. 25.

(c) Particular Situations

(i) Public and Local Authorities: Duty of Care and Statute

The tort of negligence and statute

Replace paragraph with:

2-093

Although the law of negligence is essentially judge-made, statute is increasingly important. Statute has clarified or changed existing common law duties,[311] provided the context in which common law issues have to be decided,[312] created statutory duties actionable by those for whose protection the statutory duty was enacted[313] or those specified as being entitled to bring claims,[314] and has created powers and duties to be exercised by a variety of public bodies which may give rise to common law duties of care.[315] In recent times, the courts have had to grapple with a number of novel claims against public bodies or authorities in which it has been alleged that the body or authority was in breach of a tortious duty of care in relation to the exercise (or non-exercise) of its powers, duties or functions.

[311] See, e.g. the Occupiers' Liability Act 1957 and the Occupiers' Liability Act 1984.

[312] See, e.g. *Caparo Industries Plc v Dickman* [1990] 2 A.C. 605, discussed in paras 17-054 to 17-063, below.

[313] *Clerk and Lindsell on Torts*, 23rd edn, paras 8–11 to 8–49 and see para.2-096, below.

[314] See, e.g. s.138D of the Financial Services and Markets Act 2000.

[315] *Clerk & Lindsell on Torts*, 23rd edn, Ch.13 and see paras 2-097 and 2-098, below.

Lord Browne-Wilkinson's classification

Replace footnote 318 with:

2-094

[318] See *Clerk & Lindsell on Torts*, 23rd edn, paras 13–132 to 13–142; and *Three Rivers DC v Governor and Company of the Bank of England (No.3)* [2003] 2 A.C. 1.

Breach of statutory duty simpliciter (Lord Browne-Wilkinson's first class)

Replace paragraph with:

2-096

Breach of statutory duty only gives rise to a private law cause of action if, on the true construction of the statute, the duty was imposed in order to protect a limited class of the public and Parliament intended to confer on members of that class a private right of action for breach of the duty.[322] Where there is an express provision in the statute, this principle is easy to apply.[323] It is more difficult to apply where there is no express provision. The most important factors in determining whether Parliament intended there to be a private right of action are:

1. Whether the provision was designed to protect a limited class of individuals.
2. Whether the statute provides for any other sanction for breach of the duty.
3. Whether the claimant has alternative remedies.

Of these, the first is the most important, with less weight being attached to the absence of other sanction or remedy. A broad analysis of the statute is required.[324] Analysis of the considerable body of authority as to the application of these factors is beyond the scope of this book.[325]

[322] ibid. at 731D–731E.

[323] Examples are given in para.8–11 of *Clerk & Lindsell on Torts*, 23rd edn.

[324] *Phelps v Hillingdon LBC* [2001] 2 A.C. 619 at 652D–652G per Lord Slynn.

[325] See *Clerk & Lindsell on Torts*, 23rd edn, paras 8–11 to 8–49.

The narrow scope for a common law duty of care

After paragraph 2-098, add new paragraphs 2-098A and 2-098B:

2-098A   In *N v Poole BC*,[343A] two children were the subject of harassment and abuse by a neighbouring family whilst living in accommodation provided by the defendant council under its powers as the local housing authority. A claim was brought against the council alleging breach of a common law duty of care deriving from the council's duty under statute. The Supreme Court held that no duty was owed. After an extensive review of authority, Lord Reed[343B] summarised the correct approach as follows:

> "... (1) that public authorities may owe a duty of care in circumstances where the principles applicable to private individuals would impose such a duty, unless such a duty would be inconsistent with, and is therefore excluded by, the legislation from which their powers or duties are derived; (2) that public authorities do not owe a duty of care at common law merely because they have statutory powers or duties, even if, by exercising their statutory functions, they could prevent a person from suffering harm; and (3) that public authorities can come under a common law duty to protect from harm in circumstances where the principles applicable to private individuals or bodies would impose such a duty, as for example where the authority has created the source of danger or has assumed a responsibility to protect the claimant from harm, unless the imposition of such a duty would be inconsistent with the relevant legislation."[343C]

[343A] [2019] UKSC 25; [2020] A.C. 780.

[343B] Giving a judgment with which all other members of the Supreme Court agreed.

[343C] Ibid. at [65].

2-098B   Lord Reed further made it clear that, in determining whether a public authority owes a duty of care in a given situation, it is incorrect to apply a blanket prohibition on the existence of a duty merely because policy issues arise. To this extent, the Supreme Court in *N v Poole BC*[343D] advocated a less rigid approach to that set out by the House of Lords in *X (Minors) v Bedfordshire CC*.[343E] Lord Reed set out the position as follows:

> "... in cases such as *Gorringe, Michael* and *Robinson*[343F] both the House of Lords and this court adopted a different approach (or rather, reverted to an earlier approach) to the question whether a public authority is under a duty of care. ... Rather than justifying decisions that public authorities owe no duty of care by relying on public policy, it has been held that even if a duty of care would ordinarily arise on the application of common law principles, it may nevertheless be excluded or restricted by statute where it would be inconsistent with the scheme of legislation under which the public authority is operating. In that way, the courts can continue to take into account, for example, the difficult choices which may be involved in the exercise of discretionary powers."[343G]

[343D] [2019] UKSC 25; [2020] A.C. 780.

[343E] [1995] 2 A.C. 633.

[343F] Respectively, *Gorringe v Calderdale MBC* [2004] UKHL 15; [2004] 1 W.L.R. 1057; *Michael v Chief Constable of South Wales Police* [2015] UKSC 2; [2015] A.C. 1732; and *Robinson v Chief Constable of West Yorkshire Police* [2018] UKSC 4; [2018] A.C. 736. See paras 2-064A to 2-064G, above.

[343G] [2019] UKSC 25; [2020] A.C. 780 at [75].

Supervisors and regulators

After paragraph 2-100, add new paragraph 2-100A:

2-100A   The *Yuen Kun Yeu* decision does not, however, establish that in no circumstances can a regulator be responsible for economic loss caused by a regulated person or company. This limitation upon the decision was recognised by the Court of Appeal in *Law Society v Schubert Murphy*,[360A] which concerned the defendant solicitor's claim against the Law Society for publishing on its "Find a Solicitor" website details of a solicitor who was in fact an imposter. Schubert Murphy asserted that they relied on the website details as vouchsafing the genuineness of the opposing solicitor in a conveyancing transaction. A mortgage fraud took place and the defendant was obliged to pay damages to the defrauded lender and sought contribution from the Law Society. Mitting J refused to accede to the Law Society's application to strike out the claim on the grounds that no duty of care was even arguably owed. The Court of Appeal, dismissing the appeal, held that the existence of the postulated duty turned in large part on "important issues of principle and policy", per Sir Terence Etherton MR at [57].

[360A] [2017] EWCA Civ 1295; [2018] P.N.L.R. 4.

(ii) Directors and Employees

Limited liability companies

Replace footnote 361 with:

[361] [1998] 1 W.L.R. 890. In *Fraser Turner Ltd v PricewaterhouseCoopers LLP* [2019] EWCA Civ 1290; [2019] P.N.L.R. 33 the *Williams* assumption of responsibility approach, and the emphasis upon communications that "crossed the line" between the claimant and the defendant, was applied and endorsed in a claim against joint administrators of a company—see the judgment of Sir Geoffrey Vos C at [70].   **2-102**

(iii) Sub-agents and Sub-contractors

Replace footnote 387 with:

[387] *Bowstead & Reynolds on Agency*, 21st edn, para.5–011.   **2-108**

4. THE STANDARD OF SKILL AND CARE

(b) Relevance of Defendant's Qualifications and Experience

After paragraph 2-134, add new paragraphs 2-134A and 2-134B:

The correct approach suggested above is consistent with the analysis of the Court **2-134A** of Appeal in *FB v Rana*.[483A] The claimant attended the A&E department of her local hospital where she was seen by a Senior House Officer (SHO), who failed to recognise symptoms indicative of pneumococcal meningitis. FB was discharged home, but sustained permanent brain damage. Her claim against the hospital trust was dismissed by Jay J, who considered that an A&E SHO could legitimately fail to recognise the significance of FB's presenting symptoms. The Court of Appeal, allowing FB's appeal, considered that the evidence indicated that the reasonably competent SHO would diagnose the developing meningitis. This was sufficient to dispose of the appeal, but Jackson LJ set out guiding principles to determining the correct standard of duty to apply (see [51]–[65], with which analysis Thirlwall and King LJJ agreed).

[483A] [2017] EWCA Civ 334; [2017] P.I.Q.R. P17.

First, the key issue relates to the "post" which the defendant professional "is **2-134B** fulfilling" at the time of the alleged breach of duty. This selects the appropriate standard, so if an SHO is performing a role usually occupied by an SHO (as was the case in *FB v Rana*) "the conduct ... must be judged by the standard of a reasonably competent SHO in an accident and emergency department". It follows that if, for example, an SHO is performing a role ordinarily occupied by a more senior doctor (in Jackson LJ's words, "acting up"), then "they are judged by reference to the post which they are fulfilling at the material time. The health authority or health trust is liable if the doctor whom it puts into a particular position does not possess (and therefore does not exercise) the requisite degree of skill for the task in hand". This approach also "involves leaving out of account the particular experience of the doctor or their length of service". Secondly, in claims brought in contract (even for a breach of an implied obligation to exercise reasonable skill and care), Jackson LJ mooted that "the standard of care required may be more nuanced". In particular, Jackson LJ cautioned that he did "not wish this judgment to be taken as accepting that in contractual professional negligence claims the particular experience and CV of the defendant should be ignored, as they must be in tortious claims".

(d)   Organisation Offering Professional Services

After "work in question." at the end of the paragraph, add new footnote 486A:

2-136   [486A] In *Dunhill v Brook & Co* [2018] EWCA Civ 505, Sir Brian Leveson P commented obiter that he saw merit in the proposition that the duty of care owed by a firm of solicitors to its client in relation to the conduct of litigation is fulfilled if a trainee is sent to court to accompany properly instructed counsel "provided he or she has instructions that a solicitor (preferably with the conduct of the case) is available if the need arises" (at [68]).

5.   Fiduciary Obligations

(a)   The Nature of Fiduciary Obligations

The nature of fiduciary obligations

Replace paragraph with:

2-145   So, in each case it is important to establish the extent of the trust, for that will define the extent to which equity will intervene.[516] The trust and confidence which gives rise to fiduciary obligations is not, or need not, be emotional. For example, a director owes fiduciary obligations to his company. In this sense it is to be contrasted with the confidence which is the basis for the equitable doctrine of undue influence. It is based upon reliance, but not the same sort of reliance which may underlie a tortious duty of care.[517] Nor is it simply reliance on another party to a contract to perform his obligations under it.[518] Rather it is the fact that the principal so relies on the fiduciary as to leave the principal vulnerable to any disloyalty by the fiduciary and so reliant on his good faith.[519] It follows that a commercial relationship at arm's length, with both parties on an equal footing, is unlikely to give rise to fiduciary obligations[520] and that a person may be subject to fiduciary obligations in relation to some activities but not others.[521] Per Morgan J in *Instant Access Properties Ltd v Rosser*[521A]:

> "...when a court is asked to determine whether a person owed fiduciary duties and the case is outside the paradigm cases where the principles are established, it is open to a court to hold that a person owed some of the usual fiduciary duties, but not all of them, or to hold that the specific fiduciary duty owed is a qualified form of the general fiduciary duty. This means that the court is not confined to an all or nothing response to the question."[521B]

[516] So, while usually a company director owes a fiduciary duty to the company to promote its interests, each case must be looked at on its facts. In *Plus Group Ltd v Pyye* [2002] EWCA Civ 370; [2002] 2 B.C.L.C. 201 the company had ceased to pay the director and had excluded him from its management.

The Court of Appeal held that he was not in breach of fiduciary duty when he set up his own company in the same area of business. Brooke LJ, with whom Jonathan Parker J agreed, said at [75]: "the facts and circumstances of each case must be carefully examined to see whether a fiduciary relationship exists in relation to the matter of which complaint is made."

[517] e.g. an engineer asked to design foundations may be relied upon by the building owner, but the engineer will not owe any fiduciary obligations as to the adequacy of his design.

[518] *Re Goldcorp Exchange Ltd* [1995] 1 A.C. 74 at 98C–98G. See further *Paper Reclaim Ltd v Aotearoa International Ltd* [2007] NZSC 26; [2007] 3 N.Z.L.R. 169 at [31]:

> "It is not enough to attract an obligation of loyalty that one party may have given up more than the other in entering into the contract or that the contract may be more advantageous for one party than the other. Nor is a relationship fiduciary in nature merely because the parties may be depending upon one another to perform the contract in its terms. That would be true of many commercial contracts which require cooperation. A fiduciary relationship will be found when one party is entitled to repose and does repose trust and confidence in the other. The existence of an agreement, express or implied, to act on behalf of another and thus to put the interests of the other before one's own is a frequent manifestation of a situation in which fiduciary obligations are owed. Partners are a classic example of parties in that situation. Their position is different from that of parties to a contract who may have to cooperate but are doing so for their separate advantages."

See also *Amaltal Corp Ltd v Maruha Corp* [2007] NZSC 40; [2007] 3 N.Z.L.R. 192 at [19]–[21].

[519] This sentence was cited with approval by Tomlinson LJ, with whom the other members of the Court of Appeal agreed, in *McWilliam v Norton Finance (UK) Ltd (t/a Norton Finance (In Liquidation))* [2015] EWCA Civ 186; [2015] P.N.L.R. 22 at [46]. In that case the vulnerability of the claimants, even though the defendant was not offering to advise them, resulted in a finding that there was a fiduciary relationship. The relationship between the parties had the necessary element of reliance. See also, *Hospital Products Ltd v United States Surgical Corp* (1984) 156 C.L.R. 41 at 142 per Dawson J:

> "There is, however, the notion underlying all the cases of fiduciary obligation that inherent in the nature of the relationship itself is a position of disadvantage or vulnerability on the part of one of the parties which causes him to place reliance upon the other and requires the protection of equity acting upon the conscience of that other … From that springs the requirement that a person under a fiduciary obligation shall not put himself in a position where his interest and duty conflict or, if conflict is unavoidable, shall resolve it in favour of duty and shall not, except by special arrangement, make a profit out of his position."

It follows that the directors of a company which is a fiduciary may themselves be subject to fiduciary obligations if there is the requisite kind of reliance or trust and confidence in them personally: see *JD Wetherspoon Plc v Van de Berg & Co Ltd* [2007] EWHC 1044 (Ch); [2007] P.N.L.R. 28 (Lewison J), applying *Satnam Investments Ltd v Dunlop Hayward Ltd* [1999] 3 All E.R. 652 CA. See also *Ratiu v Conway* [2005] EWCA Civ 1302; [2006] 1 All E.R. 571.

[520] (1984) 156 C.L.R. 41 at 170 per Gibbs CJ. See also *Halton International Inc (Holdings) SARL v Guernroy Ltd* [2005] EWHC 1968 (Ch); [2006] 1 B.C.L.C. 78, Patten J and *Dresna Pty Ltd v Linknarf Management Services Pty* [2006] FCAFC 193; (2006) 237 A.L.R. 687 where the Federal Court of Australia held that an arrangement between vendor and purchaser of a lease of a supermarket to pursue litigation to obtain the consent of the landlord to the assignment did not give rise to any fiduciary obligation. For a helpful review of the authorities as to whether and when one party to a commercial joint venture will be under fiduciary obligations to another, see the judgment of Lloyd LJ in *Ross River Ltd v Waveley Commercial Ltd* [2013] EWCA Civ 910; [2014] 1 B.C.L.C. 545 at [34]–[59].

[521] *New Zealand Netherlands Society "Oranje" Inc v Kuys* [1973] 2 All E.R. 1222 (PC), applied in *John Youngs Insurance Services Ltd v Aviva Insurance Service UK Ltd* [2011] EWHC 1515 (TCC), Ramsey J.

[521A] [2018] EWHC 756 (Ch); [2018] B.C.C. 751.

[521B] ibid., at [273].

The significance of the retainer

After "professional's retainer was." at the end of the paragraph, add:

It is for the claimant to prove the subject matter of that retainer. For instance, **2-146** where the claimant is a sophisticated and experienced litigator, the mere allegation that the defendant solicitor acted on a conveyance may not be sufficient to give rise to fiduciary obligations. The Court must be satisfied that the nature of the retainer gives rise to a real, not fanciful, conflict of interest.[525A]

[525A] This was the case in *Rosesilver Group Corp v Paton* [2017] EWCA Civ 158 in which the claimant failed to adduce any other evidence as to the defendant's role and the defendant solicitor's evidence was that it played no more than a routine conveyancing role in the sale of a property.

(c) Unauthorised Profits and Diversion of Opportunities

Replace paragraph 2-157 (to incorporate new text following "provide a remedy." at the end of the paragraph) with:

2-157   While acting in the interests of his principal a fiduciary may be able to further his own interests by profiting from his fiduciary position or by diverting to himself opportunities which properly belong to his principal. The classic case of the latter is *Keech v Sandford*,[565] where a trustee of a lease took the reversion personally, having failed to obtain a renewal for the trust, and was held to hold it on trust for the beneficiary. In the same way, a fiduciary whose role is to negotiate for a purchase on behalf of his principal cannot purchase for himself.[566] Nor can he exploit confidential information which he learns in his fiduciary capacity for his own benefit.[567] Again, it is important to establish the extent of the subject matter of the fiduciary obligation. In relation to bribes and secret commissions the courts have been willing to stretch the definition of fiduciary to provide a remedy.[568] Where two professionals contract with one another to divide up a secret commission, the courts have refused to award damages for breach of contract as between the professionals. This is because the courts would be permitting the claimant professional to profit from its own breach of fiduciary duty to its clients. This was the court's conclusion in *Medsted Associates Ltd v Canaccord Genuity Wealth (International) Ltd*.[568A]

[565] (1726) Sd. Cas, Ch. 61; cf. *Aberdeen Town Council v Aberdeen University* (1877) 2 App.Cas. 544. The principle was recently summarised by the Court of Appeal in *Gwembe Valley Development Co Ltd v Koshy (No.3)* [2003] EWCA Civ 1048; [2004] 1 B.C.L.C. 131 at [44]–[45] by reference to the judgment of Rich, Dixon and Evatt JJ in the High Court of Australia in *Furs Ltd v Tomkies* (1936) 54 C.L.R. 583 at 592 and to the decision of the House of Lords in *Regal (Hastings) Ltd v Gulliver* [1967] A.C. 134.

[566] *Lees v Nuttall* (1834) 2 My. & K. 891; and *Cook v Deeks* [1916] 1 A.C. 554.

[567] *Boardman v Phipps* [1967] 2 A.C. 46; and *Regal (Hastings) Ltd v Gulliver* [1967] 2 A.C. 134 (note). This may overlap with a claim for breach of confidence: see paras 2-168 to 2-196, below.
  A fiduciary who resigns from the position which gave rise to his fiduciary obligations and then exploits for himself an opportunity of which he learnt from his fiduciary position will be liable to account for the profits he makes, as will a company which he forms in order to exploit the opportunity: *CMS Dolphin Ltd v Simonet* [2001] 2 B.C.L.C. 704 (Lawrence Collins J). In any particular case, what matters is whether the opportunity was one which the fiduciary was under a duty to refer to the beneficiary. If he was, so that there was a real conflict of interest, then he will be accountable: *Bhullar v Bhullar* [2003] EWCA Civ 241; [2003] 2 B.C.L.C. 241.
  A helpful statement of the principles which apply where a fiduciary resigns from his position (in the context of a director resigning from a company) was given by Bernard Livesey QC sitting as a Deputy Judge of the High Court in *Hunter Kane Ltd v Watkins* [2003] EWHC 186 (Ch). This summary was endorsed by the Court of Appeal in *Foster Bryant Surveying Ltd v Bryant* [2007] EWCA Civ 200; [2007] 2 B.C.L.C. 239, where, after a full review of the authorities, Rix LJ, with whom Moses and Buxton LJJ agreed, described it as "perceptive and useful". A director will not be in breach of his fiduciary obligation if the business opportunity which he exploits after resigning is not a "maturing business opportunity" and the company was not pursuing further business orders or where his resignation was not prompted or influenced by the wish to acquire that business opportunity himself. There is a need to balance the proper enforcement of the fiduciary obligation of loyalty with the fiduciary's right to earn a living in his chosen field. For another decision concerning the fiduciary obligations of directors who resigned from their company, see *Shepherds Investments Ltd v Walters* [2006] EWHC 836 (Ch); [2007] 2 B.C.L.C. 202, Etherton J.

[568] *Reading v Att-Gen* [1951] A.C. 507; affirming [1949] 2 K.B. 232: ex-sergeant using uniform to assist smuggling operation.

[568A] [2017] EWHC 1815 (Comm); [2018] 1 W.L.R. 314 per Teare J at [134]–[135].

6. CONFIDENTIALITY

(a) Introduction

Replace footnote 603 with: See generally Toulson and Phipps, *Confidentiality*, **2-168**
4th edn (2020) (Toulson and Phipps). Gurry, *Breach of Confidence* (Oxford:
Clarendon Press, 1984) is also useful, if rather dated. Meagher, Gummow and
Lehane, *Equity, Doctrines and Remedies*, 5th edn (Butterworths, 2014) provide a
helpful analysis in Ch.42.

(b) Origins of the Duty of Confidence

A proprietary right?

Replace footnote 620 with:

[620] *Jeffreys v Boosey* (1854) 4 H.L.C. 814. See also *Bowstead and Reynolds on Agency*, 21st edn, para.6– **2-173**
077. In *Att-Gen v Guardian Newspapers Ltd* [1987] 1 W.L.R. 1248 at 1264D–1264F, Sir Browne-
Wilkinson VC accepted that information "is not property in any sense", but still preferred an analysis
based on "the traditional terms of equitable rights over property".

Replace footnote 622 with:

[622] [2005] EWCA Civ 595; [2006] Q.B. 1265 at [119] and [126]-[127]. Lord Upjohn's statement in **2-174**
Boardman v Phipps [1967] 2 A.C. 46 at 127 was cited as an accurate summary of the law. See also
Warwickshire CC v Matalia [2017] EWCA Civ 991; [2017] E.C.C. 25 per David Richards LJ at [26].

(c) Elements of the Cause of Action

Confidentiality of the information

After paragraph 2-183, add new paragraph 2-183A:
There are some instances in which a claimant has been able to obtain an injunc- **2-183A**
tion to protect the interests of a third party in relation to confidential information,
for example, *Ashworth Hospital Authority v MGN Ltd.*[649A] However, the basis on
which a claimant is said to be responsible for the protection of third parties' interests
in confidential information must be properly pleaded. A failure to do so may result
in a claim being struck out or injunctive relief being refused—see *Bains v
Moore.*[649B]

[649A] [2002] UKHL 29; [2002] 1 W.L.R. 2033.
[649B] [2017] EWHC 242 (QB); [2017] E.M.L.R. 20.

Disclosure justified in the public interest

After paragraph 2-188, add new paragraph 2-188A:
Another example in relation to regulatory matters can be found in *Bott-Holland* **2-188A**
v United Kingdom Council for Psychotherapy.[663A] The claimant psychotherapist applied for summary judgment against the defendant professional association. The
claimant entered into a contract with, and payed annual membership fees to, the
defendant. That contract incorporated the psychotherapists' code of conduct and its
complaints and conduct process, which provided for complaints proceedings to be
held in public. In 2011, one of the claimant's patients alleged that she had had a
consensual sexual relationship with him. The complaint was upheld and the defendant published details of the complaint on its website and in a journal. The court
refused summary judgment primarily on the ground that there was an express

contractual term which meant that the relevant information was not confidential. However, the court also allowed the defendant to argue at trial that it was in the public interest that a psychotherapist who had engaged in a sexual relationship with a patient he was treating should be identified.

663A Unreported 10 March 2017 (Ch.D.).

Detriment

After paragraph 2-191, add new paragraph 2-191A:

2-191A   When assessing financial loss in commercial cases, the court applied the following framework at [232]–[239] of *Marathon Asset Management LLP v Seddon*.671A If a claimant could not show that it had suffered financial loss, then it could nevertheless be awarded damages representing what the defendant would reasonably have had to pay to do lawfully what was done unlawfully or to obtain an equivalent benefit. If there was no alternative means by which the defendant, acting lawfully, could have obtained such a benefit and it was not reasonable to expect that the claimant would license the defendant's use of its property for a reasonable fee, it made no sense to value the benefit by postulating a hypothetical negotiation between a willing seller and a willing buyer. Accordingly, the appropriate method of valuation in such a case was to assess the amount of profit made by the defendant that was fairly attributable to its wrongful use of the claimant's property.

671A [2017] EWHC 300 (Comm); [2017] I.C.R. 791.

REMEDIES

2. DAMAGES

Replace paragraph 3-002 (to incorporate amendments to footnotes 2 and 3) with:

In most professional liability cases, the main remedy sought is damages. The **3-002** principal object of an award of damages is compensatory: to put the claimant in the position he would have occupied if the breach of duty had not occurred, so far as money can do this and subject to the rules as to remoteness[2] and mitigation of damage.[3] The classic formulation of principle is found in *Livingstone v Rawyards Coal Co.*[4] There are no general principles which apply to damages for professional negligence (as opposed to damages for negligence or breach of contract generally). The damage which professionals inflict, when things go wrong, covers the whole spectrum from personal injury through damage to property and economic loss. The most that can be said at the general level is that within individual professions or clusters of professions certain kinds of loss or damage commonly recur and these have given rise to particular rules.[5] See, for example, the solicitors' negligence cases in which the claimant loses his opportunity to bring proceedings[6] or the surveyors' negligence cases where the claimant purchases a property with defects of which he was unaware.[7] In the chapters relating to individual professions, examples are given of how the general principles governing damages are commonly applied to claims against the individual professions.[8]

[2] Following the decisions of the Court of Appeal in *Wellesley Partners LLP v Withers LLP* [2015] EWCA Civ 1146; [2016] Ch. 529 and *Wright v Lewis Silkin LLP* [2016] EWCA Civ 1308; [2017] P.N.L.R. 16, it is now clear that, where there are both contractual and tortious duties to take care in carrying out instructions, the test for recoverability of damage is the same for breach of both duties, and that the test to be applied is the more restrictive contractual one.

[3] There are very limited exceptions to the compensatory principle. In *Att-Gen v Blake* [2001] 1 A.C. 268 the House of Lords, by a majority of 4, recognised that, where the application of that principle would result in an inadequate remedy, in exceptional cases a defendant in breach of contract could be ordered to account to the claimant for the profits made from his breach. Such cases will be extremely rare: see further *Experience Hendrix LLC v Enterprises Inc* [2003] EWCA Civ 323; [2003] 1 All E.R. (Comm) 830 and *WWF—World Wide Fund for Nature v World Wrestling Federation Entertainment Inc* [2007] EWCA Civ 286; [2008] 1 W.L.R. 445. For circumstances in which the court will make an award for non-pecuniary damage other than personal injury see *Farley v Skinner (No.2)* [2001] UKHL 49; [2002] 2 A.C. 732. See, more recently, *Shaw v Leigh Day (A Firm)* [2017] EWHC 825 (QB); [2017] P.N.L.R. 26. Exemplary damages have not been awarded in negligence cases in the UK. The position is slightly less restrictive in New Zealand, where exemplary damages may be awarded in exceptional cases of negligence: see *A v Bottrill* [2002] UKPC 44; [2003] 1 A.C. 449 and *Couch v AG* [2010] NZSC 27.

[4] (1880) 5 App Cas. 25 at 39. There is a difference in principle between claims in tort and those in contract. In tort, the claimant is put in the position he would have been had the tort not been committed. In contract, he is put in the position he would have been had the contract been properly performed. However, in professional negligence there is, in reality, rarely a difference in the resulting damages. Jane Stapleton's article "The normal expectancies measure in tort damages" (1997) 113 L.Q.R. 257 provides an interesting consideration of the topic. On Stapleton's analysis the "normal expectancies" measure (rather than the "entitled result" measure) applies in most professional negligence actions. This is so whether the defendant has inflicted injury or merely failed to secure a benefit, and whether the claim is formulated in contract or in tort.

[5] Strictly speaking, these may not be "rules" at all. It may simply be that the courts, in applying the general principle of restitution to similar factual situations, inevitably adopt similar methods of assessment. See *Radford v De Froberville* [1977] 1 W.L.R. 1262 at 1268–1271; *Johnson v Agnew* [1980] A.C. 367; *Dodds Properties (Kent) v Canterbury CC* [1980] 1 W.L.R. 433; *County Personnel Ltd v Alan R Pulver & Co* [1987] 1 W.L.R. 916; *Ruxley Electronics & Construction Ltd v Forsyth* [1996] 1 A.C. 344.

[6] See paras 11-294 to 11-311.

[7] See paras 10-169 to 10-191.

[8] See the sections of the chapters concerning individual professions titled "Damages".

Banque Bruxelles Lambert SA v Eagle Star Insurance Co Ltd

After paragraph 3-003, add new paragraph 3-003A:

3-003A   In *Gabriel v Little*[16A] the Supreme Court affirmed and reinforced the decision of the House of Lords in *SAAMCO*. Lord Sumption (with whom the other members of the Supreme Court agreed) said that misunderstanding as to the decision in *SAAMCO* often arises from a tendency to overlook two fundamental features of the reasoning. The first is that, where the role of the defendant is to supply material which the client will take into account in making his own decision on the basis of a broader assessment of the risks, the defendant has no legal responsibility for the client's decision. The second, which follows from the first, is that the *SAAMCO* principle has nothing to do with causation as the expression is usually understood. Rather the focus is on the scope of the defendant's duty and whether the claimant's loss flows from a "particular feature of the defendant's conduct that made it wrongful". Lord Sumption acknowledged that the distinction between "advice" and "information" had led to confusion, largely due to the descriptive inadequacy of the labels. An "advice" case is one where the professional has to consider "what matters should be taken into account in deciding whether to enter into the transaction. His duty is to consider all relevant matters and not only specific factors". In other words the professional is "guiding the whole decision making process" and therefore is responsible for the decision to enter the transaction. In contrast, an "information" case is a case where the professional provides one part of the material on which the client relies when deciding what to do. In such a case, the process of identifying the other relevant considerations and the overall assessment of the commercial merits of the transaction are exclusively matters for the client. The professional is therefore only liable for the consequences of the information that he has provided being wrong. The fact that the material contributed by the professional is critical to the claimant's decision to enter into a transaction did not turn it into an "advice" case. On this basis, *Bristol & West Building Society v Steggles Palmer*;[16B] and *Portman Building Society v Bevan Ashford*[16C] were expressly overruled. The information which had not been reported may have been fundamental to the claimant's decision whether to proceed with the transaction, but they remained "information" cases and, as such the professional should not be held liable for all the consequences of the transaction.[16D]

[16A] [2017] UKSC 21; [2017] P.N.L.R. 23. Followed in *Ahmad v Wood* [2018] EWHC 996 (QB); [2018] P.N.L.R 28

[16B] [1997] 4 All E.R. 582.

[16C] [2000] P.N.L.R. 344.

[16D] Useful clarification of the distinction between "advice" and "information" was given by the Court of Appeal in *Manchester BS v Grant Thornton* [2019] EWCA Civ 40; [2019] 1 W.L.R. 4610. See also, in the context of a claim against auditors, *AssetCo Plc v Grant Thornton UK LLP* [2020] EWCA Civ 1151.

CHAPTER 4

CONTRIBUTION BETWEEN DEFENDANTS

3. LIABILITY OF THE PERSON CLAIMING CONTRIBUTION

(a) Basis of Liability

Replace footnote 21 with:

[21] *Hampton v Minns* [2002] 1 W.L.R. 1, where Kevin Garnett QC, sitting as a deputy High Court judge, held that the Civil Liability (Contribution) Act 1978 did not apply to a claim in debt, including a claim against a guarantor of a debtor. See also *Howkins & Harrison v Taylor* [2001] Lloyd's Rep. P.N. 1 CA. In *RSA Insurance Plc v Assicurazoni Generali SpA* [2018] EWHC 1237 (QB); [2019] 1 All E.R. (Comm) 115 the Court ruled that a claim for contribution between indemnity insurers was a claim for "damages" falling within the Civil Liability (Contribution) Act 1978 (and thus subject to a two-year limitation period).

4-008

4. THE CLAIM

(d) Time for bringing a Claim for Contribution

Replace paragraph 4-019 (to incorporate new text following the first sentence and an amendment to footnote 65) with:

Section 10 of the Limitation Act 1980 provides that a claim for contribution must be brought within two years of a judgment or arbitration award against him in favour of the original claimant or of the date of any agreement to make a payment in settlement of a claim against him.[63] Time will only start running from the date of a binding agreement as to the amount of payment. Anything short of a binding agreement on that issue (as opposed to ancillary matters) will not suffice.[63A] Where an agreement is later embodied in a consent order, time will run from when the agreement was made and not from the date of the order.[64] And when judgment is given on liability with damages to be assessed, time runs not from then, but from

4-019

the date on which damages are subsequently assessed.[65] When a claim is settled by an agreement as to the amount to be paid with the amount of costs payable to be determined or agreed at a later date, time runs from the date when damages are agreed and not from the later date when costs are determined or agreed: *Chief Constable of Hampshire v Southampton City Council.*[66]

[63] Note that the relevant date of the accrual of the right to recover contribution might vary depending on the purpose for which the question was being asked. So, in *Kazakhstan Kagazy Plc v Zhunus* [2016] EWCA Civ 1036 it was held that a party could apply for a freezing injunction in aid of a claim for contribution, once a contribution notice had been filed and served as of right or the Court had given permission to file and serve a contribution notice; before the party claiming contribution had been held liable in respect of the damage or had made or agreed to make a payment in compensation for the damage in question.

[63A] *RG Carter Building Ltd v Kier Business Services Ltd* [2018] EWHC 729 (TCC); [2018] B.L.R. 441.

[64] *Knight v Rochdale Healthcare NHS Trust* [2003] EWHC 1831 QB; [2004] 1 W.L.R. 371, Crane J. The decision (but not necessarily the reasoning) in *Knight v Rochdale Healthcare NHS Trust* [2003] EWHC 1831 (QB); [2004] 1 W.L.R. 371 was approved by the Court of Appeal in *Chief Constable of Hampshire v Southampton City Council* [2014] EWCA Civ 1541; [2015] P.I.Q.R. P5.

[65] *Aer Lingus Plc v Gildacroft Ltd* [2006] EWCA Civ 4; [2006] 1 W.L.R. 1173. The court, applying *Aer Lingus* in *Spire Healthcare Ltd v Nicholas Brooke* [2016] EWHC 2828 (QB); [2017] 1 W.L.R. 1177, held that an interim payment (whether court ordered or voluntary) did not start time running.

[66] [2014] EWCA Civ 1541; [2015] P.I.Q.R. P5.

DEFENCES

1. Exclusion or Restriction of Liability

(a) The Position at Common Law

Replace footnote 11 with:

5-003   [11] *Raiffeisen Zentralbank Österreich AG v Royal Bank of Scotland Plc* [2010] EWHC 1392 (Comm); [2011] 1 Lloyd's Rep. 123 at [313] per Christopher Clarke J (approved by Aikens LJ in *Springwell Navigation Corp v JP Morgan Chase Bank* [2010] EWCA Civ 1221; [2010] 2 C.L.C. 705 at [181] and applied by Newey J in *Avrora Fine Arts Investments Ltd v Christie, Manson & Woods Ltd* [2012] EWHC 2198 (Ch); [2012] P.N.L.R. 35 at [145]). See also the illuminating discussion in the judgments of Lewison and Leggatt LJJ in *First Tower Trustees Ltd v CDS (Superstores International) Ltd* [2018] EWCA Civ 1396; [2019] 1 W.L.R. 637.

Replace footnote 25 with:

5-009   [25] See the authorities referred to in para.12-06 of Lewison, *The Interpretation of Contracts*, 6th edn (Sweet & Maxwell, 2015) and Chitty, para.15-018.

To the end of paragraph 5-009 after "control by statute.", add:

The increasing tendency of the courts to avoid strained constructions to create ambiguities and their greater willingness to uphold exclusion clauses in contracts between commercial parties have led to the position where the guidelines in *Canada Steamship Lines Ltd v The King*[27A] may be "more relevant to indemnity clauses than to exemption clauses": *Persimmon Homes Ltd v Ove Arup and Partners Ltd*[27B] per Jackson LJ, with whom the other members of the Court of Appeal agreed.

[27A] [1952] A.C. 192.

[27B] [2017] EWCA Civ 373; [2017] P.N.L.R. 29.

(b) The Statutory Framework

Unfair Contract Terms Act 1977

Replace footnote 46 with:

5-016   [46] The operation of s.11 is briefly discussed by the House of Lords in *George Mitchell (Chesterhall) Ltd v Finney Lock Seeds Ltd* [1983] 2 A.C. 803 at 815–816. J. Adams and R. Brownsword review the earlier authorities in "The Unfair Contract Terms Act: A Decade of Discretion" in (1988) 104 L.Q.R. 94. They criticise the *George Mitchell* decision as having given rise to undue uncertainty. For a general discussion of the "reasonableness" test, see Chitty, paras 15-096 to 15-115.

The requirement of reasonableness

Replace footnote 53 with:

5-017   [53] The availability of insurance may also be a relevant factor in applying the test of reasonableness under s.11(1) (although it is not a relevant factor that the party seeking to limit or exclude liability has or has not in fact obtained insurance): see Chitty, para.15-099, fn.5589 for the relevant authorities.

To the end of paragraph 5-020 after "his agreed duties.", add:

5-020   For s.3 to apply it must be shown that the relevant party habitually uses the terms and that they have not been substantially amended in pre-contractual negotiations: *African Export-Import Bank v Shebah Exploration and Production Co Ltd.*[64A]

[64A] [2017] EWCA Civ 845; [2017] 2 Lloyd's Rep. 111.

Unfair Terms in Consumer Contracts Regulations 1999

Replace footnote 65 with:

[65] Directive 93/13. Discussed in Chitty, paras 38-220 to 38-361.   **5-021**

Replace footnote 67 with:

[67] reg.3(1). This is not the same as "dealing as a consumer" for the purposes of the Unfair Contract   **5-022**
Terms Act 1977 (as to which see fn.58 to para.5-019 above): see Chitty, paras 38-029 to 38-049 for a
full discussion of the various definitions of "consumer".

Replace footnote 79 with:

[79] See Chitty, para.38-297.   **5-024**

(c)   Exclusion of Liability to Third Parties

Replace footnote 106 with:

[106] The same principle was applied in *Omega Trust Co Ltd v Wright Son & Pepper* [1997] 1 E.G.L.R.   **5-030**
120. The defendant surveyors prepared a report for lender clients which contained the following
disclaimer: "This report shall be for private and confidential use of the clients for whom the report is
undertaken and should not be reproduced in whole or in part or relied upon by third parties for any use
whatsoever without the express written authority of the surveyors." The Court of Appeal held that this
disclaimer satisfied the test of reasonableness under the Unfair Contract Terms Act 1977; and that it
prevented any duty of care arising to lenders who were not the clients, but who relied upon the report.
See also (1) *Rehman v Jones Lang Lasalle Ltd* [2013] EWHC 1339 (QB) (HH Judge Belcher, sitting as
a High Court Judge) at [72]-[79] and (2) *Rehman v Santander UK Plc* [2018] EWHC 748 (QB) (HH
Judge Klein sitting as a High Court Judge) at [81]–[94].

Contracts (Rights of Third Parties) Act 1999

Replace footnote 112 with:

[112] See Chitty, para.15-046.   **5-031**

2.   LIMITATION IN CONTRACT AND TORT

(b)   Date when Cause of Action in Contract Accrues

Replace footnote 146 with:

[146] This sentence was cited with approval by the Privy Council in *Maharaj v Johnson* [2015] UKPC   **5-038**
28; [2015] P.N.L.R. 27, where it was held that the defendant solicitors were under no continuing duty
in contract after completion of the transaction in respect of which they had been retained.

    The decision of the Court of Appeal in *Bell v Peter Browne & Co* [1990] 2 Q.B. 495 was applied by
the Court of Appeal in *Nouri v Marvi* [2010] EWCA Civ 1107; [2011] P.N.L.R. 7, where Patten LJ, with
whom the other members of the Court of Appeal agreed, said at [38] that there needed to be "special
facts to suggest that the solicitors assumed a continuing duty". In *Morfoot v WF Smith & Co* [2001]
Lloyd's Rep. P.N. 658, HH Judge Havelock-Allan QC, sitting as an additional judge of the High Court,
applied the reasoning of the Court of Appeal in *Bell v Peter Browne & Co* [1990] 2 Q.B. 495 when
considering whether a failure to obtain a deed of release was a continuing breach of contract. He held
that it was not.

    See also *Winnote Pty Ltd v Page* [2006] NSWCA 287; (2006) 68 N.S.W.L.R. 531, where it was held
that a firm of solicitors was not under a continuing duty to provide advice about a transaction which they
had already negligently executed for their client. In so finding, the New South Wales Court of Appeal
applied a dictum of Dixon J in *Larkin v Great Western (Nepean) Gravel Ltd* [1940] HCA 37; (1940) 64
C.L.R. 221 at 236:

"If a covenantor undertakes that he will do a definite act and omits to do it within the time allowed for the purpose, he has broken his covenant finally and his continued failure to do the act is nothing but a failure to remedy his past breach and not the commission of any further breach of his covenant. His duty is not considered as persisting and, so to speak, being forever renewed until he actually does that which he promised. On the other hand, if his covenant is to maintain a state or condition of affairs, as, for instance, maintaining a building in repair, keeping the insurance of a life on foot, or affording a particular kind of lateral or vertical support to a tenement, then a further breach arises in every successive moment of time during which the state or condition is not as promised, during which, to pursue the examples, the building is out of repair, the life uninsured, or the particular support unprovided. The distinction may be difficult of application in a given case, but it must be regarded as one depending upon the meaning of the covenant."

See also *Green v Eadie* [2011] EWHC B24 (Ch); [2012] Ch. 363 (Mark Cawson QC, sitting as a Deputy High Court Judge) and *Integral Memory Plc v Haines Watts* [2012] EWHC 342 (Ch) (Richard Sheldon QC, sitting as a Deputy High Court Judge). For a rare example of a retainer which did give rise to a continuing duty see *Capita (Banstead 2011) Ltd v RFIB Group Ltd* [2014] EWHC 2197 (Comm) (Popplewell J) at [11]: retainer of specialist benefits consultancy (whose services included giving pension scheme advice) involved "considering the changes previously made, or purportedly made, and considering the implementation of the amendments in the context of subsequent dealings with the trustees".

The authority of *Midland Bank Trust Co Ltd v Hett Stubbs & Kemp* [1979] Ch. 384 has been further reduced by the decision of the Court of Appeal in *Capita (Banstead 2011) Ltd v RFIB Group Ltd* [2015] EWCA Civ 1310; [2016] Q.B. 835 where, by a majority, the Court of Appeal held that there was no continuing duty to correct earlier errors even when there was a continuing retainer.

(c)   Date when Cause of Action in Tort Accrues

(i)   Claims against Solicitors

Where client acquires less valuable rights than intended

Replace footnote 195 with:

5-051   [195] *Nouri v Marvi* [2010] EWCA Civ 1107; [2011] P.N.L.R. 7. See also *Pickthall v Hill Dickinson LLP* [2008] EWHC 3409 (Ch); [2009] P.N.L.R. 10 (claimant suffered loss when he entered transaction on less advantageous terms). Consistently with these decisions in *Davy Burton v Thom* [2008] NZSC 65; [2009] 1 N.Z.L.R. 437 the New Zealand Supreme Court held that a husband suffered loss when he entered a pre-nuptial agreement which was void and not when it was later held to be void. *Nouri v Marvi* [2010] EWCA Civ 1107; [2011] P.N.L.R. 7 was applied by Roth J in *Edehomo v Edehomo* [2011] EWHC 393 (Ch); [2011] 1 W.L.R. 2217. In the latter case the claimant's estranged husband had forged her signature on the contract for sale and transfer of a house they owned. Damage was held to have occurred when contracts were exchanged: at that point the value of the claimant's interest in the house reduced because anyone considering buying the house would be deterred by the existence of a purported contract to sell it to someone else. Roth J was not persuaded that loss was also suffered because the estranged husband's beneficial interest passed under the contract on the particular facts of the case. See also *Osborne v Follett Stock (A Firm)* [2017] EWHC 1811 (QB); [2017] P.N.L.R. 35 (damage suffered when the client entered a flawed transaction).

Previous action dismissed for want of prosecution

After paragraph 5-056, add new paragraph 5-056A:

5-056A   Where the solicitor's negligence impairs the value of an earlier claim, actionable damage is first suffered when the value of the claimant's chose in action is diminished, applying the reasoning in the cases on cases which become subject to being struck out. So in *Holt v Holley & Steer Solicitors (A Firm)*[210A] the claimant alleged that her former solicitors had negligently failed to obtain expert evidence as to the value of certain assets so that incorrect, high values were attributed to them resulting in a less favourable judgment in divorce proceedings. She contended that she only suffered loss when judgment, which was reserved, was given. Upholding the decision of the judge at first instance the Court of Appeal disagreed. The value of her chose in action was reduced by the date of the hearing at the latest (and so more than six years before proceedings were issued against the former solicitors) and, in all probability, much earlier when it became too late to introduce fresh expert evidence.

[210A] [2020] EWCA Civ 851.

(v) Claims against Financial Advisers

Replace footnote 241 with:

5-064

[241] [2008] EWCA Civ 863; [2008] P.N.L.R. 37; followed in *Davy v 01000654 Ltd (Formerly Heather Moor & Edgecomb Ltd)* [2018] EWHC 353 (QB).

(vi) Claims against Accountants

Law Society v Sephton

Replace footnote 247 with:

5-067

[247] [2010] EWCA Civ 181; [2010] 3 All E.R. 297. See also *Halsall v Champion Consulting Ltd* [2017] EWHC 1079 (QB); [2017] P.N.L.R. 32 where this reasoning was applied.

(vii) Claims against Construction Professionals

Effect of *Murphy* on *Pirelli*

Replace footnote 296 with:

5-077

[296] ibid. at 649C. In *Havenledge Ltd v Graeme John & Partners (A Firm)* [2001] P.N.L.R. 17 CA, Sir Antony Evans said at 424 that *Pirelli* remained binding as an authoritative statement of English law. In *New Islington and Hackney Housing Assoc Ltd v Pollard Thomas & Edwards Ltd* [2001] P.N.L.R. 20 at 529 Dyson J held that he was bound to follow *Pirelli* and that "the knowledge test has not been applied in English law". In *Brandley v Deane* [2017] IeSC 83 the Supreme Court of Ireland held that actionable damage was suffered not when houses were constructed with defective foundations, but when damage caused by those defective foundations manifested itself, whether reasonably discoverable or not. This is consistent with *Pirelli*.

(d) Effect of the Latent Damage Act 1986

(ii) Section 14A of the Limitation Act 1980

To the end of paragraph 5-091 after "a third party.", add:

5-091

Where a claimant has entirely entrusted his affairs to others by reason of his health or age, their knowledge will be relevant: *Lenderink-Woods v Zurich Assurance Ltd.*[339A]

[339A] [2016] EWHC 3287 (Ch); [2017] P.N.L.R. 15.

(iv) The Other Facts Relevant to the Current Action

Damage was attributable in whole or in part to the act or omission which is alleged to constitute negligence

Replace footnote 378 with:

5-102

[378] *Shore v Sedgwick Financial Services Ltd* [2008] EWCA Civ 863; [2008] P.N.L.R. 37 at [61] per Dyson LJ with whom the other members of the Court of Appeal agreed. See also *Williams v Lishman, Sidwell, Campbell & Price Ltd* [2010] EWCA Civ 418; [2010] P.N.L.R. 25: claimant knew that value of investment had fallen, so that advice given by defendant was incorrect, more than three years before issue of proceedings which were therefore statute barred. See also *Halsall v Champion Consulting Ltd* [2017] EWHC 1079 (QB); [2017] P.N.L.R. 32: knowledge that tax schemes which the claimants had been assured would succeed were the subject of negotiations with HMRC and that there might have to

be a discount to the tax relief in order to avoid the scheme being challenged before a tribunal was sufficient to justify embarking on preliminary inquiries.

(v) Constructive Knowledge

Failures by experts

Replace footnote 409 with:

5-111 ⁴⁰⁹ *Harris Springs Ltd v Howes* [2007] EWHC 3271 (TCC); [2008] B.L.R. 229 (HH Judge Raynor QC): it was reasonable for the claimant to rely upon the defendant consulting engineer whose advice did not indicate that there was a problem with the building's foundations until within three years of the issue of proceedings. It has to be reasonable for the claimant to have continued to rely upon the defendant. In *Gosden v Halliwell Landau (A Firm)* [2020] EWCA Civ 42 when they discovered that things had gone wrong, in that a property subject to a trust had been sold, the claimants consulted the individual solicitor who had acted for them in setting up a trust of the property. By this time the solicitor had moved to another firm. The solicitor did not advise the claimants that the trust's interest in the property could and should have been protected, but focused on trying to recover the proceeds of sale. The Court of Appeal agreed with the trial judge that the claimants had acted reasonably in instructing the same solicitor and so were in time for the purposes of s.14A.

(e) Special Rules re Personal Injury and Death

(ii) Discretionary Exclusion of Time Limit

The exercise of the discretion

After "s.33(3)(a)-(f) explicitly refer.", add:

5-120 Those factors are matters which experience has shown are likely to call for evaluation when exercising the discretion, but they do not fetter the exercise of the discretion, which is unfettered and requires the judge to look at the matter broadly.⁴⁴⁰ᴬ

⁴⁴⁰ᴬ *Carroll v Chief Constable of Greater Manchester Police* [2017] EWCA Civ 1992; [2018] 4 W.L.R. 32, at [42] per Sir Terence Etherton MR, with whom the other members of the Court of Appeal agreed. The judgment contains a comprehensive summary of the approach to the exercise of the court's discretion under s.33.

Replace paragraph 5-121 (to incorporate amendments to footnotes 441, 443 and 446) with:

5-121 Three factors to which the court is directed by s.33 are (a) the length and reasons for the delay in the claim being brought,⁴⁴¹ (b) the extent to which that delay may have an impact on the cogency of the evidence,⁴⁴² and (c) the conduct of the claimant during the delay.⁴⁴³ Three points should be noted about them. First, that the sheer length of the delay between the event causing injury and the bringing of proceedings may be a powerful factor against disapplying the time limit.⁴⁴⁴ Secondly, that the assessment of the claimant's reasons for the delay is subjective, rather than objective, so that the court must consider the claimant's actual state of mind, rather than what a reasonable person would think or do in the claimant's position.⁴⁴⁵ And third, that while all conduct of the claimant is relevant, only the conduct *after* the accrual of the cause of action falls within the scope of the express factor set out in s.33(3)(c). Accordingly, conduct of the claimant in the period between the relevant injury being suffered and the date of knowledge sufficient to start time running will only be considered as one of "circumstances of the case" and will be given less weight.⁴⁴⁶

⁴⁴¹ Limitation Act 1980 s.33(3)(a): "if there are no good reasons for the delay or its length, there is nothing to qualify or temper the prejudice which has been caused to the defendant by the effect of the delay

on the defendant's ability to defend the claim": *Carroll v Chief Constable of Greater Manchester Police* [2017] EWCA Civ 1992; [2018] 4 W.L.R. 32, at [42] per Sir Terence Etherton MR.

[442] ibid. s.33(3)(b).

[443] ibid. s.33(3)(c). The delay in question is that after the expiry of the primary limitation period: *Sanderson v Bradford MBC* [2016] EWHC 527 (QB), following the decision of the House of Lords in *Thompson v Brown (t/a George Albert Brown (Builders) & Co* [1981] 1 W.L.R. 744.

[444] See, e.g. *Dobbie v Medway HA* [1994] 1 W.L.R. 1234.

[445] *Coad v Cornwall HA* [1997] 1 W.L.R. 189.

[446] *Collins v Secretary of State for Business Innovation and Skills* [2014] EWCA Civ 717; [2014] P.I.Q.R. P19 at [65]-[66] per Jackson LJ, with whom the other members of the Court of Appeal agreed at [65]-[66]. The judgment of Jackson LJ contains a full and helpful analysis of the earlier authorities on delay by the claimant. See also *Malone v Relyon Heating Engineering Ltd* [2014] EWCA Civ 904 at [39]-[43] per Fulford LJ.

Replace footnote 451 with:

[451] *Nash v Eli Lilly & Co* [1993] 1 W.L.R. 782 at 807–808; *Forbes v Wandsworth HA* [1997] Q.B. 402. **5-123** It is not appropriate to conduct a mini-trial on very limited evidence: *Carroll v Chief Constable of Greater Manchester Police* [2017] EWCA Civ 1992; [2018] 4 W.L.R. 32, at [60] per Sir Terence Etherton MR.

Relevance of fault on the part of claimant's legal advisers

Replace footnote 461 with:

[461] See also (1) *Martin v Royal Free Hospital NHS Trust* [2005] EWHC 531 (QB) at [50]–[51] per **5-125** Hodge J and (2) *Carroll v Chief Constable of Greater Manchester Police* [2017] EWCA Civ 1992; [2018] 4 W.L.R. 32, at [42] per Sir Terence Etherton MR.

3.   LIMITATION IN EQUITY

(a)   Express Application of the Limitation Act 1980

To the end of paragraph 5-144 after "received trust property.", add new footnote 511A:

[511A] It is possible that some claims against trustees will be rights of action to recover a liquidated sum **5-144** and so fall within s.29(5) of the Limitation Act 1980, so that the cause of action will accrue upon any acknowledgement or part payment by the trustee: *Barnett v Creggy* [2016] EWCA Civ 1004; [2017] Ch. 273.

LITIGATION

1. Group Actions

(a) General

Replace paragraph 6-001 (to incorporate amendments to footnotes 6, 7, 9 and 10) with:

Group actions, also known as multi-party actions, and as class actions in other jurisdictions, concern the litigation of a number of claims having some similarity, usually the same claimant or defendants and similar legal and factual issues, which are administered together by the same judge. There has been an upsurge in group actions since the 1980s. They may cover a large variety of types of claims, including actions against employers for personal injury,[1] litigation alleging cancer from industrial plants,[2] transport disaster claims,[3] claims for environmental nuisance,[4] perhaps most well known of all a number of pharmaceutical product liability claims,[5] other product liability actions,[6] claims against arms of the state for negligence causing personal injury,[7] claims challenging mortgages and bank charges,[8] and claims for financial loss by investors from alleged negligent misstatements in prospectuses.[9] There have also been a number of professional negligence group actions, which will be briefly considered below. As a result of all this litigation, there has been a great deal of experience in how to manage and litigate group

6-001

actions. Some of it is reflected in reported decisions and in the provisions for group actions in the Civil Procedure Rules (CPR), but many of the techniques are necessarily of a more informal kind which is best found in the leading books on the subject.[10]

[1] The British Coal Vibration White Finger Litigation and the Respiratory Disease Litigation, which mostly resulted in success for the claimants.

[2] The Sellafield childhood leukaemia cases, which failed on causation in *Reay and Hope v British Nuclear Fuels Plc* (1994) 5 Med. L.R. 1.

[3] See, e.g. the *Herald of Free Enterprise* disaster of 1987 (where three arbitrators set landmark awards for post-traumatic stress disorder), and the Hillsborough football stadium disaster of 1989.

[4] The Docklands Nuisance actions (some of which settled, some of which were withdrawn); the Corby Group Litigation (see *Corby Group Litigation v Corby DC* [2009] EWHC 1944 (TCC)); Westmill Landfill Group Litigation (see *Barr v Biffa Waste Services Ltd* [2011] 137 Con. L.R. 125); Ocensa Pipeline Group Litigation (*Arroyo v Equion Energia Ltd* [2016] EWHC 1699 (TCC)).

[5] The Pertussis Vaccine Litigation (see *Loveday v Renton* [1989] 1 Med. L.R. 117, where the case effectively ended with failure by the claimants on a preliminary issue on causation); the Opren Litigation (where proceedings were discontinued); the Myodil Litigation (where a core cohort achieved settlements), the large and expensively unsuccessful Benzodiazepine Litigation; the Norplant Litigation (where legal aid was withdrawn shortly before trial) and the Hepatitis C Litigation where the claimants succeeded at trial (reported as *A v National Blood Authority* [2001] 3 All E.R. 289). In many of these cases, causation has been the key issue on which the claimants failed.

[6] See, e.g. the Tobacco Litigation, which ended in failure for the claimants following a preliminary issue on limitation; the litigation against Volkswagen Group companies arising from the diesel emissions scandal of 2015.

[7] The HIV Haemophiliac Litigation, which was settled following a preliminary hearing in the Court of Appeal (reported at [1996] P.N.L.R. 290); the Creutzfeldt-Jakob Disease Litigation, where the claimants succeeded in establishing liability (reported at [1996] 7 Med. L.R. 309); the Iraqi Civilian Litigation (concerning allegations of abuse by British military personnel in Iraq between 2003 and 2009) (see [2016] 1 W.L.R. 2001); the Mau Mau group actions against the Foreign and Commonwealth Office arising out of the conduct of the British Colonial Administration in Kenya.

[8] e.g. Shared Appreciation Mortgage Group Litigation.

[9] e.g. the RBS Rights Issue Litigation.

[10] See Grave, McIntosh & Rowan, *Class Actions in England and Wales* (London: Sweet & Maxwell, 2018), Hodges, *Multi-Party Actions* (Oxford, 2001) and Day, Balen & McCool, *Multi-Party Actions* (LAG, 1995). While the latter was written long before the new Civil Procedure Rules, it still provides valuable insights, and it includes helpful pleadings and orders in the appendices.

(c) Procedure

Replace paragraph 6-003 (to incorporate amendments to footnotes 18, 20, 22 and 24 and new footnote 18A) with:

6-003   CPR Pt 19 rr.10–15, and the accompanying Practice Direction, are concerned with group litigation. No similar body of rules existed before 2000. The rules can be summarised as follows. A court can make a Group Litigation Order (GLO), where there are or are likely to be a number of claims giving rise to common or related issues of fact or law ("the GLO issues").[16] A GLO must[17] contain directions about the establishment of a register,[18] specify the GLO issues to identify the claims, and identify a management court.[18A] Judgments or orders in one claim are generally binding on other claims.[19] Directions may be given[20] varying the GLO issues, providing for test claims to proceed,[21] appointing lead solicitors,[22] specifying what is to be included in a statement of case,[23] and providing for a cut-off-date for joining the litigation[24] and for publicising the GLO.[25] Co-ordinated litigation may be carried out outside the framework of GLOs in appropriate cases, for instance by the use of representative actions.

[16] CPR rr.19.10 and 19.11(1). No guidance is given in the rules as to how the court should exercise the discretion. The Practice Direction at paras 2.1–3.9 sets out a number of preliminary steps which must be undertaken before applying for a GLO, the information required for making an application, and which judges must approve any order.

[17] CPR r.19.11(2).

[18] While para.6.5 of the Practice Direction envisages that this will normally be kept by the court, it may well be more convenient for a lead solicitor to do so. In accordance with established law, a GLO will provide that a person becomes a party on the date of entry to the group register. This had a significant effect in *Kimathi v Foreign and Commonwealth Office* [2016] EWHC 3005 (QB), where one claimant had died after the issue of proceedings but before his name was added to the register. The court held that his claim was a nullity which was not capable of being cured.

[18A] There will usually be a managing judge who will conduct all hearings. This can give rise to an argument that a judge who has expressed views on the evidence in one hearing should recuse him or herself from conducting future hearings on the ground of apparent predetermination. In *Bates v Post Office Ltd (No.4)* [2019] EWHC 871 (QB), Fraser J refused such an application to recuse himself, citing authority that judges ought not to be too ready to accede to such applications in group litigation.

[19] CPR r.19.12.

[20] CPR r.19.13. In *Viner v Volkswagen Group UK Ltd* [2018] EWHC 2006 (QB), the court rejected applications to extend time for service of claim forms which were based on the argument that service had been delayed pending discussion of how to include the claims within the group litigation. The appropriate course would have been to serve the claim forms and seek a stay if necessary to discuss whether and how the claims should be included.

[21] See also para.15 of the Practice Direction.

[22] This is a necessary provision of last resort. Selection of a lead solicitor is almost always voluntary. Para.2.2 of the Practice Direction assists in this process. In *Hutson v Tata Steel* [2017] EWHC 2647 (QB); [2017] 6 Costs L.O. 753, the court refused an application to add an additional firm of solicitors as a lead firm within a group action, where the application was strongly resisted by the existing lead solicitors, and it was clear that an increase in the number of lead solicitors would add to the overall expense of the litigation, as well as the demands on the court's own resources. In *Lungowe v Vedanta Resources Plc* [2020] EWHC 749 (TCC), the court was faced with an application for a GLO made in respect of three separate sets of proceedings where the claimants were represented by two firms of solicitors. At [38], Fraser J held the following three principles to be applicable in that situation. First, parties to litigation are generally entitled to be represented by the solicitors of their choice and to have their case argued by their own representatives. However, in group litigation, that entitlement is qualified. In order properly to achieve efficient conduct and case management of the group litigation, that basic right takes second place to the advancement of the rights of the cohort. This is achieved through the role of the lead solicitor, and the use of counsel chosen and instructed by the lead solicitor. Secondly, the relationship between the lead solicitor and other firms has to be carefully defined in writing. In the absence of agreement, or in the event of deficiency in that agreement, the court will become involved. That is a reserve power and will be used only rarely. Thirdly, in group litigation the claimants would be entitled to instruct one counsel team only. Different groups of claimants are not entitled to instruct different groups of counsel. The court also reiterated at [42] the importance of co-operation between the parties in group litigation, pursuant to rr.1.4(2)(a) and 1.3 of the CPR.

[23] There is often provision for "Master pleadings", and para.14.1 of the Practice Direction envisages that "Group Particulars of Claim" may be provided. Individual claim forms are required to be issued by each claimant, under para.6.1A of the Practice Direction. However, they need only be "the simplest of documents", identifying the nature of the claim in general terms. Issues will be identified in detail by the GLO and Master Pleadings. See *Boake Allen Ltd v Revenue and Customs Commissioners* [2007] 1 W.L.R. 1386 at [28]–[32] per Lord Woolf.

[24] In *Holloway v Transform Medical Group (CS) Ltd* [2014] EWHC 1641 (QB), the court held that where a claimant had failed to apply to join a group litigation register by a cut-off date set in court directions and sought to join out of time, it was necessary for her to satisfy the criteria for relief from sanctions under CPR r.3.9. The argument that the sanction did not apply to her because she was not a party to the group litigation at the time when the order was made was rejected. An application for relief from sanction of this kind failed in the Mau Mau group action, where the claimant applying to be added to the register was doing so two-and-a-half years after it had closed and the reason for the lateness of the application was not entirely clear: see *Kimathi v Foreign and Commonwealth Office* [2017] EWHC 939 (QB). In *Hutson v Tata Steel UK Ltd* [2019] EWHC 143 (QB), the court acceded to an application to extend time where cases had not entered the register in time, in view of the fact that this would not substantially prejudice the defendant or be disruptive of the proceedings. The court also decided that it had power to extend time where cases had been entered on the register before the deadline but without

the requisite formalities having actually been satisfied. In that case and in *Crossley v Volkswagen AG* [2019] EWHC 698 (QB), the courts considered applications to add cases after cut-off dates as applications for relief from sanction. *Crossley* was a striking example, in that permission was given for over 5,000 cases to be added. However, the number was modest in the context of the case and the claimants had been named on the original claim form.

[25] See also para.13 of the Practice Direction.

Replace paragraph 6-004 (to incorporate amendments to footnotes 28 and 31) with:

6-004   The rules only lay down, and can only lay down, a very broad framework, as the circumstances of potential group actions can be very diverse. The first question will be whether a GLO should be made, and orders may be refused where actions would more efficiently or fairly be resolved by being consolidated or by representative actions or lead cases being ordered to be heard.[26] A GLO may also be refused where funding for claims is evidently lacking or the factual foundations of the claims are speculative.[27] If a GLO is made, case management will be tailored to the circumstances of the dispute.[28] A fundamental issue in many cases is likely to be whether the group action should progress by deciding generic issues without investigating any or many individual cases first, or whether individual cases should be properly pleaded and scrutinised before deciding on which generic issues should be tried.[29] In general, a high degree of co-operation is required between the lawyers for the opposing sides,[30] and judges have had to be active[31] and interventionist in these type of actions long before the Woolf reforms. Solicitors for claimants in group litigation are expected to behave professionally when advertising for and recruiting additional claimants.[32]

[26] See para.2.3 of the Practice Direction; *Hobson v Ashton Morton Slack Solicitors* [2006] EWHC 1134 (QB).

[27] See *Austin v Miller Argent (South Wales) Ltd* [2011] EWCA Civ 928; [2011] Env. L.R. 32. Or the issues may not be sufficiently common or sufficiently related to make a GLO. See *Various v Barking, Havering and Redbridge University Hospitals NHS Trust* QBD unreported 21 May 2014.

[28] In general terms, the fact that a person is a claimant in group litigation, but not a test claimant, does not prevent him from successfully making an application for an interim payment of damages, if the conditions for such a payment are met. However, there may be terms of specific GLOs which preclude this form of interim relief. See *Test Claimants in the FII Group Litigation v Revenue and Customs Comrs* [2012] EWCA Civ 57; [2012] 1 W.L.R. 2375 at [47]; *GKN Holdings Plc v Revenue and Customs Commissioners* [2013] EWHC 108 (Ch) at [22]. In *Bates v Post Office Ltd (No.2)* [2018] EWHC 2698 (QB), the court refused an application to strike out parts of statements which were made on the basis that the evidence was irrelevant to common issues. It was inappropriate to take too restrictive an approach to relevance in such an application within a group action, given the inherent difficulty of predicting the shape of the case at trial. The evidence would have to be clearly irrelevant for it to be struck out.

[29] See Hodges, op. cit., pp.15–18. When considering whether to order a preliminary trial of common or generic issues, the objective is to find the best means of dealing with a large number of claims in an expeditious, fair and proportionate way. The court should therefore be cautious about applying to the group litigation context principles which have been developed in ordinary private litigation about the ordering of preliminary issues. See *Varney v Ford Motor Co Ltd* [2013] EWHC 1226 (Ch).

[30] For instance, in the selection of test cases. In general, it will be in the interests of all parties for the test cases to include as many contentious issues as reasonably possible, and to include both strong and weak cases, so that judgment in those test cases will provide the maximum assistance in settling the remaining cases.

[31] In *XYZ v Various Companies* [2013] EWHC 3643 (QB); [2014] Lloyd's Rep I.R. 431, the court decided, in the context of group litigation relating to medical implants, that it had power to order a defendant to file a witness statement giving details of its ability to fund participation in the group litigation. This would assist the court in managing the case and was therefore a step which could be taken under CPR r.3.1. However, in a subsequent hearing in the same litigation, the court rejected an application by the insurer of one defendant to join the insurer of another defendant. The scope of insurance cover was not an issue connected to the matters in dispute in the proceedings, and so joinder could not be permitted under CPR r.19.2(2). While a general case management power could be exercised flexibly in group litigation, it could not be used to circumvent specific rules: see *XYZ v Various Companies* [2014]

EWHC 4056 (QB). See also *Re RBS Rights Issue Litigation* [2017] EWHC 463 (Ch); [2017] 1 W.L.R. 3539, where the court considered applications for disclosure of (i) the names of third party funders, and (ii) any ATE insurance policy held by the claimants.

[32] In *Saunderson v Sonae Industria (UK) Ltd* [2015] EWHC 2264 (QB) at [456]–[463], the court made critical comments regarding the practices adopted by solicitors in this regard, observing that those adopted (which included leading questionnaires, pop-up shops and cold calling of potential claimants) failed to inspire any degree of confidence.

(d) Costs

Replace paragraph 6-005 (to incorporate new text following "to achieve that effect" and new text after "in the action." at the end of the paragraph, and to make an amendments to footnotes 35 and 39) with:

As a result of the Civil Procedure (Amendment) Rules 2013,[33] the special costs rules applying where a court has made a GLO are now contained in CPR r.46.6.[34] The scheme under the old CPR r.48.6A, now repealed, remains exactly the same. The fundamental rules are that any order for common costs against group litigants will generally impose on an individual claimant several liability for an equal proportion of those costs, and that a group litigant who is the paying party will generally be liable for the individual costs of his claim and an equal proportion of the common costs.[35] These rules reflect the general practice which had already developed in a number of cases.[36] The costs of test cases are generally common, or generic, costs. It is common in practice for claimants joining a group action to become immediately responsible for an equal proportion of generic costs. When a claim is removed from the group register, the court may order that the litigant pays a proportion of the common costs to that date.[37] Where group litigation is settled, before a GLO is made, on terms that the claimants' reasonable costs will be paid, those costs will ordinarily include each claimant's proportion of the generic costs, as well as the costs specific to his claim. There is no requirement for there to be a specific agreement regarding generic costs in order to achieve that effect.[38] After a hearing on particular issues, it may be appropriate to make a costs order to reflect the success of the parties in that hearing even though the overall success of the claims has yet to be addressed.[38A] Costs budgeting rules may apply to both generic and individual costs in group actions, but in such cases it is not always desirable or practicable to carry out budgeting or to do so for all costs in the action.[39] Rules concerning applications for security for costs operate in the usual way against group claimants, including in actions financed by litigation funders.[39A]

6-005

[33] Civil Procedure (Amendment) Rules 2013 (SI 2013/262).

[34] See further the notes to the *White Book* accompanying CPR r.46.6.

[35] The court has considerable latitude to vary the default position: the broad question is what fairness demands in the particular situation. In *Greenwood v Goodwin* [2014] EWHC 227 (Ch), the court considered, in the context of group litigation brought by shareholders of a company, how costs sharing should be managed, given that there was a range of different sub-groups of litigants and that there were significant disparities between the value of the various claimants' claims. The court accepted that the default position under CPR r.46.6 involved equal sharing of costs, but noted that it should exercise latitude in adopting a solution that was fair to all the parties. A complex costs sharing scheme was ultimately decided upon, to reflect (inter alia) the value of the claims. In the *Ingenious Litigation* [2020] EWHC 235 (Ch), the court considered that it was fairer for the risks to a claimant of participating in the litigation to be proportionate to the reward that they might obtain from the litigation and that, accordingly, the claimants' liability for adverse costs should be apportioned pro rata to the size of their cash investments in the impugned tax schemes in the underlying litigation.

[36] See, e.g. *Davies (Joseph Owen) v Eli Lilly & Co* [1987] 1 W.L.R. 1136 CA; *Nationwide Building Society v Various Solicitors (No.4)* [2000] Lloyd's Rep. P.N. 71. Further guidance on costs can be found in the cases referred to in the *White Book* at paras 19.10.0 and 46.6, and in particular *Sayers v Merck SmithKline Beecham Plc* [2001] EWCA Civ 2017; [2002] 1 W.L.R. 2274 CA and *AB v Liverpool City*

Council (Costs) [2003] EWHC 1539 (QB). In *Jones v Secretary of State for Energy and Climate Change* [2013] 2 Costs L.R. 230, the court applied an overall percentage reduction of the costs recoverable by claimants in group litigation, to reflect failures on some issues of causation in some of the selected lead claims.

[37] But this may well be unfair to the claimant, see *Sayers v Merck SmithKline Beecham Plc* [2001] EWCA Civ 2017; [2002] 1 W.L.R. 2274.

[38] See *Brown v Russell Young & Co* [2008] 1 W.L.R. 525.

[38A] See *Bates v Post Office Ltd (No.5)* [2019] EWHC 1373 (QB); [2019] Costs L.R. 857, where the judge stressed the flexibility of costs rules and decided that it was appropriate to make costs orders relating to a particular common issues hearing. In doing so, he had regard to the potential duration of the litigation as a whole.

[39] See the costs budgeting judgments in the Iraqi Civilian Litigation: [2016] 3 Costs L.O. 471; [2016] 3 Costs L.O. 477. See also the costs budgeting judgment in the case of *Kalma v African Minerals Ltd* [2017] EWHC 1471 (QB) and *Hutson v Tata Steel UK Ltd* [2020] EWHC 771 (QB).

[39A] See, e.g. *Bailey v GlaxoSmithKline UK Ltd* [2017] EWHC 3195 (QB); [2018] 4 W.L.R. 7, where the court required a litigation funder that had committed to provide funding of £1.2 million for group litigation in respect of an antidepressant drug to give security for the defendant's costs up to trial of £1.75 million. See also the *Ingenious Litigation* [2020] EWHC 235 (Ch) where Nugee J made an order for security against a third-party funder in circumstances where there would be a shortfall in the event the claimants were unsuccessful in their claims even after the wealthy claimant parties had met their liabilities under a several liability order.

2. EXPERT EVIDENCE

(a) The Functions of the Expert Witness

Replace paragraph 6-006 (to incorporate an amendment to footnote 40 and new text following "the expert witnesses." at the end of the paragraph) with:

6-006 In the context of liability issues in professional negligence actions, the expert witness commonly performs two functions. First, he sets out and explains the relevant technical matters, e.g. the relevant principles of engineering and how they were applied to the building project in question, or the principles of valuation and how they were applied in the defendant surveyor's valuation or report. To this extent, the expert witness is performing a didactic role: he is explaining the technical aspects of the case in language comprehensible to laymen. Expert evidence of this sort may be largely or wholly uncontroversial. For example, the expert witnesses in a clinical negligence case may agree that the claimant's condition is the result of an adverse reaction to a new drug administered by the defendant. The court must understand and resolve any conflicts between expert evidence of this sort before it can consider the question of negligence. Where there is a dispute on questions of technical fact, the court may prefer the theory advanced by one expert witness over that advanced by another, but it will not assume technical expertise: it will not substitute a theory of its own where that theory is not supported by the evidence of any of the expert witnesses.[40] The assessment of expert evidence is a matter for the trial judge and an appeal court will be slow to interfere, since the evaluation is likely to be bound up with a wider view of matters of fact. Where the first instance court was a specialist court, such as the Technology and Construction Court, there will be particular caution in reviewing assessment of expert evidence on appeal.[40A]

[40] In the clinical negligence case *McLean v Weir* (1977) 3 C.C.L.T. 87 in the British Columbia Supreme Court, Gould J summarised the position in a manner which, it is submitted, is equally applicable in England (at 101):

"It is true that the court may accept in whole or in part or reject in whole or in part the evidence of any witness on the respective grounds of credibility or plausibility, or a combination of both. But in technical matters, unlike in lay matters within the traditional intellectual competence of the court, it cannot substitute its own medical opinion for that of qualified experts. The court has no status whatsoever to come to a medical conclusion contrary to unanimous medical evidence before it even if it wanted to, which is not the situation in this case. If the medical evidence is equivocal, the court may elect which of the theories advanced it accepts. If only two medical theories are advanced, the court may elect between the two or reject them both; it cannot adopt a third theory of its own, no matter how plausible such might be to the court."

In principle, a court or tribunal may reject uncontroverted expert evidence, or the common opinion of the experts of all parties, on an issue within the relevant scope of expertise. However, if this is to be done, then specific and adequate justification should be given. See *Al-Jedda v Secretary of State for the Home Department* [2012] EWCA Civ 358 at [102]–[107]; *Perkins v McIver* [2012] EWCA Civ 735 at [27]–[31]. For example, in *Maitland-Hudson v Solicitors Regulation Authority* [2019] EWHC 67 (Admin); [2019] A.C.D. 47 at [82]–[86], the Divisional Court held that the Solicitors Disciplinary Tribunal was not bound by the views of the parties' psychiatric experts in deciding on the appellant's ability to participate in proceedings. There are some categories of case where the court can more readily take a middle position between experts, or adopt its own approach after considering expert evidence. In the valuers' negligence case of *Capita Alternative Fund Services (Guernsey) Ltd v Drivers Jonas (A Firm)* [2012] EWCA Civ 1417; [2013] 1 E.G.L.R. 119, Gross LJ said (at [43]):

"It is as well to emphasise that a Judge is never bound by expert evidence (even, though that does not arise here, undisputed expert evidence). While a Judge must have a reasoned or rational basis for a decision—on issues of quantum as on other issues—the Judge is in no way confined to the figures contended for by the experts. This is manifestly so in a typical valuation case where the figure arrived at by the Judge may well lie somewhere in between those advanced by the rival experts. Moreover, having regard to the true nature of quantum disputes and their history as jury questions, a Judge will sometimes find himself needing to do the best he can".

[40A] *Wheeldon Bros Waste Ltd v Millennium Insurance Co Ltd* [2018] EWCA Civ 2403; [2019] 4 W.L.R. 56 at [11]–[18].

After "he was negligent.", add new footnote 40B:

[40B] In *Bot v Barnick* [2019] EWHC 3704 (QB), a clinical negligence claim was struck out because there had been a prolonged failure to serve expert evidence in support of the claim, which could not be sustained without such evidence. Yip J made the general comment at [17] that claims against professionals cannot be sustained absent supportive expert evidence.   **6-007**

(b) Cases Where Expert Evidence is not Required

Replace paragraph 6-010 (to incorporate new text following "reasonable or responsible."" at the end of (1) and an amendment to footnote 56) with:

(1) Cases in which the court considers that there is no logical basis for the body   **6-010**
of opinion in accordance with which the defendant acted. In *Bolitho v City and Hackney HA*,[51] a clinical negligence case, Lord Browne-Wilkinson said[52]:

"… the Court is not bound to hold that a defendant doctor escapes liability for negligent treatment or diagnosis just because he leads evidence from a number of medical experts who are genuinely of the opinion that the defendant's treatment or diagnosis accorded with sound medical practice. In the *Bolam* case itself, McNair J [1957] 1 W.L.R. 583, 587 stated that the defendant had to have acted in accordance with the practice accepted as proper by a '*responsible*' body of medical men'. Later, at 588, he referred to 'a standard of practice recognised as proper by a competent *reasonable* body of opinion'. Again, in the passage which I have cited from *Maynard*'s case, Lord Scarman refers to a 'respectable' body of professional opinion. The use of these adjectives—responsible, reasonable and respectable—all show that the court has to be satisfied that the exponents of the body of opinion relied upon can demonstrate that such opinion has a logical basis."

He concluded[53]:

"... if, in a rare case, it can be demonstrated that the professional opinion is not capable of withstanding logical analysis, the judge is entitled to hold that the body of opinion is not reasonable or responsible."

Although a Court may rely upon this principle to hold a defendant negligent despite expert evidence supporting his or her conduct, it is not usually appropriate for a Court to hold that a particular professional practice or opinion has no logical basis without some specific expert evidence which justifies that conclusion.[53A]

(2) Cases in which the defendant's conduct is subject to criticism and the expert evidence called by the defendant is in reality no more than the personal opinion of an expert witness as to what he would have done in the position of the defendant.[54] Such evidence does not establish that the defendant's conduct was in line with a responsible body of opinion or with a recognised *practice* within his profession. In *Midland Bank Trust Co Ltd v Hett Stubbs & Kemp*,[55] a solicitors' negligence case, Oliver J said[56]:

"Clearly, if there is some practice in a profession, some accepted standard of conduct which is laid down by a professional institute or sanctioned by common usage, evidence of that can and ought to be received. But evidence which really amounts to no more than an expression of opinion by a particular practitioner of what he thinks that he would have done had he been placed, hypothetically and without the benefit of hindsight, in the position of the defendants, is of little assistance to the court ..."

It is thought that this does not prevent the court receiving assistance from expert witnesses in cases where there is no general and approved practice or specific school of thought by reference to which the defendant's conduct can either be justified or condemned as negligent. In such cases, the court may still be assisted by the evidence of an expert witness as to how, in his experience and opinion, an ordinarily competent member of his profession would have acted in the position of the defendant. This may be quite different to the manner in which he personally would have acted.

(3) Cases in which it is not necessary to apply any particular professional expertise in order to decide whether the defendant has failed to exercise the skill and care expected of an ordinary member of his profession. For example, in the architect's negligence case of *Worboys v Acme Investments Ltd*[57] Sachs LJ recognised that there were cases where an omission on a plan was so glaring as to require no evidence of general practice and instanced a house without provision for a staircase. In the architect's negligence case of *Royal Brompton Hospital NHS Trust v Hammond (No.7)*,[58] Judge Seymour QC put it this way[59]:

"... if I am satisfied on the evidence that an obvious mistake was made which would not have been made by any careful person of whatever profession, or, indeed, of none, then I can find that the person who made that mistake was negligent. What I cannot do, as it seems to me, is to substitute my own view for that of a professional person of the appropriate discipline on any matter in respect of which any special skill, training or expertise is required to make an informed assessment."

[51] [1998] A.C. 232.

[52] ibid. at 241.

[53] ibid. at 243.

[53A] *Williams v Cwm Taf Local Health Board* [2018] EWCA Civ 1745.

[54] In *Re Barings Plc (No.6)* [1999] 1 B.C.L.C. 433 at 493, Jonathan Parker J commented that evidence amounting simply to an opinion of what the expert would have done was irrelevant. See also *JP Morgan Chase Bank v Springwell Navigation Corp* [2007] 1 All E.R. (Comm) 549 at [21] where Aikens J distinguished such evidence from legitimate expert evidence expressing a view, on assumed facts, as to whether the actions of a relevant person fell below the standard of practice in a profession.

[55] [1979] Ch. 384.

[56] ibid. at 402. This passage was approved by the Court of Appeal in *Bown v Gould & Swayne* [1996] P.N.L.R. 130 and in the architect's negligence case of *Michael Hyde & Associates Ltd v JD Williams & Co Ltd* [2001] P.N.L.R. 8 and was applied in the solicitors' negligence case of *X v Woollcombe Yonge* [2001] Lloyd's Rep. P.N. 274. See also *Linden Homes South East Ltd v LBH Wembley Ltd* 87 Con. L.R. 180 (finding of negligence by construction professionals in face of evidence of defendant's expert witness because there was no evidence of two respectable but differing bodies of opinion, merely of differing views as between the two individual experts). In *Liverpool Insurance Co Ltd v Khan* [2017] EWHC 1314 (QB), the court cited *Bown* with approval when refusing to entertain expert evidence from an orthopaedic consultant in a case where an insurer was seeking to commit a GP for contempt for allegedly preparing a dishonest report in litigation. The issue for the court was whether the GP had complied honestly with his duties to the court. The orthopaedic consultant's evidence would be no more than an assertion of what he would have done. Furthermore, even if such evidence had been warranted, it should have been from another GP.

[57] (1969) 210 E.G. 335 CA. See also the clinical negligence case of *Gold v Haringey HA* [1988] Q.B. 481 at 490 per Lloyd LJ: "If the giving of contraceptive advice required no special skill, then I could see an argument that the Bolam test should not apply."

[58] (2001) 76 Con. L.R. 148.

[59] ibid. at 170.

(c)   The Civil Procedure Rules

Replace paragraph 6-012 (to incorporate amendments to footnotes 69 and 74 and new text following "in writing only." and "is inherently weak." at the end of the paragraph) with:

Lord Woolf's final report on the civil justice system, published in July 1996,[66] **6-012** heralded a new and restrictive approach to expert evidence which has been embodied in England and Wales in Pt 35 of the Civil Procedure Rules. Under CPR r.35.4, no party may call an expert witness without the court's permission.[67] The principle which guides the court in deciding whether or not to permit expert evidence is set out in CPR r.35.1: expert evidence is to be "restricted to that which is reasonably required to resolve the proceedings."[68] Thus the use of expert evidence is now wholly subject to the control of the court[69] and the court is encouraged to exercise its powers to decide that no expert evidence shall be called upon a particular issue, that a single expert shall be jointly instructed by the parties[70] or that expert evidence should be adduced in writing only.[71] When permission is given for expert evidence, directions will usually provide for simultaneous or sequential exchange of reports and for experts in like disciplines to confer and produce a joint memorandum of points agreed and points disputed.[71A] In general, permission is required for expert evidence in all forms of hearing, including interlocutory and final hearings.[71B] The Court will exercise careful control over both the admission and scope of expert evidence. For example, in the solicitors' negligence case of *Mann v Chetty & Patel*,[72] the Court of Appeal held that expert evidence would be permitted on only one of the quantum issues which arose in the case, whereas the claimant sought to adduce expert evidence on three such issues. The Court of Appeal stated that, in deciding whether to allow expert evidence, the court had to make a judgment on at least three matters:

1.   how cogent the proposed expert evidence would be ("cogency");

2. how helpful that evidence would be in resolving any of the issues in the case ("usefulness"); and

3. how much the evidence would cost and the relationship between that cost and the sums at stake ("proportionality").

More recently, the courts have developed a composite test of asking whether the proposed expert evidence would "genuinely assist the trial judge in the determination of the issues" and have cautioned about the risk of a judge being deluged with long and complex reports straying far from the key issues.[73] In *British Airways Plc v Spencer*,[74] the court proposed a three-stage test focussed on the relevance of expert evidence to issues in the case: (i) whether the expert evidence was *necessary* to resolution of an issue; (ii) if not, whether it would be of assistance; and (iii) whether evidence which is of assistance (but not strictly necessary) is reasonably required to resolve an issue. In *Kennedy v Cordia (Services) LLP*,[75] the Supreme Court similarly rejected an absolute test of strict necessity and recommended an evaluation of the assistance the evidence could provide to the tribunal. When making decisions whether to permit expert evidence to be adduced, the court will have regard to the significance of the evidence, but it will be rare for evidence to be excluded on the basis that the claim to which it relates is inherently weak.[76] The application of the principles in this paragraph has generated particular controversy in financial services disputes, where there has been a range of decisions as to whether expert evidence is justified to comment on the suitability of financial products and the appropriateness of a professional or company recommending them. For example, in *London Executive Aviation Ltd v Royal Bank of Scotland Plc*[76A] the court refused expert evidence on product suitability issues in a swaps mis-selling case. It held that no evidence was needed on the risks of the product, which were apparent from its terms and that none was required to explain FCA Handbook rules. The application of the rules to the case was for the court.[76B] In a comparable decision going the other way, the court held in *Dudding v Royal Bank Of Scotland Plc*[76C] that the claimants were entitled to rely on expert evidence concerning the sale of derivatives by the defendant banks as such evidence was admissible and reasonably required in order for the issues to be resolved.[76D]

[66] *Access to Justice* (HMSO, 1996).

[67] This provision concerns permission to adduce the evidence of a witness. Similar permission is not required to rely upon technical literature, although of course the court may be unable to interpret or place reliance on such literature without relevant expert evidence on the subject: *Interflora Inc v Marks and Spencer Plc* [2013] EWHC 936 (Ch) at [14]–[20].

[68] In *Gumpo v Church of Scientology Religious Education College Inc* [2000] C.P. Rep. 38, Smedley J described the policy underlying r.35.1 as being to reduce "the incidence of inappropriate use of experts to bolster cases". Decisions as to the scope of expert evidence which is reasonably required to resolve relevant issues are matters of case management and will accordingly be difficult to disturb on appeal: *Blair-Ford v CRS Adventures Ltd* [2012] EWHC 1886 (QB). However, such decisions must be made in accordance with the overriding objective, and can be challenged where the court has been over-zealous in excluding potentially valuable evidence in the interests of saving costs: *British Airways Plc v Spencer* [2015] EWHC 2477 (Ch); [2015] Pens. L.R. 519 at [19]. *Evans v Frimley Park Hospital NHS Trust* QBD unreported 24 May 2012, provides an instance where a defendant made a successful application to adduce additional expert evidence. The court found that an additional haematologist's report which supported the defendant's reasoning "was likely to radically affect the outcome of a trial or have an impact on potential negotiations", and therefore granted the application.

[69] The Court can be expected to exclude opinion evidence which is "dressed up" as evidence of fact, as for example in *JD Wetherspoon Plc v Harris* [2013] EWHC 1088 (Ch); [2013] 1 W.L.R. 3296 and *Buckingham Homes Ltd v Rutter* [2018] EWHC 3917 (Ch). The requirement for permission for expert evidence cannot be circumvented by annexing to a factual witness statement a document which is intended to provide opinion evidence: see *New Media Distribution Company Sezc Ltd v Kagalovsky* [2018] EWHC 2742 (Ch). However, not every document which contains opinion evidence is governed by Pt 35. In *Rogers v Hoyle* [2014] EWCA Civ 257; [2015] Q.B. 265, the Court of Appeal held that an

Air Accident Investigation Branch report was admissible in a negligence action against a pilot who had crashed an aircraft. The narrative portions of the report were admissible as factual evidence and the opinion sections as expert evidence. In admitting the report, the Court of Appeal rejected the submission that the opinion sections had to be admitted under CPR Pt 35 and subject to its provisions. The report was not within the scope of Pt 35; it was admissible documentary evidence, but the court had a discretion under CPR r.32.1 to exclude it if justice and proportionality so dictated. The Court of Appeal drew a distinction with quasi-judicial reports, the factual findings of which are generally inadmissible. This is a significant case and it may be applied directly or by analogy in relation to other forms of report in negligence actions. The principles in *Rogers* were applied in *Mondial Assistance (UK) Ltd v Bridgewater Properties Ltd* [2016] EWHC 3494 (Ch), a landlord and tenant case in which valuation reports adduced by court order attached reports of various technical consultants that had not been obtained for the proceedings. On appeal, Nugee J held that it had been wrong to exclude those technical reports. They were relevant hearsay evidence and not governed by Pt 35. Their content, both factual and opinion, was admissible. Similarly, in *Illumina Inc. v TDL Genetics Ltd* [2019] EWHC 1159 (Pat), Henry Carr J held that CPR Pt 35 did not apply to hearsay evidence attesting to evidence given by experts in previous proceedings. However, he recognised that the court could exclude such evidence under r.32.1 if the evidence was duplicative or would result in disproportionate costs being incurred.

70 See paras 6-025 to 6-028, below.

71 CPR r.35.5(1) provides that expert evidence should be given in a written report unless the court directs otherwise. In fast-track cases (those worth between £10,000 and £25,000) experts will not be permitted to give oral evidence unless that is necessary in the interests of justice: CPR r.35.5(2). However, it should be recognised that a judge who attempts to decide between competing expert opinions is faced with a very difficult task unless the experts are called to give oral evidence, a common sense proposition acknowledged in *Preece v Edwards* [2012] EWCA Civ 902 and in *Rengasamy v Homebase Ltd* [2015] EWHC 618 (QB).

71A Failure to comply with the directions of the court may have the result that the defaulting party is not permitted to adduce the relevant expert evidence. Furthermore, a failure by a party and/or its expert to engage properly with the process of expert discussions may cause the court to withdraw permission or impose strict terms to ensure that the process is properly followed: *Mayr v CMS Cameron McKenna Nabarro Olswang LLP* [2018] EWHC 3669 (Comm).

71B See for example *B.B. Energy (Gulf) DMCC v Al Amoudi* [2018] EWHC 2595 (Comm) at [49], where an attempt to rely upon expert evidence of foreign law as an annex to a solicitor's statement in a jurisdictional dispute was rejected. Note, however, that in a security for costs application or freezing order application, a more flexible approach is taken and it is not generally necessary to comply with all the requirements of CPR Pt 35: *Pipia v Bgeo Group Ltd* [2019] EWHC 325 (Comm) (citing *Bestfort Developments LLP v Ras Al Khaimah Investment Authority* [2016] EWCA Civ 1099; [2017] C.P. Rep. 9).

72 [2001] Lloyd's Rep. P.N. 38 CA. See also the accountants' negligence case of *Barings Plc (In Liquidation) v Coopers & Lybrand* [2001] Lloyd's Rep. P.N. 379.

73 See *JP Morgan Chase Bank v Springwell Navigation Corp* [2006] EWHC 2755 (Comm); [2007] 1 All E.R. (Comm) 549. At [19], Aikens J explained that "[i]t is well established that in order to fulfil the requirement of CPR r. 35.1, a court must be satisfied that the expert evidence is properly admissible and will genuinely assist the trial judge in determining the matters which are in issue. The burden of establishing these two requirements rests upon the party that seeks permission to adduce the expert evidence concerned". This test has been repeatedly approved and applied, e.g. in *Proton Energy Group SA v Public Co Orlen Lietuva* [2013] EWHC 334 (Comm) at [30]. The case of *Mitchell v News Group Newspapers Ltd* [2014] EWHC 3590 (QB) is a good illustration of the test in practice. Having regard to the importance and value of a high-profile defamation claim, the court permitted expert evidence on phonetics to help determine whether words could be said in a given time and evidence from an optometrist and a scene reconstruction expert to help determine what could be seen from a given position. In giving permission for this evidence, the court in substance applied the test of genuine assistance, and rejected a test of absolute necessity.

74 [2015] EWHC 2477 (Ch); [2015] Pens. L.R. 519 at [68]. The court explained at [63] that at the third stage of the test, it was necessary to take into account proportionality and to consider such factors as the value of the claim, the effect of a judgment either way on the parties, who is to pay for the commissioning of the evidence on each side and any potential delay to the proceedings. The test was approved and adopted in *The RBS Rights Issue Litigation* [2015] EWHC 3433 (Ch) at [19], where the court refused permission for evidence of equity analysts to be given concerning the adequacy of information in a prospectus for investors, since it was unlikely to assist in determining what information was required to inform lay investors in accordance with statutory requirements. The test in the *British Airways* case has been applied many times since then. For example, in *English Electrical Co Ltd v Alstom UK* [2017] EWHC 1244 (QB), permission was given to call accountancy experts to comment on whether it could be inferred from accounts that a company was non-trading and without any employees. See also *Darby Properties Ltd v Lloyds Bank Plc* [2016] EWHC 2494 (Ch) and *Joint Liquidators of WR Refrigeration Ltd v WR Refrigeration Ltd* [2017] EWHC 3608 (Ch). In *Alexander Brothers Ltd v Alstom Transport*

SA [2020] EWHC 1584 (Comm), permission was given for expert evidence on the consequences under French criminal law of enforcement of an arbitral award, having regard to the potential value of the evidence; its cost; the effect on the proceedings of admitting it; and the significance of the case to the parties. In *Pilgrim v Fire and Blood Productions Ltd*, unreported, 19 February 2020, expert evidence on the safety of stunt arrangements for a film was refused when the application for its inclusion had been made shortly before trial and the factual witnesses could address the arrangements for and risks of stunts.

[75] [2016] 1 W.L.R. 597 at [45]–[49], Lords Reed and Hodge JJSC. Although a judgment in a Scottish appeal, it draws heavily on authority from England and Wales, and states principles which are in the main equally applicable to both jurisdictions.

[76] See *Neumann v Camel* [2015] EWHC 3507 (QB) at [25].

[76A] [2017] EWHC 1037 (Ch).

[76B] See also *Darby Properties Ltd v Lloyds Bank Plc* [2016] EWHC 2494 (Ch). Contrast the previous decision of the court in *St Dominic's Ltd v Royal Bank of Scotland Plc* [2015] EWHC 3822 (QB).

[76C] [2017] EWHC 2207 (Ch).

[76D] See also, to the same effect, *Fine Care Homes Ltd v Natwest Markets Plc* [2020] EWHC 874 (Ch), where expert evidence was permitted both to provide context for argument about duties owed and to ensure a level playing field between customer and bank.

After paragraph 6-012, add new paragraph 6-012A:

6-012A   Where parties attempt to introduce expert evidence after the early stages of litigation, the court will usually also consider the effects of granting permission on the other parties and any disruption to the proceedings which would result. A stricter view is now taken by the courts of non-compliance with the CPR and court directions than was once the case,[76E] such that a party attempting to adduce expert evidence at a late stage may face a heavy burden of persuasion, especially if the effect would be seriously disruptive.[76F]

[76E] In *Glaxo Wellcome UK Ltd (t/a Allen and Hanburys) v Glenmark Pharmaceuticals Europe Ltd* [2019] EWHC 3239 (Ch), the court refused an extension of time to adduce survey evidence where granting the extension would cause the expedited trial of a trade mark infringement and passing off claim to be adjourned and there was no good explanation provided for the delay in making the application that would justify extending time.

[76F] See for example *Bhaloo v Fiat Chrysler Automobiles UK Ltd* [2019] EWHC 3398 (QB), where an application to adduce evidence about lifetime exposure to asbestos was refused since it could have been obtained earlier and would cause the trial date to be lost. The judge drew on principles formulated for late amendment applications in *Quah Su-Ling v Goldman Sachs International* [2015] EWHC 759 (Comm). See also *T v Imperial College Healthcare NHS Trust* [2020] EWHC 1147 (QB) where the court rejected an application by the defendant NHS trust to adduce evidence from a single joint expert in genetics on the basis that the application had been made very late and allowing it would inevitably mean vacating the trial date.

To the end of paragraph 6-013 after "supplied to them.", add:

6-013   Guidance on expert evidence is also to be found in the various specialist court guides (Queen's Bench Division, Commercial Court, Technology and Construction Court, Chancery Division). More generally, the courts will now expect parties to co-operate in identifying the issues for expert evidence and in making arrangements for it to be produced efficiently. As well as exercising its power to specify issues for expert evidence, the court may give directions for discussions between lawyers and/or experts before first reports are produced.[77A]

[77A] See the Final Report of the Chancery Modernisation Review by Lord Justice Briggs at paras 6.28–6.34. See also the discussion of this topic in *UPL Europe Ltd v Agchemaccess Chemicals Ltd* [2016] EWHC 2889 (Ch). In that case, Chief Master Marsh said that a discussion of expert issues should be the norm and that, where scientific analysis was required, the parties should seek to agree on the method. Refusal to engage in discussions could have adverse costs consequences.

To the end of paragraph 6-014 after "of the experts.", add:

6-014   Some of those recommendations were approved by the Civil Procedure Rules Committee in May 2017 and have now come into force by way of amendments to CPR PD 35.11.

Replace the first paragraph (to amend text, incorporate new footnotes 84A and 86A and new text following "stage being disclosed." at the end of the paragraph), with:

The power of the Court to control expert evidence can also be used to support **6-015** the overriding objective of the Civil Procedure Rules and enforce proper compliance with pre-action protocols.[84A] In particular, the practices of "expert shopping" and late introduction of expert evidence will be discouraged.[85] Attempts to replace experts are treated with particular caution. In *Guntrip v Cheney Coaches Ltd*,[86] the Court of Appeal rejected an attempt by a claimant to introduce a substitute expert after his original expert had signed a joint statement, the effect of which would have been seriously adverse to the claimant's case. Lewison LJ pointed out that an expert might modify or change his opinion during a meeting with his opposite number, and stated that it was best for the revised opinion to be brought to the attention of the parties and the court as soon as possible. Such a change of mind by an expert did not necessarily have the consequence that the instructing party would be permitted to rely upon evidence from a new expert.[86A] It was necessary for the court to consider all the circumstances, including the stage at which the substitution was attempted, the nature of any change of view and the cogency of the newly expressed opinion. In *Lee v Colchester Hospital NHS Foundation Trust*,[87] the court acknowledged that *Guntrip* explained the relevant principles for such an application. However, the court permitted late substitution of an expert on the ground that his evidence had been compromised by his having been dismissed from employment. There was a very genuine reason for seeking to change expert and a prospective application would plainly have been allowed. A number of further cases have considered the consequences of an application to introduce a substitute expert, and have established the usual principle that the report of the first expert should be disclosed as a condition to such an application being allowed. In *Beck v Ministry of Defence*,[88] the Court of Appeal considered the situation where a party had instructed one named expert with permission of the court, obtained his report but subsequently sought permission to instruct a second expert on the ground that the first expert's report was not satisfactory. Permission to instruct the second expert was made conditional upon disclosure of the report of the first. In *Edwards-Tubb v JD Wetherspoon Plc*,[89] that approach was applied by extension to the instruction of experts at a pre-issue stage. In that case, the claimant had nominated experts in a pre-action protocol letter. When no objection was taken, the claimant instructed one and obtained a report from that expert, but he did not disclose a copy. He thereafter sought to rely upon a report of another expert who had not been nominated. The Court of Appeal held that permission to rely upon the expert's evidence should be subject to the same condition as in *Beck*. Such a condition should, it was said, usually be imposed where the permission of the court is sought to adduce evidence from a different expert from the one selected through the protocol procedure. However the court made clear that, parties should be free to obtain expert advice *before* embarking on the protocol, and orders should not be made conditional on reports obtained at that stage being disclosed. In *Vilca v Xstrata Ltd*,[89A] the court held that, where a party applied for a time extension to instruct a new expert to serve expert evidence, it was not obliged to impose a condition that the party disclose reports of their previous expert(s) if there was no concern about undesirable "expert shopping" or abuse of process by the party, and if there was no other good reason to impose the condition. A limitation on the power to impose such conditions was recognised in *Bowman v Thomson*,[89B] where it was held that there was no power to require provision of a previous expert's report as a condition of an existing permission for expert evidence not being withdrawn.

[84A] See for example *Obi v Patel* [2018] EWHC 3985 (QB), where permission for additional expert reports was refused on the basis that the defendant had delayed notifying the claimant of its proposed expert evidence and had done so in a tactical way. The judge observed that it was in general necessary to identify what expert evidence was required at an early stage in proceedings.

[85] See para.6-012A above. A number of cases in the professional liability field have considered whether an application to introduce expert evidence late is to be treated as one seeking relief from sanction, and thus engaging the principles discussed in *Mitchell v News Group Newspapers Ltd* [2014] 1 W.L.R. 795 and *Denton v TH White Ltd* [2014] C.P. Rep. 40. In *Bank of Ireland v Donaldsons LLP* [2014] EWHC 1957 (Ch), the claimant was permitted, in the context of a valuer's negligence claim, to adduce a supplementary expert report despite having delayed in doing so. The court rejected the submission that the request to introduce the report outside the time set in an order had to be addressed as if it were an application for relief from sanction. In *Warners Retail Ltd v National Westminster Bank Plc* [2014] EWHC 2818 (Ch), when a party in an interest rate swaps misselling action sought to introduce expert evidence late in the day and an adjournment of the trial would have been required to accommodate the new evidence, the court refused the application. It was not necessary to decide whether the *Mitchell* approach applied, since ordinary application of the overriding objective dictated the answer. In *Gladstar Ltd v Layzells* [2014] EWHC 1449 (Ch), which involved a claim for breach of a solicitor's undertaking, the claimant sought unsuccessfully to adduce expert evidence seriously out of time. Sales J concluded that the order requiring filing/service of expert evidence by a set date included an implicit sanction against non-compliance and that therefore the application to introduce the evidence late had to be treated as one for relief from sanction. In *Ellison v University Hospital of Morecombe Bay NHS Trust* [2015] EWHC 477 (QB), the court identified variable treatment of this issue in the case law, with some cases treating any late application to introduce expert evidence as engaging the robust approach in *Mitchell* and others taking a different view. On the facts of that case, it was unnecessary to decide the point.

[86] [2012] C.P. Rep. 26.

[86A] See also *Fetaj v Cohen* [2019] EWHC 2803 (Ch), where the claimants attempted to change experts on the basis that theirs had been subjected to undue pressure in an experts' meeting. The court rejected the attempt, stressing that such an allegation would have to be made clearly and the experts given an opportunity to respond.

[87] [2015] EWHC 1766 (QB).

[88] [2005] 1 W.L.R. 2206.

[89] [2011] 1 W.L.R. 1373.

[89A] [2017] EWHC 1582 (QB); [2017] B.L.R. 460. See also *TQ Delta v ZyXEL Communications* [2019] EWHC 1597 (Pat), where the court permitted the defendant to substitute one expert for another without disclosing material going beyond the new expert's report. However, the court excluded a section of the new expert's report which raised a new argument in order to preclude the defendant using it as a means of introducing a new point at a late stage.

[89B] [2019] EWHC 269 (QB).

(d)   Relevance and Admissibility of Expert Evidence

Replace paragraph 6-016 (to incorporate amendments to footnotes 95, 96 and 97 and new text following "challenge until trial." at end of the paragraph) with:

6-016   The modern approach to expert evidence encourages the Court to be vigilant in its scrutiny of expert evidence, both before and at trial. In *Kennedy v Cordia (Services) LLP*,[94] the Supreme Court identified four considerations governing the admissibility of expert evidence:

> "(i) whether the proposed [expert] evidence will assist the court in its task; (ii) whether the witness has the necessary knowledge and experience; (iii) whether the witness is impartial in his or her presentation and assessment of the evidence; and (iv) whether there is a reliable body of knowledge or experience to underpin the expert's evidence."

Accordingly, expert evidence should not be admitted if the issue to which it is directed can readily be resolved by the court without resort to expert assistance.[95] The court should guard against inappropriate expert evidence to bolster a case which properly depends on a judicial analysis of the facts.[96] Furthermore, expert evidence should be directed to assisting in the resolution of issues, and it should not ordinarily be admitted on the basis of a vague and generalised appeal to the assistance it might give the court.[97] If permission has been given to call expert evidence, objection may be made to its admissibility and this should be done as soon as possible.[98] It is no longer necessary to make such objection to the trial judge only,[99] nor is it desirable to leave such a challenge until trial. Although at an interlocutory stage the Court may reject a report wholesale on the ground of its being inadmissible, it is not usually appropriate for the Court to engage in the task of editing a report to excise inadmissible statements or passages.[99A] While it is possible for a party to apply for the court to revoke permission for expert evidence (especially if circumstances change to justify revocation), the burden in such an application will be on the applicant and the court is typically slow to revoke permission.[99B]

[94] [2016] UKSC 6; [2016] 1 W.L.R. 597 at [44].

[95] See para.6-012 above. The principles in *Kennedy v Cordia (Services) LLP* were applied in the case of *P v Home Office* [2017] EWHC 663 (QB); [2017] 1 W.L.R. 3189, where the court refused permission for expert evidence on human trafficking and the standard of care of front-line immigration officers. The proposed evidence did not in truth assist in determining the proper standard of care, and it simply sought to answer the ultimate issue.

[96] See *Liddell v Middleton* [1996] P.I.Q.R. P36 at P41–P44; *Barings Plc v Coopers & Lybrand* [2001] Lloyd's Rep. P.N. 379 at [45]; *Esure Insurance Ltd v Direct Line Insurance Plc* [2008] EWCA Civ 842; [2009] Bus. L.R. 438. In *Team Tex SAS v Wang* [2015] EWHC 1909 (QB), the court rejected an attempt to adduce evidence of an ergonomist on the issue of whether instructions for a child car seat were sufficiently clear and unambiguous. In the partnership dispute case of *Bagga v Nagpal* [2015] EWHC 398 (Ch), a party was refused permission to adduce expert evidence on the terms on which the partnership was entered into, although it was recognised that an expert might need to be called at a later stage if accounts and inquiries were ordered to be made. In *Change Red Ltd v Barclays Bank Plc* [2016] EWHC 3489 (Ch), the court refused to admit the evidence of accountancy experts in deciding whether the defendant bank had to have regard to the claimant's revised accounts in considering whether to include it in an FCA review exercise. The issue to which the evidence went was, on analysis, the meaning of "turnover" in the Companies Act 2006, which was a question for the court. In *Carr v Formation Group Plc* [2018] EWHC 3116 (Ch), an application for permission to rely upon evidence of market practice was rejected in a claim alleging unlawful conduct in payment of a commission by investment advisers to sports agents. The court concluded that the issues were of honesty and the defendants' state of mind, which were not matters for expert evidence.

[97] See *British Airways Plc v Spencer* [2015] EWHC 2477 (Ch); [2015] Pens. L.R. 519 at [21]–[24]. The judge added that, where there are technical matters requiring uncontentious explanation, that should be provided by way of agreed summary rather than by calling an expert solely to educate the court. See also *Denning v Greenhalgh Financial Services Ltd* [2017] EWHC 143 (QB); [2017] P.N.L.R. 19. In striking out a claim against financial advisers, Green J declined to give any weight to the report of a compliance expert in support of the proposition that a competent adviser owes a general duty to consider potential claims and grounds for complaint against its predecessors.

[98] In *Acamar Films Ltd v Microsoft Corp* [2012] EWHC 2682 (Pat), a late application was made which challenged the admissibility of the respondent's expert evidence. Although Arnold J found that there was room to doubt the admissibility of some passages of the report in question, he held (at [5]) that:

> "bearing in mind the lateness with which the point has been raised, as a result of which not only have I read the evidence in question but also the parties are ready to cross-examine to it, and in particular the difficulty of disentangling that which is properly admissible from that which is inadmissible, it seems to me that the better course is to admit all of the evidence and to allow any question over the evidence to be taken as one of weight rather than admissibility".

Note also *Teva Pharmaceutical Industries Ltd v Actavis UK Ltd* [2015] EWHC 2605 (Pat), where the court considered admissibility of written expert evidence filed in support of an interim injunction application. Objection was taken to the evidence on the ground that it did not contain the prescribed form of declaration. The court accepted that the provisions of CPR Pt 35 governing the form of reports applied to evidence in interlocutory applications, but admitted the evidence because as a matter of substance the report was suitable for admission as expert evidence.

[99] The position used to be more complicated. Where it was disputed whether expert evidence was admissible, the master or judge in chambers was not entitled to rule on the admissibility of such evidence: see *Sullivan v West Yorkshire Passenger Transport Executive* [1985] 2 All E.R. 134 CA. However, in *Woodford & Ackroyd v Burgess* [1999] Lloyd's Rep. P.N. 231, the Court of Appeal held that a judge who

was not the trial judge could rule on admissibility under the inherent jurisdiction. See also *Liverpool Roman Catholic Archdiocese Trustees Incorporated v Goldberg (No.2)* [2001] Lloyd's Rep. P.N. 518, where Neuberger J set out in six steps the proper approach to an application to exclude expert evidence on the grounds that it was inadmissible.

[99A] See *Moylett v Geldof* [2018] EWHC 893 (Ch), following *Hoyle v Rogers* [2014] EWCA Civ 257; [2015] Q.B. 265 (approved in *ICI v Merit Merrell* [2018] EWHC 1577 (TCC) at [214] and in *A v B* [2019] EWHC 275 (Comm); [2019] 4 W.L.R. 25).

[99B] See *Glenn v Watson* [2017] EWHC 256 (Ch), where the court refused to revoke permission for expert evidence in the field of equity investment in property opportunities. Although he applied the principles in *British Airways Plc v Spencer* [2015] EWHC 2477 (Ch); [2015] Pens. L.R. 519, Nugee J also explained that the approach of the court was different when hearing an application to revoke permission.

(ii)   The Appropriate Questions

Replace paragraph 6-018 (to incorporate an amendment to footnote 103 and new text following "the decision-maker." at the end of the paragraph:

6-018   Secondly, it is important that the evidence of an expert witness is confined to matters which are relevant to the issues before the court.[101] In *Pozzolanic Lytag Ltd v Bryan Hobson Associates*,[102] Dyson J stated that the expert witnesses should have confined themselves to the question whether there was a common practice in the engineering profession as to what engineers who are engaged as project managers do in relation to the insurance obligations of building contractors. Instead, they considered numerous other issues including contributory negligence, which was a matter for the court. He warned[103]:

> "Prolix expert reports directed to issues with which they should not be concerned merely add to the expense of litigation. Everything possible should be done to discourage this. In appropriate cases, this will include making special orders for costs."

While an expert is entitled to express opinions which would, if accepted, resolve issues in the proceedings, it is important that the expert's role should be limited to providing assistance within the scope of his or her particular expertise.[104] Moreover, the provision of expert assistance to the court "does not extend to supplanting the court as the decision-maker."[105] As well as determining the issues on which expert evidence will be given, the court exercises control over later stages of the expert evidence process to ensure that the evidence remains focused upon the issues for which permission was given. The facility to put written questions to experts under CPR r.35.6 is for the purpose of clarifying their evidence, and questions not justified for that purpose can be disallowed.[105A]

[101] Under s.3 of the Civil Evidence Act 1972, opinion evidence is admissible only on relevant matters on which the witness is qualified to give expert evidence.

[102] [1999] B.L.R. 267.

[103] [1999] B.L.R. 267 at 275. See also *Pride Valley Food Ltd v Hall and Partners (Contract Management) Ltd* [2000] N.P.C. 55, where Judge Toulmin CMG, QC concluded that the claimant's expert evidence provided little or no assistance. Amongst other criticisms, he pointed out that the report was overlong, included opinions on matters of fact and law which were questions for decision by the court and included expressions of opinion as to what the expert himself would have done in the defendant's position. The Court of Appeal did not comment on this passage: [2001] EWCA Civ 1001. See also *Stephen Donald Architects Ltd v Christopher King* [2003] EWHC 1867 (TCC) (evidence of defendant's expert architect unhelpful because he did not address the question whether any reasonably competent architect would have prepared a different design in response to the client's brief). When instructing experts to engage in discussions with each other, parties are encouraged to agree a single and focussed agenda. The aim should be to produce a joint statement of the experts which allows the Court to identify the key issues and see each expert's position on each one. See *Saunders v Central Manchester University Hospitals NHS Foundation Trust* [2018] EWHC 343 (QB) at [34]–[35].

[104] See the discussion in the Privy Council criminal appeal of *Pora v The Queen* [2015] UKPC 9; [2016] Cr. App. R 3 at [23]–[27].

[105] See *Kennedy v Cordia (Services) LLP* [2016] 1 W.L.R. 597 at [49].

[105A] See for example *Mustard v Flower* [2019] EWHC 2623 (QB), where the court disallowed a series of questions put by the claimant as being too long and complex and as amounting to cross-examination in writing. The court observed that experts should not be left having to make judgments about the appropriateness and proportionality of questions, or having to give reasons for refusals to answer.

(iii)   The Appropriate Qualifications and Experience

Replace footnote 106 with:

[106] *The Queen v Bonython* (1984) 38 S.A.S.R. 45 at 46 per King CJ, as endorsed by the Supreme Court   **6-019**
in *Kennedy v Cordia (Services) LLP* [2016] 1 W.L.R. 597 at [43], by Evans-Lombe J in *Barings Plc (In Liquidation) v Coopers & Lybrand* (2001) Lloyd's Rep. Bank 85 and by Aikens J in *JP Morgan Chase Bank v Springwell Navigation Corp* [2006] EWHC 2755 (Comm); [2007] 1 All E.R. (Comm) 549. The proposition that an expert may acquire sufficient knowledge by study was acknowledged as correct by Hamblen J in *Zeid v Credit Suisse* [2011] EWHC 716 (Comm). In *Myers v The Queen* [2015] UKPC 40; [2016] A.C. 314 (PC, Bermuda), the Privy Council accepted that police officers could probably give expert evidence of gang culture based on experience developed in practice. In *Vilca v Xstrata Ltd* [2016] EWHC 2757 (QB); [2017] B.L.R. 460, the court refused to permit expert evidence to be introduced on the topic of good practice and human rights in arranging police protection of mines in Peru. Foskett J said that there was no evidence of a recognised body of opinion on the appropriate steps to be taken. The Voluntary Principles adopted by the industry were clear and did not require expert explanation.

(iv)   Impartiality

Replace paragraph 6-021 (to incorporate new text following "an independent expert." at the end of the paragraph) with:

In *Stevens v Gullis*,[114] it was found that the defendant's expert building surveyor   **6-021**
had failed in his duty to act impartially and had also failed to comply with the requirements of the Civil Procedure Rules in relation to his report[115] and to a joint memorandum of matters agreed with the claimant's expert. The value which the court places upon the impartiality of expert evidence is demonstrated by the Court of Appeal's decision to uphold an order debarring the defendant from calling his expert, notwithstanding that both claimant and defendant had invited the court to accept his evidence. In *Great Eastern Hotel Co Ltd v John Laing Construction Ltd*,[116] the evidence of the defendant's construction management expert was rejected because, in failing to carry out thorough research, in accepting uncritically the factual account given by the defendant and in failing to take account of material evidence, he demonstrated "no concept of his duty to the court as an independent expert".[117] In *Bank of Ireland v Watts Group Plc*,[117A] the court found that the claimant's expert quantity surveyor was not a properly independent expert witness, the claimant being his principal client and providing the vast majority of his work and fees. The expert's evidence had shown a lack of realism and his criticisms were based on an unrealistic expectation of what the defendant was required to do. Further, he had attempted to mislead the court with selective reliance on RICS guidance and adopted an unreasonable approach, failing to make concessions at the experts' meeting and when giving his evidence. The court held that, in such circumstances, the evidence of the defendant's expert was to be preferred wherever there was a disagreement between the experts. In a subsequent judgment on costs in the same case, the court ordered that the defendant's costs relating to the conduct and evidence of the claimant's expert at trial would be assessed on the indemnity basis, as would the costs of the defendant's corresponding expert.[117B] *ICI v Merit Merrell*[117C] was a further case in which the court identified a lack of independence in one party's expert evidence. For example, the judge criticised a valuation expert for adopting a method favourable to the instructing party but without proper reference to the underlying contract and pleaded issues. He stressed the importance of

experts complying with the *Ikarian Reefer* guidance.[117D] On the other side of the line, the court in *Blackpool BC v Volkerfitzpatrick Ltd*[117E] found that experts instructed for one party had not acted improperly in requesting further tests from a company engaged to carry out testing for both parties, although it would have been good practice to give notice in advance.

[114] [2000] 1 All E.R. 527.

[115] CPR r.35.10(1) imposes requirements as to the contents of an expert's report, which are set out in CPR Pt 35 PD paras 3.1–3.3.

[116] [2005] EWHC 181 (TCC); 99 Con. L.R. 45.

[117] ibid. per HH Judge Wilcox at [128]. See also *London Fire and Emergency Planning Authority v Halcrow Gilbert Associates Ltd* [2007] EWHC 2546 (TCC) at [44]–[82]. In *Arroyo v Equion Energia Ltd* [2016] EWHC 1699 (TCC) at [498]–[502], Stuart-Smith J expressed serious concern about the production of expert reports where the experts had included in their reports statements and information (including comments from other expert reports) which had been provided to them by lawyers and which they had not independently verified. He observed that this cast doubt upon the integrity of the affected reports and the expert evidence process as a whole.

[117A] [2017] EWHC 1667 (TCC); 173 Con. L.R. 240.

[117B] [2017] EWHC 2472 (TCC); [2017] B.L.R. 626.

[117C] [2018] EWHC 1577 (TCC). The adverse findings about expert evidence provided part of the basis of an indemnity costs order made in that case.

[117D] Ibid per Fraser J at [236]–[237]. See also *Ashley Wilde Group Ltd v BCPL Ltd* [2019] EWHC 3166 (IPEC), where the court declined to rely on the evidence of an expert witness who had turned his initial, partisan opinion into a formal expert report, without addressing the differences between the opinion and the report, holding that the report failed to meet the requirements of objectivity and impartiality under CPR Pt 35.

[117E] [2020] EWHC 387 (TCC).

Replace footnote 119 with:

6-022

[119] ibid. at [102]. In *EXP v Barker* [2017] EWCA Civ 63; [2017] Med. L.R. 121, the Court of Appeal held that the trial judge had been fully entitled to take the view, following the non-disclosure of a close connection between the defendant and his expert witness, that the expert had so compromised his position that the weight to be accorded to his views must be considerably diminished. Irwin LJ (with whom Henderson LJ and Black LJ agreed) indicated that had the trial judge taken the decision to exclude the expert's evidence in its entirety, it would have been a proper decision.

(f) Experts' Immunity from Suit

Replace footnote 161 with:

6-032

[161] See *Siegel v Pummell* [2015] EWHC 195 (QB); [2015] 3 Costs L.O. 357 at [37]–[39]. Furthermore, in extreme cases, a party may apply to commit an expert for contempt, notably in cases where the expert has acted dishonestly. See *Liverpool Insurance Co Ltd v Khan* [2019] EWCA Civ 392; [2019] 1 W.L.R. 3833 ; *R. (on the application of Accident Exchange Ltd) v Broom* [2017] EWHC 1530 (Admin).

CHAPTER 7

HUMAN RIGHTS AND JUDICIAL REVIEW IN PROFESSIONAL LIABILITY

TABLE OF CONTENTS

5. LAWYERS

(c) Freedom of Expression/Association

Replace paragraph 7-053 (to incorporate new text following "was also dismissed." at the end of the paragraph) with:

7-053   In *National Notary Chamber v Albania*,[144] the European Court dismissed a complaint that the compulsory requirement for membership by notaries of the National Notary Chamber, a body established by the legislature to exercise a form of public control over the practice of the notary profession, was contrary to art.11. The court held that art.11 was inapplicable and compulsory membership did not infringe the right to freedom of association because the National Notary Chamber and district notary chambers were not "associations" within the meaning of the article. In *Richard Craven v Bar Standards Board*,[145] the Visitors to the Inns of Court (Silber J, Mr Kenneth Crofton-Martin, Ms Amanda Savage) dismissed an appeal against a finding by the Disciplinary Tribunal of the Inns of Court that a barrister who had sent an offensive email about a colleague to other colleagues was guilty of conduct which was likely to bring the legal profession into disrepute. Amongst other findings, they rejected the submission that the BSB proceedings against him for sending the email constituted an infringement with the appellant's art.10 right to freedom of expression. In any event, even if there was such an interference, there was no infringement of art.10 because the proceedings were in accordance with the law, necessary in a democratic society, particularly for the protection of the reputation of others, namely the legal professional, and were proportionate. A related argument based on art.8 was also dismissed. Similar arguments based on art.10 were dismissed in *Khan v BSB*[145A] and *Diggins v BSB*.[145B]

[144] (17029/05) 6 May 2008; (2008) 47 E.H.R.R. SE11.

[145] unreported 30 January 2014.

[145A] [2018] EWHC 2184 (Admin).

[145B] [2020] EWHC 467 (Admin); [2020] I.R.L.R. 686.

6. MEDICAL PRACTITIONERS

(b)   Relevant Articles in Relation to Medical Practitioners

After "of Convention articles," in the first sentence, add new footnote 148A:

[148A] Article 5 (deprivation of liberty) arguments have also been raised in this context, but to date have not been successful. See, e.g. *Gard v United Kingdom (Admissibility), App. No.39793/17*, 3 July 2017.

7-056

(i)   Article 2

Examples of the application of article 2

Replace items 1 "Abortion" and 2 "Euthanasia" of the list (to incorporate new text after "of abortion issues." and after "with art.8 rights.") with:

Article 2 has been invoked in the following situations.

7-059

1. *Abortion* Prior to the HRA, the position in English law was that an unborn child had no existence separate from its mother and could be aborted under the terms of the Abortion Act 1967.[155] In *Paton v UK*,[156] the Commission held that a foetus had no absolute right to life as the term "everyone" in art.2 generally only applied post-natally but it left open the question whether the foetus had some right to life (for example, if it was able to live independently of its mother). In *H v Norway*,[157] the Commission held that the abortion of a foetus for social reasons was not contrary to art.2 where there was "a difficult situation of life" in relation to the mother. These decisions, which allow a wide margin of appreciation in relation to the right to life, were relied on by one member of the Court of Appeal in the case of the conjoined twins in *Re A (Minors) (Conjoined Twins: Separation)*.[158] Ward LJ stated that art.2 was subject to an implied limitation that justified the balancing approach taken by the court in allowing the twins to be separated despite the fact that this would cause certain death to one of the twins.[159]

    In *Vo v France*[160] the European Court stated that it was unnecessary to answer in the abstract the question of whether the unborn child was a "person" for the purposes of art.2, thereby reinforcing the margin of appreciation of the Member States in this area and highlighting the view of the European Group of Ethics that "it would be inappropriate to impose one exclusive moral code". The Court chose to focus instead on the legal protection to which the applicant was entitled in respect of the loss of the unborn child and on the procedural requirements of art.2. The court concluded that recourse should have been made to the administrative courts, thereby allowing the applicant to prove medical negligence on the part of the doctor whose failure to examine the applicant prior to the medical procedure caused her to lose her child.

    The European Court again sought to sidestep dealing substantively with the issue of the compatibility of abortion and Convention rights in *D v Ireland*.[161] The applicant sought to complain to the ECHR about the lack of abortion services in Ireland in the case of lethal foetal abnormality. At that time, the only recognised exception to the constitutional prohibition in Ireland on abortion was "a real and substantial risk to the life of the mother" including one of suicide. The applicant asserted that she had been discriminated against as a pregnant woman with a lethal foetal abnormality.

However, the case was declared to be inadmissible by the court as a result of the applicant's failure to exhaust domestic remedies. The court relied on the *X* case as showing that the constitutional courts could develop the protection of individual rights by way of interpretation and emphasised the importance of providing those courts with the opportunity to do so. It stated that the presumption in the *X* case was that the foetus had a normal life expectancy and there was feasible argument to be made that the constitutionally enshrined balance between the right to life of the mother and of the foetus could have shifted in favour of the mother when the "unborn" suffered from an abnormality incompatible with life.

This decision can be contrasted with that reached by the court in *Tysiac v Poland*.[162] The applicant suffered from a pregnancy-related illness which resulted in a significant deterioration in her eyesight. Despite this, her treating doctors refused to certify that her pregnancy should be terminated on therapeutic grounds. The court held that there had been no breach of art.3 but that there had been a breach of art.8 given the failure of Polish law to provide an effective mechanism capable of determining whether the conditions for obtaining a lawful abortion had been met or for resolving disputes either between the woman and the doctors or between the doctors themselves. Judge Borrego's strong dissenting opinion highlights the inconsistencies between this decision and that in *D v Ireland*.

The European Court has recently been asked to revisit the approach of the Irish Government to abortion in *A, B and C v Ireland*.[163] The court (by a majority) held that the restriction imposed on abortion by the Irish Government pursued a legitimate aim of protecting morals (including the right to life of the unborn) and that this was generally a legitimate aim having regard to the right to travel abroad for an abortion with access to appropriate information and medical care in Ireland. It was held that Ireland had not breached art.8 in relation to two of the applicants (who wished to have abortions for psychological reasons) but that it had done so in relation to a third applicant (who had a rare form of cancer and who would not receive treatment for cancer in Ireland whilst pregnant, there being no accessible and effective procedure for her to use to establish whether she qualified for a lawful abortion in Ireland). The Court therefore appears to be following the *Tysiac* as opposed to the *D* approach in relation to its consideration of abortion issues.

In *R. v Secretary of State for Health Ex p. John Smeaton (on behalf of the Society for the Protection of Unborn Children)*,[164] the legality of the sale and use of the morning after pill was unsuccessfully challenged.

In *The Attorney General for Northern Ireland and the Department of Justice v The Northern Ireland Human Rights Commission*,[164A] the Court of Appeal of Northern Ireland held that it was inappropriate to make a declaration that legislative provisions were incompatible with ECHR art.8 because they prohibited abortion in cases of fatal foetal abnormalities, rape and incest. Articles 2 and 3 were also raised, but art.8 was the most relevant provision. Sections 58 and 59 of the Offences Against the Person Act 1861 and s.25 of the Criminal Justice Act (Northern Ireland) 1945 were held not to be incompatible with ECHR art.8. *A, B and C v Ireland* was applied restrictively. Morgan LCJ concluded that "each jurisdiction has a wide margin of appreciation in determining such sensitive legal and moral issues and that *A, B and C v Ireland* could not be interpreted as requiring such protection for women".

Further, in *R. (on the application of A and B) v Secretary of State for Health*,[164B] a majority of the Supreme Court held that women from Northern Ireland who travel to the UK seeking abortions are able to access the procedure without charge on the NHS. A decision whether to provide abortion services to a group of women free of charge fell within the scope of their rights under art.8 of the ECHR to respect for their private life. The decision under review had treated women usually resident in England differently from women who were UK citizens but usually resident in Northern Ireland. Such a difference in treatment had to be justified if it were not to amount to discrimination which breached art.14 of the ECHR.

2.   *Euthanasia* Article 2 confers a right to life but not a right to die. The national court's duty to respect the sanctity of human life and the refusal to sanction a course of conduct aimed at terminating life or accelerating death was affirmed at first instance in *A NHS Trust v D*.[165] The issue of euthanasia has now been extensively considered by the House of Lords and the European Court: see *Pretty v DPP and Home Secretary*[166] and *Pretty v UK*.[167] The House of Lords held that:

(a)   the right to life set out in art.2 could not be interpreted as conferring a right to die or to enlist the aid of another in bringing about one's death;

(b)   the art.3 right not to be subjected to inhuman or degrading treatment did not bear on an individual's right to live or die; it could not plausibly be suggested that the respondent was inflicting such treatment on Mrs Pretty whose suffering derived from her disease[168];

(c)   the art.8 right to respect for private life covered protection of personal autonomy in living; it did not extend to the choice not to live any longer. Further, even if art.8 applied, the present legislative regime was justifiable under art.8(2) and it was notable that the UK's response to this problem was in accordance with a broad international consensus;

(d)   a belief in the virtue of assisted suicide could not found a requirement pursuant to art.9(1) for Mrs Pretty's husband to be absolved from the consequences of criminal conduct and the same arguments on justification applied in any event;

(e)   even if one of the ECHR articles was engaged and Mrs Pretty could therefore rely in principle on art.14, s.2 of the Suicide Act 1961 did not discriminate against the disabled whilst allowing the able-bodied to commit suicide; the law conferred no right on anyone to commit suicide.

The European Court largely agreed with the English court's interpretation of the Convention, holding that:

(a)   article 2 did not impose on States a positive obligation to protect a "right to die";

(b)   a State's obligation to prevent ill treatment pursuant to art.3 could not be considered to include permitting actions designed to cause death. Nor was the State required to provide a means of lawfully committing assisted suicide;

(c)   whilst the right to refuse medical treatment was within art.8, the interference with Mrs Pretty's ability to end her life was legitimate and "necessary in a democratic society";

(d) article 9 did not protect all convictions or beliefs: a strongly held belief about assisted suicide did not fall within its meaning;

(e) the State had an objective and reasonable justification for not distinguishing in law between individuals who were and were not capable of committing suicide and therefore there had been no violation of arts 8 and 14.

However, in contrast to the *Pretty* case, in *Ms B v An NHS Hospital Trust*[169] a patient's right to refuse treatment and have the ventilator which kept her alive switched off even if this would result in her death was upheld on the ground that this amounted to refusal of treatment as opposed to active ending of life. Many commentators have called for reform of the law in light of the anomalies which arguably arise as a result of the two cases.[170]

In *Haas v Switzerland*[171] the European Court held that the applicant who was suffering from bipolar affective disorder had not had his art.8 rights infringed by reason of Switzerland's requirement for him to obtain a prescription before being able to obtain sodium pentobarbital in order to commit suicide. The requirement to obtain a prescription had the legitimate objective of preventing people from hasty decisions as well as preventing those without mental capacity from obtaining fatal doses of the drug. The case was distinguished from *Pretty* on the grounds that the applicant was able to take his own life (without drugs if necessary). In summary, whilst the court accepted that art.8 did include a right to selfdetermination in relation to the time and manner of one's own death, this right did not extent to requiring the state to provide an individual with his chosen means of committing suicide. In *R. (on the application of Tony Nicklinson) v Ministry of Justice & DPP*,[172] the English Court relied on *Haas* as authority for the proposition that whilst an individual's right to decide how and when to end his life was an aspect of art.8, the state had a wide margin of appreciation in this area. The court clarified that the ruling in *Pretty* that a blanket ban on assisted suicide was not incompatible with art.8 also applied to voluntary euthanasia and that it would be wrong to conclude that art.8 required voluntary euthanasia to afford a possible defence to murder. The court reiterated that it was for Parliament to decide whether to change the law on voluntary euthanasia.

The *Nicklinson* case has now been considered by the Court of Appeal[173] and by the Supreme Court.[174] The Court of Appeal upheld the lower court's ruling that the blanket legal prohibition on providing assistance to those wishing to die was not a disproportionate interference with art.8. In support of the appeal, an attempt was made to rely upon a recent decision of the ECHR in *Koch v Germany*.[175] However *Koch* was distinguished on the basis that the German courts had not made a ruling on the relationship between art.8 and the German law regulating the accessibility of drugs capable of terminating life despite it being incumbent on them to do so. By contrast, in the *Nicklinson* case the Divisional Court had expressly addressed this issue.

A majority of the Supreme Court dismissed the appeal reiterating that states which were parties to the Convention had a wide margin of appreciation regarding whether assisted suicide should be lawful and that a prohibition on assisted suicide such as that imposed by s.2 of the Suicide Act 1961 was within that margin of appreciation. The interference with the claimants' right to private life caused by that prohibition had to be balanced against the interests of society in protecting vulnerable people from being pressured into suicide, and on the evidence available it was impossible for the Court to make such an assessment. It was also emphasised that whether and to what extent assisted suicide should be lawful, and whether the risks to vulnerable people could be mitigated was inherently a matter for determination by the elected legislature rather than the court.

This decision has been upheld by the European Court[176] who declared the application inadmissible. The ECHR made clear that it did not consider it appropriate to extend art.8 so as to impose on the Contracting States a procedural obligation to make available a remedy requiring the courts to decide on the merits of a claim. In any event, the ECHR found that the majority of the Supreme Court had dealt with the substance of the first applicant's claim concluding that she had failed to show that developments since *Pretty* meant that the ban could no longer be considered a proportionate interference with art.8 rights.

In *R. (on the application of Conway) v Secretary of State for Justice*,[176A] the Court of Appeal overturned the refusal of the court below to allow a motor neurone disease sufferer to challenge s.2(1) of the Suicide Act 1961. He was permitted to proceed to seek a declaration under s.4(2) of the Human Rights Act 1998 that the ban on assisted dying is incompatible with the ECHR. However, the challenge was dismissed by the Divisional Court,[176B] in a judgment which was subsequently upheld by the Court of Appeal.[176C] Both courts held that the prohibition on assisted suicide was not contrary to the ECHR (in particular art.8).

[155] *Re F (in utero)* [1988] Fam. 122 CA; *St George's Healthcare NHS Trust v S* [1998] 3 W.L.R. 936 at 957A.

[156] (1980) 3 E.H.R.R. 408.

[157] (1992) 73 D.R. 155.

[158] [2001] 2 W.L.R. 480; [2000] Lloyd's Rep. Med. 425 CA.

[159] Walker LJ and Brooke LJ preferred to base their decision on the fact that the doctor's purpose in performing the operation was to save life, even if the extinction of another life was a virtual certainty and therefore this was not intentional killing. The word "intentionally" in art.2 was said to apply only where the purpose of the prohibited action was death (consistent with existing domestic law on this subject). The court's consideration of the human rights aspects of the appeal is extremely brief.

[160] (53924/00). The decision is considered in further detail in "What's the consensus? The Grand Chamber's Decision on Abortion in A, B and C v Ireland" [2011] E.H.R.L.R. 200. See also *RR v Poland* (2011) 53 E.H.R.R. 31 in which the European Court held that Poland had violated arts 3 and 8 where an applicant had been denied access to the prenatal genetic testing prior to the time limit for abortion for foetal abnormality. The woman subsequently gave birth to a baby with Turner's Syndrome and her husband left her. She was awarded €45,000 in relation to non-pecuniary damage.

[161] (26499/02) (2006) 43 E.H.R.R. SE16.

[162] (5410/03) [2007] E.H.R.L.R. 463; (2007) 45 E.H.R.R 42.

[163] (25579/05) 16 December 2010.

[164] [2002] 2 F.L.R. 146 Admin.

[164A] [2017] NICA 42.

[164B] [2017] UKSC 41; [2017] 1 W.L.R. 2492.

[165] [2000] 2 F.L.R. 677; [2000] Lloyd's Rep. Med. 411; *The Times*, 19 July 2000 per Cazalet J.

[166] [2001] 3 W.L.R. 1598; [2002] 1 All E.R. 1 HL.

[167] [2002] 35 E.H.R.R. 1. In *R. (on the application of AM) v (1) DPP (2) Solicitors Regulation Authority (3) GMC* [2012] EWHC 470 the court granted a declaration that solicitors retained by a terminally ill person wishing to end his life would not be encouraging or assisting suicide within the meaning of

the Suicide Act 1961 by obtaining information from third parties to place before the court in support of their client's case.

[168] In *R. (on the application of Q) v Secretary of State for the Home Department* [2004] Q.B. 36 the Court of Appeal approved the approach taken to art.3 in *Pretty*.

[169] [2002] 2 All E.R. 449.

[170] For further analysis of the case law in this area see "Assisted Suicide under the European Convention on Human Rights: a Critique" [2003] E.H.R.L.R. 65. See also *A Local Authority (Claimant) v MR Z (Defendant) & The Official Solicitor (Advocate to the Court)* (2005) 1 W.L.R. 959 in which Hedley J held that a local authority had a duty to investigate the position of a disabled person who wished her husband to arrange assisted suicide for her in Switzerland and to consider whether she was legally competent. However, where she was competent, the local authority had no duty to seek the continuation of an injunction restraining the husband from removing his wife from England. In the context of a person of full capacity, the right to life under art.2 of the European Convention on Human Rights 1950 did not assume primacy over the rights of autonomy and self-determination.

[171] [2011] E.H.R.L.R. 348.

[172] [2012] EWHC 2381 (Admin); (2012) 109 (32) L.S.G. 18.

[173] [2013] EWCA Civ 961.

[174] [2015] A.C. 657.

[175] (C-497/09) [2013] 1 F.C.R. 595; (2013) 56 E.H.R.R. 6.

[176] (2015) 61 E.H.R.R. SE7.

[176A] [2017] EWCA Civ 275.

[176B] [2017] EWHC 2447 (Admin).

[176C] [2018] EWCA Civ 1431.

7. PARTICULAR ISSUES ARISING UNDER THE HRA IN RELATION TO MEDICAL PRACTITIONERS

(c) Withdrawal of Treatment

To the end of paragraph 7-075 after "art.2 conventions.", add:

7-075   In *Gard v United Kingdom (Admissibility), App. No.39793/17*, 3 July 2017, the complaint was that the hospital had blocked access to life-sustaining treatment for a baby, Charlie Gard, by way of domestic legal proceedings, and not that the hospital had withdrawn life-sustaining treatment per se. The European Court nevertheless addressed the issue. It summarised the elements it takes into account in addressing the question of the administering or withdrawal of medical treatment:

(1)   The existence in domestic law and practice of a regulatory framework compatible with the requirements of Article 2.

(2)   Whether account had been taken of the applicant's previously expressed wishes and those of the persons close to him, as well as the opinions of other medical personnel.

(3)   The possibility to approach the courts in the event of doubts as to the best decision to take in the patient's interests.

After paragraph 7-076, add new paragraph:

7-076   In *In re Gard*[274A] the patient's parents proposed to obtain for their child alternative treatment which was available in the United States. It was submitted on their behalf that the test should not be what was in their child's "*best interests*" but whether or not the alternative treatment would cause their child "*significant harm*". The Court of Appeal rejected that contention, and repeated that "*best interests*" remained the relevant test.

[274A] [2017] EWCA Civ 410; [2018] 4 W.L.R. 5.

Replace paragraph 7-078 with:

In *R. (on the application of Oliver Leslie Burke) v GMC & (1) The Disability* **7-078**
*Rights Commission (Interested Party) and (2) The Official Solicitor to the Supreme
Court (Intervener)*,[279] it was held that under both the Convention and at common
law, if a patient was competent, or although incompetent had made an advance
directive which was valid and relevant to the treatment in question, his decision to
require the provision of artificial nutrition and hydration (ANH) during his dying
days was determinative of the issue. If neither such circumstances applied, the duty
would be to treat the patient in his or her best interests (with there being a strong
presumption in favour of preservation of life). It was stated that a failure to provide
life-prolonging treatment in circumstances exposing the patient to "inhuman or
degrading treatment" would in principle involve a breach of art.3. Alternatively
even if the patient's suffering had not reached the severity required to breach art.3,
a withdrawal of treatment in the same circumstances might still breach art.8 if there
were sufficiently adverse effects on his physical or moral integrity or mental
stability. Thus, at the final stage when the patient had lapsed into a coma and lacked
awareness of what was happening, there would not be a breach if ANH was
withdrawn in circumstances where its continuation was futile and of no benefit to
the patient. However, the prior authorisation of the court was required as a matter
of law where it was proposed to withdraw or withhold ANH (i) where there was
any doubt or disagreement as to the capacity (competence) of the patient; or (ii)
where there was a lack of unanimity amongst the attending medical professionals
as to either (1) the patient's condition or prognosis or (2) the patient's best interests
or (3) the likely outcome of ANH being either withheld or withdrawn or (4)
otherwise as to whether or not ANH should be withheld or withdrawn; or (iii) where
there was evidence that the patient, when competent, would have wanted ANH to
continue in the relevant circumstances; or (iv) where there was evidence that the
patient (even if a child or incompetent) resists or disputes the proposed withdrawal
of ANH; or (v) where persons having a reasonable claim to have their views or
evidence taken into account (such as parents or close relatives, partners, close
friends, long-term carers) asserted that withdrawal of ANH was contrary to the
patient's wishes or not in the patient's best interests.

[279] [2004] EWHC 1879 (Admin).

In *R. (on the application of Oliver Leslie Burke) v GMC & the Disability Rights
Commission*[280] the Court of Appeal held that there was nothing in the GMC's guidance paper on the withholding and withdrawing of artificial nutrition and hydration that was unlawful or that constituted a breach of the Convention. Where a
competent patient indicated his or her wish to be kept alive by the provision of
ANH, any doctor who deliberately brought that patient's life to an end by
discontinuing the supply of ANH would not merely be in breach of duty but would
be guilty of murder and in violation of art.2.[281] In *W (by her litigation friend B) v
(1) M (by her litigation friend the Official Solicitor) (2) S (3) a NHS Primary Care
Trust*, [282] it was emphasised that all cases relating to the withdrawal of artificial
nutrition and hydration from a person in a persistent vegetative state or minimally
conscious state should be referred to the court and that the test to be applied was
an objective one, namely what would be in the patient's best interests. The court
had to identify the factors on each side which were relevant to the patient's best
interests and carry out a balancing exercise. A balance sheet approach should be
adopted in every case save where the patient was in a vegetative state and treatment was futile. Provided this occurred, there would be no breach of arts 3 and 8.

280 [2005] EWCA Civ 1003; (2005) 3 W.L.R. 1132.

281 For a detailed commentary on this case and related issues, see Catherine Dupre's article "Human Dignity and the Withdrawal of Medical Treatment: A Missed Opportunity" [2006] E.H.R.L.R. 678.

282 [2011] EWHC 2443 (Fam); [2012] 1 W.L.R. 1653

In *R. (on the application of Tracey) v Cambridge University Hospitals NHS Foundation Trust*,[283] the Court of Appeal granted a declaration that the Trust had violated Mrs Tracey's art.8 right to respect for private life in failing to involve her in the process which led to a decision to introduce a Do Not Attempt Cardio-Pulmonary Resuscitation Notice onto her notes. The court made clear that since a DNACPR decision was one which will potentially deprive the patient of lifesaving treatment, there should be a presumption in favour of patient involvement.

283 [2014] EWCA Civ 822; [2014] Med. L.R. 273.

In *Gloucestershire Clinical Commissioning Group v (1) AB (2) CD*,[284] Baker J reiterated that in making a decision concerning life sustaining treatment, the court must have regard to the ECHR, and in particular arts 2 and 8. Article 2 imposed a positive obligation to give life sustaining treatment if this was in the best interests of the patient but did not impose an absolute obligation to treat if treatment was futile. Article 8 encompassed considerations of a patient's personal autonomy and quality of life.

284 [2014] EWCOP 49.

8. PROFESSIONAL DISCIPLINARY PROCEEDINGS

(a) Introduction

Replace the second paragraph of paragraph 7-095 with:

7-095   Where it is open to a professional to seek employment elsewhere or be self-employed, an internal disciplinary process leading to dismissal does not engage art.6: *Raj Mattu v University Hospitals of Coventry & Warwickshire NHS Trust*.[344] In *R. (on the application of G) v X School Governors and Y City Council*,[345] the Supreme Court held (Lord Kerr dissenting) that an employee's rights under art.6(1) were not engaged when he was refused legal representation during a disciplinary hearing at the school at which he was employed. His civil right to practise his profession would be directly determined by a separate decision of the Independent Safeguarding Authority and the applicable test was whether the school's disciplinary proceedings would directly determine or exert a substantial influence over that decision. Here, the ISA was required to exercise its own independent judgment both in relation to making findings of fact and assessing their significance before deciding whether it was appropriate to place a person on the barred list. The internal proceedings before the employer and the barring proceedings before the ISA were separate and distinct and not inextricably linked.

344 [2011] EWHC 2068. See also *R. (on the application of Puri) v Bradford Teaching Hospitals NHS Foundation Trust* [2011] EWHC 970; [2011] I.R.L.R. 582; [2011] Med. L.R. 280.

345 [2011] UKSC 30; [2011] 3 W.L.R. 237.

(b)   Procedural Guarantees

Independence and impartiality

To the end of paragraph 7-101 after "directing a jury.", add new footnote 372A:

372A For a decision in which allegations of apparent bias and of prejudice caused by a BSB press release were rejected see *McCarthy v Bar Standards Board* [2017] EWHC 969 (Admin).

7-101

Equality of arms

Replace footnote 375 with:

375 [2000] 1 W.L.R. 1760; see also *R. (BMA) v GMC* [2017] EWCA Civ 2191; [2018] 4 W.L.R. 31: where the chair of a tribunal is legally qualified, and accordingly no separate legal assessor is appointed, art.6 will require any new point of law which arises in the tribunal's deliberations to be raised in the parties' presence, and an opportunity given to them to make representations about it.

7-102

To the end of paragraph 7-102 after "relevant documents themselves.", add new paragraphs:

In *Smith v Bar Standards Board*380A a barrister appealed against a decision of the Bar Standards Board (BSB). A complaint had been made about his conduct of negotiations in a Family Dispute Resolution hearing, in particular for failing to achieve a "clean break" between the divorcing husband and wife. The BSB had allowed the barrister's instructing solicitors to prepare the statements for the hearing of the complaint, notwithstanding a potential conflict of interest. The BSB had also failed to take any steps to ensure the husband gave oral evidence after he made clear he did not wish to, including by issuing a witness summons. His important evidence was instead admitted on a hearsay basis. In these circumstances the court (Collins J) held that the appellant barrister had not received a fair hearing. The court recommended that no further action be taken, particularly as the BSB had "seriously mishandled" the case.

380A [2016] EWHC 3015 (Admin).

In *R. (Lewin) v Financial Reporting Council*380B a disciplinary tribunal ("the Tribunal") of the Financial Reporting Council (FRC) had made findings of misconduct against an accountancy firm and one of its partners in relation to its auditing of a public limited company. However, its final report also made findings of serious wrongdoing against a director of the public limited company, who was not a party to the proceedings and who had not been asked to give evidence or make representations. The director sought judicial review of the inclusion of references to him in the Tribunal's published report on the ground that it was contrary to both the substantive and procedural aspects of art.8 of the ECHR and unfair at common law.

380B [2018] EWHC 446 (Admin); [2018] 1 W.L.R. 2867.

The art.8 claim was rejected. The proceedings had been in public, with no reporting restrictions. The claimant was a director of a public company. In the circumstances, the claimant had no reasonable expectation of privacy arising from the proceedings or the resultant report. A balance had to be struck between his rights, the rights of the public generally, and the interests of the respondent accountancy firm and its partner, whose actions could not fairly be understood without reference to the wrongdoing of the claimant. There was a strong public interest in the report being published in full in a case of serious misconduct pursued by an independent regulatory body. Accordingly, any interference with the claimant's art.8 rights would be justified.

However, the court also held that the Tribunal's common law duty of fairness required it set out a disclaimer at the commencement or conclusion of the report, stating that (a) the claimant was not a party to the proceedings and was not invited to provide evidence; and (b) it would not be fair to treat any part of the Tribunal's findings as findings made against him as he was not represented at the Tribunal hearing and had made no representations about the matters in question.

Taveta Investments Ltd v Financial Reporting Council[380C] provides another perspective on the issues under consideration in *Lewin*. Nicklin J considered an application for interim relief brought by a third party seeking to restrain publication of an FRC settlement agreement. Annexed to the agreement were agreed particulars of fact and acts of misconduct which named the third party. Nicklin J dismissed the application for interim relief, but in reaching its conclusion rejected an argument that the FRC's duty of fairness to third parties is extinguished by the art.10 rights of the regulator and/or public to freedom of expression. Furthermore, the court held that that duty of fairness will not necessarily always be satisfied by publication of a disclaimer of the kind referred to in *Lewin*. The question of fairness is one of fact and degree. It may be necessary in some cases to invite representations from the third party before publication. Indeed, it may be in the public interest to do so, because of the risk of publishing allegations against third parties which turn out to be false. Notwithstanding these statements of principle, the court rejected the application before it, with evident reluctance, because of the high threshold for interim relief in public law cases involving restraint of publication.

[380C]   [2018] EWHC 1662 (Admin).

Right to a public/oral hearing

After paragraph 7-104, add new paragraph:

7-104   The principles in *Thompson* and *Heather, Moor and Edgcomb* were applied in *Yussouf v The Solicitors Regulation Authority*.[396A] A decision of an Adjudication Panel of the Solicitors Regulation Authority refusing a solicitor a "certificate of satisfaction" and refusing to admit her as a solicitor was quashed because the applicant solicitor had been refused an oral hearing in breach of the requirement of fairness. The character, honesty and suitability as a solicitor of the applicant had been in issue, and material facts had been in dispute which could not fairly be resolved on the basis of the documentation available.

[396A]   [2018] EWHC 211 (Admin).

9.   JUDICIAL REVIEW CHALLENGES AND PROFESSIONAL LIABILITY

(a)   Financial Ombudsman Service

(i)   FOS: Substantive challenges

Replace paragraph 7-122 with:

7-122   A decision by the FOS cannot be challenged on the basis that the FOS failed to apply the law. It is now well established that the FOS is entitled to depart from the law.[459] However, in line with the reasoning of Stanley Burton LJ in *R. (Heather Moor & Edgcomb Ltd) v Financial Ombudsman Service*,[460] any such departure must be explained in the Financial Ombudsman's decision, providing reasons for the departure. A determination may be challenged on the ground that it was inconsistent with the evidence: *R. (Garrison Investment Analysis) v Financial*

Ombudsman Service.[461] However, as with challenges to findings of fact on appeal from a trial, the question is not whether the court would have made the finding of fact which the ombudsman did, but whether there was sufficient evidential basis for the finding not to be irrational: *R. (Green) v Financial Ombudsman Service.*[462] Construction of the relevant rules, for instance those found in the FCA Handbook, is a matter for the courts. However, the application of those rules to the facts of the case is a matter for the FOS decision-maker, who will be given "considerable leeway" by the courts: *R. v Financial Ombudsman Service Ex p Norwich and Peterborough BS*[462A]; *R. (Berkeley Burke SIPP Administration Ltd) v Financial Ombudsman Service.*[462B] A decision of the FOS may be challenged on the ground of inconsistency with another of its decisions. However, inconsistency between a decision of the FOS and that of another body, created by a different statutory scheme, will generally not provide a basis for challenge: *R. (Berkeley Burke SIPP Administration Ltd) v Financial Ombudsman Service.*[462C]

[459] *R. (on the application of IFG Financial Services Ltd) v Financial Ombudsman Service* [2005] EWHC 1153 (Admin); [2006] 1 B.C.L.C. 534. See also *R. (on the application of Aviva Life and Pensions (UK) Ltd) v Financial Ombudsman Service* [2017] EWHC 352 (Admin); [2017] Lloyd's Rep. I.R. 404 and the obiter reservations of Jay J at [73] regarding the nature of the FOS's jurisdiction which "occupies an uncertain space outside the common law and statute".

[460] [2008] EWCA Civ 642; [2008] Bus. L.R. 1486.

[461] [2006] EWHC 2466 (Admin).

[462] [2012] EWHC 1253 (Admin).

[462A] [2002] EWHC 2379 (Admin); [2003] 1 All E.R. (Comm) 65.

[462B] [2018] EWHC 2878 (Admin); [2019] Bus. L.R. 437 at [82] and [137].

[462C] [2018] EWHC 2878 (Admin); [2019] Bus. L.R. 437 at [138]–[145].

Replace paragraph 7-123 (to incorporate amendments to the third sentence and to replace the final sentence) with:

One potentially promising area for challenge by way of judicial review is **7-123** jurisdiction. The issue of whether or not a complaint falls within the FOS's jurisdiction will typically depend on the application of relevant provisions of FSMA and DISP conferring or withholding jurisdiction. Examples have included: whether the complaint was brought within time (*R. (on the application of Bankole) v Financial Ombudsman Service*[463]); whether a complainant was a "consumer" (*R. (on the applicaqtion of Bluefin Insurance Services Ltd) v Financial Ombudsman Service*[464]); whether or not advice complained about was tax advice or investment advice (*R. (on the application of Chancery (UK) LLP v Financial Ombudsman Service Ltd*[465]); whether the scheme concerned was a collective investment scheme (ibid.); whether a complaint about a firm's handling of an internal complaint was about the provision or failure to provide a financial service" (*R. (on the application of Mazarona Properties Ltd) v Financial Ombudsman Service*[465A]); and whether or not advice on both regulated and unregulated investments amounted to "regulated activity" (*R. (TenetConnect) v Financial Ombudsman*[465B]). Although the court will attach weight to the expertise of persons such as the FOS in the context of jurisdictional issues, it is ultimately a matter for the courts to decide the limits of the FOS's jurisdiction. As noted by Ouseley J in *Chancery (UK) LLP* at [66], "the FSMA should not be construed so as to make the FOS master of the limits of its jurisdiction, right or wrong. It is for the Court to decide whether it has acted with or without jurisdiction." However, there is a distinction between the legal test for jurisdiction (which is for the court) and the facts to which that legal test is applied (which is for the FOS). In the words of Ouseley J at [67]: "Is there a distinction between tax advice and investment advice, and if so, on the facts found by the FOS, was advice given here which was a regulated activity? Both of these aspects are for the Court but on the facts as rationally found by the FOS". Permission to appeal the *Chancery* (UK) case was granted, but the appeal was not pursued.

[463] [2012] EWHC 3555.

[464] [2014] EWHC 3413 (Admin).

[465] [2015] EWHC 407 (Admin).

[465A] [2017] EWHC 1135 (Admin).

[465B] [2018] EWHC 459 (Admin).

Replace paragraph 7-124 (to incorporate new text following "intended to avoid." at the end of the paragraph) with:

7-124   Claims for judicial review against decisions of the FOS rejecting complaints will not usually be entertained by the court because the decision of the Financial Ombudsman in those circumstances is not binding on them and they retain the alternative remedy of bringing a civil action for damages in the courts: *R. (Duff) v Financial Ombudsman Service* at [7] per Collins J.[466] This decision has been criticised on the ground that leaving a claimant to a civil remedy involves imposing on him exactly the costs and risks the FOS scheme is intended to avoid.[467] A failure to take into account the real substance of the complaint will vitiate a decision. In *R. (Kelly) v Financial Ombudsman Service*[467A] a close analysis of the reasons given by the ombudsman for dismissing a complaint led to the conclusion that the description of the complaint was so inaccurate that it was "impossible to conclude that the decision-maker had properly in mind the issue he was supposed to be deciding". Although the ombudsman's reasons were the subject of close enquiry the claim was upheld as a matter of a substantive failure on the ombudsman's part, rather than on the basis of inadequate reasons.

[466] [2006] EWHC 1704 (Admin).

[467] *Walker's Application* [2013] NIQB 12.

[467A] [2017] EWHC 3581 (Admin) at [34].

(ii)   FOS: Procedural challenges

After "of unfair procedure." at the end of the first sentence, add new footnote 467B:

7-125   [467B] See *Full Circle Asset Management Ltd v Financial Ombudsman Service Ltd* [2017] EWHC 323 (Admin) for an example of a challenge to the procedural fairness of a FOS decision, alleging that the Ombudsman had characterised the nature of the complaint differently at different stages, and inconsistently with its description in the FOS complaint form. The challenge was dismissed by Nicol J.

(b)   Legal Ombudsman

(i)   LeO: Substantive challenges

Replace footnote 484 with:

7-131   [484] The decision in *Layard Horsfall* was followed in *R. (Ejiofor t/a Mitchell and Co Solicitors) v Legal Ombudsman* [2016] EWHC 1933 (Admin); [2016] 4 Costs L.R. 759; see also *R. (Dotcom Solicitors Ltd) v Legal Ombudsman* [2018] EWHC 2399 (Admin), in which the court repeated that LeO had jurisdiction to deal with complaints about the level of charges for the services provided, and that it is unnecessary first to use the statutory mechanism under s.70 of the Solicitors Act 1974 for challenging a solicitor's bill before complaining to LeO.

(d)   Financial Conduct Authority

In the first paragraph, after "an offer by", replace "Barlcays" with:

7-143   Barclays

After the second paragraph, add new third paragraph:

On appeal, the Court of Appeal upheld the conclusion that KPMG's decision was not amenable to judicial review, albeit for different reasons.[504] Arden LJ, with whom Newey LJ and Coulson LJ agreed, held that the Divisional Court had focussed too narrowly on the source of KPMG's power as Independent Reviewer, and should have taken a wider view of the regulatory position and factual context. The contractual source of the power did not render public law principles inapplicable. It was necessary to "stand back" and examine the function that KPMG, as Independent Reviewer, fulfilled "in the overall scheme of things". Nonetheless, the nature of the scheme was "essentially for the pursuit of private rights". There was nothing to suggest that the FSA had intended that there should be any public law challenge to a decision of the Independent Reviewer. Compensation was to be negotiated on private law principles and any agreement was to be enforceable through the courts, not by means of a system imposed by the FCA. In all the circumstances, the contractual nature of the Independent Reviewer's engagement was "all of a piece with the fact that it was not performing any public function."

[504] *R. (Holmcroft Properties Limited) v KPMG LLP* [2018] EWCA Civ 2093 at [38]–[57].

CHAPTER 8

PROFESSIONAL INDEMNITY INSURANCE

3.   THE NATURE/SCOPE OF PROFESSIONAL INDEMNITY INSURANCE

Replace paragraph 8-022 (to incorporate new text following "in Enterprise Oil." at the end of the paragraph) with:

8-022   In *Lumbermens Mutual Casualty Co v Bovis Lend Lease*,[65] Colman J held that, because the insured's liability must ordinarily be both established and quantified before any claim can be brought on any liability policy,[66] a settlement which made no allocation as between insured and uninsured losses was insufficient to "ascertain" liability in order to crystallise a right of action under the policy. While *Lumbermens* was settled before the point could be tested on appeal, in *Enterprise Oil Ltd v Strand Insurance Co Ltd*[67] Aikens J held, obiter, that *Lumbermens* was wrong since the requirement for the liability to be ascertained referred to the insured's liability to the third party and not to the amount of insurers' liability to the insured—thus it would be permissible to establish the extent of the insured liability by evidence extrinsic to the terms of the settlement with the third party. While the point remains open, the views expressed in *Enterprise Oil* are probably the less controversial. In *AIG Europe (Ireland) Ltd v Faraday Capital Ltd*,[68] Morison J sided, obiter, with the approach of Aikens J in *Enterprise Oil*. In *The Cultural Foundation v Beazley Furlonge Ltd*, the deputy judge followed the approach of Aikens J in *Enterprise Oil* and held that an insured can recover elements of a global settlement provided the settlement includes an allocation between the different losses or the insured can demonstrate which part of the settlement relates to the operation of an insured peril.[68A]

---

[65] [2005] Lloyd's Rep. I.R. 47 at [42].

[66] Which would include any professional indemnity policy.

[67] [2006] 1 Lloyd's Rep. 500 at [164]–[172] (obiter).

[68] [2007] Lloyd's Rep. I.R. 267 at [68]–[71].

[68A] [2018] EWHC 1083 (Comm) at [217].

Replace paragraph 8-028 (to incorporate amendments to the text after "of that term.") with:

Professional indemnity insurance will often exclude cover in respect of any li-   **8-028**
ability which arises purely by reason of a contractual term and which would not attach in the absence of that term. In *Impact Funding Solutions Ltd v AIG Europe
Insurance*, the Supreme Court confirmed that cl.6.6 of the SRA Minimum Terms
and Conditions (which excludes liability for trading and personal debts as well as
liabilities arising from breach of a contract or arrangement for the supply of goods
or services in the course of the Insured Firm's practice) did operate to exclude the
insured's contractual liability to a third party which had provided loans to the
insured's clients to cover disbursements in litigation.[84-85]

[84-85] [2016] UKSC 57; [2017] A.C. 73 at [29]–[30].

4. POLICY TRIGGER: CLAIMS MADE/CIRCUMSTANCES NOTIFIED

After paragraph 8-030, add new paragraph 8-030A:

In *Euro Pools v Royal & Sun Alliance*,[95A] the Court of Appeal had to consider   **8-030A**
the scope of a standard deeming provision by which "Any Claim arising from" the
circumstances notified would be deemed to have been first made in the period of
insurance. The original notification was made when the insured first became aware
that it had supplied a defective system to a client. As a result of those defects, a
remedial solution was designed and implemented which failed relatively quickly
but following renewal of the policy. Further remedial measures were therefore
implemented, the costs of which were treated by insurers as arising from the original
notification. When the overall cost began to approach the limit of indemnity under
the first policy, the insured contended that the second round of remedial costs fell
to be indemnified under the second policy. Overturning the first instance decision
of Moulder J,[95B] the Court of Appeal held that the second round of remedial works
did "arise from" the circumstances originally notified to the first policy: the connection between the original notification and the second round of remedial costs was
more than "purely coincidental"[95C]; the wording used in the deeming provision
required "some causal link", but did not impose a particularly demanding test of
causation.[95D]

[95A] [2019] EWCA Civ 808.

[95B] [2018] EWHC 46 (Comm); [2018] Lloyd's Rep. I.R. 575.

[95C] See per Dame Elizabeth Gloster at [54]–[59].

[95D] See per Males LJ at [97].

7. CONTRACTS ENTERED INTO BEFORE 12 AUGUST 2016: THE PRE-CONTRACTUAL DUTY OF UTMOST GOOD FAITH

(c) Avoidance

After paragraph 8-054, add new paragraph 8-054A:

Where an innocent (or unintentional) non-disclosure clause requires the insured   **8-054A**
to establish to the insurer's satisfaction that any non-disclosure was innocent and
free from any fraudulent conduct or intent to deceive, the insurer is subject to an

implied term that it will not exercise its decision-making powers arbitrarily, capriciously or irrationally: see *UK Acorn Finance Ltd v Markel (UK) Ltd*,[148A] applying *Braganza v BP Shipping Ltd*.[148B] In *UK Acorn Finance*, the judge found that insurers had breached their duties by failing to approach the question of dishonesty with an open mind and to consider all relevant issues.

[148A] [2020] EWHC 922 (Comm), HHJ Pelling QC.

[148B] [2015] UKSC 17.

8.   CONTRACTS ENTERED INTO ON OR AFTER 12 AUGUST 2016: THE PRE-CONTRACTUAL DUTY OF FAIR PRESENTATION

(a)   The Duty and its Scope

8-065   *Delete existing footnote 178.*

After paragraph 8-065, add new paragraph 8-065A (including new footnote 178):

8-065A   In a recent Court of Session (Outer House) decision, *Young v RSA*[178] both parties and the Court proceeded on the basis that whether or not an insurer had waived the provision of information for the purposes of s.3(5)(e) of the 2015 Act was a matter governed by the existing authorities (as to which see para.8-051(c) above). It is respectfully suggested that they were right to do so. Lady Wolffe held that the approach set out by the Court of Appeal in *Doheny v New India Assurance* (see para.8-051 above) remained good law even if it potentially fell to be applied to other communications from an insurer besides a proposal form.

[178] [2019] CSOH 32; 2019 S.L.T. 622.

9.   RULES OF CONSTRUCTION

(a)   Generally

Replace paragraph 8-072 (to incorporate amendments to footnotes 190 and 198) with:

8-072   Under English law, there is no magic to the construction of an insurance contract. The relevant principles are of application to all commercial contractual provisions and are generally well established[188]:

1.   The words used must be given their ordinary meaning albeit that they should reflect the commercial setting of the contract—thus the contract must be construed in context[189] and the meaning of the document is the meaning which would be attributed to the words in context as distinct from their dictionary definition.[190]

2.   A literal construction that leads to an absurd result or one otherwise manifestly contrary to the real intention of the parties should be rejected, if an alternative more reasonable construction can be adopted without doing violence to the language used.[191] Where one of two possible constructions would be repugnant to the commercial purpose of the contract, it will be disregarded.[192] If the apparently literal meaning of the words in a continuing warranty would produce a result inconsistent with a reasonable and business like interpretation of the warranty then it should be restricted.[193]

3.   Although commercial common sense is an important factor to take into account, it is relevant only to the question of how matters would have been

understood by reasonable people in the position of the parties at the time of contracting; a court should be very slow to reject the natural meaning of the words used simply because it appears to have been a very imprudent term for one of the parties to have agreed.[194] Earlier (but still recent) suggestions that the words used might be subservient to business common sense[195] must now be treated with caution.

4.   In the case of a genuine ambiguity,[196] the construction which is more favourable to the insured should be adopted. However, the *contra proferentem* rule is not to be invoked for the purpose of creating a doubt.[197] It is not the function of the court to punish insurers guilty of unclear and inaccurate wording,[198] still less to search out drafting infelicities in order to facilitate a departure from the natural meaning of the words used.[199]

5.   The court must recognise that commercial contracts are often imperfect instruments—it is therefore permissible to overlook obvious grammatical or linguistic errors[200] or even disregard redundant words or phrases as surplusage.[201] At the same time, the court must also be astute not to "make" for the parties a contract which they did not make for themselves.[202]

6.   Before a court can embark upon "correction of mistakes by construction", two conditions must be satisfied[203]:
   •   there must be a clear mistake on the face of the instrument;
   •   it must be clear what correction ought to be made to cure the mistake.

7.   Whilst post-contractual conduct by the parties is inadmissible as an aid to the construction of any term of the contract, such conduct is admissible for the purpose of determining whether the term in question had been agreed or even whether any contract had been concluded.[204]

8.   In construing insurance contracts, the courts should be "chary" about interfering with the interpretation given to well-known wording which has been acted upon for any considerable period of time.[205]

[188]   See generally *Investors Compensation Scheme Ltd v West Bromwich BS* [1998] 1 W.L.R. 896 at 912H–913C; *Yorkshire Water v Sun Alliance & London Insurance Plc* [1997] 2 Lloyd's Rep. 21 at 28, cited with approval in *Pilkington UK Ltd v CGU Insurance Plc* [2004] Lloyd's Rep. I.R. 891 at [46] and *Blackburn Rovers Football & Athletic Club Plc v Avon Insurance Plc* [2005] Lloyd's Rep. I.R. 447 at [9].

[189]   *Charter Reinsurance Co Ltd v Fagan* [1996] 2 Lloyd's Rep. 113 at 117, col.1; [1996] 3 All E.R. 46 at 51e.

[190]   *Gan v Tai Ping (No.2)* [2001] Lloyd's Rep. I.R. 667 at 684–685. In the *Employer's Liability Trigger Litigation* [2012] Lloyd's Rep. I.R. 371 at [19], Lord Mance stressed the need to (1) avoid overconcentrating on single words or phrases viewed in isolation; and (2) consider and construe a policy in its entirety. See also *Arnold v Britton* [2015] UKSC 36; [2015] A.C. 1619 at [14]–[22] per Lord Neuberger, and *Wood v Capita Insurance Services* [2017] UKSC 24 at [10]–14].

[191]   *Antaios Naviera SA v Salen Rederierna AB* [1985] A.C. 191 at 201; cf. *Gan v Tai Ping (No.2)* [2001] Lloyd's Rep. I.R. 667 at [85].

[192]   *Fraser v BN Furman (Productions) Ltd* [1967] 2 Lloyd's Rep. 1 at 12 where the Court of Appeal held that a clause requiring the insured under a liability policy to take reasonable precautions to prevent accidents would be breached only by reckless conduct on the part of the insured itself since to construe the clause as being breached by mere negligence would be repugnant to the commercial purpose of the contract.

[193]   *Pratt v Aigaion Insurance Co SA* [2009] 1 Lloyd's Rep. 225 at [14].

[194]   See *Arnold v Britton* [2015] A.C. 1619 at [19]–[20] per Lord Neuberger.

[195]   See, by way of example, *Rainy Sky v Kookmin Bank* [2012] 1 Lloyd's Rep. 34 at [20]–[21] per Lord Mance.

[196]   i.e. where following steps 1 and 2 there remain clearly two commercially realistic meanings which could be attributed to the words—see *Gan v Tai Ping (No.2)* Lloyd's Rep. I.R. 667 at 686, col.2.

[197]   *Cornish v Accident Insurance Co* (1889) 23 Q.B.D. 453 at 456.

[198] *Doheny v New India Assurance* [2005] Lloyd's Rep. I.R. 251 at [12]. See also *Spire Healthcare Ltd v Royal & Sun Alliance Insurance Plc* [2018] EWCA Civ 317; [2018] Lloyd's Rep. I.R. 425 at [21], where Simon LJ observed: "the Court construes the contract as it is and not as it might have been drafted. In almost any dispute over contractual terms a party can argue that a contentious term could have been better expressed to achieve the effect that the other party avows."

[199] *Arnold v Britton* [2015] A.C. 1619 at [18].

[200] *Gan v Tai Ping (No.2)* [2001] Lloyd's Rep. I.R. 667 at [83]; *Doheny v New India Assurance* [2005] Lloyd's Rep. I.R. 251 at [7]–[8] and [12].

[201] See, e.g. *Blackburn Rovers Football & Athletic Club Plc v Avon Insurance Plc* [2005] Lloyd's Rep. I.R. 239 at [13].

[202] *Charter Reinsurance Co Ltd v Fagan* [1997] A.C. 313 at 388C; *Gan v Tai Ping (No.2)* [2001] Lloyd's Rep. I.R. 667 at [85]; *Great North Eastern Railway Ltd v Avon Insurance Plc* [2001] 2 Lloyd's Rep. 649 at [34]; *Royal & Sun Alliance Plc v Dornoch* [2005] Lloyd's Rep. I.R. 544 at [16].

[203] See *Chartbrook Ltd v Persimmon Homes Ltd* [2009] UKHL 38 at [22] per Lord Hoffmann. *If* these conditions are satisfied, there is then no conceptual limit to the amount of red ink or verbal rearrangement permitted: ibid. at [25].

[204] *Great North Eastern Railway Ltd v Avon Insurance Plc* [2001] 2 Lloyd's Rep. 649 at [29]; *ED&F Man Commodity Advisers Ltd v Fluxo-Cane Overseas Ltd* [2009] EWCA Civ 406 at [20]–[21].

[205] *Hooley Hill Rubber v Royal Insurance* [1920] 1 K.B. 257 at 269 per Bankes LJ.

(b) Exclusion Clauses and Insuring Clauses

To the end of paragraph 8-078 after "construction of it.", add:

8-078   In *Impact Funding Solutions v AIG Europe Insurance*, Lord Toulson held that the fact that a provision is expressed as an exception to cover does not mean that it must necessarily be approached with a pre-disposition to construe it narrowly: such provisions must be read—as with any other—in the context of the policy as a whole; while any exclusion should be clearly expressed, it should be remembered that it is simply a way of delineating the scope of the primary obligation.[217A]

[217A] [2016] UKSC 57; [2017] A.C. 73 at [35]. See also [32] per Lord Hodge. This approach was followed in *Crowden v QBE Insurance* [2017] EWHC 2597 (Comm); [2018] Lloyd's Rep. I.R. 83, in which Peter MacDonald Eggers QC held that an "insolvency" exclusion commonly found in professional indemnity policies for independent financial advisers was effective to exclude liabilities even though the FSA handbook required IFAs to maintain insurance in respect of the self-same liabilities: as the deputy judge observed at [85], it was incumbent on the insured, not insurers, to ensure that the insured obtained sufficient professional indemnity cover.

10. CONTRACTS ENTERED INTO BEFORE 12 AUGUST 2016: CLASSIFICATION OF TERMS/CONSEQUENCES OF BREACH

(a) "Warranties"

8-085   *After "said to arise.", delete "There has, however, been little (if any) express consideration of the potential for estoppel by silence to arise in the context of an insurance policy.".*

After paragraph 8-085, add new paragraph 8-085A:

8-085A   There has, until recently, been little (if any) express consideration of the potential for estoppel by silence to arise in the context of an insurance policy. However, in *Ted Baker Plc v Axa Insurance UK Plc*,[226A] Sir Christopher Clarke held (obiter) that in circumstances where an insured had objected to the wholesale provision of information until such time as insurers had made a decision on policy liability, it was incumbent on insurers to tell the insured if they still required the insured to provide a limited category of information which should have been readily available to the insured. This conclusion was based largely on a line of authority concerning the "duty to speak" in commercial cases,[226B] rather than on the contract being uberrimae fidei, although a "duty to speak" might more readily be inferred in the latter case.[226C] In Sir Christopher's view, such a duty would arise where a reasonable in the position of the person asserting the estoppel would expect the other party, acting honestly and reasonably, to take steps to make his position plain.[226D]

[226A] [2017] EWCA Civ 4097; [2017] Lloyd's Rep. I.R. 682.

[226B] See [2017] EWCA Civ 4097; [2017] Lloyd's Rep. I.R. 682 at [72]–[77].

[226C] See [2017] EWCA Civ 4097; [2017] Lloyd's Rep. I.R. 682 at [89].

[226D] See [2017] EWCA Civ 4097; [2017] Lloyd's Rep. I.R. 682 at [82].

13. POLICY RESPONSE TO THE INSURED'S LIABILITY FOR FRAUD OR ILLEGALITY

Replace paragraph 8-116 with:

In the absence of any relevant exclusion in the policy (or any relevant limita- **8-116** tion to the scope of the insuring clause), there is no reason why a liability policy should not provide an indemnity in respect of legal liability arising out of deliberate and criminal acts of those for whom the insured is, in law, responsible.[288] This may involve issues of attribution where the insured is a limited company and the criminal acts are perpetrated by the insured's directing mind or alter ego—in such cases it would appear that the policy will respond if the criminal acts were performed for the perpetrator's own ends rather than for the benefit of the company.[289] However, this approach was rejected by the Court of Appeal in *KR v Royal & Sun Alliance*,[290] which held[291] that where the perpetrator "is to be regarded as, in effect the Company" then a policy exception in respect of the deliberate acts of the insured would be triggered.[292] Although this approach was broadly consistent with that of the majority of the House of Lords in *Moore Stephens v Stone & Rolls*,[293] in which *KR v Royal Sun Alliance* was cited, without disapproval, by Lord Phillips at [53], it is doubtful that the Court of Appeal's reasoning could survive more recent Supreme Court decisions such as *Bilta (UK) Ltd v Nazir (No.2)*.[294]

[288] See, e.g. *Hawley v Luminar Lesiure Ltd* [2006] Lloyd's Rep. I.R. 307 at [107].

[289] *KR v Royal & Sun Alliance Plc* [2006] Lloyd's Rep. I.R. 327 at [51]–[52].

[290] [2007] Lloyd's Rep. I.R. 368.

[291] At [65]. The Court of Appeal took into account the well-known dictum of Lord Atkin in *Beresford v Royal Insurance Co Ltd* [1938] A.C. 586 at 595 set out in para.8-114, above.

[292] It is implicit in the Court of Appeal's reasoning that the policy would not have responded, even if the exception had been absent, for the reasons given by Lord Atkin in the *Beresford* case.

[293] [2009] UKHL 39; [2009] 1 A.C. 1391.

[294] [2015] UKSC 23; [2016] A.C. 1.

14. CLAIMS NOTIFICATION AND CO-OPERATION CLAUSES

(a) Generally

To the end of paragraph 8-118 after "Seguros SA.", add:

However, it remains to be seen whether these authorities might now be watered **8-118** down on the basis of an argument (following the Court of Appeal's decision in *Ted Baker Plc v Axa Insurance UK Plc*)[299A] that an insurer who has repudiated the claim but nevertheless requires the provision of stipulated information is under a duty to make that clear: see para.8–085A above.

[299A] [2017] EWCA Civ 4097; [2017] Lloyd's Rep. I.R. 682.

Replace paragraph 8-119 (incorporating an amendment to footnote 300 and new text following ""claims made" basis" at the end of paragraph) with:

8-119   The obligation to notify is normally expressed as arising when the insured becomes aware of any circumstance which *may* give rise to a claim; such a requirement is logical since the insured is likely to be unable to obtain cover in any succeeding year in respect of any such circumstance.[300] Some policies, however, provide that the obligation to notify arises only when the insured is aware of circumstances which are *likely* to give rise to a claim. Such wording is more generous to an insured in terms of when the obligation to notify arises,[301] although it is better suited to other forms of liability insurance written on a "claims arising" or "liability incurred" basis rather than professional indemnity policy written on a "claims made" basis. Even if a notification obligation is not expressly qualified by reference to the insured's knowledge, it will be construed as being so qualified.[301A]

[300] *J Rothschild Assurance v Collyear* [1999] Lloyd's Rep. I.R. 6 at 22, col.2. Normally any circumstance known to the insured and/or notified to prior year insurers will be specifically excluded; however, in the (rare) absence of such an exclusion (and assuming that there is no basis for challenging the validity of the policy as a whole) the insured may be entitled to choose whether to pursue a claim under the policy to which a circumstance was notified or the policy in force at the time the ensuing claim was first made—see *The Cultural Foundation v Beazley Furlonge Ltd* [2018] EWHC 1083 (Comm) at [169]–[170].

[301] *Layher v Lowe* [2000] Lloyd's Rep. I.R. 510; *Jacobs v Coster* [2000] Lloyd's Rep. I.R. 506; *MacCaferri v Zurich Insurance* [2015] Lloyd's Rep. I.R. 594.

[301A] *Maccaferri Ltd v Zurich Insurance Plc* [2016] EWCA Civ 1302; [2017] Lloyd's Rep. I.R. 200 at [37].

Replace footnote 302 with:

8-120   [302] [2008] Lloyd's Rep. I.R. 391. In *Euro Pools v Royal & Sun Alliance* [2019] EWCA Civ 808 at [47], Dame Elizabeth Gloster cited *Kajima* with approval but explained this did not mean that a Court should "over-analyse the problem by dissecting every potential cause of the problem as a different notifiable circumstance", making clear that a higher level approach should be adopted.

To the end of paragraph 8-120 after "to a claim.", add:

In *Maccaferri v Zurich Insurance Plc*,[309A] the Court of Appeal confirmed that the possibility or likelihood of a claim, as the case may be, should be apparent to someone in the insured's position but not determined by the insured's—potentially idiosyncratic—views. In *Euro Pools v Royal & Sun Alliance*,[309B] Dame Elizabeth Gloster cited Toulson LJ's approach in *Kidsons* with approval, commenting that there was very little difference with the approach taken by Rix LJ at [72].[309C]

[309A] [2016] EWCA Civ 1302; [2017] Lloyd's Rep. I.R. 200 at [37].

[309B] [2019] EWCA Civ 808.

[309C] [2019] EWCA Civ 808 at [39].

16.   DEDUCTIBLES AND LIMITS OF INDEMNITY; AGGREGATION OF CLAIMS

(a)   Generally

After "the escrow account.", add:

8-137   Eder J's decision was upheld by the Court of Appeal.[344A]

[344A] [2017] EWCA Civ 25; [2017] Lloyd's Rep. I.R. 259.

Replace footnote 345 with:

8-139   [345] *Countrywide Assured Group Plc v DJ Marshall* [2003] Lloyd's Rep. P.N. 1 at [13]. See also *Spire Healthcare Ltd v Royal & Sun Alliance Insurance Plc* [2016] EWHC 3278 (Comm); [2017] Lloyd's Rep. I.R. 118 at [13].

To the end of paragraph 8-140 after "doomed to failure.", add:

8-140   In *AIG Europe Ltd v Woodman*,[345A] the Supreme Court stressed that aggregation clauses should be read neutrally, both because in some cases they operate in favour of the insured and, in others, in favour of the insurer; and also because—in the field of compulsory insurance—it is appropriate to balance the need for reasonable protection of the public with the cost and availability of cover.[345B]

[345A] [2017] UKSC 18; [2017] 1 W.L.R. 1168.

[345B] See [2017] UKSC 18; [2017] 1 W.L.R. 1168 at [15] and [25].

Replace paragraph 8-144 (to incorporate new text at the end of the paragraph following "sufficient causal relationship."):

A requirement in an aggregation clause that claims should "result from a related series of acts or omissions" is not satisfied simply by the identification of some common characteristic between the different claims—both because similarity does not create a relationship and also because there needs to be a sufficient causal relationship.[353] Conversely, a requirement that claims should "[arise] out of, [be] based upon or attributable to ... a series of related Wrongful Acts" was satisfied by the similarity of the acts in question even when they were separate acts, made on different occasions, causing loss to different parties and in response to different instructions; the fact of their occurrence within a broader scheme of fraudulent practice was sufficient to render them "related" and trigger the aggregation of the claims.[353A]   **8-144**

[353] *Lloyd's TSB General Insurance v Lloyds Bank Group Insurance* [2003] Lloyd's Rep. I.R. 623 at [24]–[25], [52].

[353A] *Bank of Queensland v AIG Australia* [2019] NSWCA 190; [2019] Lloyd's Rep. I.R. 639.

Replace paragraph 8-145, with:

In *AIG Europe Ltd v Woodman*,[354] the Supreme Court decided that the use of the word "related" in a provision aggregating claims as arising from "similar acts or omissions in a series of related matters or transactions" for the purposes of limb (iv) of the aggregation provision within the SRA Minimum Terms and Conditions required there to be a real connection between the transactions.[355] Whether transactions are related is an "acutely fact sensitive exercise" involving an exercise of judgment not a reformulation of the clause.[355A] Disapproving the approach taken by the Court of Appeal,[355B] the Supreme Court stressed that the courts should not take an overly narrow view of what constitutes the transaction giving rise to the claim.[355C]   **8-145**

[354] [2017] UKSC 18; [2017] 1 W.L.R. 1168.

[355] See para.22.

[355A] See para.22.

[355B] *AIG Europe Ltd v OC320301 LLP* [2016] EWCA Civ 367; [2016] Lloyd's Rep. I.R. 289.

[355C] [2017] UKSC 18; [2017] 1 W.L.R. 1168 at [23].

18.   THIRD PARTY RIGHTS

Replace footnote 369 with:

[369] *Post Office v Norwich Union Fire Insurance Society Ltd*, above; *Bradley v Eagle Star* [1989] A.C. 957. But see *Guide Dogs for the Blind Association v Box* [2020] EWHC 1948 (Ch) in which HHJ Saffman held that although there was no jurisdiction under the 1930 Act for a statutory assignee to bring an application for declaratory relief until such time as the insured's liability had been "ascertained", the court could nevertheless exercise its inherent jurisdiction to grant declaratory relief subject to the principles ordinarily applicable to the grant of such relief being satisfied.   **8-155**

Replace paragraph 8-157 with:

The 2010 Act applies unless both the insured's liability was incurred and the insured entered insolvency on or before 1 August 2016,[373] in which case the 1930   **8-157**

Act will continue to apply.[374] In *Redman v Zurich Insurance Plc*,[374A] Turner J confirmed that the relevant person "incurs a liability" for the purposes of s.1 of the 2010 Act when the cause of action is complete, not when the claimant has established a right to compensation by means of a judgment, award or settlement.

[373] See para.1 of Sch.3 to the 2010 Act.

[374] See para.3 of Sch.3 to the 2010 Act.

[374A] [2017] EWHC 1919 (QB); [2018] Lloyd's Rep. I.R. 45.

CONSTRUCTION PROFESSIONALS

1. INTRODUCTION

(a) The Construction Professionals

Quantity surveyors

To the end of paragraph 9-004 after "for its members.", add:

9-004   Quantity surveyors are also often appointed by banks to advise them about construction costs when administering facilities that are being used for construction projects.[14A]

[14A] See for example *Lloyds Bank Plc v McBains Cooper Consulting Ltd* [2018] EWCA Civ 452; [2018] P.N.L.R. 23 and *Bank of Ireland v Watts Group Plc* [2017] EWHC 1667 (TCC); [2017] T.C.L.R. 7; 173 Con. L.R. 240.

Project managers

Replace footnote 17 with:

9-006   [17] It follows that care must be taken to see that an expert witness in a claim against a project manager has the appropriate qualification(s). See *Pride Valley Foods Ltd v Hall & Partners (Contract Management) Ltd* (2001) 76 Con. L.R. 1 at 24 per Judge Toulmin CMG, QC:

"There is an initial difficulty in accepting expert opinion evidence in relation to the duties of project managers. There is no chartered or professional institution of project managers nor a recognisable profession of project managers. In so far as it may be appropriate to accept expert evidence, the nature of the evidence that might be acceptable will depend on what the project manager has agreed to do. In some cases, the project manager will be the architect who will design the project and then, acting as project manager, supervise the contractor and the sub-contractors in carrying out the work. At the other end of the scale the project manager will supervise the work of the contractor and sub-contractors and ensure that the work is carried out in conformity with the design drawings. In these circumstances the project manager will have no design function even to the extent of providing an outline specification."

The Court of Appeal did not comment on this part of the judgment: [2001] EWCA Civ 1001. For further detailed discussion of project managers' responsibilities, see C. Leong, "The duty of care in project management" (2001) 17 P.N. 250. For a case where project managers were held liable for failing to prevent works which created a risk of fire, see *Six Continents Retail Ltd v Carford Catering Ltd* [2003] EWCA Civ 1790. See also *Great Eastern Hotel Co Ltd v John Laing Construction Ltd* [2005] EWHC 181 (TCC), where the duties of a building contractor operating under a construction management contract were regarded as akin to those of a professional project manager. For a case where loss adjusters were held liable to their instructing insurers for breach of duty in managing remedial works, see *AXA Insurance UK Plc v Cunningham Lindsey UK* [2007] EWHC 3023 (TCC). In *Ampleforth Abbey Trust v Turner & Townsend Project Management Ltd* [2012] EWHC 2137 (TCC), project managers were in breach of duty in failing to procure an executed building contract and allowing construction works to proceed on the basis of letters of intent. An attack on the suitability of the claimant's expert witness failed. See also *Lloyds Bank Plc v McBains Cooper Consulting Ltd* [2018] EWCA Civ 452; [2018] P.N.L.R. 23 for consideration of the obligations of a "monitoring surveyor" (a construction professional who is appointed to inspect and report throughout the stages of a construction project, normally for the benefit of a finance lender as in this case, but sometimes for others). See also *Bank of Ireland v Watts Group Plc* [2017] EWHC 1667 (TCC); [2017] T.C.L.R. 7; 173 Con. L.R. 240 where the claim against a monitoring surveyor failed, in part, as the claimant's expert's evidence was rejected in its entirety.

2. DUTIES

(a) Duties to Client

(i) Contractual Duties

Express terms

Replace footnote 34 with:

[34] e.g. para.2.3 of the RIBA Code of Conduct (2005) states, "Members should ensure that their terms **9-013** of appointment, the scope of their work and the essential project requirements are clear and recorded in writing. They should explain to their clients the implications of any conditions of engagement ...". The failure of construction professionals to comply with good practice in this respect contributed to their later breaches of duty in regard to procurement advice, project planning and the production of timely design information in *Plymouth & South West Co-operative Society v Architecture, Structure & Management Ltd* [2006] EWHC 5 (TCC). See also *Freeborn v De Almeida Marcal (t/a Dan Marcal Architects)* [2019] EWHC 454 (TCC) in which the court held that architects have a duty of care to produce written briefs for clients, and any changes to the brief have to be recorded in writing whether by drawings, sketches and/or minutes of meetings.

Limitation of liability

Replace footnote 64 with:

[64] In *Moores v Yakeley* (1998) 62 Con. L.R. 76 the defendant architect contracted to provide his services **9-026** in connection with the construction of a new bungalow for the claimant. The contract was made on the 1992 edition of the RIB Standard Form of Agreement for the Appointment of an Architect (SFA/92), which provided that the defendant's liability for loss and damage caused by breach of the Agreement would be limited to £250,000. Since the claimant was a consumer, it was common ground that the statutory test of reasonableness under the Unfair Contract Terms Act 1977 applied. Dyson J held that the term satisfied that test. Relevant factors were that the sum referred to was based on the defendant's reasonable assessment of the likely total construction cost of the bungalow, that the sum was over 10 times the defendant's anticipated fee for the project and that the claimant was in a stronger bargaining position than the defendant (there was a severe recession in the building industry at the time, the claimant's financial resources were far in excess of the defendant's and the claimant had solicitors to protect his interest in negotiations with the defendant). The Court of Appeal unreported 23 March 2000) upheld the judge's decision for the reasons which he gave. A challenge to a financial limitation of liability clause succeeded in *Ampleforth Abbey Trust v Turner & Townsend Project Management Ltd* [2012] EWHC 2137 (TCC). A project manager's appointment sought to limit its maximum liability for breach of the appointment to the amount of the fees paid to it under the appointment. It was held that this was unreasonable for the purposes of the Unfair Contract Terms Act 1977 because the same appointment

required the project manager to maintain professional indemnity insurance cover of £10 million, the cost of which would have been passed on to the claimant as part of those fees. By contrast, in *Elvanite Full Circle Ltd v AMEC Earth & Environmental (UK) Ltd* [2013] EWHC 1191 (TCC), Coulson J (obiter) held that each of a range of contractual clauses which limited the liability of the defendant planning consultants withstood challenge under the 1977 Act. Similarly, in *Goodlife Foods Ltd v Fire Hall Protection Ltd* [2018] EWCA Civ 1371; 178 Con. L.R. 1, an exclusion clause in the standard terms of a specialist fire suppression contractor was not onerous, was reasonable and had fairly been brought to the employer's attention. Relevant factors were that the contract was a one-off supply contract and that the clause provided that liability would be reinstated if the employer elected to purchase additional insurance to cover the excluded risks.

(ii)   Duties Owed to the Client Independent of Contract

The Defective Premises Act 1972

Replace paragraph 9-032 (to incorporate new text following "of work badly." at the end of the paragraph) with:

9-032   The duty set out in s.1 applies only to work taken on after the commencement date of the Act, which was 1 January 1974. The Act applies only to "dwellings". The term is not defined in the Act. The term has been interpreted, for the purposes of other legislation, as meaning a person's home (or one of his homes).[73] It has been held that, for the purposes of the Act, a dwelling house is a building used or capable of being used as a dwelling house, not being a building which is used predominantly for commercial or industrial purposes.[74] The Act applies only to the provision of a new dwelling, whether by the construction of a new building, the conversion of an existing non-residential building or the enlargement of an existing building. It does not apply to the renovation or refurbishment of an existing dwelling unless the effect is to create a building "wholly different" from the old building.[75] Section 1 of the Act applies to the failure to carry out necessary remedial work as well as to the carrying out of work badly.[76] The duty under s.1 on a person taking on work "in connection with the provision of a dwelling" does not extend to approved inspectors who had provided building control services to ensure compliance with building regulations.[76A]

[73]   *Uratemp Ventures v Collins* [2001] UKHL 43, for the purposes of the Housing Act 1988.

[74]   *Catlin Estates Ltd v Carter Jonas* [2005] EWHC 2315.

[75]   *Jenson v Faux* [2011] EWCA Civ 423. In *Rendlesham Estates Plc v Barr Ltd* [2014] EWHC 3968 (TCC), Edwards-Stuart J examined a number of important issues arising under the Defective Premises Act 1972 and in the particular context of a building in multiple ownership. He held that a "dwelling" is the place where a person or household lives to the exclusion of members of another household. Thus each apartment in a block of flats, together with its balcony, comprised a dwelling but the common parts were not included. However, the construction of the structural and common parts would amount to "work … in connection with the provision of a dwelling" within the meaning of s.1 of the Act if those parts were physically or functionally connected with the relevant dwelling (the apartment), especially when the apartment-owner had an obligation under its lease to share the cost of maintenance and repair of the structural and common parts.

[76]   In *Andrews v Schooling* [1991] 1 W.L.R. 783 CA the purchasers of a leasehold flat claimed damages against the freehold owners and developers from whom the flat was purchased on the basis that the cellar was unfit for habitation through damp. The defendants had carried out no work to the cellar, but were held liable under s.1 of the Act for failing to do so. The Defective Premises Act 1972 does not impose a duty upon persons who build a dwelling for their own occupation, even if they later sell it on, where the development is not part of a business venture: *Zennstrom v Fagot* [2013] EWHC 288 (TCC).

[76A]   *Lessees and Management Co of Herons Court v Heronslea Ltd* [2018] EWHC 3309 (TCC); [2019] B.L.R. 401. The decision was upheld on appeal—see [2019] EWCA Civ 1423.

The scope of the concurrent duty in tort

Replace footnote 102 with:

[102] [2016] EWHC 40 (TCC); [2016] T.C.L.R. 3. The decision was upheld on appeal—see [2017] EWCA Civ 254; [2017] P.N.L.R. 25 and followed in *BDW Trading Ltd v Integral Geotechnique (Wales) Ltd* [2018] EWHC 1915 (TCC). However, the case against the architect failed on the facts—see [2018] EWHC 3166 (TCC); 181 Con. L.R. 204

(b)   Duties to Third Parties

(ii)   Negligence

Expenditure necessary to avoid liability to third parties

Replace paragraph 9-073 (to incorporate new text following "majority in Murphy." at the end of the paragraph) with:

In *Murphy*, Lord Bridge suggested the following as a possible exceptional case **9-073** wherein economic loss might be recoverable[176]:

> "... if a building stands so close to the boundary of the building owner's land that after discovery of the dangerous defect it remains a potential source of injury to person or property on the neighbouring land or on the highway, the building owner ought, in principle, to be entitled to recover in tort from the negligent builder the cost of obviating the danger, whether by repair or demolition, so far as that cost is necessarily incurred in order to protect himself from potential liability to third parties."

Lord Oliver[177] (with whom Lord Ackner agreed, whilst also agreeing with Lord Bridge) expressly deferred consideration of whether such a qualification existed whilst expressing his doubt as to its basis. If Lord Bridge is correct it would seem that the owner of a house in the centre of a city may be able to claim the cost of repairing the house so as to prevent it collapsing into a busy highway whilst the owner of an identical property set in its own land will not be able to recover. The exception was applied in *Morse v Barrett (Leeds) Ltd*.[178] The claimants, who were largely subsequent purchasers of houses, joined together to rebuild an old wall which had been rendered dangerous by the action of the defendant, the original builder of the houses. The judge found that the claim fell squarely within Lord Bridge's suggested qualification. However in *George Fischer Holding Ltd v Multi Design Consultants Ltd*,[179] Judge Hicks QC refused to follow *Morse*. Having found that a design sub-contractor owed a collateral contractual duty to the claimant, the judge went on to consider what would have been the position had he been wrong. In that case, he considered the costs of averting a danger to the public would not have been recoverable since the statements of Lords Bridge and Oliver amounted only to minority dicta and were contrary to the decision of the majority in *Murphy*. Lord Bridge's dictum was considered again more recently in *Thomas v Taylor Wimpey Developments Ltd*.[179A] The claimant owners claimed the cost of rectifying defective new-build properties they had bought from the defendant builder. After reviewing the authorities, Judge Keyser QC held that there was no exception to the general principle that the loss suffered by a building owner from an ordinary building effect was irrecoverable in tort as pure economic loss and that Lord Bridge's dictum did not represent the law.

[176] [1991] 1 A.C. at 475F.

[177] ibid. at 489C.

178 (1993) 9 Const. L.J. 158 Ch. D.

179 (1998) 61 Con. L.R. 85 at 109–111.

179A [2019] EWHC 1134 (TCC); [2019] P.N.L.R. 26.

Reliance upon a statement

Replace footnote 188 with:

9-077 188 See, for examples: *Wolverine Tube (Canada) Inc v Noranda Metal Industries Ltd* (1995) 26 O.R. 577 (Ontario Court of Appeal) (defendant prepared environmental reports for an industrial client under a contract which provided that the reports were not be used outside the client's organisation without the defendant's permission; the reports each contained a clear disclaimer of liability to third parties; a purchaser from the defendant's client relied upon the reports; held that the disclaimers and the terms of the contract with the client were such as to prevent a duty of care from arising); *McKinlay Hendry Ltd v Tonkin Taylor Ltd* [2005] N.Z.L.R. 318 (New Zealand Court of Appeal) (an express disclaimer in the defendants' report, as well as the contractual arrangements put in place by the parties, precluded a finding that the defendants were liable for negligent misstatement in a ground investigation report which was relied upon by a party which was not their client). See also *BDW Trading Ltd v Integral Geotechnique (Wales) Ltd* [2018] EWHC 1915 (TCC) (a contractual requirement for a consulting engineers' report to have been assigned to subsequent purchaser precluded a duty of care between the engineers and purchaser arising, even when no such assignment had, in fact, happened).

Duties of care to subsequent purchasers

Replace footnote 200 with:

9-084 200 [1993] C.I.L.L. 864. Similar considerations were also discussed in *BDW Trading Ltd v Integral Geotechnique (Wales) Ltd* [2018] EWHC 1915 (TCC), in which a housing developer brought an action in negligence against consulting engineers who had prepared a report on behalf of a local authority as to the presence of asbestos on the grounds of the site, which was subsequently purchased by the developer. However, in that case, there had been no assumption of responsibility in light of an express contractual requirement for the report to have been assigned to the developer even though no assignment had taken place.

(ii) Economic loss

Replace footnote 224 with:

9-093 224 ibid. at 455. For further discussion about how parties to construction projects become covered under project-wide insurance policies, and the effect of provisions expressly requiring a contractor to obtain his own insurance, see *Haberdashers' Aske's Federation Trust Ltd v Lakehouse Contracts Ltd* [2018] EWHC 558 (TCC); [2018] Lloyd's Rep. I.R. 382.

3.   THE STANDARD OF CARE

(c)   Expert Evidence

Replace footnote 270 with:

9-110 270 In *Pride Valley Food Ltd v Hall and Partners (Contract Management) Ltd*, (2001) 76 Con. L.R. 1 the claimant sought to adduce the expert evidence of an architect in support of its claim against the defendant project manager. Judge Toulmin CMG QC concluded that the evidence provided little or no assistance. Amongst other criticisms, he pointed out that the report was over-long, included opinions on matters of fact and law which were questions for decision by the court and included expressions of opinion as to what the expert himself would have done in the defendant's position. In *Royal Brompton Hospital NHS Trust v Hammond (No.7)* (2001) 76 Con. L.R. 148 the evidence of the claimant's expert architect was rejected in its entirety by the trial judge. Judge Seymour QC warned that, if experts are to give useful evidence, they must be given sufficient time to master the relevant documents. In a typical construction case, the volume of documentation which an expert will need to digest may be very large. Further, experts should avoid making assumptions (or accepting instructions to make assumptions) the accuracy of which is central to the questions which they are to address. Finally, experts should make sure that they have contemporary knowledge of practice in their own profession. The claimant's expert architect's evidence was found wanting in each of these respects. The more restrictive attitude of modern courts towards expert evidence was confirmed when the Court of Appeal upheld an order debarring the defendant from calling his expert building surveyor in *Stevens v Gullis* [2000] 1 All E.R. 527. The expert had failed in his duty to act impartially and had also to comply with the requirements of the Civil Procedure Rules in relation to his report and a joint memorandum of matters agreed with the claimant's expert. Similar failures led to the rejection of large swathes of the expert evidence in *Trebor Bassett Holdings Ltd v ADT Fire and Security Plc* [2011] EWHC 1936 (TCC) at [396]–[426] where the court denigrated in particular the parties' failure to agree a list of issues for discussion by the experts, and the experts' failures to agree a joint memorandum pursuant to CPR r.35.12(3) and jointly to conduct any necessary tests or experiments. See also *Imperial Chemical Industries Ltd v Merit Merrell Technology Ltd* [2018] EWHC 1577 (TCC); 178 Con. L.R. 89 where the court determined that none of ICI's experts was sufficiently independent of the party that instructed them and restated the importance of the principles governing expert evidence in TCC cases, as set out in *National Justice Compania Naviera SA v Prudential Assurance Co Ltd (The Ikarian Reefer) (No.2)* [2000] 1 W.L.R. 603.

(i) Special Steps and Warranty of Reasonable Fitness

Replace footnote 315 with:

315 In *Consultants Group International v John Worman Ltd* (1986) 38 B.L.R. 36 the court held that "fitness for purpose" took its meaning from the facts and meant designed and executed to the standards demanded by UK and EC requirements for grant aid. In *Trebor Bassett Holdings Ltd v ADT Fire and Security Plc* [2012] EWCA Civ 1158 it was held that a contract to design and supply a bespoke fire suppression system for a particular manufacturing process did not impose an absolute obligation to provide an effective system. A tailor-made system could not be regarded as "goods", so as to attract the statutory requirements of satisfactory quality and fitness for purpose terms implied by the Supply of Goods and Services Act 1982. On the true construction of the contract, the contractor's obligation was merely to exercise reasonable skill and care in the design of the system. Similarly, in *Sweett (UK) Ltd v Michael Wight Homes Ltd* [2012] E.W. Misc. 3 (CC) it was held that a consultant appointed to act as a quantity surveyor and employer's agent did not owe an absolute obligation to ensure that the main contractor entered into a performance bond.

9-126

After paragraph 9-126, add new paragraph:

However, an express fitness for purpose obligation may be enforced strictly, even where this imposes a requirement on a contractor to identify deficiencies in a standard industry design specification. In *MT Hojgaard v E.ON Climate and Renewables UK Robin Rigg East Ltd*,316A a contractor engaged to design and install wind turbines relied in its foundations design upon an international standard, "J101". Unknown to the industry, the standard contained a fundamental error. The contract included an express term requiring the contractor to exercise reasonable skill and care in design; but it also included a requirement for foundations with a 20-year service life. The designer's reliance on the standard, albeit consistent with the exercise of due skill and care in design, meant that the foundations did not have the required service life. The issue before the Supreme Court was whether MT Hojgaard was liable for the cost of remedial works. The Court, reversing the decision in the Court of Appeal, held that the contractor would be expected to take the risk if he agreed to work to a design that would render the structure incapable of meeting a minimum standard. It was the contractor's responsibility to identify areas where the works needed to be designed in a more rigorous way in order to comply with the stipulation as to a 20-year service life. Accordingly, MT Hojgaard was liable for the cost of remedial works.316B In *Blackpool BC v Volkerfitzpatrick Ltd*,316C the court rejected an argument that the decision in *Hojgaard* supported an argument that a design life obligation was tempered by a requirement to take reasonable skill and care and construed such a clause strictly.

9-126

316A [2017] UKSC 59; [2018] 2 All E.R. 22.

316B Express contractual requirements were also relevant to the question whether a construction professional had complied with his duty to apply reasonable skill and care in *MW High Tech Projects UK v Haase Environmental Consulting GmbH* [2015] EWHC 152 (TCC); [2015] 1 C.L.C. 449. There. the design consultant's overriding obligation was to design a waste plant using reasonable skill and care and, subject to that, to comply with a specification and delivery plan. Coulson J granted declarations to the effect that, if it was possible to comply with the specification and delivery plan by way of a non-negligent design, then that was the consultant's obligation; but if it was not possible, then the consultant was not obliged to comply with the specification or delivery plan.

316C [2020] EWHC 1523 (TCC) at [152].

4. LIABILITY FOR BREACH OF DUTY

(b)   Cost Estimates and Budgets

Replace footnote 348 with:

9-144   348 In *Stephen Donald Architects Ltd v Christopher King* [2003] EWHC 1867 (TCC) Judge Seymour QC declined to find that an architect had been in breach of duty in the steps which he took when he realised that the construction costs of his design would exceed his client's budget. In those circumstances, any reasonably competent architect would embark on the process of "value engineering", that is, the consideration with the preferred building contractor and any other members of the professional team whether there were ways in which the cost of construction could be reduced to an affordable level. If that failed, the next step was to inquire of other contractors whether they could build the design within the client's budget. By contrast, in *William Clark Partnership Ltd v Dock St PCT Ltd* [2015] EWHC 2923 (TCC) a claim that quantity surveyors and project managers were negligent in their costs monitoring advice during the construction phase of development succeeded (although the claim failed for want of causation between particular breaches and overspend on the development as a whole). In *Riva Properties Ltd v Forster & Partners Ltd* [2017] EWHC 2574 (TCC); 175 Con. L.R. 45, an architect was held negligent when it embarked on a project without considering the budget and when it provided too low a figure in respect of value engineering (although the claim succeeded only partially because the claimant had not proven causation in respect of its loss of profits).

After paragraph 9-144, add new paragraph 9-144A:

9-144A   Issues of valuation of estimated construction costs can also occur in the context of facilities obtained to fund construction projects. The bank providing the facility will often appoint a monitoring surveyor to advise the bank when requests are made to draw down against the facility. If this is not carried out with reasonable skill and care, the surveyor can be liable to the bank for money advanced in reliance on the report—see *Lloyds Bank Plc v McBains Cooper Consulting Ltd.*348A However, as the duty is to monitor, the extent of the duty owed may not be the same as a quantity surveyor instructed directly to value the works—see, for example, *Bank of Ireland v Watts Group Plc.*348B

348A [2018] EWCA Civ 452; [2018] P.N.L.R. 23.

348B [2017] EWHC 1667 (TCC); [2017] T.C.L.R. 7; 173 Con. L.R. 240.

(d)   Design and Specification

Integration of design

After "their own discipline." at the end of the second sentence, add new footnote 384A:

9-157   684A The case of *Holland Hannen* was cited in *DBE Energy Ltd v Biogas Products Ltd* [2020] EWHC 1232 (TCC) where the court rejected an argument on the facts that the design of hot water system was beyond the scope of the sub-consultant's experience.

(g)   Advice on Choice and Terms of a Building Contract

Replace footnote 400 with:

9-164   400 See the unreported decision in *Burrell Hayward & Budd v Chris Carnell and David Green* 20 February 1992, where a deputy official referee found that both the claimant quantity surveyors and the defendant architects were partially responsible for the use of an inappropriate building contract by the architect's clients; this had no causal effect, however, as the terms of the building contract were, in practice, ignored. See also *Harlequin Property (SVG) Ltd v Wilkins Kennedy (A Firm)* [2016] EWHC 3188 (TCC); [2017]

4 W.L.R. 30; 170 Con. L.R. 86 where an accountant was found to have been negligent for failing to advise a client to enter into a formal contract with a contractor.

5.   DAMAGES

(e)   Heads of Damage

(ii)   Diminution in Value

After "diminution in value", add new footnote 578A:

9-228

578A An extreme example of this is *Moore v National Westminster Bank* [2018] EWHC 1805 (TCC). Here, the mortgagee bank negligently failed to procure a Home Buyers Report and the claimants purchased the property for £135,000 (assuming that the bank had obtained a survey supporting the valuation). At first instance, the judge assessed damage not by considering diminution in value but awarding the claimants the cost of repair which, on the evidence, was found to be £115,000. The judge allowed the appeal in principle, as the correct measure of loss was diminution in value and not cost of repair and the judge was wrong to distinguish the analogous cases of negligent surveyors. However, on the facts, the judge had been entitled to take the view that the cost of repair represented the only practical indicator of what the diminution in the value of the asset was and therefore the award of £115,000 was upheld: *Moore v National Westminster Bank* [2018] EWHC 1805 (TCC) (17 July 2018). This is an extreme case on the facts as it suggests that the property was only worth £20,000 on purchase. However, the bank's only evidence was that the diminution in value was £15,000 with no intermediate position relating to cost of repair being adopted. The appeal judge noted that whilst judges would be entitled to arrive at an intermediate position, he could not be criticised for adopting one of the two extreme figures presented by the parties at trial.

(ix)   Inconvenience, Distress and Loss of Amenity

Replace footnote 603 with:

9-236

603 *Watts v Morrow* [1991] 1 W.L.R. 1421; *Farley v Skinner* [2001] UKHL 49; [2001] 3 W.L.R. 899. See also the doubts expressed by Lord Lloyd in *Ruxley v Forsyth* [1996] A.C. 344 at 374 as to the award of £2,500 in that case. For examples of the modest awards made for the inconvenience of living with defects and with subsequent remedial works, see *Eile v Southwark LBC* [2006] EWHC 1411 (TCC); *Iggleden v Fairview New Homes* [2007] EWHC 1573 (TCC); *Charlton v Northern Structural Services Ltd* [2008] EWHC 66 (TCC); *AXA Insurance UK Plc v Cunningham Lindsey UK* [2007] EWHC 3023 (TCC) (held that general damages for physical inconvenience, distress and discomfort caused by breaches of contract will not normally exceed £2,500 per person per year); *Harrison v Shepherd Homes Ltd* [2011] EWHC 8011 (TCC) (damages of £150 per person per year awarded for the physical inconvenience of living with defective foundations which caused only cosmetic defects in the superstructure). See also *West v Ian Finlay and Associates* [2014] EWCA Civ 316 (sums of £7,000, £5,000 and £2,000 awarded to different family members for just under two years' physical inconvenience and consequent distress were reduced on appeal to £2,000, £1,500 and £500); and *Rendlesham Estates Plc v Barr Ltd* [2014] EWHC 3968 (TCC) (in a claim under the Defective Premises Act 1972, occupiers of a block of apartments recovered general damages for distress and inconvenience of £750 per annum for a non-functioning intercom system and walkways subject to ponding of water, rising to £2,250 per annum where the occupier also suffered damp and mould inside his apartment). In the case of *Hart v Large* [2020] EWHC 985 (TCC), the court awarded the claimants £7,500 in damages for distress and inconvenience to reflect the fact they had lived for eight years in a leaking house which required substantial remedial work. The judge described the award as "towards the upper end but not the top end of the range".

6.   SHARED RESPONSIBILITY

(a)   Apportionment of Liability

Settlement as damage

Replace footnote 643 with:

9-259

643 Following the procedure set out in Pt 20 of the Civil Procedure Rules. The principles considered in this section will apply also when a claimant seeks to recover, as a head of consequential loss, sums paid in settlement of its alleged liability to a third party. See, e.g. *Mirant Asia-Pacific Construction (Hong*

Kong) Ltd v Ove Arup & Partners International Ltd [2007] EWHC 918 (TCC), (global settlement of a liability alleged to have been occasioned by engineers' breach of duty was unrecoverable because the project would have been delayed in any event and, further, no causal link was demonstrated between the amount paid in settlement and the engineers' breach); *Costain Ltd v Charles Haswell & Partners Ltd* [2009] EWHC 3140 (TCC) (no causal link proved between engineers' defective design and sums paid in settlement of sub-contractors' claims for loss and expense). The principles relevant to the apportionment of a global settlement where the claimant seeks only to recover part of them from a third party were discussed in *Fluor v Shanghai Zhenhua Heavy Industry Co Ltd* [2018] EWHC 1 (TCC); 178 Con. L.R. 210 per Sir Antony Edwards-Stuart at [465]–[483].

7.   ADJUDICATION

Construction operations

Replace footnote 675 with:

9-273   675   See s.105(2). The difficulties which arise when a contract provides both for works which are "construction operations" and for works which are excluded from the definition were discussed in *Severfield (UK) Ltd v Duro Felguera UK Ltd* [2015] EWHC 3352 (TCC) and repeated in subsequent proceedings in the same dispute brought following the employer's liquidation in *Severfield (UK) Ltd v Duro Felguera UK Ltd (No.2)* [2017] EWHC 3066 (TCC); 175 Con. L.R. 266.

Enforcement of adjudicator's decisions

After "be used instead.", add new footnote 692A:

9-279   692A   However, there are limits to the use of this procedure: *Hutton Construction Ltd v Wilson Properties (London) Ltd* [2017] EWHC 517 (TCC); [2018] 1 All E.R. (Comm) 524; *Actavo UK Ltd v Doosan Babcock Ltd* [2017] EWHC 2849 (TCC); 177 Con. L.R. 77; *Merit Holdings Ltd v Michael J Lonsdale Ltd* [2017] EWHC 2450 (TCC); [2018] B.L.R. 14; 174 Con. L.R. 92; *Victory House General Partner Ltd v RGB P&C Ltd* [2018] EWHC 102 (TCC).

Stay of execution

Replace paragraph 9-285 (to incorporate new text and an amendment to footnote 727) with:

9-285   The enforcement of an adjudicator's decision might work substantial injustice if, between enforcement and a subsequent reversal of the decision in arbitral or legal proceedings, the enforcing party falls into financial difficulty and is unable to repay the sum awarded by the adjudicator. Against that must be balanced the policy of HGCRA, which is designed to provide a speedy and inexpensive method of temporary dispute resolution which protects cash flow. Accordingly, special circumstances are required to justify an exercise of the court's discretion to stay execution of summary judgment enforcing an adjudicator's decision.[727] The claimant's probable inability to repay the adjudicator's award if that award were reversed in subsequent arbitration or litigation may constitute special circumstances for this purpose. Thus a stay was granted when the claimant was in liquidation.[728] Similarly, where the claimant was in administrative receivership, a stay on enforcement of an award was granted on terms that the defendant paid the sum at stake into court[729] and issued legal proceedings on the dispute within one month.[730] A stay was also granted where the evidence demonstrated a real risk that any judgment would go unsatisfied by reason of the claimant organising its financial affairs with the purpose of dissipating or disposing of the adjudication sum so that it would not be available to be repaid—see *Gosvenor London Ltd v Aygun Aluminium UK Ltd*.[730A] However a stay of execution will not be granted where the claimant was impecunious, to the defendant's knowledge, when the defendant contracted with it, since the defendant thereby accepted the risks attached to contracting with a party in that financial position.[731] Nor will a stay be granted where the claimant's impecuniosity is attributable to the defendant's failure to pay the sum awarded by the adjudicator.[732]

[727] *Grosvenor London Ltd v Aygun Aluminium UK Ltd* [2018] EWHC 227 (TCC); [2018] Bus. L.R. 1439; [2018] B.L.R. 353; 177 Con. L.R. 127, where the principles summarised in *Wimbledon Construction Co 2000 Ltd v Vago* [2005] EWHC 1086 (TCC); [2005] B.L.R. 374; 101 Con. L.R. 99 were refined at [37]–[41]; see also *Straw Realisations (No.1) Ltd v Shaftesbury House (Developments) Ltd* [2010] EWHC 2597 (TCC); [2011] B.L.R. 47.

[728] See, e.g. *Bouygues UK Ltd v Dahl-Jensen UK Ltd* [2000] B.L.R. 522 (claimant in liquidation).

[729] See, e.g. *Rainford House Ltd (In Administrative Receivership) v Cadogan Ltd* [2001] B.L.R. 416.

[730] See, e.g. *Baldwins Industrial Services Plc v Barr Ltd* [2003] B.L.R. 176.

[730A] [2018] EWHC 227 (TCC); [2018] Bus. L.R. 1439; [2018] B.L.R. 353; 177 Con. L.R. 127.

[731] *Herschel Engineering Ltd v Breen Property Ltd (No.2)* unreported 28 July 2000, *Nap Anglia Ltd v Sun-Land Development Co Ltd* [2011] EWHC 2846 (TCC).

[732] *Mead General Building Ltd v Dartmoor Properties Ltd* [2009] EWHC 200 (TCC).

CHAPTER 10

SURVEYORS

2.   GENERAL

(a)   Duties to Client

(i)   *Contractual Duties*

Terms of engagement

Replace paragraph 10-009 with:

10-009   The primary basis of a surveyor's duties to his client is the contract of engagement between himself and his client. The contract may be written or oral or inferred from the conduct of the parties. By a mandatory Professional Standard,[20] the RICS now requires a valuer to produce written terms of engagement, and to ensure that all matters material to the report have been fully brought to the client's attention and appropriately documented *before* the issue of the report. The instructions must deal, at a minimum with a total of 18 matters, including the identity of the client, purpose of the valuation, the subject of the valuation, the basis of valuation, any assumptions or special assumptions,[21] any restrictions on use, the date of the valuation, and the basis on which the fee will be calculated.[22] If he fails to do so and there is any subsequent dispute as to the terms of his instructions, he may be at a serious disadvantage.[23]

[20] RICS PS2, para.7, RICS Valuation—Global Standards, January 2020.

[21] Assumptions are matters that are reasonable to accept as fact in the context of the valuation assignment without specific investigation or verification. A special assumption is an assumption that either assumes facts that differ from the actual facts existing at the valuation date or that would not be made by a typical market participant in a transaction on the valuation date. Assumptions and special assumptions can only be made if they are "reasonable and relevant having regard to the purpose for which the valuation assignment is required." See RICS VPS1, para.3.2(k).

[22] RICS VPS1, para.3.1.

[23] See *Fisher v Knowles* [1982] 1 E.G.L.R. 154 and para.10-090, below. Note that *Fisher v Knowles* was decided at a time when the very extensive VPS1 as to the content of instructions was not in force.

For a recent example of a case where a judge criticised the absence of a confirmatory letter of instruction, see *Capita v Drivers Jonas* [2011] EWHC 2336 (Comm).

Contractual duties

Replace paragraph 10-010 (to incorporate amendments to footnotes 24 and 25) with:

10-010 A surveyor's duties will vary according to the circumstances of each case and in particular the purpose for which he is asked to report upon a particular property.[24] The RICS Practice Statements require a surveyor to use a basis of valuation recognised that is appropriate.[25] A surveyor's express duties will primarily depend upon the instructions given,[26] for example, to carry out a structural survey or valuation of a named property,[27] but the Practice Statements also define what may be required in order to carry out such instructions.[28] A surveyor will invariably be under an implied, if not an express, duty to exercise reasonable care and skill,[29] in both the work which results in the report, and the report itself.[30] In addition, certain specific duties may be implied. Thus a surveyor engaged to carry out a structural survey has been held to be under an implied duty to inspect the property so far as is reasonably practicable, whereas a surveyor carrying out a mortgage inspection and valuation may confine himself to a careful visual examination of the property.[31]

[24] See *Ker v John H Allan & Sons*, 1949 S.L.T. (Notes) 20 per Lord Birnam; but note that, where a valuation is requested, it should not make a difference to the result whether it is requested "for loan purposes" or for some other purpose; the conclusion that the valuer reaches must be his honest opinion of the true market value of the land at the relevant time: see *Singer and Friedlander Ltd v John D Wood & Co* [1977] 2 E.G.L.R. 84 at 85. RICS VPS 1, para.3.2(f) now deals specifically with the purposes of the valuation and provides that the purpose of the valuation will determine the basis of the value.

[25] See RICS VPS1, para.3.1(g).

[26] See para.10-018, below, for the problems of construction of instructions.

[27] See *Capita v Drivers Jonas* [2011] EWHC 2336 (Comm) and *Predeth v Castle Phillips Finance Co Ltd* [1986] 2 E.G.L.R. 144, and para.10-093, below.

[28] See further para.10-013 below, and see, e.g. RICS VPS2, which expressly requires that "Inspections and investigations must always be carried out to the extent necessary to produce a valuation which is professionally adequate for its purpose" and goes on to provide a substantial commentary on this requirement. In *Webb Resolutions v E. Surv Ltd* [2012] EWHC 3653 (TCC); [2013] P.N.L.R. 253, the claimant lender required completion of a "tick-box" form and positively discouraged the provision of additional information (which would "not be read by our underwriting staff"). Nevertheless, the fact that the retainer required compliance with RICS standards meant that it was incumbent upon the valuer to provide further information where those standards required it.

[29] e.g. *Kenney v Hall, Pain and Foster* [1976] 2 E.G.L.R. 29 at 33. Surveyors' negligence cases are commonly determined only by reference to whether the surveyor failed to exercise reasonable care and skill. The word "negligence" is frequently used to indicate not only the specific tort, but also breach of the implied contractual duty to exercise reasonable care and skill. Such a term is implied by the Supply of Goods and Services Act 1982 s.13. Note that a similar term is implied under s.49 of the Consumer Rights Act 2015, and that, in some circumstances, that Act implies certain other provisions. See more generally paras 2-021, 3-028 and 5-025, above.

[30] *Candler v Crane Christmas & Co* [1951] 2 K.B. 164 at 179 per Denning LJ.

[31] Commenting about the level of expertise required of this class of service, Lord Griffiths in *Smith v Bush* [1990] 1 A.C. 831 at 858 said: "It is only defects which are observable by a careful visual examination that have to be taken into account and I cannot see that it places any unreasonable burden on the valuer to require him to accept responsibility for the fairly elementary degree of skill and care involved in observing, following-up and reporting on such defects. Surely it is work at the lower end of the surveyor's field of professional expertise." See also *Whalley v Roberts & Roberts* [1990] 1 E.G.L.R. 164.

Impact of regulatory requirements

Replace paragraph 10-013 with:

10-013 Valuations carried out by members of RICS are governed by the RICS Valuation—Global Standards together with, where appropriate, the UK National Supplement, colloquially referred to as "the Red Book".[36] The purpose of these standards is to provide the profession, clients and the courts with authoritative guidance as to the assembly, interpretation and reporting of information relevant to the practice of valuation. In producing them, a conscious decision was made by the RICS to prescribe minimum standards in respect of valuations over a much wider range of services than those to which previous incarnations of the Red Book had historically applied. The Red Book Global contains Professional Standards in Part 3 and Valuation Technical and Performance Standards in Part 4. Compliance with both of these remains mandatory. Part 5 contains "Valuation Practice Guidance—Applications," which provide guidance in relation to certain specific valuation tasks. Although compliance with these statements of guidance is described as "advisory," they are nevertheless stated to represent "best practice".[37-38] The guidance covers areas such as valuations intended for inclusion in Financial Statements and valuations for secured lending.

[36] The current version of the RICS Valuation—Global Standards was effective on 31 January 2020, while the current UK National Supplement was effective from 14 January 2019. Note that it is important, when considering the obligations of a surveyor at a particular moment, to ascertain the form of the standards at the time that he carried out his work.

[37-38] See Part 1, para.15 of RICS Valuation—Global Standards. It is common for firms to assert in their reports that they have followed RICS practice guidance, see, e.g. *Craneheath Securities Ltd v York Montague Ltd* [1994] 1 E.G.L.R. 159., Jacob J; [1996] 1 E.G.L.R. 130 CA.

Surveys and valuations for lenders

Replace list item 2. (to incorporate new footnote 44A) with:

10-017   2.   a house or flat buyer's report and valuation[44A];

[44A] Until recently the RICS provided for a HomeBuyer Report, which was designed to report on the general condition of the main elements of the relevant property and particular features that affected its present value and might affect its resale. The report focused on matters that the surveyor judged to be serious and/or urgent. See UK VPGA 13.9, RICS Valuation—Global Standards 2017: UK national supplement. A RICS member carrying out a HomeBuyer Report was to comply with the relevant guidance, and use the standard documentation and report form, provided by RICS. The guidance relating to the HomeBuyer Report has been replaced by, and consolidated within, a comprehensive Home Survey Standard, published by RICS as a Professional Statement and effective from 1 June 2020, which sets out three different levels of service that can be selected as appropriate in respect of surveys of residential property.

Mutual valuers

Replace footnote 52 with:

10-020   [52] In *Darlington BC v Waring & Gillow (Holdings) Ltd* [1988] 2 E.G.L.R. 159, the appointment of an independent valuer was held not to have been carried out in accordance with the terms of the lease, the award was therefore not binding and the current rent continued. Although it will always be a question of construction of the relevant contract by which the valuer is appointed, the balance of authority is in favour of preserving access to the courts to determine questions of law relating to the jurisdiction of the expert: see *Great Dunmow Estates Ltd v Crest Nicholson Operations Ltd* [2019] EWCA Civ 1683; [2020] 2 All E.R. (Comm) 97.

Surveyors as expert witnesses

Replace footnote 58 with:

10-021   [58] CPR r.35.10(2). The question of independence of expert surveyors, in particular in the context of conditional fee arrangements, came into focus in two recent cases in the Upper Tribunal (Lands Chamber): *Gardiner LLP v David Jackson* [2018] UKUT 253 (LC); 182 Con. L.R. 127 and *Merlin*

Entertainments Group Ltd v Wayne Cox [2018] UKUT 406 (LC); [2019] R.A. 101. Conditional fee arrangements for experts are highly undesirable, and if they exist must be disclosed to the court at the outset.

(b) Duties to Third Parties

(ii) *Development of the Duty to Third Parties in Tort*

Australia

Replace footnote 149 with:

149 The principles applicable in Australia have more recently been reviewed and applied by the Full **10-050**
Court of the Federal Court in *Kestral Holdings Pty Ltd v APF Properties PTD Ltd* [2009] FCAFC 144;
(2009) 260 A.L.R. 418; see also *Propell National Valuers (WA) Pty Ltd v Australian Executor Trustees
Ltd* [2012] FCAFC 31.

(c) The Standard of Care and Skill

(ii) *General Practice and Knowledge as Evidence of the Standard*

Extent of duty determined by type of service offered

After "a particular service.", add new footnote 215A:

215A For example, a HomeBuyer Report is more limited than a building survey: see *Hart v Large* [2020] **10-069**
EWHC 985 (TCC) at [128]. Note that a surveyor could be implicated in advising on the type of survey
that is appropriate in a given case (see VPS1, para.1.2), albeit that on the facts of *Hart* the allegation of
negligence in that respect was rejected by the judge: see [130].

(iii) *Not Every Error is Negligence*

Replace footnote 231 with:

231 (1972) 230 E.G. 501 at 649; cited with approval in *Hart v Large* [2020] EWHC 985 (TCC) at [125]. **10-071**

(iv) *The Relevance of "the bracket"*

Replace footnote 238 with:

238 At [145]. The judge actually referred to seven propositions, but it is suggested that his second and **10-073**
third propositions were materially identical. A similar list was recited with approval by the Court of Appeal in *Titan Europe 2006-3 Plc v Colliers International UK Plc* [2015] EWCA Civ 1083; [2016]
P.N.L.R. 7 at [6]. Eder J's propositions were adopted in *Dunfermline Building Society v CBRE Ltd* [2017]
EWHC 2745 (Ch); [2018] P.N.L.R. 13 at [33].

The extent of the bracket

*Replace paragraph 10-075 (to incorporate amendments to footnotes 254 and 257)
with:*

In *Merivale Moore v Strutt & Parker*,252 Buxton LJ stated: **10-075**

> "the 'bracket' is not to be determined in a mechanistic way, divorced from the facts of the
> instance case. We were shown a list of figures giving either the bracket determined, or the
> percentage divergence from the true figure found nonetheless not to have been negligent,
> in a series of recent cases. I did not find that of assistance, save as a graphic reminder that
> it is not enough simply to show that the valuation was different from the true value."253

As a matter of practice, "the bracket" has usually been determined to lie in the range
10 to 20% either side of a mean figure.254 Judges have sometimes commented that

expert evidence has suggested a closer correlation between competent valuations than they would suppose. In *Beaumont v Humberts*,[255] a case involving an alleged negligent valuation for reinstatement purposes, Staughton LJ commented when dealing with the issue of breach of duty:

"It is accepted that a surveyor or valuer may be wrong by a margin of 10 per cent either way without being negligent. (That in itself seems, in my uninstructed opinion, a high standard to impose; but it is, as I have said, accepted)."[256]

Similarly, in *Nykredit Mortgage Bank Plc v Edward Erdman Group Ltd*[257] the same Lord Justice commented:

"There was evidence, which the judge accepted, that careful and skilled valuers did not inevitably arrive at precisely the same answer. If a given figure is taken as the true value, the range within which a valuer could arrive at some different amount without negligence was plus or minus 15 per cent. In the light of the sensitivity of the calculation I do not find that at all surprising."

[252] [2000] P.N.L.R. 499 at 517.

[253] See also *McIntyre v Herring Son & Daw* [1988] 1 E.G.L.R. 231, where Mr E.A. Machin QC, sitting as a deputy High Court judge, accepted at 233 that:

"The widths of such brackets reflected only the evidence in that particular case and that there is no proposition of law that in valuation cases a valuer is not negligent if his valuation falls within such a bracket. The permissible width of the bracket must be a matter to be decided upon the evidence of any particular case."

[254] See the summary from *K/S Lincoln v CB Richard Ellis* [2010] P.N.L.R. 31 at para.10-073, above. According to expert evidence in *Singer & Friedlander v John D Wood* [1977] 2 E.G.L.R. 84, the permissible margin was 10% either side of "the right figure", but in exceptional circumstances it could be extended to about 15% either way. In *Private Bank Trust & Co Ltd v S (UK) Ltd* [1993] 1 E.G.L.R. 144, the court concluded that on the evidence the defendant's valuations lay within a permissible margin of error of 15% either side of his valuation bracket. In *Banque Bruxelles Lambert SA v Lewis & Tucker Ltd* [1994] 2 E.G.L.R. 108, the evidence before Phillips J was that when valuations are based on comparables, one competent valuation may differ from another by as much as 20%. See at 118C. In *BNP Mortgages Ltd v Barton Cook & Sams* [1996] 1 E.G.L.R. 239, the evidence proved an acceptable range for the property in question to be 15%. In *Assured Advances Ltd v Ashbee & Co* [1994] E.G.C.S. 169, the valuers were approached by brokers and not the lender, and asked for a "quick £50 valuation". The court considered the proper approach was:

"to find a central accurate valuation and to establish a percentage above and below it which was the non-negligent zone. Anything outside that zone would be prima facie a negligent valuation."

There was, however, no adequate evidence of the proper valuation, so the action failed. In *Arab Bank v John D Wood Commercial* [2000] Lloyd's Rep. P.N. 173 at 195, Mance LJ plainly considered that a "bracket" of 20% above a correct figure was at the outer limits of a permissible range even for a "franking valuation"—see further para.10-069, above. In *Preferred Mortgages Ltd v Countrywide Surveyors Ltd* [2005] EWHC 2820 (Ch); [2006] P.N.L.R. 9, the judge found that the bracket for an unusual converted chapel was 15%. In *Capita v Driver Jonas* [2011] EWHC 2336 (Comm), the judge found that different components of the valuation merited different "brackets" ranging from as little as 1% either way to 20% either way for an element of assessment of likely future rentals (the case was the subject of an appeal on other points: [2012] EWCA Civ 1417). In *Paratus AMC Ltd v Countrywide Surveyors Ltd* [2011] EWHC 3307 (Ch); [2012] P.N.L.R. 12, the judge found that a bracket of 8% was applicable to the valuation of a residential flat bought in a rising market. The factors which the judge expressly took into account in arriving at this bracket included the lack of consistency amongst available comparable sales; the buoyancy of the market and the particular circumstances whereby a "glut" of desirable properties had disappeared at the time of valuation. In *Titan Europe 2006-3 Plc v Colliers International Plc* [2015] EWCA Civ 1083; [2016] P.N.L.R. 7, the Court of Appeal considered a case concerning the valuation of a very substantial commercial property in Germany. Although the Court overturned the Judge's finding as to the true value of the property (with the consequence that the valuer was not liable), there was no challenge to the finding that the appropriate "bracket" was 15% either side of such correct figure.

See also *Barclays Bank Plc v TBS & V Ltd* [2016] EWHC 2948 (QB) in which, although the defendant had faced a challenging set of circumstances involving a limited number of comparables and the valuation of a leasehold interest in a care home that was rare, the judge declined to extend the bracket beyond 15%.

255 [1990] 2 E.G.L.R. 166. See para.10-040, above.

256 ibid. at 169.

257 [1996] 1 E.G.L.R. 119 at 120. The defendants carried out a residual land valuation, acknowledged to be sensitive to the variables used in its calculation. The method was not criticised, but certain of the variables were. In *Dunfermline Building Society v CBRE Ltd* [2017] EWHC 2745 (Ch); [2018] P.N.L.R. 13 it was pointed out that a large bracket is often applied to a residual appraisal because of the particular sensitivities that are involved in that valuation approach: see [47]. The bracket in that case was held to be 15% ([194]–[196]).

3.   Liability For Breach of Duties

(d)   Failing to Make Sufficient Inquiries

The professional use of hearsay information

To the penultimate sentence after "be reliable information.", add new footnote 429A:

429A In *Barclays Bank Plc v Christie Owen & Davies Ltd* [2016] EWHC 2351 (Ch); [2017] P.N.L.R. 8, the defendant was held not to have been entitled to rely upon information about comparables provided by a third party valuer where the contents of that information were either not capable of being checked, or where the defendant had chosen not to make any independent check on them: see [171]–[172] and [181]. **10-119**

(f)   Inadequate Report

Replace footnote 456 with:

456 See *Rona v Pearce* (1953) 162 E.G. 380 per Hilbery J; also see *Hill v Debenham, Tewson and Chinnocks* (1958) 171 E.G. 835 at 837 per Judge Carter QC: "But applying the standard of the profession I entertain no doubt that the practice of the profession is 'If you do not look, you must warn'." In *Hart v Large* [2020] EWHC 985 (TCC) the judge held that the surveyor was negligent for (i) failing to advise that further inquiries be made in respect of damp proofing in circumstances in which he was unable to see visible signs of such damp proofing at the premises, and (ii) failing to advise that it was essential that a professional consultant's certificate be sought from the architect that had been involved with recent redevelopment work, given the reliance that the surveyor had been forced to place on what normal good practice would have been in relation to concealed elements of the construction. **10-127**

4.   Damages

(a)   Causation

Replace footnote 478 with:

478 In *Platform Funding Ltd v Anderson & Associates Ltd* [2012] EWHC 1853 (QB), the defendant surveyor had failed to carry out his valuation with reasonable skill and care, but because of a carefully orchestrated dishonest scheme (to which the surveyor was not a party) whereby the price of comparable properties in the same development was artificially inflated, a competently performed valuation would have reached the same result. The claim failed on causation grounds. Note that in a lending case, where prima facie the loss is calculated by reference to a "basic comparison" between (a) what the claimant's position would have been if the defendant had fulfilled his duty of care and (b) the claimant's actual position, the causation question is a purely factual one. Concepts such as reasonable contemplation of the parties might further narrow the recoverable loss on grounds of remoteness or scope of duty, but are not relevant at this prior stage: see *Tiuta International Ltd v De Villiers Surveyors Ltd* [2017] UKSC 77; [2017] 1 W.L.R. 4627 at [10] per Lord Sumption. **10-132**

Reliance

To the end of the paragraph after "in fact, occur.", add new footnote 479A:

479A The position may be different where draft reports have been provided to the claimant. Where such reports were disclosed to the client by a quantity surveyor, initial drawdowns from a loan facility were treated as having been made in reliance upon them notwithstanding the fact that the finalised report was not produced until a later date: see *Bank of Ireland v Watts Group Plc* [2017] EWHC 1667 (TCC) at **10-133**

[129]. In the event, however, the claimant failed to show that the alleged negligence (which was itself not upheld) would have made a difference to the result.

Belief that advice correct

Replace footnote 489 with:

10-135   [489] For an extreme example of such a case, see *Cavendish Funding v Henry Spencer* [1998] P.N.L.R. 122, where the Court of Appeal refused to interfere with the judge's inference that a grossly negligent valuation had been a substantial cause of the making of a loan. This was so although there were two valuations in the case; the claimant appeared to have ignored the lower valuation; the loan was made in breach of the provisions of the claimant's lending manual and there appeared reasons to doubt (at the least) the competence of the relevant lending officer who was not called to give evidence. Aldous LJ nonetheless viewed the history of the loan as being consistent only with reliance and causation. In *Bank of Ireland v Watts Group Plc* [2017] EWHC 1667 (TCC), Coulson J accepted that, in the circumstances of the case, the court should assume, in the absence of evidence to the contrary, that an employer had relied on the professional advice that he had paid for and been provided with: see [130]. In the event, however, the claimant failed to show that the alleged negligence (which was itself not upheld) would have made a difference to the result.

Novus actus interveniens

Replace footnote 504 with:

10-143   [504] [2005] EWHC 2820 (Ch); [2006] P.N.L.R. 9; see also *Hart v Large* [2020] EWHC 985 (TCC), where the judge declined to hold that apparent negligence on the part of solicitors broke the chain of causation between the surveyor's breach and the loss: see [227]–[228].

Successive loans

Replace paragraph 10-147 (to incorporate an amendment to footnote 511 and replacement text following) with:

10-147   Causation issues can also arise where successive loans are made. For example, if a lender makes a loan on the strength of a valuation provided by valuer A, and subsequently the loan is refinanced by the same lender in a greater amount on the strength of a valuation provided by valuer B in such a way that the original loan is repaid and a new loan made, the lender cannot sue valuer A, even if that original valuation was negligently carried out; the lender has suffered no loss as a result of that valuation.[511] But it does not necessarily follow that the lenders can recover for the full amount of their loss from valuer B. If that valuer had not been negligent in reporting the value of the property for the purpose of the second facility, the lenders would not have entered into the second facility, but would still have entered into the first. They would, therefore, have lost the new money lent under the second facility, but would still have lost the original loans made under the first.[512] If valuer A had been negligent, it might be open to the lenders to recover against valuer B the loss of the claim that it would otherwise have had against valuer A.[512A] But where valuer A had not been negligent, no such claim would arise.[512B]

[511] *Preferred Mortgages v Bradford & Bingley Estate Agencies Ltd* [2002] EWCA Civ 336; [2002] P.N.L.R. 35. Latham LJ, with whom Sir Martin Nourse and Buxton LJ agreed, treated any loss flowing from the first valuation as extinguished once the first loan was redeemed, applying the principles laid down in Lord Nicholls's speech in *Nykredit Mortgage Bank Plc v Edward Erdman Group Ltd (No.2)* [1997] 1 W.L.R. 1627 at 1631; see [26]–[29] of the judgment; see also *Swynson Ltd v Lowick Rose LLP* [2017] UKSC 32; [2018] A.C. 313 at [13] per Lord Sumption, and *Tiuta International Ltd v De Villiers Surveyors Ltd* [2017] UKSC 77; [2017] 1 W.L.R. 4627 at [4] per Lord Sumption. In *Barclays Bank Plc v TBS & V Ltd* [2016] EWHC 2948 (QB), Dove J held, obiter, at [93] that *Preferred Mortgages* would not have applied to a situation in which the original borrowing had been refinanced but the charge by way of mortgage had not been redeemed. It must be doubted that that reasoning can stand with Lord Sumption's explanation of *Preferred Mortgages* in *Tiuta International* at [4].

[512] *Tiuta International Ltd v De Villiers Surveyors Ltd* [2017] UKSC 77; [2017] 1 W.L.R. 4627 at [7] per Lord Sumption.

512A On the basis that, by the refinancing, valuer B's negligence had caused valuer A's liability to be extinguished: see *Tiuta International Ltd v De Villiers Surveyors Ltd* [2017] UKSC 77; [2017] 1 W.L.R. 4627 at [9].

512B *Tiuta International Ltd v De Villiers Surveyors Ltd* [2017] UKSC 77; [2017] 1 W.L.R. 4627 at [7].

(c) Scope of the Duty

To the end of the paragraph after "providers of information.", add new footnote 530A:

530A In relation to valuers, see *Hughes-Holland v BPE Solicitors* [2017] UKSC 21; [2018] A.C. 599 at [44]; see also *Bank of Ireland v Watts Group Plc* [2017] EWHC 1667 (TCC) at [151] (quantity surveyor providing an appraisal of expected cost of a development). **10-153**

After paragraph 10-155, add new paragraph 10-155A:

In *Hughes-Holland v BPE Solicitors*, the Supreme Court made clear that the burden of proving that the loss falls within the scope of the defendant's duty falls on the claimant.537A **10-155A**

537A [2017] UKSC 21; [2018] A.C. 599 at [53].

Replace footnote 538 with:

538 See Lord Hoffmann's much cited lecture to the Chancery Bar Association entitled "Common Sense and Causing Loss", 15 June 1999, and also "SAAMCO, the Scope of the Duty and Liability for Consequences" [2007] VUW Law Rw 28. Note, however, that an alternative analysis suggests that in truth the scope of the duty approach is simply a species of remoteness: see *Platform Home Loans Ltd v Oyston Shipways Ltd* [2000] 2 A.C. 190 at 208E-F; and see also *Transfield Shipping Inv v Mercator Shipping Inc, The Achilleas* [2008] UKHL 48; [2009] 1 A.C. 61 per Lord Hoffmann and Lord Hope, and the application of that case to remoteness questions in the professional liability field in *Wellesley Partners LLP v Withers LLP* [2015] EWCA Civ 1146; [2016] 2 W.L.R. 1351; *Agouman v Leigh Day* [2016] EWHC 1324 at [125]. In *Hughes-Holland v BPE Solicitors* [2017] UKSC 21; [2018] A.C. 599, Lord Sumption suggested that the *SAAMCO* principle was not comfortably expressed as simply part of the law of causation: see [36] and [38]. **10-156**

To the quoted text at the end of the paragraph after "from the transaction.", add new footnote 544A:

544A But now see *Hughes-Holland v BPE Solicitors* [2017] UKSC 21; [2018] A.C. 599 at [50]–[52]. **10-158**

To the end of the first sentence after "claims against valuers.", add new footnote 544B:

544B In *Hughes-Holland v BPE Solicitors* [2017] UKSC 21; [2018] A.C. 599 the Supreme Court confirmed that the principle stated in *SAAMCO* was a general principle of the law of damages: see [47]. **10-159**

After paragraph 10-163, add new paragraph 10-163A:

In *Bank of Ireland v Watts Group Plc*, Coulson J held, obiter, that even if the defendant quantity surveyor had been negligent in assessing the cost of a prospective development, inducing the claimant to grant a loan facility in respect of it, and even if different advice would have caused the claimant to rescind the facility, the claimant had still failed to prove that it had suffered a loss that fell within the scope of the defendant's duty.554A **10-163A**

554A [2017] EWHC 1667 (TCC) at [154].

(d)   Measure of Damages

(i)   Negligent Survey or Valuation for a Purchaser who Completes a Purchase

The use of hindsight in assessing damages

After "if correctly described.", add new footnote 624A:

10-180   624A   In *Hart v Large* [2020] EWHC 985 (TCC), the defendant surveyor argued that "the true value if correctly described" could not include an assessment of latent defects that would not have been unearthed even on a competent survey. The judge rejected that argument on the basis that the surveyor's breach involved a failure to give clear and unequivocal advice that there were risks relating to the building that simply could not be assessed and against which the claimants needed protection if they were to proceed. See [246]–[254].

Relevance of cost of repairs

Replace footnote 653 with:

10-186   653   [1989] 1 E.G.L.R. 159 CA at 161. The cost of repairs was used as a cross-check against the diminution in value in the Scottish case of *Wood v McVicar* [1990] G.W.D. 37–2143, Lord Morton of Shuna. See also *Moore v National Westminster Bank* [2018] EWHC 1805 (TCC) in which the judge was held to have been entitled to adopt the cost of repair as a proxy for the diminution in value in the absence of reliable valuation evidence.

5.   SHARED RESPONSIBILITY

(a)   Contributory Negligence

The percentage reduction

Replace footnote 853 with:

10-243   853   There are numerous other examples of cases that have considered the appropriate reduction. In *Cavendish Funding Ltd v Henry Spencer & Sons Ltd* [1996] P.N.L.R. 554, the Court of Appeal held that the claimants' failure to review two valuations of the proposed security property received from different valuers at the same time in the light of their differences was negligent, and reduced the damages by 25%. In *UCB Bank Plc v David Pinder Plc* [1998] P.N.L.R. 398, the claimant lender was held one-third to blame, principally for failing properly to investigate the value of the borrower's covenants. In *Mortgage Corp Plc v Halifax (SW)* [1999] Lloyd's Rep. P.N. 159 at 178, the claimant lender was held 20% to blame, for failing to make proper enquiries as to the borrower's ability to service a very large loan and as to whether there were arrears on any existing or previous mortgages. In *Omega Trust & Co Ltd and Banque Finindus v Wright Son & Pepper (No.2)* [1998] P.N.L.R. 337, Douglas Brown J held that the failings of Omega were extensive and assessed the appropriate reduction at 70%. The instances of Omega's failure included ignoring the obvious inadequacies of the valuation reports; failing to act on their knowledge of the borrowers' adverse financial history; failing to appreciate that a clearing bank had declined the loan proposal; failing to give even ordinary scrutiny to the borrower's accounts; disregarding the contents of an Infolink search which revealed county court judgments against the director of the borrower and 46 recent credit searches against the borrower; most seriously in failing to challenge the director of the borrower who had certified to Omega that there was no litigation outstanding or threatened against himself or the borrower when in fact, as Omega knew from the Infolink search, there were already three judgments in existence with two more pending; failing to verify the freehold property allegedly owned by the director of the borrower; and failing to obtain banking references. In *First National Commercial Bank Plc v Andrew S Taylor Commercial Ltd* [1997] P.N.L.R. 37, the surveyor was held not negligent, but if negligence had been found, then the trial judge would have found contributory negligence by the claimant lender of 75% in failing to make adequate enquiries of the borrower and the guarantor. In *Speshal Investments Ltd v Corby Kane Howard Partnership* [2003] EWHC 390, the defendant valuers made grossly negligent valuations which, as the lender knew, although the valuer did not, exceeded the amount of the purchase price of the properties concerned and were also called into question by other valuations (of which both the valuer and the lender were aware). Hart J found that the lenders should have either withdrawn from the transaction or made further inquiries. He assessed the appropriate reduction for contributory negligence as 20% stating:

"A higher reduction would in my view be unjust. A valuer who gives negligent valuations as egregiously wrong as these cannot lightly be excused any part of his prima facie liability to pay for the full consequences of his negligence. A lesser reduction would risk appearing to be a recognition of an almost token nature only of some minor carelessness on the claimant's part."

In *Barclays Bank Plc v Christie Owen & Davies Ltd* [2016] EWHC 2351 (Ch); [2017] P.N.L.R. 8, a failure on the part of the claimant lender to take proper account of dishonesty on the part of the borrower in respect of a prior loan led to a reduction for contributory negligence as against a negligent valuer on a later loan of 40%. In *Bank of Ireland v Watts Group Plc* [2017] EWHC 1667 (TCC), Coulson J held (obiter, because the defendant was not liable in any event) that the bank was the author of its own misfortune by reason of a catalogue of errors that had been made during the course of making the decision to lend; but had he had to decide an apportionment, he would have attributed 75% to the claimant, albeit that that was "about the maximum that can be deducted in circumstances such as this": see [180]. In *Lloyds Bank Plc v McBains Cooper Consulting Ltd (No.2)* [2018] EWCA Civ 452; [2018] P.N.L.R. 23, the Court of Appeal increased the level of contributory negligence from one-third to two-thirds on the basis of a failure to adhere to elementary banking principles which gave rise to a formidable catalogue of responsibility on the part of the lender.

6. LIMITATION

Replace footnote 867 with:

[867] In most cases where the claimant has purchased an asset for a price that exceeded what it was worth **10-251** as a result of reliance upon a negligent survey, this will be the point at which the claimant became contractually committed to the transaction: see *Byrne v Hall Pain & Foster* [1999] P.N.L.R. 565. But in lender cases, the cause of action will not generally accrue until the value of the security together with the value of the borrower's covenant is less than the amount owed by the borrower: see para.5-061, above. The claimant may bear an evidential burden to show that the value of the borrower's covenant was sufficient to prevent loss being suffered more than six years prior to the issue of the claim form, see *Bridging Loans Ltd v Toombs* [2017] EWCA Civ 205. Note also *Kitney v Jones Lang Wootton* [1988] 1 E.G.L.R. 145, where the cause of action in respect of organising repair works necessary in order to fulfil a covenant for repair accrued when the stipulated period for the works to be done expired rather than when the court subsequently held that the works had not been carried out.

CHAPTER 11

SOLICITORS

Table of Contents

1.   GENERAL

(a)   Duties to Client

(i)   Contractual Duties

Formation of the retainer

Replace footnote 15 with:

11-004   [15] See *Bristol & West Building Society v Fancy & Jackson (A Firm)* [1997] 4 All E.R. 582 at 604j–605b per Chadwick J. In *Aroca Seiquer & Asociados v Roger Adams* [2018] EWCA Civ 1589; [2018] P.N.L.R. 32, UK purchasers of Spanish holiday homes instructed Spanish solicitors. The solicitors wrote letters to them headed "Dear client", which was an offer to act for them, and that offer was accepted by agents making appointments for the purchasers to see the solicitors.

The need for writing

Replace footnote 32 with:

11-006   [32] [1997] 1 Lloyd's Rep. 525. Applying those observations in *Dymocks Franchise Systems (China) Ltd* *v Norton Rose Fulbright Hong Kong* [2019] HKCFI 1602; [2019] 3 HKLRD 742, the defendant solicitor failed to prove that their retainer to assist and advise in relation to the potential termination of a franchise was limited to a property law question, and thus extended to giving advice about the effect of the Transfer of Business (Protection of Creditors) Ordinance. cf. *Silver v Morris* (1995) 139 N.S.R. (2d) 18, Nova Scotia CA, the defendant solicitor was retained by an experienced businesswoman in the sale of a business, in which he would be expected to give advice on tax implications. As he had orally made it clear to the claimant that he knew nothing about tax, it was held that the solicitor was not retained to give tax advice.

(iii)   Fiduciary Duties

(1)   Undue influence

To the end of the paragraph after "suggest the contrary.", add:

Solicitors acting for patients or minors often advise that the proceeds of personal **11-016** injury litigation are paid into a personal injury trust, where the trustees are connected with the solicitors. In *AKB v Willerton*[91A] Norris J held that this gave rise to a rebuttable evidential presumption of undue influence, which would typically be rebutted by evidence showing that the settlor had had independent advice. Where the settlement was £1m or more, a separate partner in the firm should, at the firm's expense, instruct chancery counsel to advise the claimant or his litigation friend in writing.

[91A] [2016] EWHC 3146 (QB); [2017] 4 W.L.R. 25.

Canadian and other commonwealth cases

Replace footnote 130 with:

[130] *Davey v Woolley, Hames, Dale Dingwall* (1982) 133 D.L.R. (3d) 647 Ontario CA, distinguished in **11-025** *Simmons v Hamber* 2011 ONCA 7; (2011) 329 D.L.R. 716 where there was in fact no conflict of interest. In *Salomon v Matte-Thompson* 2019 SCC 14; (2019) 432 D.L.R. 1 a solicitor wrongly encouraged a client to invest in offshore hedge funds. While his close friendship with the head of the investment corporation was disclosed, his blind confidence caused him to neglect his duty to undertake due diligence into the proposed investments.

No confidential information

Replace footnote 149 with:

[149] [2000] Lloyd's Rep. P.N. 452. Contrast the following cases. In *Davies v Davies* [1999] 3 F.C.R. 745 **11-028** CA, a solicitor was disqualified from acting for the husband in divorce proceedings where the solicitor had been consulted by the wife six years earlier about problems in the marriage. The facts and conclusions were similar in *Re Z (Restraining Solicitors from Acting)* [2009] EWHC 3621 (Fam); [2010] 2 F.L.R. 132, where the solicitor had been consulted by the husband for an extensive time some seven years before. In *Ball v Druces & Attlee (A Firm)* [2002] P.N.L.R. 23, the defendant solicitors acted for the Eden Trust in litigation brought by the claimant. He alleged that the solicitors had acted for him in setting up the Eden project, and that there was a risk that they would give their clients confidential information to his prejudice. Burton J held that there was an arguable case that the claimant's retainer of the solicitors had existed and that confidential information imparted to the solicitors might remain in their hands. He therefore granted an interlocutory injunction, as he was not satisfied that there was no risk of disclosure, on the basis of a cross-undertaking and guarantee in relation to the solicitors' potential lost profits and the Eden Trust's potential expense of instructing new solicitors. cf. *Re Recover Ltd (In Liquidation)* [2003] EWHC 536 (Ch); [2003] 2 B.C.L.C. 186, where Pumfrey J required the alleged confidential information to be properly particularised, which it was not, and thus no injunction was granted. In *E-Clear (UK) Plc v Elia* [2012] EWHC 1195 (Ch); [2012] B.P.I.R. 732 the third defendant claimed that the claimant had acted for her son in previous litigation and had confidential information, but the judge held that the solicitors never had acted for him. In *Maxwell-Smith v S & E Hall Pty Ltd* [2014] NSWCA 146; (2014) N.S.W.L.R. 481 there was no relevant confidential information, and thus no action lay against the solicitors. In *Western Avenue Properties Ltd v Soni* [2017] EWHC 2650 (QB); [2018] P.N.L.R. 10 a solicitor acting for tenants defending a claim by their landlords had previously worked in-house for the claimant landlords for eleven months, and was injuncted from acting for the tenants. It was neither possible nor necessary to identify each and every item of confidential information, and a

waiver by the tenant of any right to be told of confidential information did not assist the defendant, in particular because confidential information may be used subconsciously.

Adequate barriers

Replace footnote 152 with:

11-029   152 See also *Halewood International Ltd v Addleshaw Booth & Co* [2000] P.N.L.R. 788. Neuberger J held that the solicitor who had acted for the claimant in litigation and moved firms had probably obtained confidential information that might be relevant to other proceedings where the defendant firm acted for a client. The judge held that the defendant solicitors then had a heavy evidential burden to show that there was no real risk of disclosure. They had set up an information barrier, and as the size of their intellectual property department in Leeds was relatively small and only one solicitor had confidential information, such a system would be easier to police than in the *Bolkiah* case. However, the judge thought that there was still a small risk of disclosure of confidential information as the solicitor worked in the same building as the team involved in the new litigation. The defendant solicitors were prepared to undertake that the solicitor would work in a different building, and on that basis the judge did not grant the injunction. In *Glencairn IP Holdings Ltd v Product Specialities Inc* [2020] EWCA Civ 609; [2020] P.N.L.R. 25 solicitors for the new defendant had acted for another defendant whom the claimant had previously sued for infringement of the same registered design, where the claim had settled at mediation. The claimant alleged that the solicitors had confidential information concerning the mediation including its negotiating position and the terms on which it was prepared to settle. The Court did not grant an injunction to prevent the solicitors from continuing to act for the defendant. There was an information barrier in place and although the firm was a small one (which increased the risk of breach) the court concluded that the risk of disclosure was small. Higher safeguards would be required where the solicitors had acted for the claimant and would owe a continuing fiduciary duty to their former client. The Court of Appeal upheld the decision.

Commonwealth cases

Replace paragraph 11-031 (to incorporate amendment to footnote 160 and new text at the end of the paragraph following "similar to England.") with:

11-031   The position in the Commonwealth varies. In *MacDonald v Martin*[155] the Supreme Court of Canada adopted a twofold approach. First, could the solicitor rebut the inference that he had received confidential information, without revealing any such information?[156] Secondly, was there a risk of using that information to prejudice the client? The court left open the possibility of professional bodies adopting effective screening rules, which subsequently happened. In Australia, the test is whether there is a real and sensible possibility of a breach of confidence,[157] and *Bolkiah* has been followed and applied.[158] In New Zealand, the test used for granting injunctions to restrain breaches of confidence is similar to that found in *Bolkiah*, but in addition a balancing exercise is undertaken.[159] An injunction was granted by the New Zealand Court of Appeal in favour of a party which had not been a client of the solicitors in *Carter Holt Harvey Forests Ltd v Sunnex Logging Ltd*.[160] The solicitors acted for Sunnex in proceedings against Carter Holt. An injunction was granted as they had acted in a very similar claim by Rua against Carter Holt. The earlier litigation had ended in a mediation in which the lawyers had participated, and where they had signed a comprehensive confidentiality agreement on which Carter Holt were entitled to rely. The law in Hong Kong is similar to England.[161] In *Ecclesiastical Insurance Office Plc v Whitehouse-Grant-Christ*[161A] a majority of the Inner House of Sessions followed English law, and the solicitors in question did not have any confidential information.

155 [1990] 3 S.C.R. 1235, which has been applied in many subsequent cases, for which see the Canadian Abridgement and the index to the *Dominion Law Reports*. For a recent application, see *Wallace v Canadian Pacific Railway* 2011 SKCA 108; (2012) 340 D.L.R. (4th) 402.

156 cf. the approach in Australia in *Carindale Country Club Estate Pty Ltd v Astill* (1993) 115 A.L.R. 112, where the complainant has to identify the confidential information. But in *Unioil International Pty Ltd v Deloitte Touche Tohmatsu* [1997] 17 W.A.R. 98 the High Court followed the *McDonald v Martin*

approach. For a helpful explanation of some aspects of the law, see C. Edmonds, "Trusting lawyers with confidences" (1997–98) 17 *Australian Bar Review* 222.

[157] *National Mutual v Sentry* (1989) A.L.R. 539 and *Murray v MacQuarie Bank Ltd* (1992) 105 A.L.R. 612, both Federal Court of Australia. However, in *Spincode Pty Ltd v Look Software Pty Ltd* [2001] VSCA 248; (2001) 4 V.R. 501, the Victoria Court of Appeal rejected the English law that an injunction could only be granted where there was a risk of disclosure of confidential information, and considered that an order could also be made on the basis of breach of a duty of loyalty or a solicitor's conduct being offensive to fairness and justice. No such injunction was granted in relation to a previous retainer as there was no continuing duty of loyalty in *Dealer Support Services Pty Ltd v Trades Assoc of Australia Ltd* [2014] FCA 1065; (2015) 318 A.L.R. 507.

[158] *Newman v Phillips Fox* (1999) 21 W.A.R. 309 Sup Court.

[159] *Russell McVeagh McKenzie Bartleet & Co v Tower Corp* [1998] 3 N.Z.L.R. 641 NZCA.

[160] [2001] 3 N.Z.L.R. 343. In *Glencairn IP Holdings Ltd v Product Specialities Inc* [2020] EWCA Civ 609; [2020] P.N.L.R 25 at [77] the Court of Appeal held that *Carter Holt* did not represent English law in applying the *Bolkiah* burden of proof, see fn.152 above.

[161] *Wright v Hampton Winter & Glynn* [2008] 2 H.K.L.R.D. 341 High Court (plaintiff failed to establish that the defendants had information which was confidential to him).

[161A] [2017] CSIH 33; 2017 S.L.T. 697.

(iv)   Trust Duties

Trusts and lender claims

Replace paragraph 11-036 (to incorporate an amendment to footnote 179 and new text following "Edmunds & Co (A Firm)." at the end of the paragraph) with:

A number of recent cases have considered breach of trust in the context of lenders' claims. In the leading case of *Lloyds TSB Bank Plc v Markandan & Uddin (A Firm)*,[179] solicitors paid away monies without receiving the documents required to register title, but did receive an undertaking by the vendor's purported solicitor to provide such documents. The purported solicitor was in fact a fraudster, and the money was lost. The transaction was on the standard CML terms, which required by cl.10.3.4 that the loan should be held on trust until completion. The Court of Appeal held that "completion" did not mean registration of title, but it did require that the defendant should have received the completed transfer and other documents necessary to obtain and register title, or the vendor's solicitors' undertaking to provide them. As there were no documents provided, and no solicitors' undertaking, the defendants were in breach of trust. The Court stated, obiter, that the release of mortgage funds in exchange for forged documents would be in breach of trust, but innocent solicitors were adequately protected by s.61 of the Trustee Act 1925, which gives a Court a discretion to excuse a trustee who acted reasonably. It would appear that the documents necessary to complete transfer which the solicitor should obtain may not include a Stamp Duty Land Tax certificate, see *D B UK Bank Ltd v Edmunds & Co (A Firm)*.[180] In both *P&P Property Ltd v Owen White & Catlin LLP* and *Dreamvar v Mishcon de Reya*[180A] the Court of Appeal concluded that the vendor's solicitors could only release the monies when there was a genuine completion, and there was no such completion when the vendor was a fraudster who did not own the property.

11-036

[179] [2012] EWCA Civ 65; [2012] 2 All E.R. 884. For a helpful commentary on this case see J. Hall, "Breach of trust by conveyancing solicitors—the strongest of all lender claims?" (2012) 28 P.N. 109. In *Broker House Insurance Services Ltd v OJS Law* [2010] EWHC 3816 (Ch); [2011] P.N.L.R. 23, solicitors acted for an intended second charge holder, and their instructions were not on the terms of the CML Handbook. They paid away monies without obtaining the first chargeholders' permission to a second charge, but, applying *Bristol & West Building Society v Mothew* [1997] 1 Ch. 1, the language of the relevant special condition was not clear enough to make the breach a payment away made without authority.

180   [2014] P.N.L.R. 12 Ch. D.

180A [2018] EWCA Civ 1082; [2018] P.N.L.R. 29.

Replace paragraph 11-037 (to incorporate amended text and new text following "are relevant considerations)." at the end of the paragraph) with:

11-037   Subsequent cases have considered the circumstances in which relief should be given pursuant to s.61 of the Trustee Act 1925, whereby the Court may excuse the breach of trust if the trustee has acted honestly and reasonably and ought fairly to be excused.[181] There are two important issues to consider. First, the relevant standard of conduct, which has been expressed in slightly different ways in three cases. In *Lloyds TSB Bank Plc v Markandan & Uddin (A Firm)*,[182] this appeared to be equated with "exemplary professional care and efficiency" and being "careful, conscientious and thorough". In contrast, in *Nationwide Building Society v Davisons Solicitors*,[183] it was held that the standard applied to a solicitor did not "predicate that he has necessarily complied with best practice in all respects." In *Santander UK Plc v RA Legal Solicitors (A Firm)*,[184] the Chancellor held that "s.61 must be interpreted consistently with equity's high expectation of a trustee discharging fiduciary obligations" but pointed out that the test was not "perfection".[185] The second issue is whether the trustee ought fairly to be excused. This usually entails considering whether there is a causal connection between the solicitors' conduct and the loss.[186] In *Santander UK Plc v RA Legal Solicitors (A Firm)*,[187] the Court of Appeal held that the test is whether the solicitors' impugned conduct was *connected* with the loss by increasing the risk of loss, rather than *causative* of the loss in the sense that but for it the loss would not have happened. In that case, the fraud would have succeeded even if the solicitors had acted reasonably, but the court did not grant relief pursuant to s.61. The Court of Appeal held that it is for a trustee to satisfy the court that none of his or her conduct has played any material part in the occasioning of the loss. If a trustee cannot satisfy the court that his or her conduct did not materially contribute to the opportunity for loss, or the risk of loss, he or she cannot rely on s.61. In *Purrunsing v A'Court & Co (A Firm)*,[188] the judge made clear, following *Santander UK Plc v RA Legal Solicitors*, that: (i) the relevant conduct had to be taken as a whole and in the round rather than considering each complaint separately; and (ii) in the exercise of the discretion took account of the effect of granting relief on both parties, so that the financial strength of the loser and the availability of insurance were relevant considerations. In *P&P Property Ltd v Owen White & Catlin LLP* and *Dreamvar v Mishcon de Reya*[188A] the purchaser's solicitors conceded that they were in breach of trust in releasing the purchase money to the solicitors of a fraudster who did not own the property. While they acted honestly and reasonably, a majority of the Court of Appeal did not grant relief under s.61. Professional trustees should be treated strictly, the purchaser was a small company without insurance, and any distribution of liability should be by contribution proceedings with the vendor's solicitors.

181   See further P. Davies: "Section 61 of the Trustee Act 1925: Deus Ex Machina?" (2015) 79 Conv 379.

182   [2012] EWCA Civ 65; [2012] 2 All E.R. 884 at [60]–[61].

183   [2012] EWCA Civ 1626; [2013] P.N.L.R. 12 at [48]. In that case the defendants paid away trust money to fraudsters on an undertaking which they believed was from solicitors, and were in breach of trust. However, relief was granted under s.61 as the defendants had checked the existence and office of the solicitors with the Law Society and the SRA.

184   [2014] EWCA Civ 183; [2014] P.N.L.R. 20, The defendant solicitors were in breach of trust in releasing monies against a forged transfer provided by solicitors acting for the purported vendor. They were not relieved of liability pursuant to s.61, as they had failed to follow up unclear Replies to Requisitions. See further on this case S. Charlwood, "Conveyancing solicitors' liability for breach of trust" (2014) 30

P.N. 102. It must be doubted that the earlier case of *Ikbal v Sterling Law* [2013] EWHC 3291 (Ch); [2014] P.N.L.R. 9 was correctly decided.

[185] ibid. at [111]. cf. Briggs LJ at [21] and [30], who followed *Davisons* in identifying the test as reasonableness not perfection. Proudman J agreed with both judgments. See also *Agouman v Leigh Day (A Firm)* [2016] EWHC 1324 (QB); [2016] P.N.L.R. 32 at [135].

[186] The court may also have to consider conduct again, e.g. if there is a dispute over what conduct is relevant to the loss.

[187] [2014] EWCA Civ 183; [2014] P.N.L.R. 20 at [24]–[25] and [110].

[188] [2016] EWHC 789 (Ch); [2016] P.N.L.R. 26 at [38]. In this case neither the registered conveyancer who acted for the purchaser, nor the solicitors who acted for the fraudster purporting to be the vendor, were excused, and between them they bore equal liability for the loss.

[188A] [2018] EWCA Civ 1082; [2018] P.N.L.R. 29.

Dishonest assistance

Replace footnote 198 with:

[198] [1995] 2 A.C. 378, a case which did not involve a claim against solicitors. *Tan* was applied in an **11-041** orthodox manner in a claim against a solicitor in *Eden Refuge Trust v Hohepa* [2011] 1 N.Z.L.R. 197, upheld by the New Zealand Court of Appeal sub. nom. *Fletcher v Eden Refuge Trust* [2012] NZCA 124; [2012] 2 N.Z.L.R. 227, which made clear that following client's instructions was not a defence to dishonest assistance. That case and *Sandman v McKay* [2019] NZSC 41; [2019] 1 N.Z.L.R. 519 applied *Barlow Clowes International Ltd v Eurotrust Ltd* [2006] 1 W.L.R. 1476. A claim for dishonest assistance succeeded in *Frank Houlgate Investment v Biggart Baillie* [2014] CSIH 79; [2015] P.N.L.R. 3, as the solicitor made a continuing implied representation that he knew nothing suggesting his client was dishonest in relation to the relevant security, when he did, and he was therefore objectively dishonest. Two of the judges also considered that there was a duty of honesty on a solicitor which founded an implied representation that he did not know that the information provided by his client was untrue.

Further cases

Replace footnote 204 with:

[204] [2016] EWCA Civ 73; [2016] P.N.L.R. 18. In *Group Seven Ltd v Nasir* [2017] EWHC 2466 (Ch); **11-042** [2018] P.N.L.R. 69 Morgan J held that a claim for dishonest assistance failed against a solicitor when he did not know that a company was not able to deal with funds which were paid away as its own, and had not deliberately refrained from asking questions about it. Although the court found that the solicitor had dishonestly handled in the monies in breach of the Solicitors' Accounts Rules, he had not dishonestly assisted in a breach of trust. The solicitor was however found liable for unconscionable receipt.

(b)   Duties to Third Parties

(i)   General

The general law

Replace paragraph 11-043 (to incorporate new text following "between the parties" at the end of the paragraph) with:

The starting point is *Hedley Byrne Co Ltd v Heller Partners Ltd*, which **11-043** established liability for negligent misstatements relied upon by claimants.[207] Since then, there has been considerable uncertainty about the test to be applied for determining whether a duty of care is owed to third parties. One approach has been the "tripartite test" developed in *Smith v Bush*,[208]*Caparo v Dickman*,[209]*Spring v Guardian Assurance Plc*[210] and *Marc Rich Co v Bishop Rock Marine Co Ltd*[211] of foreseeability, proximity, and whether it is just and reasonable to impose a duty of care. Side by side with this general test, as a result of *Murphy v Brentwood DC*,[212] the courts have adopted an incremental approach from decided cases. Following this approach, *Hedley Byrne* has been interpreted as imposing liability when there has been a voluntary assumption of responsibility, and this was applied by all of the House of Lords in *Henderson v Merrett Syndicates Ltd*,[213] a minority in *Spring v Guardian Assurance Plc*,[214] a majority in the solicitor's negligence case of *White v Jones*,[215] and all their Lordships in *Williams v Natural Life Ltd*.[216] Assumption of responsibility was also regarded as the crucial feature in *Caliendo v Mishcon de Reya*[217] where the court found that solicitors retained to act for a football club also assumed responsibility to act for the directors of the club in their capacity as directors in certain limited regards. In *Customs and Excise Commissioners v Barclays Bank Plc*,[218] the House of Lords held that the various tests disclose no single common denominator, and the court should focus on the detailed circumstances of the case and the relationship between the parties. In the Scottish solicitors' case of *NRAM Plc v Steel*[218A] the Supreme Court held that the assumption of responsibility was the foundation of liability for negligent misstatement leading to economic loss, based on the reasonableness and foreseeability of reliance. It rejected the tripartite test.

[207] [1964] A.C. 465.

[208] [1990] 1 A.C. 831 at 865A per Lord Griffiths.

[209] [1990] 2 A.C. 605 at 617H–618B per Lord Bridge and 633B–633C per Lord Oliver.

[210] [1995] 2 A.C. 296 per Lords Keith, Slynn and Woolf.

[211] [1996] A.C. 211.

[212] [1991] 1 A.C. 398.

[213] [1995] 2 A.C. 145.

[214] [1995] 2 A.C. 296 (Lords Goff and Lowry).

[215] [1995] 2 A.C. 207. This case is discussed below at para.11-052.

[216] [1998] 1 W.L.R. 830.

[217] [2016] EWHC 150 (Ch), see [713] of the judgment.

[218] [2006] UKHL 28; [2007] 1 A.C. 181.

[218A] [2018] UKSC 13; [2018] 1 W.L.R. 1190. See E. Gordon: "Out with the old, in with the older? Hedley Byrne reliance takes centre stage." [2018] C.L.J. 251.

No duty

Replace footnote 242 with:

11-049   [242] [2012] EWHC 1471 (Admin); [2012] P.N.L.R. 27. Similarly, in *First Asia Finance International Ltd v Tso Au Yim & Yeung* [2017] 5 H.K.L.R.D. 746 no duty of care was owed to the plaintiff in relation to a settlement agreement drafted by solicitors for the other contracting party, not least because there was a conflict of interest. Nor was any duty owed in *Joseph v Farrer & Co LLP* [2017] EWHC 2072 (Ch); [2018] P.N.L.R. 1 by solicitors acting for the beneficiary of a trust who had executed a letter of wishes that the trustees fund payments to his intimate companion, the claimant, in part because their interests may diverge.

(iii)   Duty of Care to the Other Side

General considerations

After paragraph 11-060, add new paragraph 11-060A:

11-060A   In the Scottish solicitors' case of *NRAM PLC v Steel*[295A] a solicitor acting for a borrower who was partly redeeming a loan emailed the lender wrongly stating that the whole loan was being repaid, and requested the execution of draft deeds of discharge of the security. The lender relied on the email. The Supreme Court held that the assumption of responsibility was the foundation of liability for negligent misstatement leading to economic loss, based on the reasonableness and foreseeability of reliance. It was neither reasonable for the lender to rely on the representation, nor foreseeable that it would do so. The misrepresented fact was wholly within the knowledge of the lender.

[295A] [2018] UKSC 13; [2018] 1 W.L.R. 1190.

Judicial comments on *Gran Gelato*

Replace paragraph 11-062 (to incorporate replacement text at the end of the paragraph) with:

The decision in *Gran Gelato* was referred to with approval by Lord Goff in *White v Jones*.[298] However, the Court of Appeal in *McCullagh v Lane Fox Partners Ltd*[299] considered that the reasoning in *Gran Gelato* was inconsistent with *Punjab National Bank v De Boinville*,[300] unless it was confined to a special rule applicable to solicitors in conveyancing transactions, and the court was not wholly confident in identifying why such cases should differ. In *First National Bank Plc v Loxleys*,[301] the Court of Appeal refused to strike out a similar action against solicitors who negligently replied to standard enquires before contract, and despite the existence of a disclaimer. However, in *Dean v Allin & Watts (A Firm)*,[302] the Court of Appeal appeared to approve of *Gran Gelato*. In the Scottish solicitors' case of *NRAM Plc v Steel*[303] the Supreme Court appeared to approve of *Gran Gelato*. In *P&P Property Ltd v Owen White & Catlin LLP* and *Dreamvar v Mishcon de Reya*[303A] the Court of Appeal held that *Gran Gelato* was good authority for the general rule that a solicitor for a vendor owes no duty to the buyer.

11-062

[298] [1995] 2 A.C. 207 at 256D. In *Trend Publishing (HK) Ltd v Vivien Chan & Co (A Firm)* [1996] 2 H.K.L.R.D. 227, the High Court of Hong Kong followed *Gran Gelato* in deciding that the landlord's solicitor owed no duty of care to the tenant in drafting the tenancy agreement. In *Primosso Holdings Ltd v Alpers* [2006] 2 N.Z.L.R. 455, the New Zealand Court of Appeal held that a solicitor owed no duty to the other party to a transaction to check that his client was not using the solicitor to deceive the other party.

[299] [1996] 1 P.N.L.R. 205 at 226-234.

[300] [1992] 1 Lloyd's Rep. 7 CA.

[301] [1997] P.N.L.R. 211.

[302] [2001] Lloyd's Rep. P.N. 605.

[303] [2018] UKSC 13; [2018] 1 W.L.R. 1190 at [29]. See also the discussion in *P&P Property Ltd v Owen White & Catlin LLP* [2018] EWCA Civ 1082; [2018] P.N.L.R. 29 at [70]. There, solicitors acting for a fraudster who did not own the property were held not to owe a duty of care to the purchasers to check the identity of its customer.

[303A] [2018] EWCA Civ 1082; [2018] P.N.L.R. 29.

Exceptions to the general rule: reliance on solicitor's representations

Replace paragraph 11-063 (to incorporate replacement text at the start of the paragraph and an amendment to footnote 304) with:

One example of the reasonableness and foreseeability of reliance, establishing a voluntary assumption of responsibility, will be where the solicitor gives a formal report or certificate on which he intends the representee to rely. This is illustrated by the New Zealand case of *Allied Finance and Investment Ltd v Haddow & Co*.[304] The plaintiffs lent $25,000 to one Hill on the security of a yacht, which they understood that he was buying. In fact, the yacht was bought by E. Ltd, a company owned and controlled by Hill. Before the transaction was entered into, Hill's solicitors, who were the defendants, sent a letter to the plaintiffs' solicitors stating: "we

11-063

... certify that the Instrument by way of Security is fully binding on Roger Kenneth Hill ... We certify, on behalf of our client, that there are no other charges whatsoever on the yacht ..." This letter failed to disclose that Hill was not buying the yacht himself. The Court of Appeal held that the defendant solicitors owed a duty of care to the plaintiffs in respect of the letter and that the letter was misleading and negligent. Cooke J stated:

> "I agree ... that the relationship between two solicitors acting for their respective clients does not normally of itself impose a duty of care on one solicitor to the client of the other ... But surely the result of established principles is different when on request a solicitor gives a certificate on which the other party must naturally be expected to act. That is a classic duty of care situation ..."[305]

[304] [1983] N.Z.L.R. 22, cited with approval in *NRAM Plc v Steel* [2018] UKSC 13; [2018] 1 W.L.R. 1190 at [26].

[305] ibid. at 24. Richardson J (at 30-31) and McMullin J (at 35-36) came to the same conclusion by applying the two-stage test formulated by Lord Wilberforce in *Anns v Merton LBC* [1978] A.C. 729. See also *Connell v Odlum* [1993] 2 N.Z.L.R. 257. Under s.21 of the New Zealand Matrimonial Property Act 1978, people who had married or intended to marry could contract out of the provisions of the Act. This required a certificate signed by a solicitor, stating that he had explained the implications of the deed and given her independent legal advice. The defendant solicitor had signed such a certificate for Mrs Odlum. Six years later, Mrs Odlum succeeded in setting the deed aside on the basis that it had not been properly explained to her. The New Zealand Court of Appeal concluded that there was no conflict of interest between the duties owed by the solicitor to Mr and Mrs Odlum, and that Mr Connell owed a duty of care to Mr Odlum by signing such a certificate. The Court therefore refused to strike out Mr Odlum's action against the solicitor.

Replace footnote 307 with:

11-064   [307] ibid. at 616. The decision was cited with approval in *NRAM PLC v Steel.* [2018] UKSC 13; [2018] 1 W.L.R. 1190 at [27] and [33], approving the fourth factor.

Other exceptions to the general rule

Replace paragraph 11-065 (to incorporate deletion of some text and an amendment to footnote 312) with:

11-065   In *Searles v Cann and Hallett (A Firm)*,[309] a duty of care was owed applying a different test. The solicitor acted for a businessman who borrowed money from the plaintiffs on the security of their property, and he prepared a deed of assignment of insurance policies in favour of the plaintiffs, which referred to a nonexistent legal charge. Applying *White v Jones*,[310] the borrower would not suffer any loss from the solicitor's negligence, but the unrepresented plaintiffs would do so. The duty of care was only to carry out the terms of the agreement between the parties, and there was thus no conflict between the duties owed by the solicitor to the plaintiffs and to his client. While there was negligence in preparing a composite charge over the property, there was no loss as it was effectively worthless. Similarly, a duty of care was held to be owed in *Dean v Allin & Watts (A Firm)*.[311] The solicitor acting for the borrower gave an undertaking to hold the deeds of a flat which belonged to an associate of the borrower to the claimant's order. The form of security, which was ineffective, had not been agreed before the solicitor had been instructed. There was therefore a potential conflict between the duties of the solicitor to his client and to the claimant. The Court of Appeal held[312] that where there was such a conflict the court should be slow to find that the solicitor had assumed a duty of care, which would ordinarily be an improbable assumption. However, a duty was owed in that case where the retainer was to take the necessary steps to provide effective security which was a necessary part of the transaction, the unsophisticated lender was known not to be instructing solicitors and would rely on the solicitors, there was no disclaimer of a duty, there was in fact an identity of interest in providing effective security, and in default only the lender would suffer loss. Contrast *BDG Roof-Bond Ltd v Douglas*[313-314] where no duty of care was held to be owed. The defendants were solicitors for a client who sold his 50% shareholding in the claimant company to that company. The transaction was invalid, and after the company went into liquidation the liquidator sought to recover the £135,000 paid to the client from his solicitors. It was held that the solicitors were not retained by the company, and that they owed it no duty of care. Park J observed that the general trend was a reluctance to find that a professional adviser owed a common law duty to someone who was not his own client. There was not a sufficiently proximate relationship between the parties, and it was not just and fair to impose a duty of care, as the company was on the opposite side of the transaction. Nor did the solicitors voluntarily assume responsibility to the company.

[309] [1999] P.N.L.R. 494 QBD.

[310] [1995] 2 A.C. 207.

[311] [2001] Lloyd's Rep. P.N. 605. In *Chief Land Registrar v Caffrey & Co* [2016] EWHC 161 (Ch); [2016] P.N.L.R. 23, Master Matthews held that solicitors acting for a dishonest client owed no duty to a bank in relation to a forged DS1 discharging its charge, but did owe a duty to the Land Registry when it made negligently false representations to it.

[312] Applying the tripartite test, but also, in the case of Lightman J, on the basis of an assumption of responsibility. *NRAM Plc v Steel* [2018] UKSC 13; [2018] 1 W.L.R. 1190 at [31] and [32] approved of the decision, but on the basis of assumption of responsibility (which included foreseeability and reasonableness of reliance). The decision did not apply the tripartite test.

[313-314] [2000] P.N.L.R. 397.

Other commonwealth cases

Replace footnote 317 with:

[317] See *NRAM Plc v Steel* [2018] UKSC 13; [2018] 1 W.L.R. 1190 noted at 11-060A above. See also *Frank Houlgate Investment v Biggart Baillie* [2009] CSOH 165; [2010] P.N.L.R. 13. The same conclusion was reached on a rehearing, [2011] CSOH 160; [2012] P.N.L.R. 2. Note however that it was also held that a solicitor acting for a recipient of money in a transaction involving a charge makes a continuing implied representation to the solicitor for the transferor that he is not aware of any fundamental dishonesty or fraud that might make the security worthless. **11-066**

(iv) Solicitors' Liability on Undertakings

Replace heading footnote 332 with:

General[332]

[332] See J. Adam, "Solicitors' undertakings—an analysis of legal and professional conduct aspects" (1990) 6 P.N. 58; H. Evans, "The unpredictability of undertakings" (1996) 12 P.N. 90; H. Evans, *Lawyers' Liabilities*, 2nd edn (2002), Ch.6. Undertakings given to the court are of course different, and can give rise to applications for committal for contempt. For an example see *Discovery Land Co LLC v Jirehouse* [2019] EWHC 2249 (Ch); [2020] P.N.L.R. 1. **11-070**

Construction of the undertaking

Replace footnote 349 with:

[349] See *Reddy v Lachlan* [2000] Lloyd's Rep. P.N. 858 CA, which is authority for the propositions in the first two sentences of this paragraph. The principle that ambiguous undertakings are construed in favour of the recipient was applied in *Templeton Insurance Ltd v Penningtons Solicitors LLP* [2006] EWHC 685 (Ch); [2007] W.T.L.R. 1. Lewison J construed the context of an undertaking, where the purpose of the loan was stated to be completion of the purchase of particular property, as an express undertaking to apply monies for that sole or exclusive purpose. In *Thomas v Conor Agnew* [2017] NICh **11-073**

28; [2018] P.N.L.R. 18 an undertaking to "furnish a copy of the land registry letter of confirmation of completion of registration to you when received…. You will be aware that your client was formally released from her mortgage obligations…" was not reasonably understood as an undertaking to release the petitioner from her mortgage obligations, which had not taken place.

Replace second paragraph (to incorporate new text following "may be negligent." at the end of the paragraph) with:

The Divisional Court held that this was a personal undertaking, otherwise it would mean nothing as the client would be liable by the order of the magistrate in any event. However, even an undertaking by a client may impose an enforceable duty on his solicitors to act when their client is relying on them to implement it.[351] An undertaking need not use the word "undertaking", as is illustrated by *John Fox v Bannister King & Rigbeys*.[352] The plaintiff had acted as solicitors for Mr Watts, and was owed moneys by him. The defendants acted for Mr Watts in selling two properties, and in relation to some of the proceeds they informed the plaintiff: "… no doubt you and [Mr Watts] will sort out as to the £18,000 which is still in my account and which of course I shall retain until you have sorted everything out". The Court of Appeal held that this was an undertaking not to part with the £18,000. Furthermore, an undertaking may be oral rather than in writing,[353] although it is good practice for the recipient to confirm it in writing.[354] Solicitors' undertakings to lenders are generally not construed to impose absolute obligations.[355] An imprecisely drafted undertaking may be negligent.[356] In *P&P Property Ltd v Owen White & Catlin LLP* and *Dreamvar v Mishcon de Reya*[356A] the Court of Appeal construed an undertaking "to have the seller's authority to receive the purchase money on completion" to mean that the authority must be of the real vendor.

[351] As in *Refson Co v Saggers* [1984] 1 W.L.R. 1025, Nourse J, although no action was taken against the solicitors in that case.

[352] [1988] Q.B. 925. Note that the undertaking there was to the solicitors. It is often a matter of construction whether the undertaking was given to the solicitor on the other side or his client. For an illustration of the latter see *Kutilin v Auerbach* (1989) 34 B.C.L.R. (2d) 23; for the facts, see below.

[353] Nor need it be embodied in an order of the court even though it be given in the context of litigation, see *Williams v Williams and Partridge* (1910) 54 Sol. Jo. 506 CA.

[354] *Udall v Capri Lighting Ltd* [1988] Q.B. 907 at 919H-920A per Kerr LJ.

[355] See paras 11-009 and 11-010 above, and in particular *Barclays Bank Plc v Weeks Legg & Dean (A Firm)* [1999] Q.B. 309. In that case, Millet LJ observed that money, supplied pursuant to an undertaking to apply any sums received solely to acquire a good and marketable title, was held on trust to be applied only in accordance with the terms of the undertaking. In *Twinsectra v Yardley* [2000] Lloyd's Rep. P.N. 239 at 254 col.1, the Court of Appeal suggested that the observation should be applied more widely to money received by a solicitor from a third party to be held by him on express terms. An undertaking to apply the monies received in a particular way is likely to create a trust, see *Twinsectra v Yardley* [2002] UKHL 12; [2002] 2 A.C. 164 and para.11-035, above. For the meaning of an undertaking "to effect completion" see *1st Property Finance Ltd v Martin & Haigh (A Firm)* [2006] P.N.L.R. 29 Ch D.

[356] *Auckland Standard Committee v W* [2011] 3 N.Z.L.R. 117.

[356A] [2018] EWCA Civ 1082; [2018] P.N.L.R. 29.

Impossibility and compensation

Replace footnote 381 with:

11-077 [381] In the Irish case of *National Irish Bank v O'Ceallaigh* [2011] IEHC 216; [2012] 1 I.L.R.M 428, it was held that in order for the court to assess appropriate compensation, all relevant facts had to be disclosed in an affidavit. For a slightly different approach see *115 Place Co-op Housing Assn v Burke* (1994) 116 D.L.R. (4th) 657 British Columbia CA, where the plaintiff paid the defendant solicitors moneys owing to their client on an undertaking to deposit those moneys in their own name in a trust company. The trust company mistakenly paid out the moneys to the client. The plaintiff obtained judgment against the client, which later ceased to exist. The solicitors and the trust company were ordered to recreate the fund. They were not entitled to become involved in the assessment of damages against the client, but they could contest whether there were deficiencies in the contract covered by the undertaking. In *Allied Irish Bank Plc v Maguire & Co* [2016] IESC 57; [2017] P.N.L.R. 6, solicitors gave an undertaking to discharge a prior charge in 2007, but did not do so, and in 2009 the security property was sold, leaving nothing for the plaintiff lender. The Supreme Court of Ireland held that compensation should be assessed on the basis of the value of the property in 2007, and not the much lower value in 2009.

(v)   Other Liabilities

Breach of warranty of authority

Replace paragraph 11-081 with:

11-081   Liability for breach of warranty is strict, as it is based on a contractual analysis.[411] The claimant has to prove reliance rather than mere inducement.[412] The scope of the warranty given has been subject to contrasting decisions. In *P&P Property Ltd v Owen White & Catlin LLP*[413] solicitors acted for a fraudster who purported to be the vendor but did not own the property. A warranty of authority was given where the solicitors signed and exchanged contracts on behalf of a person named in the document as the seller. The opposite conclusion was reached on different facts in the combined appeal in *Dreamvar v Mishcon de Reya*. In *Penn v Bristol West Building Society*[414] a husband instructed a solicitor to carry out the sale of a house that was owned by him and his wife. She was ignorant of the transaction and did not instruct the defendant solicitor, although the solicitor mistakenly thought that he was acting for both husband and wife. The conveyance was in fact achieved by the forgery of the husband. As a result, the purchaser obtained no title to the property, and the building society which had loaned him money suffered loss. The Court of Appeal held that the solicitors were liable to the building society for breach of warranty of authority. In *Penn*, the solicitors did not act for the building society, which had its own lawyers. It was suggested by Chadwick J in *Bristol & West Building Society v Fancy Jackson (A Firm)*[415] that solicitors could also be liable for breach of warranty of authority if they acted for borrowers and lenders, but the Court of Appeal held in *Zwebner v The Mortgage Corp Ltd*[416] that the true position is that there is a duty to take any steps necessary to make up for the absence of such a warranty.[416A]

---

[411] *Younge v Toynbee* [1910] 1 K.B. 215 CA; *Babury Ltd v London Industrial Plc* (1989) 139 N.L.J. 1596, Steyn J. Thus solicitors were strictly liable when purportedly acting for a company in a boardroom dispute on the instruction of directors who had been invalidly appointed, see *Grand Field Group Holdings Ltd v Tsang Wai Lun Wayland (No.2)* [2010] 4 H.K.L.R.D. 487 High Court. For a criticism of the supposed contractual basis of the law see H. Evans, "Warranty of authority in litigation" (2010) 26 P.N. 96. As to the extent of a solicitor's authority, see para.11-155, below.

[412] *P&P Property Ltd v Owen White & Catlin LLP* [2018] EWCA Civ 1082; [2018] P.N.L.R. 29. See also *Donsland Ltd v Van Hoogstraten* [2002] EWCA Civ 253; [2002] P.N.L.R. 26 (where the Court of Appeal stated at [14] that it remained to be decided whether the representee had to prove that he had relied on the warranty or been induced to incur costs as a result of it); *Penn v Bristol & West Building Society* [1997] 1 W.L.R. 1356 at 1363A (where the Court of Appeal appeared to conclude that inducement was not required); *Excel Securities v Masood* [2010] Lloyd's Rep. P.N. 165 QBD (where it was suggested at [54] that reliance was required); *Zoya Ltd v Ahmed (t/a Property Mart) (No.2)* [2016] EWHC 2249 (Ch); [2016] 4 W.L.R. 174 (reliance required, see [39]).

[413] [2018] EWCA Civ 1082; [2018] P.N.L.R. 29. For commentaries see R. Kennedy: "Conveyancing fraudsters – who picks up the bill after P&P and Dreamvar?" (2018) 34 P.N. 205, and F. Reynolds: "Of warranty of authority and related topics" (2018) 134 L.Q.R. 511. In contrast, in *Excel Securities v Masood* [2010] Lloyd's Rep. P.N. 165 QBD solicitors were instructed by an imposter for a Mr Goulding, and confirmed to the lender's solicitors that they were instructed by Mr Goulding. It was held that the warranty was only that they had authority to act for a person identifying himself as Mr Goulding who claimed to be the owner of the relevant property. *Excel* was followed in *Stephenson v Singh* [2012] EWHC 2880 (QB). The judge relied on *SEB Trygg Liv AB v Manches* [2005] EWCA Civ 1237; [2006]

1 W.L.R. 276, on which see the next paragraph. To similar effect see *Frank Houlgate Investment v Big-gart Baillie* [2009] CSOH 165; [2010] P.N.L.R. 13, which held that the warranty is that the solicitor acts for his client, not that the client is the registered title holder, and similarly on a rehearing at [2011] CSOH 160; [2012] P.N.L.R. 2. The same result was reached in *Cheshire Mortgage Corp Ltd v Grandison* [2012] CSIH 66; [2013] P.N.L.R. 3, where the Inner House expressly followed *Excel*. The decision in *Excel* remains controversial.

414 [1997] 1 W.L.R. 1356.There was no one purporting to be the wife. In a similar case in Singapore, a solicitor purportedly acted for a company pursuant to a forged resolution in a sale of property, and was found liable to the prospective purchaser for breach of warranty of authority, see *Fong Maun Yee v Yoong Weng Ho Robert* [1997] 2 S.L.R. 297 CA.

415 [1997] 4 All E.R. 582 at 612F–613E.

416 [1998] P.N.L.R. 769.

416A [2002] EWCA Civ 253; [2002] P.N.L.R. 26.

Replace paragraph 11-082 (to incorporate amendments to footnotes 417, 419 and 420) with:

11-082   In litigation, a solicitor acting for a client warrants that he has a client who has authorised the proceedings,[417] but not that the client had the name by which he appeared in the proceedings, nor that the client was solvent or had a good cause of action.[418] In an appeal from a winding up order where solicitors had instructions from the former directors, there was no breach of warranty because the issue of authority was known to be controversial and the litigation was to provide an answer to it, and the other side were as well placed to know if the authority had come to an end as the solicitors.[419] There is a summary jurisdiction to award damages against a solicitor who commenced proceedings without authority, which requires that the solicitor has a reasonable opportunity to make representations. However, Colman J refused such an application in *Skylight Maritime SA v Ascot Underwriting Ltd*[420] because it was a complex case which was unsuitable for summary determination, and required a separate action instead. The judge also held that, as the damages were compensatory, the applicants could not be in a better position than if they had been successful against the apparent party, and there was an issue as to whether the latter had any assets against which an order for costs could have been enforced. In *Padhiar v Patel*,[421] the court reduced the amount of costs payable for breach of warranty of authority in the exercise of its summary jurisdiction where the defendants were in a position to know the status of the company.

417 On this the law is the same in Ireland, see *Jabaar Ltd v Townlink Construction Ltd* [2011] IEHC 111; [2011] 1 I.R. 767. To similar effect, although without the citation of authority, see *Ferreira v St Mary's General Hospital* 2018 ONCA 247; (2018) 422 D.L.R. (4th), where costs on an indemnity basis were awarded against a solicitor who instituted proceedings on behalf of a person with brain damage to prevent withdrawal of his life support when she had no authority to do so.

418 See *Nelson v Nelson* [1997] 1 W.L.R. 233 CA, and *SEB Trygg Liv AB v Manches* [2005] EWCA Civ 1237; [2006] 1 W.L.R. 276 CA. *SEB* decides that the obiter conclusion of McCowan LJ in *Nelson*, that the solicitor warrants that the client did bear the name of the party to the proceedings, was wrong. Quaere whether lack of due diligence must be shown if the solicitors' authority ceases during the proceedings, see *Wilson v Leek General Commissioners* [1994] S.T.C. 147, Knox J. In *Carpathian Resources Ltd v Hendricks* [2012] FCA 496; (2012) 290 A.L.R. 252, no personal costs order was made against solicitors acting for the company in a dispute as to who were the directors of a company, and where those purporting to act for the company were found at trial not to be directors, as it was impossible to predict the outcome of the trial.

419 *Aidiniantz v The Sherlock Holmes International Society Ltd* [2016] EWHC 1392 (Ch); [2016] P.N.L.R. 31. Reported sub. nom.*The Sherlock Holmes International Society Ltd*. It was followed in *Zoya Ltd v Ahmed (t/a Property Mart) (No 2)* [2016] EWHC 2249 (Ch); [2016] 4 W.L.R. 174, where there was no warranty of authority after the Master had directed the determination of a preliminary issue on the client's claim to be a director of the claimant. There was, however, a breach of warranty before that time, but the applicant had failed to show that it relied on the warranty. To similar effect as to whether a warranty had been given, see *Bronze Monkey LLC v Simmons & Simmons LLP* [2017] EWHC 3097 (Comm); [2018] P.N.L.R. 14.

[420] [2005] EWHC 15 (Comm); [2005] P.N.L.R. 25. Similarly, in *Attis v Ontario (Minister of Health)* 2011 ONCA 675; (2012) 343 D.L.R. (4th) 263, a claim for breach of warranty of authority failed because the apparent party had no assets, and thus the claim failed on causation, but in any event the failure to explain costs properly to the client did not invalidate the client's consent to proceedings. Where solicitors had acted in breach of warranty in purporting to act for a company, the court's jurisdiction to determine the company's claim against the solicitors in negligence could also be exercised summarily provided that it was clear that a liability in damages existed and would extend to the sums claimed, see *Griffith v Gourgey* [2018] EWHC 1484 (Ch); [2018] 3 Costs L.R. 605.

[421] [2001] Lloyd's Rep. P.N. 328 QBD.

(c)   The Standard of Skill and Care

(vi)   General Observations

Illegality

Replace paragraph 11-112 (to incorporate new text following "parties' respective culpability)." at the end of the paragraph) with:

In *Sweetman v Nathan*,[512] it was held to be no defence to a claim in negligence that the solicitor and client were both engaged on a fraud, as the action could be pleaded and proved without reliance on the alleged fraud. However, the reliance test has now been abolished and replaced by the Supreme Court in *Patel v Mirza*[513] with a more flexible approach based on whether it would offend public policy to allow a claimant who was involved in a fraud to recover damages, which in turn involves considerations of the underlying purpose of the prohibition which has been transgressed, other relevant public policy considerations, and whether the denial of the claim would be a proportionate response, the latter including factors such as the seriousness of the parties' conduct, its centrality to the issues, whether it was intentional and whether there was marked disparity in the parties' respective culpability. Applying *Patel v Mirza*, in *Stoffel & Co v Grondona*[513A] the Supreme Court held that solicitors who negligently failed to register title to property had no defence based on illegality where the underlying transaction was a mortgage fraud. The deception involved their client, Ms Grondona, posing as the purchaser of the property and obtaining a mortgage, where the true owner was unable to obtain one. However, Ms Grondona and the true owner did intend legal title to pass to her (whatever their intentions may have been regarding the beneficial ownership). The public policy of deterrence would not be significantly undermined, the protection of mortgagees would not be enhanced, there was a public interest in not allowing the solicitors to avoid their professional obligations, the illegal conduct was not central to the firm's breach of duty, and the claimant would not be helped to profit from her own wrongdoing which was in any event not the proper focus of the illegality defence. In *Day v Womble Bond Dickinson (UK) LLP*[513B] the claimant pleaded guilty to unauthorised interference with a site of special scientific interest, and was fined £450,000 and ordered to pay a similar sum in costs. He sued his solicitors alleging that they should have advised him to insist on a trial in the magistrates' court, where the penalty was limited to £20,000, and if they had advanced an abuse of process argument he would have been convicted. The Court of Appeal upheld the striking out of the claim on the basis of ex turpi causa as it applied to a penalty for culpable criminal conduct, an established principle which was approved in *Patel v Mirza*.

11-112

[512] [2003] EWCA Civ 1115; [2004] P.N.L.R. 7.

[513] [2016] UKSC 42; [2017] A.C. 467.

[513A] [2020] UKSC 42. For commentary on the Court of Appeal decision see Z. Tan: "Illegality and professional negligence: applying the "range of factors" approach" (2019) 35 P.N. 121.

[513B] [2020] EWCA Civ 447; [2020] P.N.L.R 19. The claim was also an inadmissible collateral attack on the claimant's conviction.

(d)   Specific Defences to a Claim for Breach of Duty

(ii)   Abuse of Process

Hall v Simons

Replace footnote 518 with:

11-114   [518] [2002] 1 A.C. 615. For earlier Court of Appeal cases see: *Somasundaram v M Julius Melchior & Co* [1988] 1 W.L.R. 1394; *Walpole v Partridge Wilson* [1994] Q.B. 106 (Lord Hoffmann's suggested in *Hall v Simons* that Ralph Gibson LJ's judgment was "admirable" and the result correct, see [2002] 1 A.C. 615 at 703G at 706E, but it may be doubtful whether the reasoning in the case is in fact consistent with *Hall v Simons*); and *Smith v Linskills (A Firm)* [1996] 1 W.L.R. 763. Is is clear from *Smith v Liinskills* that the motive of the claimant is irrelevant, see *Workman v Deansgate 123 LLP* [2019] EWHC 360 (QB); [2019] P.N.L.R. 18.

Criminal cases

Replace footnote 529 with:

11-116   [529] [1994] Q.B. 106. For an example of a failed attempt to expand the exceptions to the abuse of process principle, see *Day v Womble Bond Dickinson (UK) LLP* [2020] EWCA Civ 447; [2020] P.N.L.R 19, noted at para.11-112 above.

Civil cases

Replace footnote 533 with:

11-117   [533] ibid. at 706G–706H. His comments were relied on by *Feakins v Burstow* [2005] EWHC 1931 (QB); [2006] P.N.L.R. 6, Jack J, in holding that an allegation that a solicitor had failed to produce documentary evidence in a trial which was lost was not an abuse of process. To similar effect see *Rogers v Roche (No.1)* [2016] QCA 340; (2017) 2 Qd. R. 307.

Other cases on abuse of process

Replace footnote 538 with:

11-118   [538] [2008] EWCA Civ 1146; [2008] P.N.L.R. 11. For another illustration see *Ridgewood Properties Group Ltd v Kilpatrick Stockton LLP* [2014] EWHC 2502 (Ch); [2014] P.N.L.R. 31. The claimant had entered a contract with a landowner permitting it to develop filling stations owned by the landlord. The claimant had sued the landlord for breach of contract, which claim failed on the basis that planning permissions had lapsed for reasons unconnected with the breach, and the claimant did not pursue an appeal. The claimant's subsequent claim against its solicitors for failing to advise it about its right to terminate the agreement for repudiatory breach was held to be an abuse of process, as it was a collateral attack on the earlier decision of the Court. In contrast, in *Ferrara v Lorenzetti, Wolfe Barristers and Solicitors* 2012 ONCA 852; (2013) 357 D.L.R. (4th) 480 a claim against solicitors was not an abuse of process although the same issue was raised in proceedings against another defendant as there was no possibility of inconsistent results, and the solicitors had repeatedly said they had acted correctly. In *Smith v McCarthy* [2017] IECA 168; [2017] P.N.L.R. 28 solicitors acted for the claimants in relation to a loan from a bank. When the bank issued proceedings for repayment, the claimants attempted to defend the claim on the basis that the solicitors had wrongfully confirmed to the bank that other lands had been sold, but the bank succeeded in obtaining summary judgment. The claimants then sued the solicitors on the basis of the same allegation, but the Court of Appeal of Ireland held that the claim was abusive as it sought to relitigate matters determined in the earlier proceedings by the bank. In *Ahmad v Wood* [2018] EWHC 996 (QB); [2018] P.N.L.R. 28 the claimant sued his former solicitors alleging that at an ancillary relief hearing they had contributed to an impression in the District Judge's mind that he was dishonest, and caused the District Judge to arrive at conclusions which were contrary to the documents before him. Following *Laing v Taylor* both allegations were struck out as a collateral attack on the previous decision of the Court.

(e)   Solicitor's Liability for Costs

Replace footnote 571 with:

[571] Prosecution of Offences Act 1985 s.19A, and Costs in Criminal Cases (General) Regulations 1986 **11-126**
regs 3A–3D, and *Practice Direction (Costs in Criminal Proceedings) 2015* [2015] EWCA Crim 1568
para.4.2. There are similar provisions in employment tribunals, see the Employment Tribunals (Constitu-
tion and Rules of Procedure) Regulations 2004 Sch.1 para.48(4), which require a representative to be
acting in pursuit of profit before a wasted costs order can be made against him, which was not the case
in *Lloyd v Cambridgeshire CC* [2011] P.N.L.R. 32. As to attempts to limit the scope of the jurisdiction,
see para.12-013, below. As to the last clause of subs.51(7), this may be relevant, for instance, where costs
were reasonably incurred on behalf of a litigant but the action was later struck out as a result of the
litigant's solicitors' defaults, see *Snowden v Ministry of Defence* [2001] EWCA Civ 1524; [2002] Costs
L.R. 249 CA at [26]. There are similar provisions in relation to tribunals, see *Awuah v Secretary of State
for the Home Department* [2017] UKFTT 555 (IAC); [2018] P.N.L.R. 7 (which decided that wasted costs
orders could not be made against Home Office Preventing Officers). CPR r.44.11 permits a Court to
disallow all or part of the costs being assessed, or order the payment of the costs incurred, when a party
of its legal representative acted unreasonably or improperly (but not negligently), a jurisdiction similar
to the wasted costs jurisdiction, on which see *Gempride v Bamrah* [2018] EWCA Civ 1367; [2019] 1
W.L.R. 1545 and *GSD Law Ltd v Craig Wardman* [2017] EWCA Civ 2144; [2017] 6 Costs L.R. 1253.

The inherent jurisdiction

Replace footnote 574 with:

[574] [1940] A.C. 282. There, the order was made against a solicitor for the defaults of his clerk. Similarly, **11-127**
in *Kelly v Jowett* [2010] NSWCA 278; (2009) 76 N.S.W.L.R. 405, the court made an order against a
firm for the defaults of its employee. The inherent jurisdiction remains the basis for wasted costs in much
of the commonwealth, see: *Harley v McDonald* [2001] UKPC 18; [2001] 2 A.C. 678, PC, a New Zealand
appeal; *White Industries (QLD) Pty Ltd v Flower Hart (A Firm)* (1999) 163 A.L.R. 744, Federal Court
of Australia, Full Court; *Knaggs v JA Westaway Sons* (1996) 40 N.S.W.L.R. 476 CA; *Steindl Nominees
Pty Ltd v Laghaifar* [2003] QCA 157; [2003] 2 Qd. R. 683 CA; *Young v Young* [1993] 4 S.C.R. 3
Supreme Court of Canada (which emphasised the need for caution); and *Hunter v Hunter* [2001] 4
W.W.R. 28 Manitoba CA. But in Ontario, for instance, the jurisdiction arises from procedural rules, see
Carleton v Beaverton Hotel (2010) 314 D.L.R. (4th) Ontario Div Ct (which emphasised that wasted costs
orders should only be made sparingly, with care and discretion, and only in clear cases) and for a similar
case see *Galganov v Russell (Township)* 2012 ONCA 410; (2012) 350 D.L.R. 679. The law in Hong
Kong is similar to the inherent jurisdiction, see *HKSAR v Harjani* [2017] 3 H.K.L.R.D. 1.

Parties and the limits of the jurisdiction

Replace footnote 583 with:

[583] [1997] C.O.D. 430. However, a wasted costs order cannot be made against a non-party who applies **11-128**
to the Court for the release of documents, see *In re Soni (Sadhana)* [2019] EWCA Crim 1304; [2019] 4
W.L.R. 103.

The position of the respondent lawyer and privilege

Replace footnote 597 with:

[597] [2002] UKHL 27; [2003] 1 A.C. 120, discussed at para.12-015, below. In *Dura v Hue (No 5)* [2014] **11-131**
VSC 400; (2014) 48 V.R. 1 inadequate material was placed before the court to allow a conclusion that
privileged communication existed which would give any benefit of doubt to the solicitors, and a wasted
costs order was made for pursuing hopeless litigation.

Procedure

Replace footnote 609 with:

[609] See now CPR Pt 48 PD at para.53.5., which echoes this, a point reiterated in *Hedrich v Standard* **11-134**
Bank London Ltd [2008] EWCA Civ 905; [2009] P.N.L.R. 3. While in most circumstances cross-
examination of the representative against whom costs are sought will be inappropriate, it may be
proportionate and fair in some circumstances, see *Godfrey Morgan v Cobalt* [2011] 6 Cost L.R. 1006,
where cross-examination was correctly permitted as the representative no longer acted for the party,
privilege had been waived, an oral hearing had been fixed, and there was a conflict on the facts. The summary nature of the procedure means that a court does not have to be satisfied document by document

that the impugned litigation was made at the instigation of the person against whom the wasted costs order is sought, see *MA Lloyd & Son Ltd (In Administration) v PPC International Ltd (t/a Professional Powercraft)* [2016] EWHC 2162 (QB); [2017] P.N.L.R. 1.

Causation

Replace footnote 630 with:

11-138   630   See also the following. In *R. v M (Wasted Costs Order)* [2000] P.N.L.R. 2 solicitors issued a witness summons in unfortunately wide terms. The Court of Appeal held that no costs had been wasted, as a hearing would have been necessary at some stage, and the judge in fact dealt with the substance of the matter at the hearing of the defective summons in any event. Costs unnecessarily incurred as a result of negligent conduct of litigation were awarded for a period of delay of four years under the wasted costs jurisdiction in *Padhiar v Patel* [2001] Lloyd's Rep. P.N. 328 QBD. In *Mitchells (A Firm) v Funkwerk Information Technologies York Ltd* [2008] P.N.L.R. 29, the Employment Appeal Tribunal set aside a wasted costs order against a solicitor in part because the tribunal had failed to consider whether there was any causation between the alleged negligence and the claimed loss, as they did in part for the same reason in *Robinson v Hall Gregory Recruitment Ltd* [2014] I.R.L.R. 761. A litigant in person in criminal proceedings could recover no wasted costs, because under statute such costs were not recoverable, see *R. (on the application of Crowch) v DPP* [2008] EWHC 948 (Admin); [2009] P.N.L.R. 1. A claim for a wasted costs order made in an employment tribunal failed on appeal, inter alia, on causation in *KL Law Ltd v Wincanton Group Ltd* [2019] P.N.L.R. 1.

Difficulties with public funding

Replace footnote 650 with:

11-142   650   [1997] P.I.Q.R. 494. In *HKSAR v Apelete (No.1)* [2019] HKCA 1189; [2019] 5 H.K.L.R.D. 574 it was held that even if there were funding issues before legal aid was granted, solicitors were on record and had not ceased to act, and thus were obliged to comply with the court's directions.

Errors concerning documents

Replace footnote 662 with:

11-146   662   [2008] EWCA Civ 1120; [2009] 2 Costs L.R. 269. It should not be assumed that a failure to disclose documents was by the legal representative, see *KL Law Ltd v Wincanton Group Ltd* [2019] P.N.L.R. 1.

(h)   Authority, Attribution and Vicarious Liability

Liability of partners

Replace footnote 706 with:

11-154   706   [2002] UKHL 48; [2003] 2 A.C. 366. In *Various Claimants v Wm Morrison Supermarkets Plc* [2020] UKSC 12; [2020] 2 W.L.R. 941 (a case which did not directly concern partnership but employment) the Supreme Court re-examined *Dubai Aluminium* in detail and made clear that what is "fairly and properly" regarded as part of the ordinary course of business of a firm is not an invitation to judges to decide cases in accordance with their own personal sense of justice. The Supreme Court also considered the relevance of the fact that the tortfeasor in that case had deliberately inflicted harm in order to further his own interests. In *Re Bell's Indenture* [1980] 1 W.L.R. 1217 Vinelott J held that a solicitor had implied authority in the ordinary course of business to accept trust moneys, but not to accept office as a trustee. In *Scarborough Building Society v Howes Percival* (1998) 76 P. & C.R. D4 CA, partners were liable for a fraudulent solicitor acting in the ordinary course of the firm's business. In *Walker v Stones* [2001] Q.B. 902 the Court of Appeal held that breaches of trust committed by a solicitor trustee fell outside the ordinary business of a partnership and could not give rise to vicarious liability under s.10. Cases decided before *Dubai* need to be treated with some caution.

Liability for staff

Replace paragraph 11-156 (to incorporate amendments to footnotes 711 and 713) with:

11-156   A firm of solicitors is vicariously liable for breaches of duty committed by its own staff.[711] This will generally include liability for the fraud of the employee.[712] A firm will normally be liable for breaches committed by other solicitors acting as their agents within the scope of their authority.[713] Similarly if a solicitor entrusts his practice to a locum while he is away from the office for any reason, he will be liable for any breaches which the locum may commit. A solicitor will not, however, normally be liable for the defaults of a foreign lawyer he has instructed, who is an independent expert in the same way as an expert witness or counsel would be.[714]

[711] e.g. *Creech v Mayorcas* (1966) 198 E.G. 1091 Ch D; *Heywood v Wellers* [1976] Q.B. 446 CA. The ostensible authority of both a partner and an employed solicitor has been considered in a number of cases and in particular *United Bank of Kuwait Ltd v Hammoud* [1988] 1 W.L.R. 1051 CA, see further para.11-071, above. In *Nayyar v Denton Wilde Sapte* [2010] EWHC 3218 (QB); [2010] P.N.L.R. 15, an employee of the defendants introduced the claimants to a third party in order to be appointed sales agent for Air India. The claimants made a large payment to the third party, and received nothing. The claim for the loss of the payment failed as it was a bribe and contrary to public policy. Further, the firm's employee acted as an independent deal broker, which was not solicitorial in nature and went beyond her role in business development, so they were not liable for her defaults. Subject to any possible defence based on co-insurance, the firm would be entitled to an indemnity from the employee; e.g. see *Lee Siew Chun v Sourgrapes Packaging Products Trading Pte Ltd* [1993] 2 S.L.R. 297 Singapore High Court. Members of staff should be properly supervised, see *Kim v Oh* [2013] NZHC 925; [2013] 2 N.Z.L.R. 825. For the general test of vicarious liability for the wrongful conduct of employees see *Various Claimants v Wm Morrison Supermarkets Plc* [2020] UKSC 12; [2020] 2 W.L.R. 941 (a case which did not concern solicitors but which examines in detail the underlying principles about the type of act for which an employer is liable, and its necessary connection to the employer's business).

[712] e.g. see: *Lloyd v Grace Smith & Co* [1912] A.C. 716 (managing agent undertaking conveyancing work procured title deeds and stole the property); *Uxbridge Permanent Benefit Building Society v Pickard* [1939] 2 K.B. 248; and *Balfron Trustees Ltd v Karsten Peterson* [2002] Lloyd's Rep. P.N. 1, Laddie J, who emphasised that the relevant principles of vicarious liability are now to be found in *Lister v Hesley Hall Ltd* [2002] 1 A.C. 215.

[713] *Re Ward, Simmons v Rose, Weeks* v Ward (1862) 31 Beav 1: solicitor held liable for negligent representations made by London agent. Solicitors will also be liable for independent costs draftsmen who they instruct, see *Gempride v Bamrah* [2018] EWCA Civ 1367; [2019] 1 W.L.R. 1545. The general test is that a defendant will be liable for acts of someone who was not their employee if the relationship was sufficiently analogous to employment to make it fair, just and reasonable to impose liability, but not if they were carrying on business on their own account, see *Various Claimants v Barclays Bank Plc* [2020] UKSC 13; [2020] 2 W.L.R. 960 (a case which did not concern solicitors).

[714] *Gregory v Shepherds* [2000] P.N.L.R. 769 CA. The solicitors were found liable on other grounds, see para.11-209, below for the facts.

2. LIABILITY FOR BREACH OF DUTY

(c) Failing to Give Advice

As to the progress of the cause or matter

Replace footnote 760 with:

[760] In *Tamlura NV v CMS Cameron McKenna* [2009] EWHC 538 (Ch); [2009] Lloyd's Rep. P.N. 71, **11-166** Mann J held that there was no duty to inform the client of an advantageous change from the heads of agreement which appeared in the other side's solicitors' draft agreement, as that was an error, and there was no duty to seek to take advantage of that mistake rather than correct it. In *Gabriel v Little* [2012] EWHC 1193 (Ch); [2013] W.T.L.R. 419, the solicitor had learned that the other side intended to use a loan, which was to be provided by his client and was to be evidenced by a facility letter, mostly to purchase a property, rather than to develop it, and he was negligent in failing to pass this on to the client, and also negligent in failing to make it sufficiently clear in the facility letter that the loan was only to be used for development. The appeal on breach was dismissed by the Court of Appeal, [2013] EWCA Civ 1513. The issue of breach was not appealed to the Supreme Court, sub. nom. *Hughes-Holland v BPE Solicitors* [2017] UKSC 21; [2018] A.C. 599.

In respect of matters which he is not asked to investigate or advise upon

Replace footnote 767 with:

[767] See the following further examples: *Amersfort Ltd v Kelly Nichols & Blayney* [1996] E.G.C.S. 156 **11-168** Ch D (defendant solicitors answered the three questions asked of them, but had not been asked to review

the plaintiffs' lease generally; they had no duty to bring to the clients' attention any unusual features of the lease beyond answering the three questions); *Bartter v Gambrill* (1932) 76 S.J. 868 (plaintiff agreed with S, an adjoining landowner, to exchange part of her garden for a portion of S's land; after the agreement was made, the defendant solicitor was instructed to carry out the conveyancing, but the plaintiff subsequently regretted the transaction; Luxmoore J held that "a solicitor was not obliged to point out to the person instructing him that he was not legally bound to carry out his bargain."); *Griffiths v Evans* [1953] 1 W.L.R. 1424 (plaintiff sustained an accident at work and thereafter received weekly payments from his employers under the Workmen's Compensation Acts, and consulted the defendant solicitor, because he feared a reduction of the weekly payments; they advised the plaintiff in respect of his claim under the Workmen's Compensation Acts, but not whether he had a claim for damages at common law in respect of the accident; the Court of Appeal (Denning LJ dissenting) held that the defendant was not negligent); *Swain Mason v Mills & Reeve (A Firm)* [2011] EWHC 410 (Ch); [2011] S.T.C. 1177; upheld on appeal at [2012] EWCA Civ 498; [2012] W.T.L.R. 1827 (no duty to advise a client not to enter a management buy-out until after a heart operation (which proved fatal) because of the tax consequences if the client died, despite the retainer including advising on the tax consequences of that buy-out, when the information about the heart operation was conveyed to the solicitors by the client in an email which was blind-copied to them and did not seek any advice from them); *Stone Heritage Developments Ltd v Davis Blank Furniss (A Firm)* [2007] EWCA Civ 765; [2007] Lloyd's Rep. P.N. 33 (developers instructed solicitors that the proposed development was not to concern certain land held on possessory title, and the solicitors therefore had no duty to advise that the licence provisions of a development agreement should be extended to enable development of part of that land); *Woodward v Wolferstans (A Firm)*, *The Times*, 8 April 1997; [1997] N.P.C. 51 (defendant solicitors were retained by the plaintiff's father in relation to the purchase of property, where he was acting as guarantor; while they owed her a duty of care, there was no breach in failing to explain the details of the transaction to her, as the retainer from the father was simply to secure a good and marketable title). *Minkin v Landsberg* [2015] EWCA Civ 1152; [2016] 1 W.L.R. 1489 (instructions to draft consent order, no duty to give advice to the client on the merits of it); *Flynn v King (p/a J F Williams & Co)* [2017] IEHC 735; [2018] P.N.L.R. 15 (after contracts for the sale of land signed, no duty to make enquiries about the purchaser's ability to complete the transaction).

The duty to warn against particular risks

Replace footnote 786 with:

11-172   [786] [2001] EWCA Civ 1360; [2002] P.N.L.R. 14. For criticism of the decision, see S. Gee, "The Solicitor's duty to warn that a court might take a different view" (2003) 19 P.N. 363. Similarly, in *Hermann v Withers LLP* [2012] EWHC 1492 (Ch); [2012] P.N.L.R. 28, Newey J held that the defendant solicitors came to a reasonable view that the construction of an Act of Parliament meant that their clients were entitled to enter and use a communal garden, but negligently failed to explain to them that there was scope for different opinions on the matter. Following these cases, in *Balogun v Boyes Sutton and Perry* [2017] EWCA Civ 75; [2017] P.N.L.R. 20 the Court of Appeal held that a solicitor's interpretation of a clause in a lease was correct, but they were negligent in failing to point out that there was a risk of argument about its true construction, although on the facts that caused no loss. In *Barker v Baxendale Walker Solicitors (A Firm)* [2017] EWCA Civ 2056; [2018] 1 W.L.R. 1905; [2018] P.N.L.R. 16 solicitors gave advice on whether a transfer was exempt from inheritance tax pursuant to s.28(1) of the Inheritance Tax Act 1984, which was not alleged to be negligent. However, the Court of Appeal held that the solicitors were negligent in failing to advise that a court might come to a different interpretation. Asplin LJ explained at [61] that such matters are highly fact-sensitive, if the provision is clear it is very likely that the threshold of a significant risk would not be met so no advice needed to be given, and there is more likely to be a duty to point out the risks if litigation is already on foot or the point has already been taken.

Advice on matters of business.

Replace footnote 802 with:

11-176   [802] See *Clarke v Boyce Mouat* [1994] 1 A.C. 428 and *Pickersgill v Riley* [2004] UKPC 14; [2004] P.N.L.R. 31 noted at para.11-168, above. Contrast *Salomon v Matte-Thompson* 2019 SCC 14; (2019) 52 CCLT (4th) 175 where a solicitor negligently advised the client to invest in Ponzi schemes, wrongfully recommending investment in an undiversified offshore hedge fund when the client wished to preserve capital and without performing any due-diligence.

(d) Misconduct of Litigation

Funding of litigation

Replace paragraph 11-182 (to incorporate amendments to footnotes 822 and 824) with:

A solicitor is obliged to discuss with the client how his litigation is to be **11-182** funded.[822] In the context of a claim by a passenger injured in a vehicle driven by someone in the same household, the Court of Appeal gave guidance as to what a solicitor should do in *Sarwar v Alam*,[823] relying on the provisions in what was then the Client Care Code 1999. He should normally advise the client to bring to the first interview any relevant motor insurance policy, household insurance policy, or before the event (BTE) policy belonging to him or any spouse or partner living in the same household. It is desirable for solicitors to send a standard form letter requesting sight of such documents. The solicitor should inquire whether a third person such as a trade union or employer might pay the costs, and should generally ask a passenger to obtain a copy of the driver's insurance if reasonably practicable. The solicitor's inquiries should be proportionate to the amount at stake. In most cases worth less than £5,000, the solicitor should refer the client to any BTE insurer, rather than seek After the Event insurance. The *Sarwar* test has been qualified in *Garrett v Halton BC*,[824] where the Court of Appeal emphasised that what it laid down was guidance only, and the suggestion that the client should be invited to bring any relevant policy to a first interview had no application in high volume, low value litigation conducted on referral by claims management companies.

[822] The Solicitors Code of Conduct 2011 gives as indicative behaviour at IB1.16: "discussing how the client will pay, including whether public funding may be available, whether the client has insurance which may cover the fees, and whether the fees may be paid by someone else such as a trade union." The Solicitors Code of Conduct 2007 at r.2.03(1)(d) was to similar effect, and at r.2.03(1)(g), it was also directed that the liability for another party's costs should be discussed, including whether it may be covered by existing insurance or by specially purchased insurance (i.e. after the event insurance). See also *Andrews v Messer Beg Ltd* [2019] EWHC 911 (Ch); [2019] P.N.L.R. 23.

[823] [2001] EWCA Civ 1401; [2002] 1 W.L.R. 125. There is an obligation to explain a costs agreement even if there is no formal retainer yet, see *McNamara Business & Property Law v Kasmeridis* [2007] SASC; (2007) 97 S.A.S.R. 129, South Australia CA. In *David Truex (A Firm) v Kitchin* [2007] EWCA Civ 618; [2007] P.N.L.R. 33, solicitors were told by their client that she had no money and was borrowing from her parents, and the Court of Appeal held that they were negligent in failing to advise her at the outset that she may be eligible for public funding.

[824] [2006] EWCA Civ 1017; [2007] 1 W.L.R. 554. See also *Lyons v Fox Williams* [2018] EWCA Civ 2347; [2019] P.N.L.R. 9 where the Court of Appeal held that a solicitor instructed to deal with a client's claim under an accident, death and disablement insurance policy had not been under a duty to advise his client about his rights under a long-term disability insurance policy which was not covered by the retainer.

Evidence

To the end of the paragraph after "advice of counsel.", add:

It is not negligent to pursue settlement in accordance with the client's instruc- **11-190** tions despite reliable evidence not being available given the expense of pursuing litigation to obtain such evidence, see *Seery v Leathes Prior (A Firm)*.[851A]

[851A] [2017] EWHC 80 (QB); [2017] P.N.L.R. 14.

Delay in defending proceedings

Replace footnote 876 with:

11-196 ⁸⁷⁶ e.g. *Godefroy v Jay* (1831) 7 Bing. 413; *Dual Homes Pty Ltd v Moores Legal pty Ltd* [2016] VSC 86; (2016) 50 V.R. 117 (failure to attend court to defend a winding up petition despite instructions to do so).

Settlement: the merits

Replace footnote 889 with:

11-199 ⁸⁸⁹ Sending letters to a client of limited education and understanding of legal concepts was not suf-ficient, and, even in group litigation with an element of commoditisation, a meeting or telephone call was needed, see *Procter v Raleys Solicitors* [2015] EWCA Civ 400; [2015] P.N.L.R. 24. In *Thomas v Hugh James Ford Simey Solicitors* [2017] EWCA Civ 1303; [2018] P.N.L.R. 5 there were two meet-ings in the same litigation with the claimant. He had decided not to pursue a special damages claim, and no advice needed to be given on the value of such a claim or the possibility of an interim payment. It was not the job of a solicitor to tempt a client to make a claim once it was clear there was no evidence to support it.

To the end of the paragraph after "the settlement negotiations.", add:

Independent legal advice may also be needed where the proceeds of litigation are paid into a personal injury trust where the trustees are connected with the solici-tors, see *AKB v Willerton*,⁸⁹³ᴬ noted at para.11-016 above.

⁸⁹³ᴬ [2016] EWHC 3146 (QB); [2017] 4 W.L.R. 25.

(e) Misconduct of Non-contentious Business

(i) Conveyancing

Communicating with the client

Replace paragraph 11-207 (to incorporate amendments to footnotes 924 and 933) with:

11-207 The Law Society's Conveyancing Handbook provides a checklist of matters to be considered when acting for a purchaser, some of which expressly require advice to the client.⁹²⁰ The solicitor should explain the effect of the conveyance, in particular any unusual or important provisions⁹²¹:

> "A person who goes to a lawyer with respect to a land transaction is entitled to expect that lawyer to investigate the state of any title that is germane to the matter and to explain to the client exactly what it is that is portrayed by the state of the title."⁹²²

A solicitor will generally have no duty to advise on the commercial implications of matters he draws to his client's attention.⁹²³ He should, though, advise his client about important matters that come to his notice, such as the existence of a right of way over the property,⁹²⁴ the absence of planning permission,⁹²⁵ or the existence of a "contracts race".⁹²⁶ He should warn his client about risks that the client may not appreciate, particularly unsophisticated clients,⁹²⁷ such as: the risks which a purchaser ran by moving in and carrying out works of repair before contracts were exchanged⁹²⁸; of the dangers which they ran by exchanging contracts for the purchase of new property, before the prospective purchaser of their existing property had paid a deposit⁹²⁹; of the nature and effect of a restrictive covenant and the risks attached to it⁹³⁰; that the solicitor's interpretation of a restrictive covenant was open to dispute⁹³¹; on the sale of land and proposed reconveyance of a flat after construction, that the client may be left without any interest if the builder became insolvent[932]; and of the absence in the proposed contract which was conditional on planning permission of any provision allowing the clients to cancel the contract if planning permission was subsequently challenged successfully.[933] In *Atkins v Atkins*,[934] the solicitors failed to explain the real purpose of the transaction to the plaintiff, which was to raise money on her house for her son, and was held to be negligent. Contrast *Haigh v Wright Hassall & Co*,[935] where a solicitor exchanged contracts on being assured by his client that a deposit cheque would be available that afternoon. The solicitor was held not to be liable; he had no duty to question how secure was the availability of the deposit cheque. However, the answer might have been different if the client was wholly inexperienced. There is generally no duty to repeat advice already given after exchange of contracts.[936]

[920] A1.9.1. This includes advice about funding the purchase price, survey arrangements, insurance, how the property is to be held by co-owners, and advice on completing a Stamp Duty Land Tax Return.

[921] See paras 11-173 onwards.

[922] *Graybriar Industries Ltd v Davis & Co* (1992) 46 B.C.L.R. (2d) 161 at 181 British Columbia Sup Court per Thackray J. Similarly, in *Behrooz Siasati v Bottoms & Webb (A Firm)* [1997] N.P.C. 20; [1997] E.G.C.S. 22 QBD, the solicitor had a duty to a foreign client with limited English to take all reasonable steps to explain, if necessary through an interpreter, the nature and scope of the obligations of the lease of old commercial property which he intended to take on, of the risks involved, and to take reasonable steps to ensure that the client understood the advice, which should generally be reduced to writing so the client could obtain a translation.

[923] *Reeves v Thrings & Long* [1996] P.N.L.R. 265 CA. See generally paras 11-176 onwards.

[924] *Piper v Daybell, Court-Cooper & Co* (1969) 210 E.G. 1047. Similarly, a solicitor should advise that planning enquiries revealed that a nearby school site was to be redeveloped into a larger school, *Orientfield Holdings Ltd (a company registered and incorporated in the British Virgin Islands) v Bird & Bird LLP* [2015] EWHC 1963 (Ch); [2015] P.N.L.R. 34. An appeal on causation was dismissed at [2017] EWCA Civ 348; [2017] P.N.L.R. 31.

[925] *Lake v Bushby* [1949] 2 All E.R. 964.

[926] *Nash v Phillips* (1974) 232 E.G. 1219 Ch. D, and (in relation to informing the other side) *Jenmain v Steed & Steed* [2000] P.N.L.R. 616 CA. The client will be fixed with knowledge communicated by the other side to the solicitor: *Strover v Harrington* [1988] 1 Ch. 390 Ch D, but cf. *Halifax Mortgage Services Ltd v Stepsky* [1996] Ch 207 CA.

[927] In *O'Brien v Hooker Homes* (1993) A.S.C. 56–217 Supreme Court NSW, a solicitor who arranged finance for the purchase of property by uneducated clients owed a duty to spell out the workings of their interest obligations. In *Keep Point Development Ltd v Chan Chi Yim* [2000] 3 H.K.L.R.D. 166 the solicitors were found liable for failing to explain to unsophisticated clients the unusual danger of selling their property for option agreements on land which was not registered. cf. *Carvin v Dunham Brindley & Linn* [1997] E.G.C.S. 90: part of the garden of a house was used as a storm drain which had not been adopted, and the purchaser was initially granted only a licence over it. It was intended that the remaining land would be conveyed to the purchaser in due course when the position had been finalised. The Court of Appeal upheld the judge's decision that the solicitor was not in breach of his duty to the prospective purchaser, a successful man of business, as he had explained the nature of the licence and the fact that the plaintiff would not immediately be acquiring the title to the whole property.

[928] *Attard v Samson* (1966) 110 S.J. 249 QBD. Similarly, in *Baird v Hastings & Co (Solicitors)* [2013] NIQB 143; [2014] P.N.L.R. 17 (on appeal [2015] NICA 22) solicitors were held to be negligent in failing to advise the clients of the risks of purchasing a new property with a bridging loan before their house had sold in circumstances where the Northern Irish "Home Charter" scheme required advice to be given about the consequences of any mortgage. Upheld on appeal (although the issue of causation was remitted) at [2015] NICA 22. In *Xenakis v Birkett Long LLP (A Firm)* [2014] EWHC 171 (QB); [2014] P.N.L.R. 16, solicitors were found to be negligent in failing to advise clients that their guarantees of a lease ran from the date of completion of the lease by the landlords and failing to advise about the risks of releasing the documents and procuring the claimants' company to go into occupation before such completion, which caused their guarantee to last nearly a year longer than they had contemplated.

[929] *Morris v Duke-Cohan & Co* (1975) 119 S.J. 826; *The Times*, 22 November 1975 QBD.

[930] *Bittlestone v Keegan Williams* [1997] E.G.C.S. 8; [1997] N.P.C. 3 Ch. D, unless the solicitor could satisfy himself that it was plainly unenforceable.

931 *Queen Elizabeth's Grammar School Blackburn v Banks Wilson* [2001] EWCA Civ 1360; [2002] P.N.L.R. 14.

932 *Boateng v Hughmans (A Firm)* [2002] EWCA Civ 593; [2002] P.N.L.R. 40. And in failing to advise fully on the risks faced in paying a deposit for the purchase of an apartment to be built, including the vendor, a company of no substance, not having any rights to the land on which it was to be built or funding to do so, see *Tauranga Law v Appleton* [2015] NZSC 3; [2015] 1 N.Z.L.R. 814. However, the claim failed on causation.

933 *Stoll v Wacks Caller (A Firm)* [2010] EWHC 2299 (Ch); [2010] P.N.L.R. 4, relying on a dictum of Bingham LJ in *County Personnel (Employment Agency) Ltd v Alan R Pulver & Co* [1987] 1 W.L.R. 916 at 922E quoted at para.11-172, above. In *Blackwell v Edmonds Judd* [2016] NZSC 40; [2016] 1 N.Z.L.R. 1001 solicitors were held negligent in failing (inter alia) to strongly advise that an informal agreement that an option to purchase should not be exercised by the tenant before the death of the lessor should be included as a formal term of the agreement.

934 [1993] E.G.C.S. 54 Ch. D.

935 [1994] E.G.C.S. 54 CA. See also *Park Hall School v Overend* [1987] 2 I.R. 1 Irish High Court, where a solicitor acted for a school in the proposed sale of land. The land had previously been sold at auction, although the sale had not gone ahead. Given the uncertain state of the law, it was not clear whether there existed a binding contract with the original proposed purchaser. The solicitor was found not to be negligent when he failed to warn his client that it might be already liable to convey the property, given that the original proposed purchaser had made no suggestion that he would assert his possible rights.

936 *Elland Developments Ltd v Smith* [1995] E.G.C.S. 141, Rattee J, and see para.11-175, above.

Wider duties

To the end of the paragraph after "breach of duty.", add:

11-212   If a solicitor acting for the purchase discovers a previous sale at a substantially lower price, he should tell the client, see *Eden (NI) Ltd v Mills Selig (A Firm)*,936A applying *Mortgage Express Ltd v Bowerman & Partners*936B (see para.11-219) where a similar duty was owed to a lender. Solicitors acting on the purchase of land for £5.4m negligently failed to inform their client that it had been purchased shortly before for £3.3m.

936A [2016] NIQB 71; [2017] P.N.L.R. 2.

936B [1996] 2 All E.R. 836.

(ii)   The Investment of Money and Claims by Lenders

Basic principles

Replace footnote 993 with:

11-218   993 *Roe v Cullinane Turnbull & Steele Partners (No.2)* [1985] 1 N.Z.L.R. 37, Quillam J: on a sale of land to a company without capital for payment which was mostly deferred, the vendor's solicitor was negligent in not obtaining personal guarantees when he knew that the security over the land was worth less than the debt; *County Natwest Ltd v Pinsent & Co* [1994] 4 Bank L.R. 4, Hobhouse J: solicitors failed to point out mismatch between the duration of insurance cover and loan facility. *Pegrum v Fatharly* (1996) 14 W.A.R. 92, Western Australia CA: if the solicitor has reason to suspect that the borrower may be insolvent or the securities are inadequate in value, he should advise his client; *Midland Mortgage Corp v Jawl Bundon* (1999) 8 W.W.R. 535 British Columbia CA: solicitors were not negligent in failing to advise a lender of the riskiness of a mortgage over a short term lease, as their only duty was to implement lender's agreement with developer. *Beazer v Tollestrop Estate* [2017] ABCA 429; [2018] 4 W.W.R. 5113: solicitors negligently drafted mortgages by not amending them to reflect the fact that they were intended to secure past obligations, and only enforceable on death or sale, as they knew was contemplated.

(iii) Wills

Taking instructions

Replace footnote 1049 with:

[1049] The New Zealand Court of Appeal has held in *Knox v Till* [2000] P.N.L.R. 67 that there would be **11-230**
no duty to refuse to act if there were doubts about testamentary capacity, and in any event whether a
testator has testamentary capacity is outside a solicitor's professional expertise. See also *Ryan v Public
Trustee* [2000] 1 N.Z.L.R. 700, where it was suggested that if there was doubt about capacity the will
should be executed and the opinions on capacity recorded. In *Sandman v McKay* [2019] NZSC 41;
[2019] 1 N.Z.L.R. 519 the Supreme Court of New Zealand observed that if the circumstances suggested that issues about capacity may later be raised, the advice given and steps taken should be carefully documented, it should be suggested that a medical certificate be obtained, and the reasons for provisions in the will, the process of taking instructions and making sure they had been correctly understood
should be documented. The position in Canada is summarised in the decision of the Manitoba Court of
Appeal in *Slobodianik v Podlasiewicz* (2003) 228 D.L.R. (4th) 610, that if there were suspicious
circumstances as to testamentary capacity, the solicitor should satisfy himself that capacity did exist, and
if there were any possible doubt a note of the observations and conclusions should be made. If it were
clear that the patient lacked capacity, the will should not be executed, see *Hall v Estate of Bruce Ben-
nett* [2003] W.T.L.R. 827, (2003) 227 DLR (4th) 263.

3. DAMAGES

(a) Remedies for Breach of Fiduciary Duty and Breach of Trust

The modern law

Replace footnote 1095 with:

[1095] [2014] UKSC 58; [2015] P.N.L.R. 10 (applied in *LIV Bridging Finance Ltd v EAD Solicitors LLP* **11-241**
[2020] EWHC 1590 (Ch); [2020] P.N.L.R. 24, where the court held that in a transaction where a professional had not guided the whole decision-making process, a claimant seeking equitable compensation
for breach of fiduciary duty consisting of knowingly paying out mortgage money in breach of instructions was only able to recover losses falling within the scope of the professional's duty to obtain a first
charge). For helpful commentary see S. Charlwood: "AIB Group Plc v Mark Redler & Co Solicitors:
the last word on lenders' breach of trust claims against solicitors?" (2015) 31 P.N. 60, L. Ho, "Equitable
compensation on the road to Damascus?" (2015) 131 L.Q.R. 213, P. Turner: "the new fundamental norm
of recovery for losses to express trusts" [2015] C.L.J. 188, and S. Televantos and L. Maniscalco, "Stay
on Target: compensation and causation in breach of trust claims" (2015) 79 Conv. 348. And see P.
Davies: "Remedies for breach of trust" (2015) 78 M.L.R. 681 at para.11-241. In *Various Claimants v
Giambrone and Law (A Firm)* [2017] EWCA Civ 1193; [2018] P.N.L.R. 2 purchasers paid large deposits
for an Italian development. Their solicitors failed to advise them that the developer's bank guarantees
did not comply with Italian law, and the Court of Appeal upheld the judge's decision to award equitable
compensation for breach of trust, which was the same measure of damages as in contract. There was
also a breach of trust in failing to pay out a substantial part of the deposit as commission. The decision
has been questioned, see P Davies: "Equitable compensation and the SAAMCO principle" (2018) 134
L.Q.R. 165.

(b) Claims at Common Law: Remoteness

(i) Causation

"But for" causation

*Replace paragraph 11-247 (to incorporate amendments to footnotes 1107 and 1110)
with:*

Whether the claim is brought in contract or tort, it is first necessary to determine **11-247**
whether the solicitor's breach of duty was "the cause" of the alleged damage.[1106] The
burden of proof is on the claimant to prove causation.[1107] However, in *Levicom
International Holdings BV v Linklaters*,[1108] the Court of Appeal considered that
where solicitors advise a client that it has a strong case and it starts litigation, it

should rebuttably be inferred that the advice was causative and thus the client would not have gone ahead but for that advice.[1109] Clearly, the breach of duty was not the cause if the damage would have occurred in any event.[1110] In *Sykes v Midland Bank Executor Trustee Co Ltd*,[1111] for example, the Court of Appeal held that the plaintiffs would have entered the under-lease in question, even if they had been properly advised by their solicitors. Accordingly, nominal damages only were awarded.[1112] Some cases seek to draw a distinction about what the claimant needs to prove in a case where his solicitor has failed to give him proper advice, as opposed to cases where his solicitor has given him incorrect advice or information. In the former type of case, it is necessary for the claimant to prove that if proper advice had been given he would have acted differently, and it is not enough merely to prove that he relied on the solicitors' advice. The position may be different where the claim is that a solicitor has given incorrect advice or information, although this is doubtful and it is not easy to draw a distinction between the two types of case.[1113]

[1106] For a statement of the general principles, see *McGregor*, 19th edn, paras 8–005 to 8–079 (in relation to tort) and paras 8-137 to 8-154 (in relation to contract).

[1107] See *Wilsher v East Essex Area HA* [1988] A.C. 1074, which was applied in a solicitor's negligence case by the British Columbia Court of Appeal in *Haag v Marshall* (1989) 1 C.C.L.T. (2d) 99 with the qualification that "in a situation where it is impossible, as a practical matter, to prove whether the breach of duty caused the loss, it is more in keeping with a common sense approach to causation as a tool of justice to let the liability fall on the defendant"; however evidence could have been led in that case and the claim against the solicitor failed. See also *BSA Investors Ltd v Mosly* (2007) 283 D.L.R. (4th) 21, where the British Columbia Court of Appeal held that circumstantial evidence should be used to decide causation, and no inference should be drawn as to causation. In *Etridge v Pritchard Englefield* [1999] P.N.L.R. 839 the solicitors were negligent in failing to give the plaintiff any advice about charges she was making on her property to raise money for her husband. The Court of Appeal held that there was no presumption that the client would have followed the advice which should have been given to her, and the burden remained on the plaintiff to prove on the balance of probabilities that she would have done so. Further, in *Boateng v Hughmans (A Firm)* [2002] EWCA Civ 593; [2002] P.N.L.R. 40, the Court of Appeal emphasised that in all cases where failure to advise was alleged against a solicitor, the claimant had to plead and prove what he would have done if he had been properly advised. The claimant in that case failed to prove that he would have acted differently. See also *E Surv v Goldsmith Williams Solicitors* [2015] EWCA Civ 1147; [2016] 4 W.L.R. 44 and *Capital Home Loans Ltd v Hewitt & Gilpin Solicitors Ltd* [2016] NIQB 13; [2016] P.N.L.R 24 (both cases in which the court held that the claimants had failed to put adduce adequate evidence to prove causation). An appeal on the issue of causation failed in *Capital Home Loans Ltd v Hewitt & Gilpin Solicitors Ltd* [2016] NICA 45; [2017] P.N.L.R. 12. Similarly, the claimants failed to prove that on balance they would have done anything different but for the defendant's negligence in *Taray Investments Ltd v Gateley Heritage LLP* [2020] EWHC 716 (QB); [2020] P.N.L.R. 21.

[1108] [2010] EWCA Civ 494; [2010] P.N.L.R. 566,

[1109] In *Luffeform Ltd v Kitsons LLP* [2015] EWHC B10 (QB), [2015] P.N.L.R. 30, Recorder Acton Davis QC found that in a case where defendant solicitors had failed to advise purchasers of a public house about the lack of covenant restraining competition from a chef employed at the public house, the evidential burden shifted to the defendant solicitors to show that its negligence was not causative.

[1110] Unless there are concurrent causes of the damage, as in *Baker v Willoughby* [1970] A.C. 495, cf. *Jobling v Associated Dairies Ltd* [1982] A.C. 794. In *Rochpion Properties (4) LLP v Hill Dickinson LLP* [2019] EWHC 2354 (TCC); [2020] P.N.L.R. 11 a claim was brought against several professional defendants for loss caused by the late discovery that the claimant did not own land on which it was building an electricity substation. It was held that it was not fatal were damage to have been suffered by the claimant even if individual defendants had not been at fault, and where the serial act of negligence of several defendants combined to cause a claimant loss, the claimant could recover in full against each of them

[1111] [1971] 1 Q.B. 113. For the facts see para.11-173. This decision has been applied in a number of cases: *GP&P Ltd v Bulcraig & Davies* (1986) 2 E.G.L.R. 148, although with the opposite result (see para.11-265); *Stratton Ltd v Weston, Financial Times*, 11 April 1990, Ch. D: a solicitor negligently failed to register a client's lease; there was no loss as the landlord would have sold free of the lease anyway under a prior equitable mortgage; *Polischuk v Hagarty* (1985) 14 D.L.R. (4th) 446 (reversing the first instance decision at (1983) 149 D.L.R (3d) 65): the solicitor for the purchaser accepted an undertaking from the vendor's solicitor without first consulting his client, who would not have accepted it; *Income Trust Co v Watson* (1984) 26 B.L.R. 228 Ontario High Court; *Hanflex Pty Ltd v NS Hope Associates* [1990] 2 Qd. R. 218 Queensland Full Court.; *Hall v Foong* (1995) 65 S.A.S.R. 281 Full Court of South

Australia: the plaintiff had not proved what she would have done if the defendant solicitor had not been negligent, and thus awarded her only nominal damages, as did the Supreme Court in *Smith v Moloney* [2005] SASC 305; (2005) 223 A.L.R. 101. A similar result was reached in *Chaster (Guardian ad litem of) v LeBlanc* 2009 BCCA 315; (2009) 66 C.C.L.T. 227 British Columbia CA, where it was held that the plaintiff would have accepted the settlement on offer at mediation whether or not the defendant lawyers had prepared for the mediation more competently. For another case where the claimant failed to prove causation, see *Westbury v Sampson* [2001] EWCA Civ 407; [2002] 1 F.L.R. 166. The defendant solicitors acted for the claimant husband in ancillary relief proceedings, and failed to inform him that any lump sum settlement could be later varied by the court pursuant to s.31 of the Matrimonial Causes Act 1973, as in fact happened. The Court of Appeal held that the claimant could not establish causation as there was no way to protect him from the effect of s.31.

[1112] See, however, paras 11-269 onwards on the differing approach taken in evaluating a chance.

[1113] In *Bristol & West Building Society v Mothew* [1998] Ch. 1, the Court of Appeal held that where a client sued his solicitor for negligently giving him incorrect advice or information (rather than failing to give him proper advice), the client did not have to show that he would not have acted as he did if he had been given the proper advice or correct information but merely that he had relied on the incorrect advice or information. Millett LJ said as follows:

> "In considering the issue of causation in an action for negligence brought by a client against his solicitor it appears from *Downs v Chappell* that it is necessary to distinguish between two different kinds of case. Where a client sues his solicitor for having negligently failed to give him proper advice, he must show what advice he should have been given and (on a balance of probability) that if such advice had been given he would not have entered into the relevant transaction or would not have entered into it on the terms he did. The same applies where the client's complaint is that the solicitor failed in his duty to give him material information .... Where, however, a client sues his solicitor for having negligently given him incorrect advice or for having negligently given him incorrect information, the position appears to be different. In such a case it is sufficient for the plaintiff to prove that he relied on the advice or information, that is to say, that he would not have acted as he did if he had not been given such advice or information. It is not necessary for him to prove that he would not have acted as he did if he had been given the proper advice or the correct information. This was the position in *Downs v Chapell* [1997] 1 W.L.R. 426."

Hobhouse LJ subsequently suggested Millett LJ's interpretation was wrong in *Swindle v Harrison* [1997] 4 All E.R. 705 at 728. Millett LJ's interpretation is also criticised by J. O'Sullivan in "Acts, omissions and negligence professionals: confusion over counterfactuals" (2001) 17 P.N. 272. In *White v Paul Davidson & Taylor (A Firm)* [2004] EWCA Civ 1511; [2005] P.N.L.R. 15, the Court of Appeal held that in order to establish causation, it was necessary for the clamant to prove that if the proper advice had been given, he would have acted differently and it was not sufficient merely to prove that he relied on his solicitor's advice in acting as he did. However, the court was content to apply the *Mothew* distinction, despite scepticism about whether it was correct, observing that every case of giving incorrect advice necessarily involved a failure to give proper advice. The Court of Appeal also made clear that the special policy reasons in *Chester v Afshar* [2005] 1 A.C. 134, where the House of Lords afforded a remedy to a claimant who could not satisfy traditional causation principles, did not apply in professional negligence claims outside clinical negligence.

(ii)   Foreseeability

General rules

Replace footnote 1133 with:

[1133] [2015] EWCA Civ 1146; [2016] 2 W.L.R. 1351. For commentary see A. Taylor: "Whither Remoteness? Wellesley Partners LLP v Withers LLP" (2016) 79 M.L.R. 679 and I. Matthews: "Understanding the relationship between duties in contract and the tort of negligence" (2019) 35 P.N. 155. *Wellesley* was subsequently applied in *Agouman v Leigh Day (A Firm)* [2016] EWHC 1324 (QB) and in *Wright v Lewis Silkin LLP* [2016] EWCA Civ 1308; [2017] P.N.L.R. 16. In the latter case, negligent advice on jurisdiction in an employment contract providing £10m in the event of the employee claimant's constructive dismissal caused the delay of English proceedings, during which time the guarantor became insolvent. The loss of the chance to enforce the judgment against the guarantor was not foreseeable. While *Wellesley* was not cited, applying contractual principles claimants recovered for the loss of a chance of obtaining rental income from some alternative property investment from the property investment they should have been advised not to enter in *Leggett v Giambrone Law LLP (In Liquidation)* [2020] EWHC 724 (QB); [2020] P.N.L.R. 18.

11-254

(iii)   The Scope of the Duty

The principle

After paragraph 11-258, add new paragraphs 11-258A and 11-258B:

11-258A   In *Hughes-Holland v BPE Solicitors*[1152A] the Supreme Court considered for the first time the scope of duty in relation to a claim against solicitors. The claimant businessman agreed to lend £200,000 to a builder and developer on the understanding that the loan was to be used to develop the buildings on the secured property, when in fact it was used to purchase the building by a special purpose vehicle. The solicitors negligently confirmed the claimant's misunderstanding of the purpose of the loan, and if they had not the client would not have proceeded with the transaction, in which he lost all his money. The Supreme Court, in the sole judgment of Lord Sumption, applied *SAAMCO*, and held that it was an information case, the loan would have been lost even if the monies had been applied to the development of the property, and the claimant could not recover damages from the defendant.

[1152A]   [2017] UKSC 21; [2018] A.C. 599.

11-258B   Four points from the judgment of Lord Sumption are particularly important. First, a valuer or a conveyancer will rarely supply more than information. The information/advice distinction should be understood as distinguishing cases where the professional contributes a limited part of the material on which the client will rely in deciding to enter a transaction from those where he has a duty to consider all relevant matters in deciding whether the client should do so. In this regard, the fact that the professional's advice is critical does not turn it into an advice case. Secondly, if the information which has not been provided would have shown that the transaction was not viable, or reveals an actual or potential fraud, then this does not make the case an advice one, overruling a previous line of cases.[1152B] Thirdly, Lord Sumption approved Lord Hoffmann's principle in *SAAMCO* that a professional is not responsible for losses which would have occurred even if the information had been correct, adding that the maximum measure of the professional's liability is the increased risk to which he exposed the client. Fourthly, the claimant must plead and has the burden of proof in showing what loss was within the scope of the defendant professional's duty.[1152C]

[1152B]   Discussed at para.11-315.

[1152C]   For a commentaries see: H. Evans: "Solicitors and the scope of duty in the Supreme Court" (2017) 33 P.N. 193; D. Ryan "SAAMCO re-explored: BPE and the law of professional negligence" (2018) 34 P.N. 71; and J. Thomson: "SAMCO revisited" [2017] C.L.J. 476.

Solicitors generally provide information and not advice

Replace paragraph 11-259 (to incorporate new text following "in the property." at the end of the paragraph) with:

11-259   It is submitted that solicitors advising in commercial transactions, like other professional advisers, are generally under a duty to provide specific information or advice, and not to advise on the wisdom of transactions in general, and thus the loss for which they are responsible will be limited to the consequences of the specific information or advice being accurate. Of course the facts of any particular case may show that the solicitor is under a wider duty to advise on the wisdom of the transaction as a whole. In *Cottingham v Attey Bower & Jones (A Firm)*,[1153] Rimer J expressly agreed with this statement, and added that there were no fundamentally different considerations in a domestic conveyancing transaction. In that case, solicitors acting for vendors of property failed to obtain a copy of building regulations consent for substantial renovations which had never in fact been granted. As the duty was only to provide information, the solicitors were liable for the overpayment due to defects which had not been noted in the survey report which the claimants had obtained and which assumed that building regulations had been complied with, but not for all the defects identified in the property. In *Hughes-Holland v BPE Solicitors*[1153A] the Supreme Court confirmed that a conveyancer will rarely supply more than information.

[1153] [2000] P.N.L.R. 557. cf. *Michael Gerson Investments Ltd v Haines Watts (A Firm)* [2002] P.N.L.R. 34, noted at para.11-260 below.

[1153A] [2017] UKSC 21; [2018] A.C. 599. But see *Various Claimants v Giambrone and Law (A Firm)* [2017] EWCA Civ 1193; [2018] P.N.L.R. 2.

Recovery of the whole loss

Replace paragraph 11-260 (to incorporate new text after "to giving information." at the end of the fourth sentence and new text following the quotation ending "of its loss.") with:

Claimants have recovered the whole of their loss in broadly three categories of cases. First, in some cases, the solicitors may be held to be providing advice about the transactions, and not merely information. Thus in *Carter v TG Baynes & Sons*,[1154] the defendant solicitors failed to note that there were restrictive covenants preventing development of the site which the plaintiff intended to purchase, and advised him to go ahead with the transaction. The plaintiff recovered for all foreseeable losses, including those resulting from a fall in the market, as the advice had been to proceed with the works, and it was not limited to giving information. In *Various Claimants v Giambrone and Law (A Firm)*[1154A] purchasers paid large deposits for an Italian development, which was in fact never completed, and they lost their deposits. Their Anglo-Italian solicitors failed to advise them that the developer's bank guarantees did not comply with Italian law or that the contract was inadequate in failing to provide for termination for delay, failed to undertake due diligence which they had agreed to do, and other breaches. The deposit monies were paid away by the solicitors, and the Court of Appeal upheld the judge's decision that the damages were the lost deposit. Applying the scope of duty principle, and taking into account the decision in *Hughes-Holland v BPE*, the solicitors were guiding the whole decision-making process. Secondly, the whole loss has been recovered in claims where the reliability of the borrower should have been reported to the claimant. In *Portman Building Society v Bevan Ashford (A Firm)*,[1155] a solicitor failed to report matters relating to the borrower's financial condition to the lender and was liable for the whole lost. The Court of Appeal stated:

> "... where a negligent solicitor fails to provide information which shows that the transaction is not viable or which tends to reveal an actual or potential fraud on the part of the borrowers, the lender is entitled to recover the whole of its loss."[1156]

This dictum has been expressly overruled by the Supreme Court in *Hughes-Holland v BPE Solicitors*,[1156A] and this second category of cases where claimants may recover their whole loss no longer exists. Thirdly, there may be some further cases where the scope of the duty may include all of the losses suffered by the claimant. In *McLoughlin v Jones*,[1157] the claimant alleged that as a result of the

11-260

defendant solicitors' negligent handling of his criminal trial he was imprisoned, which caused his psychiatric illness. The Court of Appeal held that it was arguable that the purpose of the defendants' engagement was to minimise the risks of wrongful conviction and of suffering psychiatric illness. They applied the tests of the scope or purpose of the duty, the assumption of responsibility, and the tripartite test of foreseeability, proximity and justice and reasonableness.

¹¹⁵⁴ [1998] E.G.C.S. 109 Ch. D. In *Kirkton Investments Ltd v VMH LLP* [2011] CSOH 200; [2012] P.N.L.R. 11 solicitors negligently advised developers that they had a legally enforceable right to erect a flue which was necessary for a development, and after a dispute arose that they had a strong case, and as a result the development was delayed. Lord Doherty held that the advice was not merely the provision of information, and the solicitors were held liable for the losses sustained from the downturn of the property market, but he also relied on the mitigation exception, see para.11-258. Similarly, a claim by developers for losses caused by the fall in the market was not struck out in *Henderson (t/a Henderson Group Development) v Wotherspoon* [2013] CSOH 113; [2013] P.N.L.R. 28. cf. *Michael Gerson Investments Ltd v Haines Watts (A Firm)* [2002] P.N.L.R. 34 it was alleged that the defendant solicitors, by releasing documents in a tax saving scheme, impliedly advised that good title was available for the containers which underlay the scheme. The solicitors gave no tax advice but were only concerned with the question of good title. Rimer J held that it was arguable that they gave advice rather than information, and were responsible for the wasted expenditure of the scheme which failed. In *Rosbeg Partners Ltd v L.K.Shields (A Firm)* [2018] IESC 23; [2018] P.N.L.R. 26 solicitors negligently failed to register title to land as a result of which a sale was lost, and the market value of the land then fell. The Supreme Court of Ireland held that the loss for which the solicitors were responsible was the cost of remedying the defect by registering the land, and the loss in value from the fall in the market until the point when the defect could reasonably have been remedied.

¹¹⁵⁴ᴬ [2017] EWCA Civ 1193; [2018] P.N.L.R. 2. The decision has been questioned, see P Davies: "Equitable compensation and the SAAMCO principle" (2018) 134 L.Q.R. 165.

¹¹⁵⁵ [2000] P.N.L.R. 344, and see *Clack v Wrigleys Solicitors LLP* [2013] EWHC 413 (Ch); (2013) 163 N.L.J. 17 and *Morkot v Watson & Brown Solicitors* [2014] EWHC 3439 (QB); [2015] P.N.L.R. 9. The distinction between information and advice, and the scope of the solicitor's duty, has also been explored in cases where lenders have sued the solicitors they instructed, which are summarised at paras 11-314 onwards.

¹¹⁵⁶ See further para.11-315.

¹¹⁵⁶ᴬ [2017] UKSC 21; [2018] A.C. 599.

¹¹⁵⁷ [2002] Q.B. 1312.

Cases limiting damages to losses within the scope of duty

Replace paragraph 11-261 (to incorporate amendments to footnotes 1159 and 1163) with:

11-261   Four Court of Appeal cases concerning a variety of factual circumstances have limited damages to those within the scope of duty. In *Pearson v Sanders Witherspoon*,¹¹⁵⁹ the defendant solicitors were negligent in failing to prosecute their client's action timeously against Ferranti, which went into administration. The Court of Appeal held that (a) a solicitor's duty when conducting litigation is to act with all due expedition and not to cause delays which resulted in the loss of the right of action, and (b) an inability to enforce a judgment is not within the scope of the solicitor's duty, unless such duty was expressly assumed by the solicitor, or the solicitor was given sufficient notice of the impecuniosity of the original defendant to make it fair, just and reasonable to extend the duty. In *Jenmain v Steed & Steed*,¹¹⁶⁰ the defendant solicitors acted for the vendors in a contract race. They were also retained by the claimants, who were some of the proposed purchasers, in a limited capacity which the court found required the solicitors to pass on the fact that they were also dealing with another proposed purchaser. The purpose of the duty, based on r.6A of the Solicitors' Practice Rules 1990, was to avoid purchasers incurring wasted costs in proceeding towards completion in ignorance of a contracts race. The judge found the claimant purchasers would have obtained the property if properly advised by the defendants. The Court of Appeal held that they could recover any wasted costs and also the difference between the price they would have paid and the value of the property. However, they could not recover the profits they would have made from the proposed development of the property. In *Petersen v Personal Representatives of Rivlin*,[1161] the claimant purchased property which was subject to litigation with a neighbour, and in respect of which he gave an indemnity for 90% of any liability and of the costs of the proceedings from the date of the contract. The defendant solicitor negligently failed to explain the indemnity provision properly, and the claimant would have withdrawn from the transaction if it had been explained. The failure to advise was a failure to provide information, and the claimant's claim for the vendors' legal fees in the proceedings with the neighbour were not within the scope of the duty, as he did understand and accept that the indemnity applied to costs liabilities incurred by the vendors after the exchange of contracts. In *Haugesund Kommune v Depfa ACS Bank*,[1162] the defendant bank obtained no contractual rights against the claimant municipalities in swaps transactions, as they were ultra vires, and the third party lawyers were negligent in failing to advise about this. However, no damages were recovered because the bank's loss resulted from the municipalities' impecuniosity. That loss was not within the scope of the duty broken. The Court of Appeal distinguished *Portman Building Society v Bevan Ashford (A Firm)*,[1163] as there was a difference between failing to advise a lender about a borrower who was lying about the equity he was putting into a property, and failing to advise about an honest borrower's capacity to enter into a transaction.[1164] Nor was it an "advice" rather than an "information" case.[1165]

[1159] [2000] P.N.L.R. 110. Similarly, in *Wright v Lewis Silkin LLP* [2016] EWCA Civ 1308; [2017] P.N.L.R. 16, the lost chance of enforcement was not within the scope of the solicitors' duty where negligent advice was given on jurisdiction in an employment contract providing payment to the employee claimant if he were constructively dismissed, and the English proceedings were delayed as a result of arguments about jurisdiction, during which time the guarantor became insolvent. In *Ahmad v Wood* [2018] EWHC 996 (QB); [2018] P.N.L.R. 28, it was held that the correct measure of damages for negligence in conducting litigation was the value of the chance of obtaining a better result, and claims for further consequential loss such as the equity in property transferred to settle enforcement proceedings, were struck out.

[1160] [2000] P.N.L.R. 616. cf. *Joyce v Bowman Law Ltd* [2010] EWHC 251 (Ch); [2010] P.N.L.R. 22, and *Watts v Bell & Scott, WS* [2007] CSOH 108; 2007 S.L.T. 665; [2007] P.N.L.R. 30, noted at para.11-291, where compensation for loss of profits was awarded, and *Keydon Estates Ltd v Eversheds LLP* [2005] EWHC 972; [2005] P.N.L.R. 40, noted at para.11-291 where the hypothetical rents from another suitable property would have been awarded.

[1161] [2002] Lloyd's Rep. P.N. 386.

[1162] [2011] EWCA Civ 33; [2011] P.N.L.R. 14; [2011] 3 All E.R. 655.

[1163] [2000] P.N.L.R. 344, supra. *Portman Building Society v Bevan Ashford (A Firm)* has been overruled by the Supreme Court in *Hughes-Holland v BPE Solicitors* [2017] UKSC 21; [2018] A.C. 599.

[1164] [2011] EWCA Civ 33; [2011] P.N.L.R. 14; [2011] 3 All E.R. 655 at [61].

[1165] ibid. at [74]; Gross LJ at [101] considered that it did not matter which type of case it was.

(c) Measure of Damages at Common Law

(ii) Credit for Benefits

General principle

Replace footnote 1185 with:

[1185] See also the discussion of IFA cases at paras 15-088 onwards. See also *Fulton Shipping Inc of Panama v Globalia Business Travel SAU of Spain* [2015] EWCA Civ 1299; [2016] 1 W.L.R. 2450 at   **11-265**

[23], overturned on the facts by the Supreme Court [2017] UKSC 43; [2017] 1 W.L.R. 2581, a case which did not concern solicitors, cited by the Court of Appeal in *Bacciottini v Gotelee & Goldsmith* [2016] EWCA Civ 170; [2016] 4 W.L.R. 98 at [49], and *LSREF III Wight Ltd v Gateley LLP* [2016] EWCA Civ 359; [2016] P.N.L.R. 21 at [40], on which see para.11-292 below. In both of those cases the benefits of mitigation (or which would have arisen but for the failure to mitigate) were taken into account. On collateral benefits, see also *Swynson Ltd v Lowick Rose LLP* [2017] UKSC 32; [2018] A.C. 313, where loans were made by the claimant S to E relying on a due diligence report by the defendant accountants. The repayment of the loans to E funded by S's owner were not treated as collateral benefits.

(iii)   Evaluation of a Chance

What a third party would have done

Replace footnote 1194 with:

11-270   1194   [1995] 1 W.L.R. 1602. Approved by the Supreme Court in *Perry v Raleys* [2019] UKSC 5; [2019] 2 W.L.R. 636.

Broad-brush assessments of the loss of a chance

Replace footnote 1196 with:

11-271   1196   See also: *Abraxas Computer Services Ltd v Rabin Leacock Lipman (A Firm)* [2000] E.G.C.S. 70; N.P.C. 63 QBD (due to the defendants' negligence, the claimant had limited time to resolve its accommodation needs, and lost the chance of obtaining a better deal on some other property equivalent to that into which it did move, damages assessed at 35% of the difference between what the claimant paid and the offer from an alternative bidder); *Finley v Connell Associates (A Firm)* [2002] Lloyd's Rep. P.N. 62 (if properly advised, development 60% likely to commence by May 1990, profits reduced by £30,000 if development started later, damages reduced by £12,000); *Football League Ltd v Edge Ellison (A Firm)* [2006] EWHC 1462 (Ch); [2007] P.N.L.R. 2, Rimer J (were liability established, 70% chance of obtaining guarantees to £160m, and 50% for the remaining £155m); *Motor Crown Petroleum Ltd v SJ Berwin Co* [2000] Lloyd's Rep. P.N. 438 CA (40% chance of obtaining planning permission if the solicitors had challenged in time the local council's designation of the land on which they wished to build a petrol station as open countryside); *Rey v Graham & Oldham (A Firm)* [2000] B.P.I.R. 354, McKinnon J (failure to apply for an adjournment of bankruptcy proceedings, 80% chance of avoiding bankruptcy, damages reduced by 20%); *Talisman Property Co (UK) Ltd v Norton Rose (A Firm)* [2006] EWCA Civ 1104; [2006] 3 E.G.L.R. 59 (notice served wrongly opposing the grant of a new tenancy, in relation to loss of rent and loss of capital 35% chance of tenant going to counsel on the status of its own tenancy and then reaching agreement on new tenancy, plus 50% chance of avoiding statutory compensation); *Wright v Lewis Silkin LLP* [2015] EWHC 1897 (QB); [2015] P.N.L.R. 32 (on a failure to advise on a jurisdiction clause in an employment contract, causing a delay in subsequent proceedings as jurisdiction was challenged, there was a 20% chance of enforcement before the employer became insolvent); reversed on appeal, [2016] EWCA Civ 1308; [2017] P.N.L.R. 16, on the basis that the loss of the chance of enforcement was neither foreseeable nor within the scope of the solicitors' duty); *Commodities Research Unit International (Holdings) Ltd v King & Wood Mallesons LLP* [2016] EWHC 727 (QB); [2016] P.N.L.R. 29 (if proper advice had been given on a term in an employment contract there was a 35% chance of avoiding vesting the remaining 25% of an incentive in the CEO employee); *Trillium Motor World Ltd v Cassels Brock & Blackwell LLP* [2017] ONCA 544; (2017) 41 CCLT (4th) 177 (55% chance of dealers negotiating increased payments from termination of dealerships to $218m, rather than the $143.5m offered); *Leggett v Giambrone Law LLP (In Liquidation)* [2020] EWHC 724 (QB); [2020] P.N.L.R. 18 (75% prospect of obtaining rental income from an alternative property investment).

Detailed assessments of the loss of a chance

Replace footnote 1200 with:

11-272   1200   [1997] N.P.C. 49 QBD. See also *Joyce v Bowman Law Ltd* [2010] EWHC 251 (Ch); [2010] P.N.L.R. 22 (29% chance of developing property based on 85% chance of obtaining option to purchase from third party, 50% chance of obtaining planning permission, and 85% chance of funding development); *Kirton Investments Ltd v VMH LLP* [2011] CSOH 200; [2012] P.N.L.R. 11 (a development was delayed beyond the fall in the market, and the Judge held there was a 40% chance of selling all the town houses, 60% of selling the apartments, and 55% of selling sufficient properties to clear the bank indebtedness before the market turned down). In *Xenakis v Birkett Long LLP (A Firm)* [2014] EWHC 171 (QB); [2014] P.N.L.R. 16 negligence in failing to advise that going into occupation and releasing documents to the landlord before completion caused the claimants to be liable under a guarantee for nearly a year longer than they had contemplated due to the delays in completing the lease, and there was a 50% chance of renegotiating the terms and an 80% chance of getting the lease completed earlier. In *Wellesley Partners*

LLP v Withers LLP [2014] EWHC 556 (Ch); [2014] P.N.L.R. 22 solicitors negligently drafted an agreement for an LLP giving a bank the ability to withdraw monies within 41 months rather than after 42 months, as a result of which profits were lost, including a 15% chance of being awarded a sole mandate from a bank in New York and a 45% chance of a half mandate. This was upheld on appeal, [2015] EWCA Civ 1146; [2016] 2 W.L.R. 1351 (save that the partner's time for dealing with the dispute was increased from one to four months). In *Moda International Brands Ltd v Gateley LLP* [2019] EWHC 1326 (QB); [2019] P.N.L.R. 568 the claimant had agreed to sell land to M for redevelopment in return for 35% of the profits, but the defendant solicitors did not include part of the land in the development agreement. The judge assessed the prospects of the parties actually reaching a binding agreement to include the land in that agreement on a sliding basis where there was (1) a 50% chance of agreeing a 35% profit share, (2) a 30% chance of agreeing a 17.5% profit share, and (3) a 20% chance of no agreement. Applying the first two figures, he found that the claimant had lost 22.5% of the entire profits. The fact that the third party, M, had given evidence did not alter the fact that the matter was to be assessed on the basis of the loss of a chance.

The limits of the principle

Replace footnote 1211 with:

[1211] *Cancer Research Campaign v Ernest Brown & Co* [1998] P.N.L.R. 592 at 604 (where Harman J found that the claimant had not proved that the testator may have acted differently; for a contrary view of what the judge found, see J. Murphy, "Probate solicitors, disappointed beneficiaries and the tortious duty to advise on tax avoidance'" (1998) 14 P.N. 107). Similarly, in *Feltham v Freer Bouskell* [2013] EWHC 1952 (Ch); [2013] W.T.L.R. 1363 (in that case the lost chance was 100%). But, in *Shah v Forsters LLP* [2017] EWHC 2433 (Ch); [2018] P.N.L.R. 8, in a claim brought by executors, it was held, obiter, that the claimants have to prove that, with different advice, the deceased would have acted differently on the balance of probabilities.

11-275

(d)   Heads of Damage

(ii)   Difference in Value of Property

The normal rule

Replace footnote 1242 with:

[1242] [1996] 1 P.N.L.R. 361. The court held that here were no special circumstances requiring a later date of assessment. For further examples see *Lake v Bushby* [1949] 2 All E.R. 964 KBD: property less valuable by reason of the absence of planning permission for the bungalow standing on it. The diminution was assessed at £100; *Piper v Daybell Court-Cooper & Co* (1969) 210 E.G. 1047, Nield J: property less valuable by reason of a right of way running across it. Diminution assessed at £200; *Collard v Saunders* (1972) 221 E.G. 797, Mocatta J: property less valuable by reason of defects. Diminution assessed at £250; *Trask v Clark & Sons* [1980] C.L.Y.B. 2588, Talbot J: a footpath ran across plaintiff's property, diminution assessed at £1,500; *Walker v Giffen Couch & Archer* [1988] E.G.C.S. 64, Peter Gibson J: diminution in value from a public footpath through property assessed at £8,000; *Twidale v Bradley* [1990] 2 Qd. R. 464, Queensland Supreme Court: a grocery business was less valuable without secure title of premises; *Owen v Fielding* [1998] E.G.C.S. 110, Steel J: diminution in value assessed at 20% as part of the land was subject to rights of common; *Greymalkin Ltd v Copleys (A Firm)* [2004] EWHC 1155 (Ch); [2004] P.N.L.R. 44; [2004] EWCA Civ 1754; [2005] P.N.L.R. 20: diminution of £45,000 awarded for three charges on title of hotel. *644036 Alberta Inc. v Cameron Horne Law Office* 2011 ABQB 708; (2012) 343 D.L.R. (4th) 756: solicitors failed to obtain part of property purchased; diminution in value of the whole property, after subsequent division of titles (less sums received from subsequent foreclosure).

11-285

(iii)   Loss of Opportunity to Bring Proceedings

Claimant's claim statute-barred: *Kitchen*

Replace footnote 1283 with:

[1283] [1958] 1 W.L.R. 563. The general approach was approved by the Supreme Court in *Perry v Raleys Solicitors* [2019] UKSC 5; [2019] 2 W.L.R. 636 esp. at [32] and [34].

11-294

After paragraph 11-294, add new paragraph 11-294A:

11-294A **The two stage test** In *Perry v Raleys*[1284A] the Supreme Court made it clear that there was a two stage test, consistent with *Allied Maples Group Ltd v Simmons & Simmons*.[1284B] First the claimant has to prove on the balance of probabilities that he would have brought the relevant claim in time. Secondly, the value of the claim will be assessed on the basis of the loss of a chance. But at the first stage, the claim would have to be an honest one. In that case the claimant claimed that as a result of his solicitors' negligence he had lost a "service award" (for inability to carry out domestic tasks) in the vibration white finger claim brought by miners. However, the subsequent claim against the solicitors failed as the claimant could not have made an honest claim for a service award.

[1284A] [2019] UKSC 5; [2019] 2 W.L.R. 636, esp at [20]–[26].

[1284B] [1995] 1 W.L.R. 1602, on which see paras 11-270 et seq.

The general approach

Replace footnote 1288 with:

11-295 [1288] See, e.g. *Melanson v Cochrane Sargeant, Nicholson Paterson* (1968) 68 N.B.R. (2d) 370 New Brunswick CA and *Rose v Mitton* (1994) 111 D.L.R. 217 Nova Scotia CA. But see *Fisher v Knibbe* (1992) 3 Alta. L.R. (3d) 97 and see *Jarbeau v McLean* [2017] ONCA 114; (2017) 410 D.L.R. (4th) 246.P.

Presumption in favour of the claimant

Replace footnote 1289 with:

11-296 [1289] [1998] P.N.L.R. 493. This dictum has been cited and relied on in a large number subsequent lost litigation cases, e.g. *Sharif v Garrett & Co (A Firm)* [2001] EWCA Civ 1269; [2002] 1 W.L.R. 3118 and *Sharpe v Addison* [2003] EWCA Civ 1189; [2004] P.N.L.R. 23, and approved by the Supreme Court in *Perry v Raleys Solicitors* [2019] UKSC 5; [2019] 2 W.L.R. 636 esp. at [34].

No trial within a trial

Replace paragraph 11-299 with:

11-299 It might be thought, consistent with Lord Evershed MR's dictum in *Kitchen v Royal Air Force Association*,[1300] and with *Sharif v Garrett & Co (A Firm)*,[1301] that where a fair trial is possible, the original action should be tried in the normal way, and the loss of chance approach should not be followed. Two cases make it clear that this is not correct.[1302] In *Hanif v Middleweeks*,[1303] the claimant's counterclaim against his insurers for an indemnity for the loss of his night club by fire was struck out. In the professional negligence action, the judge determined that the claimant had only a 25% chance of proving that his co-owner[1303A] had not set fire to the nightclub. The Court of Appeal held that the judge had and should have determined the chances of proving the claimant's co-owner's dishonesty in the original action rather than whether the claimant had in fact set fire to his property.[1304] The court stated that the fact of delay or absence of witnesses was only one set of reasons why the court assesses the prospects of success on a percentage basis, and only if the evidence or law showed that the prospects were overwhelming or negligible would a claim be assessed at 100% or nothing. Other reasons included the fact that other witnesses may have been called at a notional trial, the judge at the notional trial may have taken a different view of the matter, and that account should be taken of the prospects of settlement.[1305] Following that analysis, Rix LJ held in *Dixon v Clement Jones Solicitors (A Firm)*[1306] that:

"there is no requirement in such a loss of a chance case to fight out a trial within a trial, indeed the authorities show as a whole that is what should be avoided. It is the prospects and not the hypothetical decision in the lost trial that have to be investigated."

That case concerned lost litigation against accountants, where the judge assessed the value of the lost claim at 30% because he thought that the claimant would on balance have pressed on with what turned out to be a disastrous business venture even if the accountants had given her the negative advice they should have done. The Court of Appeal upheld this conclusion. However, in *Perry v Raleys*[1306A] the Supreme Court reserved its position as to whether causation in the underlying claim had to be determined on loss of chance principles when the key question in that underlying claim related to the claimant's own acts rather than those of a third party.

[1300] [1958] 1 W.L.R. 563.

[1301] [2001] EWCA Civ 1269; [2002] 1 W.L.R. 3118.

[1302] cf. the approach in Alberta. In *Fisher v Knibbe* (1992) 3 Alta. L.R. (3d) 97 the Court of Appeal considered that the plaintiff would be awarded the value of the lost opportunity, rather than 100% of the lost damages or nominal damages, only where a "trial within a trial" was impossible. In that case, the trial judge had decided that the original defendant was not negligent, and thus only nominal damages were awarded. The decision was applied in *Stealth Enterprises Ltd v Hoffman Dorchik* [2003] ABCA 58; [2003] 5 W.W.R. 205 Alberta CA. However, in *Henderson v Hagblom* 2003 SKCA 40; [2003] 7 W.W.R. 590, the Saskatchewan Court of Appeal rejected that approach in favour of the English one.

[1303] [2000] Lloyd's Rep. P.N. 920.

[1303A] The dishonesty was by the co-owner, and thus the claimant could honestly bring a counterclaim and thus had lost something of value, see *Perry v Raleys Solicitors* [2019] UKSC 5; [2019] 2 W.L.R. 636 esp. at [35]–[36].

[1304] Similarly, the claim should not be denied on public policy grounds as the judge had not found that the claimant had been the arsonist.

[1305] [2000] Lloyd's Rep. P.N. 920 at [13]-[15], [21] and [56]. cf. the remarks of Smith LJ in *Dudarec v Andrews* [2006] EWCA Civ 256; [2006] 1 W.L.R. 3002 at [60] that when the only issue is quantum and the evidence before the trial judge is substantially the same as would have been available at the notional trial, the judge should simply assess the damages on the basis of that evidence.

[1306] [2004] EWCA Civ 1005; [2005] P.N.L.R. 6 at [27].

[1306A] [2019] UKSC 5; [2019] 2 W.L.R. 636 at [39]–[40].

Examples of the evaluation

Replace footnote 1308 with:

[1308] [1997] 3 All E.R. 909. cf. *Folland v Reardon* (2005) 249 D.L.R. (4th) 167 where the Ontario Court of Appeal held that a plaintiff who had been wrongly convicted and imprisoned allegedly as a result of his lawyer's negligence would have to prove on the balance of probabilities that he would have avoided that result if his lawyers had acted competently. Quaere whether *Acton* was correctly decided in the light of *Perry v Raleys Solicitors* [2019] UKSC 5; [2019] 2 W.L.R. 636, on which see para.11-294A above.

11-300

The lower threshold

Replace footnote 1317 with:

[1317] See the following examples. A claim in relation to libel and related actions where the claim form expired before service was struck out as the underlying claims were unsustainable in *Al-Ruby v Quist Solicitors* [2007] EWHC 2297 (QB); [2007] Lloyd's Rep. P.N. 35. In *Jemma Trust Co Ltd v Kippax Beaumont Lewis* [2005] EWCA Civ 248; [2005] W.T.L.R. 533, the deceased's landed estate was left to his nephew upon trust for life for his wife, who suffered from severe senile dementia, and then his nephew. The executors decided to mitigate liability to inheritance tax on the wife's death by advancing a sum to her on her releasing her life interest, and an application was made to the Court of Protection to enable this, which was opposed, but the opposition was withdrawn when the sum offered increased to £750,000. The solicitors were negligent in failing to deal properly with the opponents, failing to obtain an actuarial report, and failing to make the application timeously. However, it was pure speculation that, but for the negligence, the opposition to the application would have been withdrawn for any smaller

11-302

price, and the claimant failed to obtain any damages. In *Miller v Garton Shires (A Firm)* [2006] EWCA Civ 1386; [2007] P.N.L.R. 11, the claimant's claim against the lawyers for allowing his personal injury claim to become statute-barred was struck out, as the original claim would have failed, and thus the claimant had suffered no loss. In *Nichols v Warner Scarborough, Herman & Harvey* 2009 BCCA 277; (2009) 95 B.C.L.R. (4th) 133, there was no prospect of success in a claim by an injured motorcyclist against the owners of a pole by the road into which he crashed. In *Webb v Birkett* 2011 ABCA 13; [2011] 3 W.W.R. 20, the plaintiff was unable to show that the further information which her solicitors should have obtained would have led to a better settlement. In *Ladner v Wolfson* 2011 BCCA 370; (2012) 343 D.L.R. (4th) 299 it was held that the alleged failure to pursue a claim for a constructive trust failed because there was no basis to pursue such a claim. In *Waraich v Ansari Solicitors (A Firm)* [2019] EWHC 1038 (Comm); [2019] P.N.L.R. 24 the claimants only recovered nominal damages for failing to issue proceedings against solicitors in time concerning the negligent handling of their application for leave to remain, as there was only a speculative chance that they would have been granted further leave to remain any earlier.

Cost of the original action

Replace footnote 1332 with:

11-305   [1332] See further H. Evans, *Lawyers' Liabilities*, 2nd edn (2002), Ch.11, and ibid., "Damages for solicitors' negligence: (1) the loss of litigation" (1991) 7 P.N. 201, where further dicta are cited. For an argument that insufficient attention is paid to the impact of costs on uncertain litigation in valuing bungled litigation, see, ibid. "Bungled litigation and costs" (2019) 35 P.N. 87. The point may develop a different significance in the context of conditional fee agreements. For further illustrations see *McNamara v Martin Mears & Co* (1983) S.J. 69 where Peter Pain J gave a discount of a third from the award of £12,000 "for the costs and hazards of litigation, and for the acceleration of payment." and *Thompson v Howley* [1977] 1 N.Z.L.R. 1 at 27, where Somers J held that the plaintiff would have won his case, and deducted a sum of $150 for irrecoverable costs, apparently on the agreement of counsel.

The prospects of settlement

Replace footnote 1339 with:

11-306   [1339] [2000] Lloyd's Rep. P.N. 89; see para.11-301 for the facts. In *Hanbury v Hugh James Solicitors* [2019] EWHC 1074 (QB); [2019] P.N.L.R. 25 Yip J valued the lost chance of a claim against several employers for negligently exposing the deceased to asbestos causing him lung cancer. She concluded that there were good prospects of the claim succeeding at trial and as a result the claim was highly likely to have settled. The judge rejected multiple discounts relating tor the chance of counsel advising in favour of the issue of proceedings, and then of obtaining supportive engineering evidence as those discounts were effectively for the same risks in valuing the lost litigation.

The significance of the notional date of trial

Replace paragraph 11-309 (to incorporate new text following "on that footing." at the end of the paragraph) with:

11-309   The principles discussed above have been qualified by the Court of Appeal in three cases. In *Charles v Hugh James Jones & Jenkins (A Firm)*,[1352] the plaintiff suffered personal injuries in a road accident in 1990, and the defendant solicitors negligently allowed her subsequent action to be struck out. The judge held that the original action would have been tried in January 1996, but in assessing damages he took into account evidence in relation to the deterioration of the claimant's condition obtained after that date. The Court of Appeal held the court should consider evidence of the claimant's condition which would have been available at the notional trial date, even if the evidence in fact only emerged later. Furthermore, if a condition was of uncertain prognosis at the notional trial date, but became clearer afterwards, it was appropriate to admit later evidence of what in fact happened.[1353] The court tentatively considered that evidence of some entirely new condition which manifested itself only after the notional trial date should not be admitted. In *Dudarec v Andrews*,[1354] the claimant was injured in a road traffic action, but his solicitors negligently delayed the action so that it was struck out for want of prosecution in 1996. He issued proceedings against his solicitors in 2002, and a preliminary issue was ordered to decide whether the claimant failed to mitigate his damage by not having an operation to correct an aneurism which he said prevented him working. A scan in 2004 showed that there was in fact no aneurism. The experts agreed that they would have wanted the 2004 scan performed in 1996 for the notional trial, and the Court of Appeal therefore held that it would not have been unreasonable in 1996 to refuse an operation for a problem that did not exist, and damages for loss of earnings were awarded until 2004. Smith LJ went on to agree with the comments made in *Charles*, and suggested that if the claimant died of unrelated causes between the notional and actual trial date, or won the lottery and gave up work, those matters should be taken into account. Finally, in *Whitehead v Searle*,[1355] PM gave birth to a child with spina bifida, and claimed that this should have been diagnosed antenatally and that she would have had a termination. The claim was progressed negligently slowly by the defendant solicitors, and PM committed suicide after the time at which the claim should have been brought to trial. In a claim brought by the estate, the Court of Appeal held that there would be a windfall if PM's death was ignored, and the court should not proceed to assess damages on that footing. In *Edwards v Hugh James Ford Simey (A Firm)*[1355A] the claimant claimed damages for negligent undersettlement by solicitors of a miners' claim for vibration white finger. The deceased miner had a potential claim for services in the underlying claim, as he was allegedly unable to undertake particular tasks due to his condition. The judge below assessed the value of the claim against the negligent solicitors on the basis of an expert's report made a decade after the original claim settled, which concluded that the deceased's condition was such that he did not require any assistance. The judge rejected the claim, as the deceased would have had an uncovenanted windfall if his services claim had succeeded, when it in fact had no value. The Court of Appeal reversed the decision. Under the settlement scheme of the original claims, services were assessed without the use of any medical evidence beyond the report which had already been obtained and which supported the deceased's claim. Subsequent medical evidence was therefore not relevant. Events after the notional trial which could not and would not have been known then should only alter the outcome if there was a significant or serious scale to the consequences of the supervening event. The Supreme Court dismissed a further appeal, but did not consider this last point.[1355B]

[1352] [2000] 1 W.L.R. 1278.

[1353] ibid. at 1290G, cf. 1295D–1295E per Swinton Thomas LJ, with whom Robert Walker LJ agreed, but Sir Richard Scott VC reserved his position. These comment were obiter see *Dudarec v Andrews* [2006] EWCA Civ 256; [2006] 1 W.L.R. 3002 at [33] per Waller LJ. They were doubted, obiter, by the Outer House in *Campbell v Imray* [2004] P.N.L.R. 1, where the potential problems with the reasoning were explained.

[1354] [2006] EWCA Civ 256; [2006] 1 W.L.R. 3002. For commentary see T. Dugdale, "Chance, Certainty and Risk" (2007) 23 P.N. 43, and more generally H. Evans, "Lost litigation and later knowledge" (2007) 23 P.N. 204.

[1355] [2008] EWCA Civ 285; [2009] 1 W.L.R. 549 (reported sub. nom. *Whitehead v Hibbert Pownall & Newton* [2008] P.N.L.R. 25). A similar result was reached, effectively on the grounds of remoteness, in *Witcombe v Talbot Olivier* [2011] WASCA 107; (2011) 280 A.L.R. 177.

[1355A] [2018] EWCA Civ 1299; [2018] P.N.L.R. 649. See H. Evans: "Valuing bungled litigation and later facts" (2019) 35 P.N. 75.

[1355B] [2019] UKSC 54; [2019] 1 W.L.R. 6549.

Interest after date of trial

Replace paragraph 11-310 (to incorporate new text following "by the courts." at the end of the paragraph) with:

11-310   If the claimant would have recovered damages at a particular date which has been assessed, then those damages would have attracted judgment debt interest thereafter if they had not been paid. The Court of Appeal decided in *Pinnock v Wilkins & Sons*[1356] that such interest is recoverable in an action against solicitors who have lost the plaintiffs' right of action by their negligence. However, in *Harrison v Bloom Camillin*,[1357] Neuberger J held that the appropriate rate of interest was a matter of discretion, and although many cases had awarded judgment rate interest, he considered it just to award the more flexible short-term investment rate. In *Nicholson v Knox Ukiwa & Co (A Firm)*,[1358] Saunders J held, obiter, that judgment rate was appropriate in that case where the delay was some 15 years, as it compensated in part for the fact that the claimant would have obtained a compound return on his damages, whereas only simple interest was awarded by the courts. In *Perry v Raleys Solicitors*[1358A] the Court of Appeal awarded interest at judgment rate because it more adequately compensated the claimant for being kept out of his money and because of the conduct of the defence of the claim.

[1356] *The Times,* 29 January 1990. See further, on the issue of interest, paras 3-024 onwards, above,

[1357] [2000] Lloyd's Rep. P.N. 404; see para.11-301 for the facts. Neuberger J's reasoning was followed, albeit not in the context of lost litigation, in *Griffiths v Last Cawthra Feather (A Firm)* [2002] P.N.L.R. 27 TCC. In *Browning v Brachers (A Firm)* [2004] EWHC 16 (QB); [2004] P.N.L.R. 28, Jack J awarded interest at the ordinary commercial rate, broadly reflecting the cost of the claimants' borrowings.

[1358] [2008] EWHC 1222 (QB); [2008] P.N.L.R. 33.

[1358A] [2017] EWCA Civ 314; [2017] P.N.L.R. 27. The Supreme Court ([2019] UKSC 5; [2019] 2 W.L.R. 636), allowed an appeal in the case, but did not discuss the question of interest.

(v)   Losses on Loans Secured by Mortgages

The basic calculation

Replace footnote 1363 with:

11-313   [1363] See the discussion in paras 10-147 and 10-166 et seq., above. For earlier cases see: *Wilson v Rowswell* (1970) 11 D.L.R. (3d) 737, Supreme Court of Canada; followed in *Collin Hotels Ltd v Surtees* [1988] 1 W.W.R. 272, Saskatchewan CA.

An exception: dishonest borrowers

Replace paragraph 11-315 with:

11-315   In one of the cases in *Bristol & West Building Society v Fancy & Jackson (A Firm)*,[1371]*Steggles Palmer*, Chadwick J held that the consequence of the solicitors' breach was that the plaintiff loaned money to a borrower whom they would not otherwise have wanted to lend to, as the circumstances of the loan were suspicious, and the defendants were held liable for the full amount of the plaintiff's loss (subject to mitigation and contributory negligence). Blackburne J adopted the same approach in the *Nationwide Building Society v Balmer Radmore (A Firm)* litigation.[1372] The approach of these two cases was approved by the Court of Appeal in *Portman Building Society v Bevan Ashford (A Firm)*,[1373] where the solicitor failed to report matters relating to the borrower's financial condition. As a result, the plaintiff thought that there was no second charge and that the borrower was paying the balance of the purchase from his own resources, when in fact he had no personal equity and had fraudulently deceived the lender. The plaintiff was entitled to recover its full loss. The Court of Appeal cast the relevant principle in very wide terms:

"... where a negligent solicitor fails to provide information which shows that the transaction is not viable or which tends to reveal an actual or potential fraud on the part of the borrowers, the lender is entitled to recover the whole of its loss."

This statement of principle has been followed by the Court of Appeal in *Lloyds Bank Plc v Crosse & Crosse*.[1374] All of the cases discussed in this paragraph where claimant lenders recovered their full loss from the solicitors have been overruled by the Supreme Court in *Hughes-Holland v BPE Solicitors*,[1375-1377] which expressly disapproved the dictum in *Portman Building Society v Bevan Ashford (A Firm)*. They all effectively gave full recovery in any claim where the claimant would not have entered a transaction if properly advised by the professional, whereas *SAAMCO* had rejected the distinction between no transaction and successful transaction cases.

[1371] [1997] 4 All E.R. 582. Contrast the *Colin Bishop* case.

[1372] [1999] P.N.L.R. 606. Thus the full loss was recovered in *Nationwide BS v JR Jones* [1999] Lloyd's Rep. P.N. 414. Contrast *Nationwide BS v ATM Abdullah* [1999] Lloyd's Rep PN 616.

[1373] [2000] P.N.L.R. 344.

[1374] [2001] P.N.L.R. 34.

[1375-1377] [2017] UKSC 21; [2018] A.C. 599.

(vi)   Loss of Some Other Financial Advantage

Diminution in value of shareholding and the reflective loss principle

Replace paragraph 11-321 with:

Shareholders and directors sometimes sue their company's solicitors for their **11-321** own losses. In many cases contractual or tortious duties will be owed to them by the solicitors, and they may seek to recover the diminution in value of their shareholdings. The circumstances in which they may do so was reviewed by the House of Lords in *Johnson v Gore Wood & Co (A Firm)*.[1386] However, that decision was recently re-examined by the Supreme Court in *Sevilleja v Marex Financial Ltd*,[1387] which was not a claim brought against solicitors. The majority decided held that it is necessary to distinguish between (a) cases which are brought by a shareholder in respect of loss he has suffered in that capacity, in the form of diminution of share value or distributions, which is the consequence of loss sustained by a company and in respect of which the company has a cause of action and (b) cases where claims are brought by a shareholder or anyone else (such as a creditor) which do not fall within that description, even if the company has a right of action in respect of the same loss. In respect of claims in class (a) a shareholder cannot bring proceedings because he has no legal or equitable interest in the company's assets and only the company has a cause of action. Although there may be cases where even a company's cause of action does not ensure that the value of a shareholder's shares is fully replenished or where a company declines to sue, the shareholder's remedies are confined to remedies such as a derivative action or unfair prejudice petition. Claims in class (b) by contrast, do not infringe principles of company autonomy. They might involve concerns about double recovery but this issue should be dealt with by other means (such as prioritising one claim over another, or subrogation).[1388-1389]

[1386] [2002] 2 A.C. 1. For the analogous Canadian position, see *Martin v Goldfarb* (1999) 41 O.R. (3d) 161. Note the extensive criticism of Lord Millett's speech in *Johnson v Gore Wood* in the judgment of the majority in *Sevilleja v Marex Financial Ltd* [2020] UKSC 21; [2020] 3 W.L.R. 255. The majority held that, properly understood, *Johnson v Gore Wood* is authority for the proposition that a shareholder is unable to sue for the recovery in the diminution in the value of his shareholding or the distributions he receives as shareholder, which flow from the loss suffered by the company in respect of which the company has a cause of action, even if the company has declined or filed to make good that loss.

[1387] [2020] UKSC 31; [2020] 3 W.L.R. 255.

[1388-1389] In *Webster v Sandersons Solicitors (A Firm)* [2009] EWCA Civ 830; [2009] P.N.L.R. 37. the Court of Appeal applied the then rule that the claimant shareholder could not recover losses which were merely reflective of the losses of the company, which encompassed all payments which the claimant might have obtained from the company. They held that this included dividends, losses to the company's pension fund and thus to the claimant's pension prospects, and a personal guarantee to the bank for the company's indebtedness. However, a claim for loss of income due to the company's collapse was arguable.

(ix)   Wasted Expenditure

Original solicitors' costs

Replace footnote 1413 with:

11-327   [1413] e.g. *Cox v Leech* (1857) 1 C.B. (N.S.): attorney sued in the wrong court, but was entitled to recover the costs of sending letters before action. "These letters are distinguishable. They might have produced the desired result." See also *Shaw v Arden* (1832) 9 Bing. 287. In *Shaw v Leigh Day* [2018] EWHC 2034 (QB); [2018] P.N.L.R. 2, where the claim failed, Andrews J held, obiter, that the provision of negligent services did not entitle the claimant to her money back, as the costs the claimant had incurred were not wasted.

(xi)   Physical Injury, Inconvenience and Distress

Application of the rule

Replace footnote 1439 with:

11-334   [1439] [2002] EWCA Civ 353; [2002] P.N.L.R. 41. In *Shaw v Leigh Day (A Firm)* [2017] EWHC 925 (QB); [2017] P.N.L.R. 26 a claim for damages for distress resulting from an allegedly bungled retainer in relation to an inquest was not struck out. The claimant failed to prove negligence, but the judge stated that she might have been minded to make an award for injured feelings, see *Shaw v Leigh Day* [2018] EWHC 2034 (QB); [2018] P.N.L.R. 2 at [103].

(e)   Mitigation of Damage

Examples of failure to mitigate: generous treatment of the claimant

Replace footnote 1446 with:

11-335   [1446] See the following illustrations. *Whiteman v Hawkins* (1878) 4 C.P.D. 13: the security for a loan proved to be subject to an equitable charge. The court rejected the argument that the plaintiff should enforce other securities which were available, rather than sue his solicitor. *Transportation Agency Ltd v Jenkins* (1972) 223 E.G. 1101, Kerr J: the plaintiffs were not obliged to iron out the difficulties caused by a lease including a covenant against cooking with their landlords and to make the business viable, and were entitled to have simply withdrawn from the transaction. *King v Hawkins & Co, The Times,* 28 January 1982, Mars-Jones J: the purchaser of property discovered a defect in title owing to his solicitors' negligence. He refused to abandon his plans for improving the property. Held that the purchaser was not in breach of his duty to mitigate. *Barnes v Hay* (1988) 12 N.S.W.L.R. 337 CA: it was not unreasonable for a tenant to refuse to go out of business when the solicitor's negligence enabled the lessor to harass him causing the business loss, because it was not unreasonable to expect that the position would improve when changes to the shopping complex were complete. *Fairbrother v Gabb & Co* [2002] EWCA Civ 803; [2002] 23 E.G. 119: after solicitors gave wrong advice on the time limits for an application for a new tenancy, the claimants refused to accept a new lease without a break clause, which a court would have ordered, but they did not act unreasonably. *Hayes v Dodd* [1990] 2 All E.R. 815 CA: the purchaser of two properties discovered that there was no right of way over the only convenient means of access; it was not unreasonable to attempt to sell both properties together, which had been done on advice, and caused a four-year delay before they were sold. *Rosbeg Partners Ltd v L.K.Shields (A Firm)* [2016] IECA 161; [2016] P.N.L.R. 30: as a result of the defendant's failure to register title to property which the plaintiff bought in 1994, a sale fell through at €10m in 2007. The plaintiff did not fail to mitigate its loss in not accepting subsequent offers of €8m and €6m in 2008, as it was not at fault in failing to foresee the subsequent falls in the property market.

Fresh litigation: the general rule

Replace footnote 1449 with:

[1449] [1953] Ch. 770. See also the following examples. In *Treloar v Henderson* [1968] N.Z.L.R. 1085, High Court, the solicitor's negligence resulted in the client being liable under a contract; it was reasonable for the plaintiff not to attempt to avoid the contract, because he would have been sued and probably lost. In *Williams v Glyn Owen & Co* [2003] EWCA Civ 750; [2004] P.N.L.R. 20 the vendor delayed the completion of the sale of a Welsh hill farm to the claimant, who as a result lost the profits he would have made if he had been able to purchase breeding ewes in time. His solicitors, the defendants, negligently failed to serve a completion notice. The Court of Appeal held that the claimant had no duty to mitigate his loss and sue the vendor for damages, particularly as the solicitor had not recommended such a course of action. Similarly, in *Cottingham v Attey Bower & Jones (A Firm)* [2000] P.N.L.R. 557, the claimants had not been advised by solicitors that there was no building regulation consent for what were defective renovation works. Rimer J held that they were not obliged to mitigate their loss by suing the surveyors who had also advised them. In *Luft v Taylor, Zinkhofer & Conway* [2017] ABCA 228; [2017] 10 W.W.R. 39 the defendant solicitors negligently gave away the plaintiffs' right to trial and bound them to a binding judicial dispute resolution. A majority of the Alberta Court of Appeal held that the plaintiffs did not fail to mitigate their loss by pursuing such resolution, as they desired an open process with a right of appeal, and the judge would not have been able to consider a claim for defamation.

11-336

Exceptions to the general rule on fresh litigation

Replace footnote 1454 with:

[1454] (1990) 6 P.N. 205 at 211. In *Ueland v Lynch* 2019 BCCA 431; (2020) 31 B.C.L.R. (4th) 33 the plaintiff's personal injury claim was ordered to be dismissed as he had failed to attend medical examinations. He failed to mitigate his loss by making a prompt application to overturn the order, which would have succeeded.

11-337

4.   SHARED RESPONSIBILITY

(a)   Contributory Negligence

Circumstances in which contributory negligence cannot be claimed

Replace footnote 1485 with:

[1485] As in *Bristol & West Building Society v Kramer, The Times,* 6 February 1995. But see para.11-010, above. Similarly, breaches of three terms of the CML Lenders' Handbook were also held not to give rise to a defence of contributory negligence in *Mortgage Express v Iqbal Hafeez Solicitors* [2011] EWHC 3037 (Ch) at [74]. Quaere whether that conclusion is correct, particularly given cl.1.4 of the Handbook which imposed the standard of care of a reasonably competent solicitor.

11-345

(b)   Apportionment of Liability

Successive solicitors

Replace footnote 1494 with:

[1494] [1983] V.R. 573 Supreme Court Victoria, Full Court. The first solicitors failed to institute proceedings for two years and nine months. There was a delay in forwarding their file to the second solicitors, who wrongly assumed that a writ had been issued. The apportionment was 80% to the first solicitors and 20% to the second solicitors. In *Dual Homes Pty Ltd v Moores Legal pty Ltd* [2016] VSC 86; (2016) 50 V.R. 117 two firms (one of which was the successor to the first) failed to act in relation to a winding

11-347

up application against their client resulting in its winding up. The second was held to be two-thirds responsible because of its greater causative responsibility.

CHAPTER 12

BARRISTERS

1. GENERAL

(e) Immunity

Replace footnote 46 with:

[46] [2016] HCA 16; (2016) A.L.R. 1, which held that immunity did not apply to negligent advice which **12-009** led to the settlement of proceedings between the parties, followed in *Kendirjian v Lepore* [2017] HCA 13; (2017) 343 A.L.R. 86.

(g) Liability for Costs

Guidelines

Replace footnote 54 with:

[54] The need to show causation of loss is illustrated by *Harrison v Harrison* [2009] EWHC 428 (QB); **12-012** [2009] 1 F.L.R. 1434. Mackay J dismissed an application for wasted costs against a barrister because the other party to the litigation whom the barrister had represented had had a costs order made against her, much of which had been paid, and all of which was expected to be paid. In any event, the wasted costs proceedings were disproportionate to any benefit they might bring. In *Le Brocq v Liverpool Crown Court* [2019] EWCA Crim 1398; [2019] 4 W.L.R 108 a wasted costs order against a barrister was quashed on the grounds of causation. He had made inappropriate comments in his closing speech, and the judge had discharged the jury. However, the judge should not have done so, but should have directed the jury to ignore the offending part of the speech.

Misjudgments on timing

Replace footnote 92 with:

12-021   [92] [1997] P.N.L.R. 489. In *HKSAR v Harjani* [2017] 3 H.K.L.R.D. 1 the Hong Kong Court of Appeal upheld a wasted costs order, applying the more rigorous tests applicable to Hong Kong criminal cases, against a barrister who conducted himself improperly at trial by protracted and irrelevant cross-examination.

2.   LIABILITY FOR BREACH OF DUTY

Advising where not instructed to do so

Replace footnote 144 with:

12-035   [144] [2009] EWCA Civ 369; [2009] P.N.L.R. 28. A barrister owes no duty to advise a client on how to fund litigation, unless instructed to do so, and even then did not owe a continuing duty to give such advice, see *Andrews v Messer Beg Ltd* [2019] EWHC 911 (Ch); [2019] P.N.L.R. 23.

CHAPTER 13

MEDICAL PRACTITIONERS

[145]

2.   DUTIES

(a)   Duties to Patient

(iii)   Duty of Care in Tort

Replace paragraph 13-005 (to incorporate new text following "in other circumstances." at the end of the paragraph) with:

13-005   A medical practitioner owes a duty of care in tort in advising, diagnosing and treating a patient, even where no contract exists between them.[10] The duty of care arises out of the relationship between practitioner and patient. It may arise even when the practitioner renders his services gratuitously or entirely voluntarily, as in rescue situations. A doctor will be taken as assuming a duty of care to the victim of a road accident by attending to the victim.[11] A duty of care may also arise in other circumstances.[12] Undoubtedly, a medical practitioner is under a duty not to act in such as a way as foreseeably to cause a patient to sustain physical injury. This duty encompasses a duty to take reasonable care not to provide misleading information which may foreseeably cause physical injury.[12A]

[10] For an early example, see *Gladwell v Steggall* (1839) 5 Bing (N.C.) 733.

[11] See *Capital & Counties Plc v Hampshire CC* [1997] Q.B. 1004 CA. Stuart-Smith LJ stated at 1035D–1035E that in such circumstances a doctor would be under no general obligation to provide assistance to such a victim and would only owe a duty of care to the victim should he choose to do so. Further, "if he volunteers his assistance his only duty as a matter of law is not to make the victim's condition worse". However, in relation to the ambulance service, it owes a duty to attend a member of the public within a reasonable time and its duty goes beyond that of a rescuer: see *Kent v Griffiths* [2001] Q.B. 36.

[12] e.g. a duty of care owed by a doctor to parents after the death of a baby in explaining the purpose of a post-mortem examination and alerting parents to them to the possibility of organs being retained, depending on whether a doctor-patient relationship existed between the doctors and the parents when seeking consent for a post mortem: *A&B v Leeds Teaching Hospital NHS Trust* [2004] EWHC 644 QB; [2005] Q.B. 506.

[12A] *Darnley v Croydon Health Services NHS Trust* [2018] UKSC 50; [2018] 3 W.L.R. 1153. A receptionist at the defendant's A&E department had provided the claimant with misleading information as to the time within which medical attention might be available. The Court held that in determining whether a duty of care was owed in such circumstances, it was inappropriate to distinguish between medically qualified professionals and administrative staff.

(b)   Duties to Third Parties

Replace the first paragraph up to and including "a genetic condition." with:

13-010   The general principles governing liability to third parties are treated in Ch.2.[20] Usually, a doctor's negligence will only cause personal injury to his patient.[21] However, there are exceptions, for example where a male sterilisation procedure fails and the patient's partner becomes pregnant.[22] A doctor may also owe a duty of care to prevent harm to those who come into contact with his patient who, for example, is infectious or suffers from a psychiatric disorder.[23] There is now scope to argue that an NHS trust owes a duty of care to the family of a patient suffering from a genetic condition. [24]

[20] See Ch.2 and paras 2-124 to 2-130, above.

[21] In the Canadian case of *Urbanski v Patel* (1978) 84 D.L.R. (3d) 650, where a defendant doctor negligently created a situation in which organ donation was required urgently and was found to owe a duty to the third party who donated a kidney.

[22] See, e.g. *McFarlane v Tayside Health Board* [2000] 2 A.C. 59, where it was confirmed that the wife of a patient has a claim for damages for the pain, suffering and loss of amenity of pregnancy and birth. The cost of bringing up a healthy child is not recoverable—but the extra cost of bringing up a disabled child is recoverable (see *Rees v Darlington Memorial NHS Trust* [2003] UKHL 52; [2004] 1 A.C. 309—although this is not a third party case). See also *ARB v IVF Hammersmith* [2018] EWCA Civ 2803; [2019] 2 W.L.R. 1094 in which the Court of Appeal confirmed that the legal policy barring damages for the wrongful conception or birth of a child in cases of negligence also applied to a wrongful birth arising from a breach of contract.

[23] A claimant must establish foreseeability and proximity. There is more extensive case law in the US and Canada than in the UK, but that case law is not explored in detail here. Where a practitioner treats an infectious patient, it is likely he owes a duty of care to those he should foresee are likely to be infected (see the Canadian case of *Pitman Estates v Bain* (1994) 112 D.L.R. (4th) 257). A duty may be found to warn a patient not to undertake activities which could be hazardous to third parties (see the Canadian case of *Spillane v Vasserman* (1992) 13 C.C.L.T.267.) The limits of such duty are likely to be closely circumscribed—see *Goodwill v British Pregnancy Advisory Service* [1996] 1 W.L.R. 1397. The defendants negligently carried out a vasectomy and advised the patient that there was no need to use contraception. The patient began a sexual relationship with the claimant, who became pregnant. She brought an action for the costs of the child. The Court of Appeal struck the claim out on the basis that the defendant owed no duty of care to the claimant, as the claimant had failed to establish proximity. As to the potential liability of psychiatrists to persons who may foreseeably be injured by their patients, see *Palmer v Tees HA* [1999] Lloyd's Rep. Med. 351. See also *Selwood v Durham CC* [2012] EWCA Civ 979: the Court of Appeal set aside an order striking out a claim by a social worker, employed by the defendant local authority, who had been attacked by a voluntary patient of two defendant NHS trusts (with whom the local authority worked closely). The defendants had failed to warn the social worker of threats made by the patient that he would harm the social worker if he saw her. Although not a "third party" case, it engages with the issue of when a health professional owes duties in respect of actions threatened by a mentally ill patient.

[24] In *ABC v St George's Healthcare NHS Foundation Trust* [2017] EWCA Civ 336, the Court of Appeal overturned the decision at first instance, in which the judge had struck out a claim brought by the daughter of a patient with Huntington's disease. The daughter complained that she should have been informed of her father's diagnosis sooner because as a result she had a 50% chance of developing the condition. The Court of Appeal found that it was arguably fair, just and reasonable to impose a duty of care on the respondent trust to disclose the father's diagnosis to the daughter. However the claim ultimately failed as whilst the trust had owed the daughter a duty of care to balance her interest in being alerted to her father's diagnosis against the duty of confidentiality owed to him (and the public interest in maintaining confidentiality) there had been no breach of duty in that case [2020] EWHC 455 (QB). In *Bot v Barnick* [2018] EWHC 3132 (QB), the claimant sought to rely on the decision in *ABC* in order to claim damages for economic loss sustained as a result of misleading information provided to him by the defendants about his partner's (the patient's) mental state following the birth of their child. However, the Court distinguished *ABC* on the basis that the claim in *ABC* was not one for pure economic loss. Further, the Court held that *ABC* was: "a case limited to very specific facts (disclosure of a hereditary disease in a family member)" (at [28]).

Replace footnote 26 with:

[26] See, e.g. *Julia Ward v Leeds Teaching Hospitals NHS Trust* [2004] EWHC 2106 (QB), reported at [2004] Lloyd's Rep. Med. 530; *Taylor v Somerset HA* [1993] 4 Med. L.R. 34; *Tredget and Tredget v Bexley HA* [1994] 5 Med. L.R. 178 (Central London County Court); *Walters v North Glamorgan NHS Trust* [2002] Lloyd's Rep. Med. 227. Contrast the approaches to a need for a traumatic external event in *Sion v Hampstead HA* [1994] 5 Med. L.R. 170 and *Taylor v Somerset HA* (above). See also *Liverpool Women's Hospital NHS Foundation Trust v Ronayne* [2015] EWCA Civ 588, where the defendant's appeal was allowed. On the facts of the case, the necessary element of suddenness did not exist and what the claimant husband saw was not horrifying by objective standards. The Court of Appeal applied *Shorter v Surrey and Sussex Healthcare NHS Trust* [2015] EWHC 614 (QB). For an example of a case in which a claimant satisfied the *Alcock* criteria, see *Farnworth v Wrightington Wigan and Leigh NHS Foundation Trust* unreported 21 December 2016 CC (Manchester). The claimant father witnessed his partner's negligently managed labour that resulted in the death of his child shortly after birth. The issue was whether the father satisfied the second criteria, i.e. that the injury for which damages were claimed arose from the sudden and unexpected shock to his nervous system. The court found that it did. For another case in which the claimant could not establish that his illness was caused by a sudden shocking event, as opposed to a series of distressing events over a significant period of time see *O'Connor v Royal Bournemouth and Christchurch Hospitals NHS Foundation Trust* unreported 13 July 2018 County Court Central London. See also *YAH v Medway NHS Foundation Trust* [2018] EWHC 2964 (QB); [2019] 1 W.L.R. 1413 in which a mother who suffered psychiatric injury following the birth of her baby was clas-

sified as a primary victim. She suffered injury consequent on negligence which occurred before her daughter was born and did not cease to be a primary victim at the moment of birth. In *Paul (A Child) v Royal Wolverhampton NHS Trust* [2020] EWHC 1415 (QB), the appellant children successfully appealed against the striking out of their claims for psychiatric harm, on the basis of the hospital trust's allegedly negligent failure to diagnose their father with ischaemic heart disease. This led to his collapse and death from a heart attack fourteen-and-a-half months later, witnessed by his children. See however *Purchase v Ahmed*, unreported 5 June 2020 in which a county court struck out a claim for damages for psychiatric injury brought by a woman who found her daughter dead two days after a GP failed to diagnose her daughter's pneumonia, finding that (following *Taylor v A Novo (UK) Ltd* [2013] EWCA Civ 194) the death and aftermath could not be the "relevant event" for the purposes of determining the issue of proximity.

(c)   The Standard of Skill and Care

(ii)   The Advisory Role

The advisory duty

Replace paragraph 13-016 (to incorporate new footnote and text following "may be involved." and an amendment to footnote 42) with:

13-016   The Supreme Court rejected the *Bolam* test as the appropriate test in determining whether the consultant had been negligent in omitting to advise the claimant of the risk of shoulder dystocia. It is not relevant that the omission may have been accepted as proper by a responsible body of medical opinion. A doctor is under a duty to take reasonable care to ensure that a patient is aware of any *material* risks involved in any recommended treatment and of any reasonable alternative or variant treatments. This can be understood, within the traditional framework of negligence, as a duty of care to avoid exposing a person to a risk of injury which she would otherwise have avoided. It is also the counterpart of the patient's entitlement to decide whether or not to incur that risk. There is "a fundamental distinction" between (1) the doctor's role when considering possible investigatory or treatment options and (2) the doctor's role in discussing with the patient any recommended treatment and possible alternatives, and the risks of injury which may be involved.[41A] The first is an exercise of professional skill and judgment. In contrast, the doctor's advisory role is not solely an exercise of medical skill. It must take into account the patient's entitlement to decide what risks to health to run, which may be influenced by non-medical considerations.[42]

[41A] In *Webster v Burton Hospitals NHS Foundation Trust* [2017] EWCA Civ 62, the Court of Appeal found that the judge had wrongly followed the *Bolam* approach of basing his decision on whether the doctor had acted in accordance with a responsible body of expert opinion, when the judge should have followed the approach in *Montgomery*. The patient should have been told of the evidence of increased risk of delaying labour in her specific circumstances and her baby would then have been delivered sooner than had been the case. The judge's decision on liability was reversed. This case was followed in *Bayley v George Eliot Hospital NHS Trust* [2017] EWHC 3398 (QB), in which the Court considered the question of what is a "reasonable alternative" treatment, stating that it was necessary to take into account all of the relevant evidence (not only expert medical evidence). See also the consideration of the authorities in respect of consent in *Pepper v Royal Free London NHS Foundation Trust* [2020] EWHC 310 (QB).

[42] [2015] UKSC 11 at [82], [87]. See also the Scottish case of *LT v NHS Lothian Health Board* [2019] CSIH 20, at [61], where the Court held that the *Montgomery* duty arose "Only if there was a risk and the relevant clinician was or should have been aware of it".

Materiality of risk

After "significance to it.", add new footnote 42A:

13-017   [42A] There is a prior stage. See *Duce v Worcestershire Acute Hospitals NHS Trust* [2018] EWCA Civ 1307 ([30]–[42]) in which the Court of Appeal found that whilst the judge at first instance had correctly considered *Montgomery*, he had not needed to address the issue of materiality because he had found that the claim failed at the first hurdle, i.e. there was no proof that the medic was or should have been aware of the relevant risks.

Informed decision

Replace paragraph 13-018 (to incorporate new footnotes 43A and 43B) with:

Moreover, a doctor's advisory role involves dialogue with the aim of ensuring the patient understands the seriousness of his or her condition, and the anticipated benefits and risks of the proposed treatment and any reasonable alternatives. The patient is then enabled to make an informed decision.[43A] For the advisory role to be effective, the information provided must be comprehensible.[43B] The doctor's duty is not fulfilled by "bombarding the patient" with technical information which the patient cannot reasonably be expected to grasp. Nor is it fulfilled by routinely demanding the patient's consent on a consent form.[44] An advisory duty of the like stated in *Montgomery* may also arise in the context of advice on post-operative risks, that is outside the context of the adequacy of advice given to a patient upon which they decide whether or not to undergo a particular treatment.[45]

13-018

[43A] See *R. v Lanarkshire Health Board* [2016] CSOH 133, the judge confirmed that where there were two alternative approaches to the management of the patient's labour, those ought to have been explained to her together with the risks of the alternative approaches. This would have provided the patient with sufficient information to make an informed choice. The case fell within the ratio of *Montgomery*.

[43B] In both *Thefaut v Johnston* [2017] EWHC 497 (QB) and *Rajatheepan v Barking, Havering and Redbridge NHS Foundation Trust* [2018] EWHC 716 (QB), the importance of "dialogue" was emphasised. In the second case, this was in the context of a failure to communicate effectively with a new mother, who spoke very limited English.

[44] [2015] UKSC 11 at [90].

[45] *Spencer v Hillingdon Hospital NHS Trust* [2015] EWHC 1058 (QB) at [32]. The judge observed that whilst the ratio decidendi of *Montgomery* was confined to such cases, there was force in the contention that the basic principles and duty of care defined in *Montgomery* are likely to be applied to all aspects of the provision of advice given to patients, and that insofar as *Montgomery* emphasised the need for a court to take into account the patient's point of view as to the significance of information for a patient, it was relevant to the facts of the case.

Justification

Replace footnote 47 with:

[47] [2015] UKSC 11 at [74]–[81]. As was pointed out in *Holdsworth v Luton and Dunstable University Hospital NHS Foundation Trust* [2016] EWHC 3347 (QB) the fact that a patient may be insistent about receiving certain treatment cannot itself justify such treatment being provided.

13-020

(iii)   Diagnosis and treatment roles

Bolam test applies

Replace footnote 49 with:

[49] *Maynard v West Midlands Regional HA* [1984] 1 W.L.R. 634. See *Penney v East Kent HA* [1999] Lloyd's Rep. Med. 123, for a case where the *Bolam* test was found not to apply in the context of cytoscreening, in part because it involved a mechanical process, not diagnosis. The finding of liability against the health authority was upheld on appeal [2000] Lloyd's Rep. Med. 41. In *Muller v King's College Hospital NHS Foundation Trust* [2017] EWHC 128 (QB), the judge stated that the authorities applying the conventional *Bolam* approach do not sufficiently differentiate between cases where diagnosis is alleged to be negligent and those where the alleged negligence consisted of a decision to treat the condition in a particular way. The judge in *Bolam* did not have in mind a "pure diagnosis" case. However, even in such a case, the *Bolitho* exception applies, i.e. an expert's view can only be rejected if it is untenable in logic or otherwise flawed in such a way that its conclusion is indefensible and impermissible.

13-021

Standard of skill and care determined by reference to the current state of Knowledge

Replace footnote 54 with:

13-023   ⁵⁴ See, e.g. *Chin Keow v Government of Malaysia* [1967] 1 W.L.R. 813 at 817. For a particularly clear illustration, see *Roe v Ministry of Health* [1954] 2 Q.B. 66. For statutory recognition of this principle, see s.1(5) of the Congenital Disabilities (Civil Liability) Act 1976. In *Watts v Secretary of State for Health* [2016] EWHC 2835 (QB), the judge emphasised that when applying the *Bolam* test, the issues must be judged by the standard of a reasonably competent medical practitioner applicable when the claimant was born in 1993 and not by today's standards. The claimant's expert had not appreciated the importance of basing her opinions on standards applicable in 1993. See also *Sullivan v Guy's and St Thomas' NHS Foundation Trust* [2017] EWHC 602 (QB). The medical practitioner is to be judged by the standards applicable at the time the treatment in question was administered. However there is an issue not yet decided by the courts as to whether a doctor can be vindicated by subsequent events in respect of the prescription of a drug whose use was not accepted as appropriate at the time but was accepted as appropriate later: *Jones v Taunton and Somerset NHS Foundation Trust* [2019] EWHC 1408 (QB); [2019] All E.R. (D) 49.

Undertaking work beyond one's competence

Replace footnote 56 with:

13-025   ⁵⁶ See, e.g. *Djemal v Bexley HA* [1995] 6 Med. L.R. 269 and *Brooks v Home Office, The Times,* 18 February 1999. The standard of care to be expected of junior hospital doctors was considered in detail in *Wilsher v Essex AHA* [1987] Q.B. 730. See also the Scottish case of *Andrews v Greater Glasgow Health Board* [2019] CSOH 31; 2019 S.L.T. 727. The defendant argued that the doctor who had treated the claimant had discharged his duty of care by seeking advice from a senior colleague. The Court held that this did not have the effect of exonerating him from his failure to exercise reasonable care (at [108]).

Expert evidence

Replace paragraph (to incorporate an amendment to footnote 65 and new text following "by expert evidence." at the end of the paragraph) with:

13-029   In the context of clinical negligence, as elsewhere, the expert witness has two principal functions. First, the expert witness has an explanatory or didactic function involving an explanation of the patient's condition, treatment, and its consequences.⁶¹ Where there is dispute upon an issue of medical fact, the court may prefer the evidence of one party's experts to that of the other's experts: the *Bolam* test does not apply to opinion evidence on matters of fact.⁶² The second function of the expert witness is to assist the court in deciding whether the acts or omissions of the defendant constituted negligence.⁶³ Ultimately, however, it is for the court to decide, on the totality of the evidence and applying the *Bolam* test, and the necessary logical analysis, whether the defendant exercised the requisite degree of skill and care.⁶⁴ The evidence of a particular expert witness may be rejected on grounds that the expert has become partial or on grounds that his evidence lacks internal consistency or logic.⁶⁵ Where no general practice or relevant school of thought exists, the decision whether reasonable care and skill was exercised will be informed but not constrained by expert evidence.⁶⁶ There are circumstances in which a judge will be justified in finding that he is unable to resolve an issue of fact, for example where expert evidence is difficult and shifting. ⁶⁶ᴬ

⁶¹ The court cannot speculate upon medical matters or come to conclusions or diagnoses which are not supported by at least one of the experts: see *McLean v Weir* (1977) 3 C.C.L.T. 87 at 101, a decision of the British Columbia Supreme Court which it is submitted is equally applicable in England. See also *Roughton v Weston AHA* [2004] EWCA Civ 1509.

⁶² See *Loveday v Renton* [1990] 1 Med. L.R. 117 at 182 per Stuart-Smith LJ.

⁶³ So, amongst other matters, the expert will recount the current state of knowledge at the material time; give his view on what the general and approved practice was and/or what different schools of thought

were relating to the patient's condition; he will explain the risks attaching to particular courses of treatment and procedure; he may state what is the experience of skill usually displayed by medical practitioners with the relevant specialisation.

[64] See *C v North Cumbria University Hospitals NHS Trust* [2014] EWHC 61 (QB).

[65] e.g. in *Murphy v Wirral HA* [1996] 7 Med. L.R. 99 the evidence of an expert witness for the defence was rejected because the witness had lost his objectivity, his views were unsupported by the literature and his argument did not withstand analysis when tested by the views of other expert witnesses. For an example of a successful appeal on grounds of serious procedural or other irregularity under CPR r.52.11(3)(b), see *Breeze (As personal representative of the Estate of Leonard Breeze, deceased) v Saeed Ahmad* [2005] EWCA Civ 223, where an expert made a mistake as to the contents of some academic papers. See also *Rachael Brown (A patient by her litigation friend Angela Brown) v (1) Birmingham & Black Country Strategic HA (2) Patricia May Shukru (widow and personal representative of Umit Shukru, deceased) (3) Medical Defence Union* [2005] EWHC 1098 (QBD), for an instance where the claimant's expert was criticised for loss of objectivity. In *EXP v Barker* [2017] EWCA Civ 63, the Court of Appeal found the judge had been entitled to take the view that an expert's approach was highly compromised and that the weight to be given to his views considerably diminished. The expert had failed to disclose his association with the defendant and there was good reason to doubt his approach to the issues in the case. The judge was entitled to reject his evidence and would have been justified in excluding it entirely.

[66] See, e.g. *AB v Tameside and Glossop HA* [1997] 8 Med. L.R. 91.

[66A] *Barnett v Medway NHS Foundation Trust* [2017] EWCA Civ 235, in which the judge found that the claimant had failed to discharge the burden of proof, where there was considerable uncertainty in the expert evidence about the onset and progression of an infection.

Res Ipsa Loquitur

Replace footnote 68 with:

[68] See *Ratcliffe v Plymouth and Torbay HA* [1998] Lloyd's Rep. Med. 162. especially at 184: the evidence of the claimant is likely to be buttressed by expert evidence to the effect that the matters complained of do not ordinarily occur in the absence of negligence. For examples of claims which were assessed not to be ones of res ipsa loquitur, see *Thomas v Curley* [2013] EWCA Civ 117 and *O'Connor v Pennine Acute Hospitals NHS Trust* [2015] EWCA Civ 1244. See also *Rowley v King's College Hospital NHS Foundation Trust* unreported 20 November 2016, in which the judge found that the patient had raised a prima facie claim against the hospital trust, based on a combination of fact and inference, and that the trust had failed to rebut the inference of negligence. *Ratcliffe* followed.

13-030

(d)   Consent to Treatment

(iii)   Informed Consent

Replace footnote 82 with:

[82] Lady Hale attributes this to a combination of the 2008 Guidance provided by the GMC, the decision of the Court of Appeal in *Pearce v United Bristol Healthcare NHS Trust* [1999] P.I.Q.R. P.53 and the decision of the House of Lords in *Chester v Afshar* [2005] 1 A.C. 134. There is no separate or freestanding cause of action for wrongful invasion of personal autonomy caused by the failure to obtain informed consent. Such a claim should be formulated as an action in negligence/breach of duty. See *Shaw v Kovac* [2017] EWCA Civ 1028.

13-035

3.   BREACH OF DUTY

(b)   Failing to Explain Treatment or Warn of Risks

Risk of disability of unborn baby

Replace paragraph 13-054 (to incorporate amendments to the final sentence and footnote 129) with:

Claims may be brought on the basis that if the defendant had properly advised the claimant as to the condition of the foetus she was carrying, then the claimant would have had an abortion.[127] The liability issues in these cases usually are (i) what

13-054

tests were or should have been done, and (ii) what inferences should have been drawn from the results of such tests. It is normally accepted that full disclosure of any defects discovered in the foetus should be made, since the prime object of the tests is to obtain such information for the parents.[128] There is now scope to argue that a medical practitioner is under a duty of care to disclose a patient's diagnosis to family members in the case of an inheritable condition. [129]

[127] See, e.g. *Lillywhite v University College London Hospitals NHS Trust* [2005] EWCA Civ 1466 and *Farraj v King's Healthcare NHS Trust* [2009] EWCA Civ 1203.

[128] See also *P v Taunton and Somerset NHS Trust* [2009] EWHC 1965 and *Carver v Hammersmith & Queen Charlotte's Special HA* unreported 25 February 2000 QBD in respect of tests for Down's syndrome.

[129] *ABC v St George's Healthcare NHS Foundation Trust* [2017] EWCA Civ 336, overturning the decision in *ABC v St George's Healthcare NHS Foundation Trust* [2015] EWHC 1394 (QB).

(e)   Wrong Diagnosis

General

Replace footnote 138 with:

13-058 [138] See, e.g. *Djemal v Bexley HA* [1995] 6 Med. L.R. 269, where an inexperienced casualty officer failed to elicit a full history from the patient or the patient's wife and so failed to realise that advice from an ENT specialist was called for. See also *Drake v Pontefract HA* [1998] Lloyd's Rep. Med. 425: senior house officer negligently failed to diagnose (and accordingly failed to treat) the claimant's agitated depression, resulting in her depressive condition deteriorating until an attempt to commit suicide resulted in serious injury and disablement. See also *FB v Rana* [2017] EWCA Civ 334, in which the Court of Appeal reversed the decision in the court below. There was no difference in the standard of care required of an A&E senior house officer as compared to a more senior doctor in the context of taking patient history in A&E and eliciting an important symptom in a child precipitating a hospital visit. *Rana* is cited in *SC (A Child) v University Hospital Southampton NHS Foundation Trust* [2020] EWHC 1610 (QB).

4.   DAMAGES

(a)   Scope of Duty

Replace footnote 162 with:

13-071 [162] See generally on scope of duty *Caparo Industries v Dickman* [1990] 2 A.C. 605 at 627 per Lord Bridge; *Rahman v Arearose Ltd* [2001] Q.B. 351 at 367–368, [33] per Laws LJ; *Fairchild v Glenhaven Funeral Services Ltd* at [54] per Lord Hoffmann; *South Australia Asset Management Corp v York Montague Ltd (SAAMCO)* [1997] A.C. 191. In the medical context see, e.g. *R. v Croydon HA* [1998] Lloyd's Rep. Med. 44; *Brown v Lewisham and North Southwark HA* [1999] Lloyd's Rep. Med. 110 at 118; *Thompson v Bradford* [2005] EWCA Civ 1439; [2006] Lloyd's Rep. Med. 95. See also *Less v Hussain* [2012] EWHC 3513 (QB), where the defendant gynaecologist, from whom the claimant mother had sought advice about the safety of pregnancy, argued that, since a stillbirth was caused by hypercoiling of the umbilical cord, which was not a matter about which her advice was sought by the claimant nor a risk or complication which the defendant should have addressed, the subsequent stillbirth and the claimant's consequent psychiatric injury were outside the scope of the defendant's duty. The argument failed: it was held that given that this was advice about conception, loss of the baby during term was a kind of loss in respect of which a duty was owed, and it made no difference that the precise mechanism was not foreseen. See also *Khan v Meadows* [2019] EWCA Civ 152; [2019] 4 W.L.R. 3, where the Court found that the doctor had no duty to prevent the birth of a child with autism and that the purpose and scope of the doctor's duty was to advise and investigate in relation to haemophilia, not other risks of pregnancy including the risk of autism.

(b)   Factual Causation

Material contribution

Replace footnote 169 with:

13-074 [169] See, e.g. *Hotson v East Berkshire AHA* [1987] A.C. 750, discussed by Waller LJ in *Bailey v Ministry* *of Defence* (above) at [46]. *Hotson* was also applied in *Hussain v Bradford Teaching Hospital NHS Foundation Trust* [2011] EWHC 2914: the claimant failed to establish causation where a hospital had been negligent in failing to diagnose and treat his Cauda Equina Syndrome. On the expert evidence, on the balance of probabilities the claimant would not have made a good recovery even if the Syndrome had been diagnosed and treated non-negligently, given its rapid onset. The claimant's "fall-back" case that earlier treatment might have resulted in some general improvement to his condition was too speculative and impressionistic to succeed. See also the obiter comments on causation in *Beech v Timney* [2013] EWHC 2345 (QB). See also *R. (on the application of Chidlow) v HM Senior Coroner for Blackpool and Fylde* [2019] EWHC 581 (Admin); [2019] Med. L.R. 313. General statistical evidence alone was unlikely to be sufficient to prove causation, and being a figure in a statistic did not prove causation: *Hotson* followed.

Loss of a chance

After "or materially contributed to) the injury,", add new footnote 189A:

13-080

[189A] See the application of *Gregg v Scott* in *Schembri v Marshall* [2020] EWCA Civ 358; [2020] Med. L.R. 240, which concerned the death of the respondent's wife from an untreated pulmonary embolism, in particular in respect of the proper role of statistical evidence. The judge was entitled to conclude on the evidence as a whole that the patient's survival prospects absent negligence would have been very high.

Warnings

After "a later date.", add new footnote 192A:

13-081

[192A] *Chester v Afshar* was considered in *Correia v University Hospital of North Staffordshire NHS Trust* [2017] EWCA Civ 356; [2017] Med. L.R. 292. The Court of Appeal emphasised that it was a crucial finding in *Chester* that, if warned of the risk, the claimant would have deferred the operation. If a claimant was to rely on the exceptional principle of causation established by that case, the claimant had to plead the point and support it by evidence ([28]). See also *Duce v Worcestershire Acute Hospitals NHS Trust* [2018] EWCA Civ 1307.

(e)   Measure of Damages

(iii)   *Damages in Wrongful Birth and Wrongful Conception Claims*

Unwanted pregnancy leading to unwanted but healthy child

After "child, is irrecoverable.", add:
This is so irrespective of whether the claim is brought in tort or in contract.[225A]

13-099

[225A] *ARB v IVF Hammersmith* [2018] EWCA Civ 2803; [2019] 2 W.L.R. 1094, at [39]. The Court held that "the legal policy which prevented recoverability of the cost of the upbringing of a healthy child in the tortious claims in *Rees* and *McFarlane* applies to [the Claimant's] claim for breach of contract."

Impact of the Human Rights Act 1998

Replace footnote 232 with:

13-104

[232] *Groom v Selby* [2001] Lloyd's Rep. Med. 39 (affirmed in the Court of Appeal at [2001] EWCA Civ 1522; [2002] P.I.Q.R. P18; [2002] Lloyd's Rep. Med. 1, although this point was not considered on appeal); *Greenfield v Irwin* [2001] 1 W.L.R. 1279; [2001] EWCA Civ 113 at [31]–[37], and [48]. In *Meadows v Khan* [2017] EWHC 2990 (QB), *Parkinson* was followed. The claimant was negligently informed that her child ran no risk of haemophilia, when in fact the claimant was a carrier. The son in fact suffered from both haemophilia and autism. The Court held that the costs of raising a disabled child born as a result of a doctor's negligence were recoverable, even where there was no link between the negligence and a disability (here, autism).

CHAPTER 14

REGULATION OF FINANCIAL SERVICES

TABLE OF CONTENTS

1. GENERAL

(a) The Regulators

Replace footnote 16 with:

[16] Established under the Tribunals, Courts and Enforcement Act 2007. FSMA Pt IX originally established a Financial Services and Markets Tribunal (FISMAT) but its functions were transferred to the Upper Tribunal by SI 2010/22. There is an appeal on a point of law to the Court of Appeal (TCEA 2007 s.13). See *Financial Services Authority v Fox Hayes* [2009] EWCA Civ 76; [2009] 1 B.C.L.C. 603 (successful appeal by the FSA from FISMAT on whether approvals of advertisements by authorised persons contravened the *FSA Handbook* (COBS Module), see para.14-055 onwards). See also *Winterflood Securities Ltd v Financial Services Authority* [2010] EWCA Civ 423; [2010] 2 B.C.L.C. 502 (an unsuccessful appeal by the appellant in relation to an FSA market abuse determination) and *Burns v Financial Conduct Authority* [2017] EWCA Civ 2140; [2018] 1 W.L.R. 4161 (unsuccessful appeal by approved person). See also *Jeffery v Financial Services Authority* [2012] EWCA Civ 178 (successful appeal from Tribunal decision on point of law relating to time limit under FSMA s.66(5)(a)); *Financial Conduct Authority v Hobbs* [2013] EWCA Civ 918; [2013] Bus. L.R. 1290 (FCA traders successful appeal against Tribunal decision); *7722656 Canada Inc (formerly Swift Trade Inc) v Financial Services Authority* [2013] EWCA Civ 1662; [2014] Lloyd's Rep. F.C. 207 (appeal against FSA in market abuse context dismissed); *Abdul Razzaq v Financial Services Authority* [2014] EWCA Civ 770 (applicant refused permission to appeal Tribunal decision); *Financial Conduct Authority v Macris* [2017] UKSC 19; [2017] 1 W.L.R. 1095 (on FSMA 2000 s.393: Tribunal ruling against FCA reversed). And see *Bayliss & Co (Financial Services) Ltd, Clive John Rosier v Financial Conduct Authority* [2015] UKUT 265 (TCC) (the Tribunal issued recommendations to the FCA regarding its procedures in relation to the publication of decision notices that had been referred to the tribunal).

14-004

Limited immunity

Replace footnote 27 with:

[27] Noted at para.15-034, below. [1996] 3 All E.R. 558, upheld on appeal to the House of Lords: [2001] UKHL 16; [2003] 2 A.C. 1. Note also *Hall v Bank of England* [2000] Lloyd's Rep. Bank 186 CA where an allegation of dishonesty against the Bank of England as banking regulator was not made out. For another unsuccessful claim (this time against the FCA) for, inter alia, misfeasance in public office, see *AAI Consulting Ltd v Financial Conduct Authority* [2016] EWHC 2812 (Comm).

14-005

Other functions

Replace footnote 28 with:

[28] Payment Services Regulations 2017 (SI 2017/752) (implementing the so-called PSD2, Directive 2015/2366/EU), replacing the Payment Services Regulations 2009 (SI 2009/209) (implementing the so-called PSD1, Directive 2007/64/EC), making provisions for the regulation of those payment services providers that are not already regulated by the FSA. See also: (i) the Regulated Covered Bonds Regulations 2008 (SI 2008/346); (ii) the Cross-Border Payments in Euro Regulations 2010 (SI 2010/89) (implementing Regulation 924/2009); (iii) the Recognised Auction Platforms Regulations 2011 (SI 2011/2699) (implementing the Emission Allowance Auctioning Regulation (Commission Regulation 1031/2010)).

14-006

(b)   The General Prohibition

Territorial scope

Replace footnote 39 with:

14-008   ³⁹ In *Financial Services Authority v Bayshore Nominees Ltd* [2009] EWHC 285 (Ch); [2009] Lloyd's Rep. F.C. 398, it was confirmed that "inward" advice from persons outside the UK, targeting UK investors, was carried on "in the United Kingdom". See also *Financial Conduct Authority v Capital Alternatives Ltd* unreported 26 March 2018 ChD (2018 WL 01472533) (location of establishment and operation of collective investment scheme). But note that there are significant exclusions in the RAO (as to which see para.14-024, below) for investment business activity by "overseas persons" (defined in RAO art.3), e.g. RAO art.72(1)(2).

(d)   Authorised Persons

After paragraph 14-012 add new paragraph 14-012A:

14-012A   The "sandbox"   To facilitate innovation in the financial market, the FCA has a facility known as "the regulatory sandbox"⁶⁵ᴬ that allows businesses (for example FINTECH businesses) to test innovative products, services, business models and delivery mechanisms in the real market, with real consumers, without the need to obtain full authorisation. Instead such businesses can obtain "restricted authorisation" (that is, authorisation restricted to allow firms only to test their new business as agreed with the FCA) and have the benefit of individual guidance, rule modifications or waivers and no enforcement action letters whilst they test their new business.

⁶⁵ᴬ See its website: *https://www.fca.org.uk/firms/regulatory-sandbox* [Accessed 7 August 2018].

(e)   Approved Persons, etc

After paragraph 14-013, add new paragraph 14-013A:

14-013A   The Bank of England and Financial Services Act 2016 (Commencement No.6 and Transitional Provisions) Regulations 2019 (SI 2019/1136), published on 18 July 2019, extend the SM&CR to insurers with effect from 10 December 2018, and provide for a further extension of the SM&CR to FCA solo-regulated firms (except for benchmark administrators), from 9 December 2019. As a consequence the SM&CR will replace the approved persons regime for most firms.⁶⁸ᴬ

⁶⁸ᴬ See the Bank of England and Financial Services Act 2016 (Commencement No.6 and Transitional Provisions) Regulations 2019 (SI 2019/1136).

(g)   Appointed Representatives

(ii)   Liability of Principal under FSMA

Replace paragraph 14-017 (to incorporate amendments to footnotes 87, 88 and 89 and to the text of the fourth sentence) with:

14-017   Apart from ordinary common law principles,⁸⁵ which will apply to render the principal liable for certain activities of his appointed representative, FSMA makes further provision clarifying the responsibility of the principal.⁸⁶ Nevertheless, these provisions only apply in relation to business for which the principal has accepted responsibility.⁸⁷ First, whatever the position at common law,⁸⁸ the principal is responsible for *anything* done or omitted to be done by his appointed representative in carrying out business for which the principal has accepted responsibility "to the same extent as if he had expressly permitted it".[89] Thus the principal will be liable to third parties and accountable to his regulator, for the activities of his appointed representative, as if the principal had given express permission for the relevant activities of the appointed representative. In particular, the principal will be liable to third parties on contracts made by his representative without the third party having to prove that the representative was actually (or ostensibly) authorised by the principal to act. Further, he may be liable as joint tortfeasor with the appointed representative on the basis that he is taken to have expressly permitted any tort the appointed representative engages in. Secondly, special provision is made in respect of determinations as to whether the principal has complied with a provision contained in or made under the Act (only). Here again, anything done (or omitted) by the appointed representative in carrying on the business for which the principal has accepted responsibility is attributed to the principal.[90] Once more the wording of this subsection is apt to cover both civil and criminal[91] (in addition to disciplinary) liability, but only under the Act. In particular, the wording enables the regulator to hold the principal responsible for all the activities of the appointed representative but only in deciding if the principal has complied with the regulatory regime. There is no direct attribution (for example, by analogy with the vicarious responsibility of an employer for the torts of his employee) of breaches by the appointed representative to the principal. There is only attribution of the representative's acts and omissions for the purposes of deciding if the principal himself has been in breach.[92]

[85] Especially in relation to agency (see paras 15-026 to 15-027, below) and, as to criminal law, principles of vicarious liability.

[86] FSMA s.39.

[87] Thus in *Emmanuel v DBS Management Plc* [1999] Lloyd's Rep. P.N. 593 (a decision under the 1986 Act s.44), the principal was not liable for activities which were held to be outside the scope of the business for which he had accepted responsibility and for activities undertaken before the agent became an appointed representative. See further as to this case, para.15-044 fn.99, below. cf. *Martin v Britannia Life Ltd* [2000] Lloyd's Rep. P.N. 412 (considered further at paras 15-027 and 15-057, below). In *Anderson v Sense Network Ltd* [2019] EWCA Civ 1395; [2020] 1 B.C.L.C. 555 the Court of Appeal confirmed that a principal was not liable for losses resulting from the claimants' investment in a fraudulent ponzi scheme operated by the appointed representative. The Court placed significant weight on the terms of the s.39 Agreement. Nor was the principal vicariously liable at common law, as the representative was found to have carried out a separate business.

[88] Which to some extent limits the extent to which a principal is responsible for the activities of his agent.

[89] FSMA s.39(3), applied in *Ovcharenko v InvestUK Ltd* [2017] EWHC 2114 (QB).

[90] FSMA s.39(4).

[91] But note s.39(6) attribution of knowledge or intentions in criminal context only to be done where "in all the circumstances it is reasonable".

[92] The last two sentences of this paragraph were referred to with approval in *Page v Champion Financial Management Ltd* [2014] EWHC 1778 (QB) at [12]

(i) European Aspects

Replace the second paragraph of paragraph 14-020 with:

The future of such EU-derived law in the UK in the wake of the "Brexit" **14-020** referendum is unclear at the time of writing. The Government has made statutory instruments to cater for the eventuality of a no-deal Brexit under the European Union (Withdrawal) Act 2018; see for example the Financial Services and Markets Act 2000 (Amendment) (EU Exit) Regulations 2019 (SI 2019/632), the EEA Passport Rights (Amendment, etc., and Transitional Provisions) (EU Exit) Regulations 2018 (SI 2018/1149), the Collective Investment Schemes (Amendment etc.) (EU Exit) Regulations (SI 2019/325) and the Deposit Guarantee Scheme and Miscellaneous Provisions (Amendment) (EU Exit) Regulations 2018 (SI 2018/1285).

2. APPLICATION OF THE FSMA REGULATORY REGIME

(a) Regulated Activities

The RAO

Replace paragraph 14-025 (to incorporate amendments to footnotes 150 and 161) with:

14-025   The scheme of Pt II of the RAO[141] is, broadly, to incorporate under "chapters" a series of articles relating to a "specified activity." The first article in the chapter defines the substantive activity and other articles define specific exclusions or contain supplemental provisions. In addition, there are some general exclusions that apply to several specified kinds of activity.[142] Regulated activities that are specified activities relating to an "investment" (also as specified in the RAO)[143] comprise the following: (1) accepting deposits[144]; (2) issuing electronic money[145]; (3) effecting and carrying out contracts of insurance[146]; (4) dealing in investments as principal[147]; (5) dealing in investments as agent[148]; (6) bidding in emissions auctions[149]; (7) arranging deals in investments[150]; (8) credit broking[151]; (9) operating an electronic system in relation to lending (i.e. so-called "P2P lending")[152]; (10) managing investments[153]; (11) assisting in the administration and performance of a contract of insurance[154]; (12) activities in relation to debt[155] (13) safeguarding and administering investments[156]; (14) sending dematerialised instructions[157]; (15) establishing, etc. a collective investment scheme[158]; (16) establishing, etc. a pension scheme[159]; (17) providing basic advice on stakeholder products[160]; (18) advising on investments[161]; (19) advising, managing and arranging activities in relation to Lloyd's[162]; (20) entering as provider into a funeral plan contract[163]; (21) activities in relation to regulated credit agreements[164]; (22) activities in relation to regulated hire agreements[165]; (23) entering into a regulated mortgage contract or administering the same[166]; (24) entering into a regulated home reversion plan (HRP) or administering the same[167]; (25) entering into a regulated home purchase plan (HPP) or administering the same[168]; (26) entering into a regulated sale and rent back agreement (SRA) or administering the same[169]; (27) activities of reclaim funds in meeting repayment claims and managing dormant account money[170]; (28) activities in relation to specified benchmarks[171]; and (29) agreeing to carry on certain specified activities.[172] Each of such activities is defined in considerable detail in the RAO and it is essential to have regard to the definitions including any applicable exclusions.[173]

[141] RAO Pt II arts 4–72H.

[142] RAO Pt II arts 66–72H.

[143] RAO Pt III arts 73–89.

[144] i.e. banking. RAO Pt II Ch.II art.5; it is subject to the exclusions in arts 5–9AC and 72A.

[145] RAO Ch.IIA art.9B; it is subject to the exclusions in arts 9C–9G (but see art.9BA) and 72A; see also supplemental provisions in arts 9H–9K. This chapter was extensively amended on the implementation of the Second E-Money Directive 2009/110, by SI 2011/99 (and see PERG3A of the *FCA Handbook*).

[146] RAO Ch.III art.10; it is subject to the exclusions in arts 11–12A and 72A; see also provision in art.13 in relation to Lloyds.

[147] RAO Ch.IV art.14; it is subject to the exclusions in arts 15–20, 66, 68–72A.

[148] RAO Ch.V art.21; it is subject to the exclusions in arts 22–24, 67–72B, 72D and 72E.

[149] RAO Ch.VA arts 24A–24B.

[150] RAO Ch.VI arts 25–25E. The exclusions (see arts 26–36, 66 to 72E) vary, depending on the category of "arrangements" and investments involved. See *Re Inertia Partnership LLP* [2007] EWHC 539 (Ch); [2007] 1 B.C.L.C. 739 on the meaning of "arrangements" in the RAO art.25, followed in *Watersheds Ltd v DaCosta* [2009] EWHC 1299 (QB); [2009] 2 B.C.L.C. 515. But note that the FSA "clarified" the effect of *DaCosta* in its Handbook (now the *FCA Handbook*), PERG 2.7.2B adding that the judgment "should be considered in the light of the case to which it relates". See also, *Personal Touch Financial Services Ltd v SimplySure Ltd* [2016] EWCA Civ 461; [2016] Bus. L.R. 1049, followed in *Financial Conduct Authority v Capital Alternatives Ltd* unreported 26 March 2018 ChD (2018 WL 01472533)

[151] RAO Ch VIA arts 36A–36G.

[152] RAO Ch VIB, arts 36H–36J.

[153] RAO Ch.VII art.37; it is subject to the exclusions in arts 38 and 39, 66, 68,69 72A,72C and 72E.

[154] RAO Ch.VIIA arts 39A and 39B; it is subject to the exclusions in arts 39C, 66 and 67, 72A–72D.

[155] RAO Ch.VIB arts.39D–39M.

[156] RAO Ch.VIII art.40; it is subject to the exclusions in arts 41–44, 66–69, 71, 72A, 72C and 72E.

[157] RAO Ch.IX art.45; it is subject to the exclusions in arts 46–50, 66, 69 and 72A.

[158] RAO Ch.X arts 51–51A; it is subject to the exclusions in arts 51A, 72A and 72E. Note the extensive amendments to Ch.X as a result of the implementation of the AIFMD (Alternative Investment Fund Managers Directive 2011/61) by the Alternative Investment Fund Managers Regulations 2013 (SI 2013/1773).

[159] RAO Ch.XI art.52, as amended; it is subject to the exclusions in arts 52A and 72A.

[160] RAO Ch.XIA art.52B, added by SI 2004/2737 and replaced by SI 2005/593. It is subject to the exclusion in s.52C (providing pensions guidance under Pt 20A).

[161] RAO Ch.XII arts 53–53D, as amended by SI 2017/488 (transposing the MiFID II definition of a "personal recommendation"). The exclusions (see arts 54 to 55, 66–70, 72, 72A, 72B, 72D and 72E) vary depending on the category of investments involved. For case law discussing the meaning of "investment advice", see: *Re Market Wizard Systems (UK) Ltd* [1998] 2 B.C.L.C. 282; *Martin v Britannia Life Ltd* [2000] Lloyd's Rep. P.N. 412 (considered further at paras 15-027 and 15-057, below); *Walker v Inter-Alliance Group Plc (In Administration), Scottish Equitable Plc* [2007] EWHC 1858 (Ch); [2007] Pens. L.R. 347, considered further at para.15-083, below; *Financial Services Authority v Bayshore Nominees Ltd* [2009] EWHC 285 (Ch); [2009] Lloyd's Rep. F.C. 398.

[162] RAO Ch.XIII arts 56–58; it is subject to the exclusion in arts 58A and 72A.

[163] RAO Ch.XIV art.59; it is subject to the exclusions in arts 60, 60A and 72A.

[164] RAO Ch.XIVA arts.60B–60M.

[165] RAO Ch.XIVB arts.60N–60S.

[166] RAO Ch.XV art.61; it is subject to the exclusions in arts 62–63A, 66, 72 and 72A. This chapter was extensively amended as a result of the Mortgage Credit Directive (Directive 2014/17).

[167] RAO Ch.XVA art.63B, added by SI 2006/2383. Article 63B(2) is subject to the exclusions in arts 63C–63D. The whole of art.63B is subject to the exclusions in, 66, 72 and 72A.

[168] RAO Ch.XVB art.63F, added by SI 2006/2383. Article 63F(2) is subject to the exclusions in arts 63G–63I. The whole of art.63F is subject to the exclusions in, 66, 72 and 72A.

[169] RAO Ch.XVC art.63J, added by SI 2009/1342. Article 63J(2) is subject to the exclusions in arts 63–63L. The whole of art.63J is subject to the exclusions in, 66, 72 and 72A.

[170] RAO Ch.XVD art.63N, added by SI 2009/1389. There are no exclusions.

[171] RAO Ch.XVE arts 63O–63R.

[172] RAO Ch.XVI art.64; it is subject to the exclusions in arts 5, 9B, 10, 25D, 51, 52, 63N, 65, 72 and 72A.

14-034 *Change title of section:*

4. REGULATORY RULES AND THE FCA HANDBOOK AND PRA RULEBOOK

(b) FCA Handbook

To the end of paragraph 14-035 after "the relevant time(s).", add:

14-035   Extensive amendments have been made to the Handbook in order to implement the requirements of MiFID II, Directive 2014/65/EU.[239A] In its Business Plan for 2020, published on 17 April 2019, the FCA stated that as part of its review of the FCA Handbook it was considering how firms interpret and interact with its regulatory standards, focusing upon where they incur cost, and exploring the possibility of a machine readable and executable Handbook (and machine executable regulatory reporting).

[239A] The FCA has issued a series of Policy Statements concerning implementation. Note in particular PS17/14: Markets in Financial Instruments Directive II implementation – Policy Statement II. This details amendments to the Handbook.

(i) Structure of FCA Handbook

After "of 30 September", replace "2016" with:

14-037   2017

The Business Standards block

14-040 *Replace table with:*

Reference Code	Title	Subject matter[243]
COBS	*Conduct of Business sourcebook*	Applies to all firms accepting deposits, conducting designated investment business and carrying on long-term business in relation to life policiess
ICOBS	*Insurance Conduct of Business sourcebook*	Applies to non-investment business of insurerss
MCOB	*Mortgages and Home Finance: Conduct of Business sourcebook*	Applies to firms conducting regulated mortgage activities and home finances
BCOBS	*Banking Conduct of Business sourcebook*	Applies to firms that accept deposits from banking customers
CMCOB	Claims Management	Applies to claims management firms which were regulated by the FCA as of 1 April 2019
CASS	Client Assets	Rule s and guidance on holding client assets and client moneys

Reference Code	Title	Subject matter[243]
MAR	Market Conduct	Applies to wholesale and professional markets

[243] As described in the Reader's Guide.

Regulatory Guides

Replace table with: **14-046**

Reference Code	Title
COLLG	Collective Investment Scheme Information Guide
EG	The Enforcement Guide
FCG	Financial Crime Guide: A Firm's guide to countering financial crime risks
FCTR	Financial Crime Thematic Reviews
PERG	The Perimeter Guidance Manual
RPPD	The Responsibilities of Providers and Distributors for the Fair Treatment of Customers
UNFCOG	The Unfair Contract Terms and Consumer Notices Regulatory Guide
WPDG	The Winding-down Planning Guide
M2G	The MiFID 2 Guide

(d) Statements of Principle and Code of Practice for Approved Persons (APER)

Replace paragraph (to replace all references to "controlled function" with "accountable function" and "significant influence position" with "accountable higher management function") with:

The "Statements of Principle for Approved Persons",[265] presently seven in   **14-054**
number, are similar in concept to the FCA's Principles for Businesses applicable to
authorised persons[266] but are tailored to the position of approved persons.[267] While
the latter focus on an authorised person's responsibilities when undertaking
regulated activities, the Statements of Principle for Approved Persons focus on approved
persons' responsibilities when undertaking "accountable" functions[268] in the
context of regulated activities. When issuing such Statements of Principle, the FCA
was required also to issue a Code of Practice to help determine compliance with
them.[269] The Code, divided into general and specific matters, was issued and is
incorporated together with the *Statements of Principle as a sourcebook* (referenced
APER) in the Handbook. The first four Statements of Principle relate to every approved
person. These statements require integrity, due skill and diligence and proper
standards of market conduct in carrying out his accountable function and open and
co-operative dealings with the FCA and other regulators and disclosure of information
of which the FCA would reasonably expect notice. The other three Statements
of Principle relate to those approved persons who perform an "accountable
higher management function" in relation to his sphere of responsibility in his accountable
function. They require the taking of reasonable steps to ensure proper
organisation, regulatory compliance and the exercise of competence in

management. Contravention of a Statement of Principle does not of itself give rise to any right of action[270] or affect the validity of any transaction but may attract disciplinary sanctions.[271]

[265] They were originally issued by the FCA under powers conferred under FSMA s.64 to enable the FCA to issue statements of principle as to the conduct of approved person. They did not originally have the status of *rules* of conduct. FSMA was amended (by the Financial Services (Banking Reform) Act 2013 s.30) so as to provide for the repeal of s.64 and the addition of new ss.64A and 64B. Under ss.64A and 64B the FCA is enabled to make rules of conduct in relation to persons approved by it (the PRA is similarly enabled). With effect from 7 March 2016 when FSMA s.64 was repealed and FSMA s.64A and s.64B (apart from subs, (5)) were brought fully into force (see SI 2015/490 arts 2(1)(b) and 2(1)(d) as amended by SI 2015/2055), the Statements of Principle are made by the FCA under powers conferred under FSMA s.64A and have the status of *rules* of conduct (though the FCA in its Handbook retains their original name as Statements of Principle).

[266] See para.14-053, above.

[267] See further para.14-013, above.

[268] Defined to include three categories of functions including, first, "FCA controlled functions" and second, "PRA controlled functions". Such "controlled functions" are not to be confused with "controlled activities" in relation to the financial promotion restriction, as to which see para.14-009 and 14-027 above.

[269] Originally by FSMA s.64(2).

[270] See FSMA s.64(8) prior to its repeal with effect from 7 March 2016 (see fn.292 above) and FSMA s.138D(5)(za) with effect from 25 July 2014 (see the Financial Services (Banking Reform) Act 2013 s.35 and Sch.3 para.9 which was brought into force on that date by SI 2014/1819 art.2(4)).

[271] See FSMA s.66. This section was amended with effect from 7 March 2016 (see Financial Services (Banking Reform) Act 2013 s.32(1)(a) and (b), and SI 2015/490 art.2(1)(c) as amended by SI 2015/2055 art.2(3)).

(e)   Conduct of Business Sourcebook (COBS)

(i)   Arrangement

14-056   *Replace table with:*

Reference Code	Title
COBS 1	Application
COBS 2	Conduct of business obligations
COBS 3	Client categorisation
COBS 4	Communicating with clients, including financial promotions
COBS 5	Distance communications
COBS 6	Information about the firm, its services and remuneration
COBS 7	Insurance Distribution
COBS 8	Client agreements
COBS 9	Suitability (including basic advice)
COBS 10	Appropriateness (for non-advised services)
COBS 11	Dealing and managing
COBS 11A	Underwriting and placing
COBS 12	Investment research
COBS 13	Preparing product information
COBS 14	Providing product information to clients

Reference Code	Title
COBS 15	Cancellation
COBS 16	Reporting information to clients
COBS 17	Claims handling for long-term care insurance
COBS 18	Specialist Regimes
COBS 19	Pensions supplementary provisions
COBS 20	With-profits
COBS 21	Permitted Links and conditional permitted links
COBS 22	Restrictions on the distribution of certain complex investment products

(v)   Communicating with Clients

Replace footnote 320 with:

[320]   COBS 6.1ZA.7B(2)(b).

14-062

5.   FSMA IMPOSED REGULATORY LIABILITIES

(b)   Liabilities Imposed on Authorised Persons

(iv)   Authorised Persons' Liability for Contravention of Regulatory Rules

Replace footnote 407 with:

[407]   The FSMA (Rights of Action) Regulations 2001 (SI 2001/2256): see para.14-076 above. For a case under the predecessor provision (1986 Act ss.62, 62A) where the claimant failed as he was not a "private customer", see *Diamantides v JP Morgan Chase Bank* [2005] EWHC 263 (Comm) (not considered on appeal at [2005] EWCA Civ 1612). See also *Titan Steel Wheels Ltd v Royal Bank of Scotland Plc* [2010] EWHC 211 (Comm); [2010] 2 Lloyd's Rep. 92; *Camerata Property Inc v Credit Suisse Securities (Europe) Ltd* [2012] EWHC 7 (Comm); [2012] P.N.L.R. 15; *Nextia Properties Ltd v Royal Bank of Scotland* [2013] EWHC 3167 (QB); *Gestmin SGPS SA v Credit Suisse (UK) Ltd* [2013] EWHC 3560 (Comm); *Bailey v Barclays Bank Plc* [2014] EWHC 2882 (QB); *Thornbridge Ltd v Barclays Bank Plc* [2015] EWHC 3430 (QB); *London Executive Aviation Ltd v Royal Bank of Scotland Plc* [2018] EWHC 74 (Ch). See also *Gorham v British Telecommunications Plc* [2000] 1 W.L.R. 2129 (statutory duty not owed to claimant), considered further at para.15-041, below.

14-081

Replace paragraph 14-082 (to incorporate amendments to footnotes 415, 416 and 418) with:

As discussed below,[414] contravention of a rule may well give rise to concurrent civil liability in tort or contract and so, in practice, s.138D liability may not add to the liability already existing at common law.[415] In particular the standard of the duty of care in negligence is likely to be largely coextensive with that imposed by the regulatory rules.[416] However, being able to point to an explicitly imposed duty that has been broken with consequent liability under s.138D, will often result in a more easily established liability[417] and hence it is now routinely pleaded in addition to the usual common law claims.[418] However, in contrast to contravention of the general prohibition and the financial promotion restriction, breach of a regulatory rule does not of itself give rise to any *criminal* liability,[419] nor does a breach of a rule as such generally provide a ground for vitiating any transaction.[420] Nevertheless, conduct which is impugnable not only as a breach of a rule but also on other common law grounds, such as a misrepresentation, presumably may vitiate a transaction at common law. A person is not to be regarded as having contravened a rule if the "rule-making instrument" had not been published sufficiently widely at the time.[421]

14-082

[414] See paras 15-021 to 15-024, below.

[415] See (under the predecessor provision, 1986 Act s.62): *Loosemore v Financial Concepts* [2001] Lloyd's Rep. P.N. 235; considered further in paras 15-022 and 15-058; *Gorham v British Telecommunications Plc* [2000] 1 W.L.R. 2129, considered further at paras 15-041, 15-043 and 15-081, below; *Seymour v Ockwell* [2005] EWHC 1137 (QB); [2005] P.N.L.R 39, considered further at paras 15-039 and 15-060, below. See also *Redmayne Bentley Stockbrokers v Isaacs* [2010] EWHC 1504 (Comm), followed in *Wilson v MF Global UK Ltd* [2011] EWHC 138 (QB), where Hamblen J saw no point in implying the rule as an implied term in the contract (as there was already liability under s.150). See, to the same effect, *Basma Al Sulaiman v Credit Suisse Securities (Europe) Ltd* [2013] EWHC 400 (Comm); [2013] 1 All E.R. (Comm) 1105, Cooke J: the common law "adds little or nothing" to a s.150 (as it then was) claim.

[416] See cases in previous note. See also *Gestmin SGPS SA v Credit Suisse (UK) Ltd* [2013] EWHC 3560 (Comm). But in *Green v Royal Bank of Scotland Plc* [2013] EWCA Civ 1197; [2014] Bus. L.R. 596 it was held that (the statutory claim being time-barred) the common law duty would not be *extended* so as be to coextensive with the statutory duty. *Green* was applied in *Flex-E-Vouchers Ltd v Royal Bank of Scotland Plc* [2016] EWHC 2604 (QB) and *CGL Group Ltd, J v Royal Bank of Scotland Plc* [2017] EWCA Civ 1073; [2018] 1 W.L.R. 2137 (denial of s.135D claim where this would upset the architecture of FCA redress scheme (see para.14-131)).

[417] This is especially the case where the claimant wishes to make a claim under the compensation scheme established under Pt XV of FSMA (see paras 14-132 to 14-17, below). See also *In the matter of Barings Plc (In Liquidation)* [2002] 1 B.C.L.C. 401 (s.150 claims in liquidation of firm).

[418] See the case law at fn.395, especially (i) *Loosemore v Financial Concepts* [2001] Lloyd's Rep. P.N. 235; (ii) *Gorham v British Telecommunications Plc* [2000] 1 W.L.R. 2129; (iii) *Martin v Britannia Life Ltd* [2000] Lloyd's Rep. P.N. 412; (iv) *Seymour v Ockwell* [2005] EWHC 1137 (QB); [2005] P.N.L.R. 39; (v) *Walker v Inter-Alliance Group Plc (In Administration), Scottish Equitable Plc* [2007] EWHC 1858 (Ch); [2007] Pens. L.R. 347; (vi) *Wilson v MF Global UK Ltd* [2011] EWHC 138 (QB); (vii) *Redmayne Bentley Stockbrokers v Isaacs* [2010] EWHC 1504 (Comm); (viii) *Bank Leumi (UK) Plc v Wachner* [2011] EWHC 656 (Comm); [2011] 1 C.L.C. 454; (ix) *Rubenstein v HSBC Bank* [2011] EWHC 2304 (QB); [2012] P.N.L.R. 7 (reversed on appeal on an unrelated point ([2012] EWCA Civ 1184; [2013] P.N.L.R. 9)); (x) *Green v Royal Bank of Scotland Plc* [2013] EWCA Civ 1197; [2014] Bus. L.R. 596; (xi) *Gestmin SGPS SA v Credit Suisse (UK) Ltd* [2013] EWHC 3560 (Comm).

[419] FSMA s.138E(1).

[420] FSMA s.138E(2)—but see the exceptions in s.138E(3). See *Thakker v Northern Rock (Asset Management) Plc* [2014] EWHC 2107 (QB): the predecessor s.151(2) applied so that alleged breaches of MCOB in a mortgage transaction did not made the right to possession unenforceable (as the contravention of an MCOB rule did not make the transaction void or unenforceable).

[421] FSMA s.138G(6). Note also s.138H as to verification of regulatory rules in legal proceedings.

6. FSMA REMEDIES

(a) Remedies Available to Regulators

Replace paragraph 14-088 (to incorporate amendments to footnotes 448 and 449) with:

14-088   FSMA confers a number of important enforcement powers (more extensive than those that existed under the 1986 Act[447]) which enable regulators to act on behalf of investors and obtain various remedies in the event of actual or potential breaches of the regulatory regime. The regulators (or sometimes the Secretary of State) may apply to the court for injunctions, "remedial orders" and "restitution orders" against persons contravening the regulatory regimes as well as against persons "knowingly concerned in the contravention".[448] The FCA may also so apply against persons engaging in market abuse.[449] Moreover the regulators are empowered to act extra-judicially and obtain "restitution" from authorised persons (only) contravening the regulatory regime.[450] The FCA may do so from any persons engaging in market abuse.[451]

[447] 1986 Act ss.6 and 61. In relation to s.6, see *Securities and Investments Board v Pantell SA* [1990] Ch. 426 (*Mareva* injunction available) (noted Lomnicka [1989] J.B.L. 509); *Securities and Investments Board v Pantell SA (No.2)* [1993] Ch. 256 (noted Lomnicka [1993] J.B.L. 54); *Securities and*

Investments Board v Lloyd-Wright [1993] 4 All E.R. 210 (no undertaking in damages for interlocutory relief and see now *FSA v Sinaloa Gold Plc*, para.14-089, below); *Securities and Investments Board v Scandex Capital Management A/S* unreported but noted (1997) Co. Lawyer 217 and affirmed on appeal [1998] 1 W.L.R. 712. Similar powers were conferred on the Bank of England to apply to the court in respect of contraventions of the Banking Act 1987 in ss.48, 49 and 93 of that Act.

[448] FSMA ss.380, 382, see para.14-094. For case law see *Financial Services Authority v Fradley* [2004] EWHC 3008 (Ch); [2004] All E.R. (D) 297, per Martin QC, and on appeal [2005] EWCA Civ 1183; [2006] 2 B.C.L.C. 616; *Financial Services Authority v Matthews* [2004] EWHC 2966 (Ch); [2005] Pens. L.R. 241 (failure to comply with PIA Ombudsman award); *Financial Services Authority v Martin* [2004] EWHC 3255 (Ch); [2005] 1 B.C.L.C. 495, appeal dismissed [2005] EWCA Civ 1422; [2006] P.N.L.R 11 (solicitors "knowingly concerned" in clients' breach); *Financial Services Authority v Shepherd* (2009) 153 (22) S.J.L.B. 34; [2009] Lloyd's Rep. F.C. 631; *Financial Services Authority v Anderson* [2010] EWHC 1547 (Ch) (breach of s.19); *Financial Conduct Authority v Capital Alternatives Ltd* unreported 26 March 2018 ChD (2018 WL 01472533).

[449] ibid. ss.381, 383. For the market abuse regime, see MAR, the EU Market Abuse Regulation (Regulation (EU) No 596/2014) and FSMA Pt VIII.

[450] ibid. ss.384(1) and 386.

[451] ibid. ss.384(2) and 386.

(ii)   Persons against whom Orders Available

Persons knowingly concerned

Replace paragraph 14-094 with:

Relevant orders may also be obtained against "any other person who appears to **14-094** have been knowingly concerned" in the contravention.[472] The phrase "knowingly concerned" has been transplanted from the 1986 Act,[473] but its precise meaning is unclear,[474] although some clarification has been given in the case law, especially *Financial Conduct Authority v Capital Alternatives Ltd*.[475] The phrase has two components, one pertaining to the state of mind of the person ("knowingly") and one pertaining to their involvement ("concerned"). In *Capital Alternatives Ltd* it was confirmed that mere passive knowledge was not enough but that the concept of "involvement" was a broad one and could cover both "those who pulled the strings at a directorial and/or managerial level" as well as "in an appropriate case, those who were involved at a lower level, depending on their knowledge and participation in the contravention".[476] A person who knowingly received the proceeds of another's wrongdoing was assumed to be "knowingly concerned" in the wrongdoing in the first of two decisions in the same case.[477] In a related decision[478] it was accepted that solicitors acting for the wrongdoer could also be knowingly concerned and "a person who was the moving light behind a company" was given as another example.[479] In another case it was stated that a director could be someone "knowingly concerned" in the company's breach[479A] and that a person could be so concerned "if he merely knew the facts giving rise to the breach, even if he erroneously thought a breach of the law was not occurring".[479B] In relation to market abuse, a relevant order may only be made against the person concerned, i.e. in actual or potential market abuse.[479C]

[472] FSMA ss.380(2), (3), 382(1).

[473] 1986 Act ss.6(2), 61(1).

[474] See Lomnicka, "'Knowingly concerned?' Participatory liability to regulators" (2000) 21 Co. Lawyer 120.

[475] unreported 26 March 2018 ChD (2018 WL 01472533). Cited with approval and applied in *Financial Conduct Authority v Avacade Ltd* [2020] EWHC 1673 (Ch).

[476] So it covered both "front office" and "back office" functions performed with the necessary knowledge.

[477] *Securities and Investments Board v Pantell SA* [1990] Ch. 426 (noted Lomnicka [1989] J.B.L. 509).

[478] *Securities and Investments Board v Pantell SA (No.2)* [1993] Ch. 256 (noted Lomnicka [1993] J.B.L. 54). See also: *Financial Services Authority v Martin* [2004] EWHC 3255 (Ch); [2005] 1 B.C.L.C. 495 (a decision under FSMA 2000).

[479] See also *Financial Conduct Authority v Capital Alternatives Ltd* unreported 26 March 2018 ChD (2018 WL 01472533).

[479A] *Securities and Investments Board v Scandex Capital Management A/S* unreported 26 March 1997 ChD but noted (1997) 18 Co. Lawyer 217, per Carnwath J.

[479B] *Securities and Investments Board v Scandex Capital Management A/S* [1998] 1 W.L.R. 712 CA; following *Burton v Burton* [1980] Ch. 240 at 246–247. See also (decisions under FSMA 2000): *Financial Services Authority v Fradley* [2004] EWHC 3008 (Ch); [2004] All E.R. (D) 297, per Martin QC, and on appeal [2005] EWCA Civ 1183; [2006] 2 B.C.L.C. 616, *Financial Services Authority v Martin* [2004] EWHC 3255 (Ch); [2005] 1 B.C.L.C. 495 and *Financial Conduct Authority v Capital Alternatives Ltd* unreported 26 March 2018 ChD (2018 WL 01472533) (*Scandex Capital Management* followed and *Fradley* applied).

[479C] FSMA ss.381, 383. However, market abuse can be committed "jointly or in concern", which could (in the right circumstances) cover a person who is "knowingly concerned".

(iii)   Orders Available

Restitution orders

Replace paragraph 14-100 (to incorporate an amendment to footnote 503 and a new footnote 505A at the end) with:

14-100   In *FSA v Shepherd*,[503] the judge noted that the discretion conferred by the statute was in extremely wide terms, but held that the court order had to be fair and just. Hence he regarded the culpability and means of the defendants as relevant. He also considered the relationship between the provision on "remedial orders"[504] and that on "restitution orders"[505] and held that a restitution order was more appropriate in the case before him, in that (unlike a remedial order) it did not require the "unravelling" of transactions (which entailed the investors choosing to do so and/or difficult factually issues).[505A]

[503] (2009) 153 (22) S.J.L.B. 34; [2009] Lloyd's Rep. F.C. 631 (Jules Sher QC, sitting as a Deputy High Court Judge), followed in *Financial Services Authority v Anderson* [2010] EWHC 1547 (Ch) (s.382 order for unlawful deposit-taking in breach of s.19). See also *Financial Services Authority v Upton & Co Accountants Ltd* [2010] EWHC 2345 (Ch) (reimbursement of money laid out rather than anticipated notional loss of profit, was the basis of restitution ordered under FSMA 2000 s.382). *Shepherd* and *Anderson* were applied in *Financial Conduct Authority v Capital Alternatives Ltd* unreported 26 March 2018 ChD (2018 WL 01472533) where it was held that "the default position was that restitution orders would usually extend to the losses sustained by investors".

[504] FSMA s.380(2), see para.14-097, above.

[505] FSMA s.382.

[505A] See also *Financial Conduct Authority v Avacade Ltd* [2020] EWHC 2175 (Ch) in which the court discussed the principles underpinning both final and interim restitution orders.

(iv)   The Regulators' Extra-judicial Power to Require Restitution

Replace footnote 507 with:

14-101   [507] ibid. As to market abuse, see MAR, the EU Market Abuse Regulation (Regulation (EU) No 596/2014) and FSMA Pt VIII.

7.   THE OMBUDSMAN SCHEME

(a)   Introduction

Replace footnote 537 with:

14-110   [537] FSMA s.225(1). For a general discussion, see Morris, "The intersection of commercial powers and complaints: the Financial Ombudsman Service, consumer protection and the courts" [2009] L.M.C.L.Q. 344. See also Samuel, *Consumer Financial Services Complaints and Compensation* (Thomson Reuters, 2017).

Scope of jurisdictions

Replace paragraph 14-113 (to incorporate amendments to footnotes 557 and 558 and new text following "Act 1973 s.6." at the end of the paragraph) with:

As to the legal status of FOS, it has been held that the FOS is a "tribunal" and that its final determinations are "judgments" for the purposes of the merger doctrine (whereby a claimant's rights are extinguished by a "judgment" of a "tribunal").[557] In Scotland, it has been held that the FOS is not an "arbitrator" for the purposes of the Prescription and Limitation (Scotland) Act 1973 s.6[558] as in an arbitration both parties were bound by the decision whereas the complainant to FOS had the option of either accepting or rejecting the decision.[558A] That decision was followed in *Berkeley Burke SIPP Administration LLP v Charlton*,[558B] where it was held that an agreement between a complainant and firm that the FOS reconsider, as an alternative to a judicial review application, a (positive outcome of the) complaint was not an "arbitration agreement" within the Arbitration Act 1996,[558C] in that the FOS operated under the statutory FSMA scheme. Hence the reconsidered FOS decision was not an "arbitration award" to which the appeals procedure under the Arbitration Act 1996 applied.[558D]

14-113

[557] *Andrews v SBJ Benefit Consultants* [2010] EWHC 2875 (Ch); [2011] P.N.L.R. 29, see para.14-124, below. This case was approved in *Clark v In Focus Asset Management & Tax Solutions Ltd* [2014] EWCA Civ 118; [2014] 1 W.L.R. 2502. Hence a complainant cannot pursue civil proceedings for further compensation, having accepted a FOS determination.

[558] *Clark v Argyle Consulting Ltd* [2010] CSOH 154; 2011 S.L.T. 180 (Outer House of the Court of Session).

[558A] See para.14-124.

[558B] [2017] EWHC 2396 (Comm); [2018] 1 Lloyd's Rep. 337; [2018] C.T.L.C. 1.

[558C] s.6.

[558D] s.69.

(b) Compulsory and Voluntary Jurisdiction

(i) The Compulsory Jurisdiction

Replace paragraph 14-144 (to incorporate amendments to footnotes 559 and 560) with:

This is imposed upon all authorised firms[559] and extends to cover[560] all regulated activities,[561] payment services, consumer credit activities, lending money secured by a charge on land, lending money (other than "restricted credit" (as defined)), paying money by a plastic card,[562] and the provision of ancillary banking services. The latter category includes the provision and operation of cash machines, safe deposit boxes, etc.

14-114

[559] See FSMA s.226(2). In January 2018 the FCA amended the Compulsory Jurisdiction of the FOS to ensure that it can consider complaints about investment services provided by CRD credit institutions and investment firms authorised under MiFID (DISP 2.3.1A).

[560] DISP 2.3. These activities include any "ancillary activities, including advice, carried on by the firm in connection with" those activities. Complaints about firms that are members of designated professional bodies and which relate to any otherwise exempt regulated activity (see para.14-018, above) cannot be handled under the Compulsory Jurisdiction of the FOS but must go to the professional body. For a case held to be outside the jurisdiction, see *R. (on the application of Mazarona Properties Ltd) v Financial Ombudsman Service* [2017] EWHC 1135 (Admin); [2017] A.C.D. 94. In *R. (on the applica-*

tion of Chancery (UK) LLP) v Financial Ombudsman Service [2015] EWHC 407 (Admin); [2015] B.T.C. 13 the FOS held that the compulsory jurisdiction applied to tax advice given by a firm to its client when entering a film scheme. The Court rejected the application for judicial review.

561 FSMA s.226(4) limits the activities which may be covered by the Compulsory Jurisdiction to activities which are "regulated activities or which could be made regulated activities by an order under section 22 [of FSMA]".

562 Excluding a store card where that is not a "consumer credit activity" (as defined).

(c) Complaint Handling Procedures for Firms

Replace footnote 569 with:

14-116   569 DISP 1.4. In *Davis v Lloyds Bank Plc* [2020] EWHC 1758 (Ch) the claimant argued that an IRHP review in which he participated was a complaints process conducted in breach of the DISP Handbook. The court rejected the claim on a preliminary issue, determining that he had made no "complaint" and even if he had, the IHRP review was not a complaints handling mechanism to which DISP obligations attached.

(e) The Investigation

Replace paragraph 14-119 (to incorporate new text added to the second sentence after "into the complaint.") with:

14-119   The Ombudsman may dismiss a complaint without considering its merits in a number of circumstances.580 Otherwise, he will proceed to carry out an investigation into the complaint. It was confirmed in *R. (on the application of Williams) v Financial Ombudsman Service* that the "jurisdiction is inquisitorial not adversarial".580A He has a considerable discretion as to the procedure to be adopted during the course of any investigation. The starting point for any investigation will generally be the complaint form which complainants are required to complete at the outset. That complaint form will usually be sent to the respondent and a response to the complaints invited. Directions can be and frequently are given by the Ombudsman as to the issues that he wishes to be addressed, the evidence that he requires, how such evidence should be given and the like. Representations and submissions, either in writing or at a hearing, frequently are invited.581 The Ombudsman is also empowered to require a party to provide specified information or documents to assist in his investigation if the information or documents in question are necessary for the determination of the complaint.582 A failure to comply with a request for information or documents without reasonable excuse can be referred to the court, which may deal with the defaulter as if he were in contempt.583 For respondents that are "authorised persons" under FSMA,584 the failure may also be referred to the regulators for possible disciplinary action. The Ombudsman has also, on occasion, published guidance as to the material he requires parties to particular types of complaints to provide.585

580 See DISP 3.3.4. Those circumstances include: (1) if the complainant has suffered no financial loss, material distress or material inconvenience; (2) if the complaint has no reasonable prospect of success; (3) if the respondent has already made a fair and reasonable offer of compensation which remains open for acceptance; (4) if the matter has already been considered by the FOS or a predecessor scheme; (5) if the complaint has been the subject of court proceedings in which there has been a decision on the merits; (6) if the complaint is at that time the subject of court proceedings, unless those proceedings have been stayed for the purpose of referring the complaint to the FOS; (7) the complaint is about investment performance; (8) there is some other compelling reason why it is inappropriate for the FOS to deal with the complaint. If the Ombudsman is minded to dismiss a complaint on any such basis he must give the complainant an opportunity to submit representations as to why he should not do so.

580A [2008] EWHC 2142 (Admin) per Irwin J at [26].

581 The Ombudsman is not fettered by the rules of evidence that would be applied by a court. He is permitted either to exclude evidence that would otherwise be admissible in a court or to include evidence that would not be admissible: DISP 3.5.8.

582 FSMA s.231(1).

583 FSMA s.232(2).

584 See para.14-011, above.

585 Such guidance has for example been given in relation to complaints about endowment and zero dividend preference share misselling.

Replace paragraph 14-121 (to incorporate amendments to footnotes 589 and 590 and new text following "of the case." at the end of the paragraph) with:

While this "fair and reasonable jurisdiction" undoubtedly increases the scope for **14-121** uncertainty over what decision the Ombudsman may reach, guidance has been given as to factors that he is obliged to take into account when reaching that decision. In particular, the Ombudsman must consider: (1) relevant law, regulations, regulators' rules, guidance and standards and codes of practice and (2) where appropriate, what he considers to have been good industry practice at the relevant time.588 Hence it is clear that he is not obliged to make a decision strictly in accordance with English law. If he considers that the result under English law would not be fair and reasonable, he is free to make an award at variance with that result provided that he has taken into account the matters identified above. In *R. (on the application of Heather Moor & Edgecomb Ltd) v Financial Ombudsman Service*,589 the Court of Appeal confirmed that FOS determinations may be made by reference to what the Ombudsman considers to be "fair and reasonable" and not necessarily in accordance with the law. In an earlier decision,590 it was held that the Ombudsman was free to make an award which differed from that which a court applying the law would make (and which, on the facts, differed from the advice given by a QC to the effect that the claimants were not liable for loss caused by the unforeseeable dishonesty of an investment manager), provided that the award was one which was "fair and reasonable" in all the circumstances of the case. This state of affairs led one judge to opine that "[t]he court had concerns about a jurisdiction, such as the ombudsman's, which occupied an uncertain space outside the common law and statute. The relationship between what was fair and reasonable, and what the law laid down, is not altogether clear."590A

588 DISP 3.6.4.

589 [2008] EWCA Civ 642; [2009] 1 All E.R. 328. See [80]: the Ombudsman "is dealing with complaints, and not legal causes of action".

590 *R. (on the application of IFG Financial Services Ltd) v Financial Ombudsman Service Ltd* [2005] EWHC 1153 (Admin); [2006] 1 B.C.L.C. 534, Burnton J especially [12], [74]–[76]. See now DISP 3.7.2. And see *R. (on the application of Bamber & BP Financial Services) v Financial Ombudsman Service Ltd* [2009] EWCA 593 (FOS could determine a complaint outside the statutory limitation periods).

590A *R. (on the application of Aviva Life and Pensions (UK) Ltd) v Financial Ombudsman Service* [2017] EWHC 352 (Admin); [2017] Lloyd's Rep I.R. 404 per Jay J at [73].

Replace footnote 593 with:

593 For examples of (unsuccessful) challenges to decisions of the Ombudsman see (i) *R. (Norwich &* **14-122** *Peterborough Building Society) v Financial Ombudsman Service Ltd* [2002] EWHC 2379; [2003] 1 All E.R. (Comm) 65; (ii) *R. (Green Denman) v Financial Ombudsman Service Ltd* [2003] EWHC 338 (Admin); (iii) *R. (IFG Financial Services Ltd) v Financial Ombudsman Services Ltd* [2005] EWHC 1153 (Admin); [2006] 1 B.C.L.C. 534; (iv) *R. (Heather Moor and Edgecomb Ltd) v Financial Ombudsman Service Ltd* [2008] EWCA 643; [2009] 1 All E.R. 328 (fee-charging regime (whereby all firms, even those where complaints were dismissed, had to pay fees to FOS)) was upheld as not irrational; (v) *R. (on the application of Keith Williams) v Financial Ombudsman Service* [2008] EWHC 2142 (Admin); (vi) *R. (Bamber & BP Financial Services) v Financial Ombudsman Services* [2009] EWCA 593, and further cases cited below. For successful challenges see: (i) *R. (Garrison Investment Analysis) v Financial Ombudsman Service* [2006] EWHC 2466 (Admin) (decision quashed as being "irrational" in that it was based on an assumption that was unsupported by the evidence); (ii) *R. (British Bankers Association) v Financial Services Authority* [2011] EWHC 999 (Admin); [2011] Bus. L.R. 1531; (iii) *R. (Kelly) v*

Financial Ombudsman Service Ltd [2017] EWHC 3581 (Admin); [2018] C.T.L.C. 107. For other unsuccessful challenges to FOS, see also *R. (Green) v Financial Ombudsman Service Ltd* [2012] EWHC 1253
(Admin); (iii) *R. (Aviva Life and Pensions (UK) Ltd) v Financial Ombudsman Service* [2017] EWHC
352 (Admin); [2017] Lloyd's Rep. I.R. 404 (FOS determination quashed on basis that it was flawed for
inadequacy of reasons); *R. (Bankole) v Financial Ombudsman Service* [2012] EWHC 3555 (Admin);
R. (Calland) v Financial Ombudsman Service Ltd [2013] EWHC 1327 (Admin); *R. (London Capital
Group) v Financial Ombudsman Service Ltd* [2013] EWHC 2425 (Admin); [2014] A.C.D. 3; *R. (Fisher)
v Financial Ombudsman Service* [2014] EWHC 4928 (Admin); *Westscott Financial Services Ltd v
Financial Ombudsman Service* [2014] EWHC 3972 (Admin); *R. (Bluefin Insurance Ltd) v Financial
Ombudsman Service Ltd* [2014] EWHC 3413 (Admin); [2015] Bus. L.R. 656; [2015] Lloyd's Rep. I.R.
457; *R. (Chancery (UK) LLP) v Financial Ombudsman Service* [2015] EWHC 407 (Admin); [2015]
B.T.C. 13; (vii) *Full Circle Asset Management Ltd v Financial Ombudsman Service Ltd* [2017] EWHC
323 (Admin); *R. (TenetConnect Services Ltd) v Financial Ombudsman* [2018] EWHC 323 (Admin);
[2018] 1 B.C.L.C. 726; [2018] C.T.L.C. 116. For leave to appeal to challenge FOS, see: *R. (London
Capital Group Ltd) v Financial Ombudsman Service Ltd* [2013] EWHC 218 (Admin).

After paragraph 14-122, add new paragraph:

The Ombudsman has the power to reconsider a complaint if (instead of proceeding to judicial review) the complainant and firm agree he should do so.[595A]

[595A] *Berkeley Burke SIPP Administration LLP v Charlton* [2018] 1 Lloyd's Rep. 337; [2018] C.T.L.C.
1.

(f) The Award

Money awards.

Replace paragraph 14-127 with:

14-127   The maximum money award that the Ombudsman may make is now £355,000
for a complaint concerning an act or omission taking place on or after 1 April 2020;
£350,000 where it takes place between 1 April 2019 and 31 March 2020; and
£160,000 where it takes place before 1 April 2019. There is an indexation provision to adjust the maximum award going forward.[609] The award is exclusive of costs
and interest.[609A] In addition, if the Ombudsman considers that the award necessary
to compensate the complainant exceeds the limit, he can recommend that the
respondent should pay the difference on a voluntary basis. However, that recommendation is not enforceable and the respondent is under no obligation to meet any
higher money award.[609B]

[609] DISP 3.7.4(R).

[609A] DISP 3.7.5G.

[609B] DISP 3.7.6G.

8. FINANCIAL SERVICES COMPENSATION SCHEME

(d) Qualifying Conditions for Compensation

Replace footnote 642 with:

14-136   [642] COMP 3.2.1. The eligibility requirements for deposit and policyholder claims are now set out in the
PRA's Depositor Protection and Policyholder Protection Rules. In respect of claims under protected
contracts of insurance there is one additional qualifying condition, namely that it is not reasonably
practicable or appropriate to take steps to secure continuity of insurance or to provide assistance to an
insurance undertaking in financial difficulties.

(ii) Protected Claims

Replace footnote 650 with:

14-138   [650] COMP 5.2.1 and the PRA Depositor Protection and Policyholder Protection Rules.

(v) Assignment of Rights

Replace paragraph 14-141 (to incorporate deletion of footnote 655 and amendments to footnotes 657 and 658) with:

As a pre-condition to a payment of compensation, the COMP rules provide that **14-141** the FSCS may require a claimant to assign the whole or any part of his rights against the relevant person or against any third party to the FSCS on such terms as it thinks fit.[656] Where this is done the FSCS is obliged to make "such recoveries as it reasonably can" through the rights so assigned.[657] It is also obliged to pay any recoveries made through the pursuit of the assigned claim to the claimant, unless equivalent compensation has already been paid by the FSCS to him.[658] In *FSCS Ltd v Abbey National Treasury Services Plc*,[659] a challenge on the basis that these rules were ultra vires the powers of the FSA to make compensation rules under FSMA failed. In addition, it was held that, as assignee, the FSCS did not have to give credit for the compensation received by the assignors when recovering (as assignee) for the loss they had suffered.

[656] COMP 3.2.1(3), 7.2.1: see *Financial Services Compensation Scheme v Larnell Insurance* [2005] EWCA Civ 1408. Where such an assignment is required, there is no obligation on the part of the FSCS to provide the claimant with an indemnity against any liability for costs that might arise in any future proceedings pursued by the FSCS against the relevant body: *R. v Investors Compensation Scheme Ltd Ex p. Bowden* [1994] 1 W.L.R. 17; [1996] A.C. 261.

[657] COMP 7.4.1. For examples of one of the FSCS's predecessor schemes taking such steps, see *Investors Compensation Scheme Ltd v West Bromwich Building Society* [1999] Lloyd's L. Rep. P.N. 496 and *Investors Compensation Scheme Ltd v Cheltenham & Gloucester Plc* [1996] 2 B.C.L.C. 165. See now *FSCS Ltd v Abbey National Treasury Services Plc* [2008] EWHC 1897 (Ch).

[658] COMP 7.6.1.

[659] [2008] EWHC 1897 (Ch), following (a decision under the predecessor provision in the Financial Services Act 1986) *Investors Compensation Scheme Ltd v West Bromwich Building Society (No.1)* [1998] 1 B.C.L.C. 493.

(e) Compensation

(i) Offers of Compensation

Replace paragraph 14-142 (to incorporate amendments to footnotes 660 and 665) with:

The FSCS is obliged to ensure that a claimant does not suffer any disadvantage **14-142** by promptly accepting any offer of compensation that might be made to him by the FSCS.[660] The amount of compensation payable to a claimant in respect of any type of protected claim (except in the case of "protected deposits"[661]) is the amount of his "overall net claim" against the relevant person at the "quantification date".[662] A claimant's overall net claim is the sum of the protected claims of the same category that he has against a relevant person in default, less the amount of any liability which the relevant person may set off against any of those claims.[663] The FSCS will therefore (except in the case of bank deposits) offset against any award of compensation, monies to which the relevant person could properly claim to be entitled from the claimant. It will also offset monies that the relevant person (or a third party) has already paid to the claimant, if such payment was connected with the relevant person's liability to the claimant.[664] The quantification date varies according to the type of protected claim in issue.[665]

[660] COMP 7.6.1.

[661] This qualification was inserted after the 2008 financial crisis to facilitate the swift payment out of compensation for bank deposits with a failed bank, without waiting to calculate the net liability of the bank to the customer.

[662] COMP 12.2.1. In addition, COMP 12.4–12.6 identifies a number of specific matters of which the FSCS must take account when assessing appropriate compensation under particular categories of protected claims.

[663] COMP 12.2.4.

[664] In *R. v Investors Compensation Scheme Ex p. Bowden* [1996] A.C. 261 investors challenged the decision of the ICS to make deductions from the compensation that was offered to them so that the amount offered fell below the investors' overall net claim. The House of Lords found that the ICS was entitled to exclude elements of a claim which it considered were not essential to provide fair compensation to investors and also to place a reasonable limit on the sums payable to investors in respect of their professional fees. It is doubtful whether the COMP rules would be interpreted so as to permit the FSCS to apply similar deductions or limitations.

[665] COMP 12.3.

Replace paragraph 14-143 (to incorporate replacement text at the end of the paragraph) with:

14-143   The FSCS may make reduced or interim offers of compensation if the amount of compensation payable is uncertain or if the claimant has reasonable prospects of recovering part of his loss from any other person.[666] Any offer of compensation made by the FSCS must remain open for 90 days unless it appears during that period that no offer should in fact have been made, or the offer is rejected in that period. Upon the expiry of 90 days, the FSCS may withdraw the offer unless its size has been disputed and consideration is being given to making a reduced or interim offer.[667] No offer of compensation will exceed the limits payable by the FSCS for protected claims.[668] For protected deposits or protected dormant accounts, the limit is now 100% of the claim up to £85,000. For a protected contract of insurance when the contract is a relevant general insurance contract and for protected non-investment insurance mediation, the limit is: (i) 100% of the claim (to an unlimited maximum) where the claim is in respect of a liability subject to compulsory insurance, and (ii) 100% of the claim (to an unlimited maximum) in all other cases. For protected investment business and protected home finance mediation, the limit is now 100 per cent to a maximum payment of £85,000.[669] Customers of firms who have failed and were declared in default prior to 1 April 2019 will still be covered up to the previous £50,000 limits; the new higher limits, however, apply only to claims against firms that fail on or after 1 April 2019.

[666] COMP 8.3.2 and COMP 11.2.4–11.2.5.

[667] COMP 8.3.1. The offer may also be withdrawn if it is rejected.

[668] See in COMP 10.2. Interest, which may be paid on the compensation sum under COMP 11.2.7, is not to be taken into account when applying limits on the compensation sum payable.

[669] COMP 10.2.3, Rule 4.1 of the PRA Depositor Protection Rulebook and Rule 17 of the PRA Policyholder Protection Rulebook.

(ii)   Acceptance of Offers of Compensation

Replace paragraph 14-145 (to incorporate amendments to footnotes 671, 672 and 673) with:

14-145   The FSCS is obliged[670] to pay a claim as soon as reasonably possible after it has satisfied itself that the qualifying conditions for compensation have been met and the amount of compensation due to the claimant has been calculated and in any event, generally within 20 working days for a protected deposit and three months in relation to any other claim.[671] With limited exceptions,[672] payment will be made to the claimant or to the order of the claimant unless arrangements have been or are to be made to secure continuity of insurance or the FSCS is taking measures to safeguard the claimant in respect of an insurance undertaking in financial difficulty.[673]

670 COMP 9.2.1.

671 COMP 9.2.1 and Annex 1 of the PRA Depositor Protection Rulebook. The FCA may extend these deadlines to 30 working days and six months. COMP 9.2.2 does permit the FSCS in extremely limited circumstances to postpone paying compensation to a claimant.

672 See COMP 11.2.2–11.2.2A.

673 Rule 18.1(1) of the PRA Policyholder Protection Rules.

(iii) Insurance

Replace paragraph 14-146 (to incorporate amendments to footnotes 674–677) with:

14-146 Insurance, and in particular long-term insurance, can cause difficulty when the issue of compensation is considered. If, for example, a life policy is payable only upon the death of the policyholder or upon the policyholder reaching a certain age, and he is below that age at the material time, it is not obvious how best to compensate the policyholder. Particular provision is therefore made in FSMA for the FSCS to make arrangements *not* to make an immediate payment of monetary compensation to such persons. The FSCS may instead secure continuity of insurance for policyholders whose insurer is unable, or appears to be unable, to satisfy claims against it.[674] This may involve either securing or facilitating the transfer of all or part of the long-term insurance business of the relevant person in default to another firm or securing the issue of policies by another firm to eligible claimants in substitution for their existing policies.[675] The FSCS may also take measures to safeguard a policyholder whose insurer encounters financial difficulty.[676] This may involve securing or facilitating the transfer of all or part of the business of the relevant person which consists of carrying out contracts of insurance to another firm. Alternatively, it may involve the provision of assistance to the relevant person to enable it to continue to effect or carry out contracts of insurance.[677]

674 FSMA s.216. The rules governing the circumstances in which the FSCS is obliged to make arrangements to secure continuity of insurance are set out in Rule 4 of the PRA Policyholder Protection Rules.

675 Rule 4.2.

676 FSMA s.217. The rules governing the circumstances in which the FSCS is obliged to take measures to safeguard eligible claimants where the relevant person about whom complaint is made is an insurance undertaking in financial difficulty are set out in Rule 5.1.

677 Rule 5.2.

FINANCIAL PRACTITIONERS

2.   Duties and Liabilities

(d)   The Misrepresentation Act 1967

(i)   Relevance

Replace footnote 9 with:

15-014   9 See generally *Chitty on Contracts*, 33rd edn, Ch.7. For a successful s.2 claim in the investment context, see *Taberna Europe CDO II Plc v Selskabet (Formerly Roskilde Bank A/S) (In Bankruptcy)* [2015] EWHC 871 (Comm). However on appeal the court held that the bank was entitled to rely upon a disclaimer; [2016] EWCA Civ 1262.

(ii)   Representations as to Fact or Opinion: Suitability

Replace footnote 10 with:

15-015   10 See generally, Chitty, op. cit., paras 7–007 to 7–024. But for findings that statements, in the investment context, were only of "opinion", see *IFE Fund SA v Goldman Sachs International* [2007] EWCA Civ 811; *Springwell Navigation Corp v JP Morgan Chase Bank* [2010] EWCA Civ 1221 (considered further at paras 15-036 and 15-051, below); *Cassa di Risparmio ella Repubblica di San Marino SpA v Barclays Bank Ltd* [2011] EWHC 484 (Comm).

(e)   Contractual Duties

(iii)   Incorporation of Regulatory Duties in Contract

Replace paragraph 15-021 (to incorporate amendments to footnotes 30, 31 and 37) with:

15-021   Regulatory duties such as those imposed by the FCA Handbook, market codes of practice or other codes also may be incorporated as contractual duties, whether expressly or by implication. Contravention may then be actionable at common law as a breach of contract as well as, in some cases, being actionable by reason of a regulatory statute, although in two first instance cases the court did not see the necessity to imply such a term if the statutory requirement was in any event actionable.[28] What terms fall to be implied in a contract is a question of law[29] to be determined in accordance with usual principles for implication of terms.[30] These principles were considered in a financial services context in *Clarion Ltd v National*

Provident Institution.[31] It was alleged that the defendant mutual life office had agreed to grant the claimant investment advisers a special block switching arrangement for their clients' investments. The defendant contended that the SIB Principles[32] were implicitly incorporated as a term of that agreement.[33] Rimer J rejected the contention. He reasoned, first, since both claimant and defendant already were subject to the SIB Principles at the time that the agreement was made, there was no point in incorporating those principles into the contract. Secondly, a number of the SIB Principles were either irrelevant or inapplicable to the relationship between claimant and defendant. Thirdly, there was no basis for classifying the agreement between the parties as a generic type which required the implication of the SIB Principles. A contrasting conclusion was reached obiter in *Larussa-Chigi v CS First Boston Ltd,*[34] in which Thomas J held that relevant agreements between the parties expressly incorporated the London Code of Conduct.[35] He went on to opine that, had this not been the case, the code would have been incorporated as an implied term since it was not intended that the foreign exchange transactions in question be unregulated. The implied term to exercise reasonable care and skill[36] may provide another, indirect, route to the incorporation of regulatory rules or code of practice. Thus such rules or code will usually be relevant in ascertaining what is required in order to meet the standard in question.[37]

[28] *Redmayne Bentley Stockbrokers v Isaacs* [2010] EWHC 1504 (Comm) at [94], Hamblen J; *Wilson v MF Global UK Ltd* [2011] EWHC 138 (QB) at [14], Eady J.

[29] *Mosvolds Rederi A/S v Food Corp of India* [1986] 2 Lloyd's Rep. 68 at 70.

[30] See generally *Chitty on Contracts*, 33rd edn, paras 14-001 to 14-036. See, recently, *Marks & Spencer Plc v BNP Paribas Securities Services Trust Co (Jersey) Ltd* [2015] UKSC 72.

[31] [2000] 1 W.L.R. 1888. See also *Bear Stearns Bank Plc v Forum Global Equity Ltd* [2007] EWHC 1576 (Comm), considered further at para.15-093, below (Loan Market Association rules not implied) and *Redmayne Bentley Stockbrokers v Isaacs* [2010] EWHC 1504 (Comm), above. *Clarion* was applied in *Flex-E-Vouchers Ltd v Royal Bank of Scotland Plc* [2016] EWHC 2604 (QB) (COB rules not implied where s.138D claim not available as upholding the claim would undermine the limits of the statutory scheme).

[32] Similar to the FCA's "Principles for Business", see para.14-053, above.

[33] The defendant contended both that it was a matter of obvious inference that the SIB Principles were incorporated and that the agreement with the claimant was of a particular generic type which required the implication of the SIB Principles.

[34] [1998] C.L.C. 277.

[35] i.e. promulgated by the Bank of England and applicable to the defendant as a listed institution under the 1986 Act s.43. The full title of the code is "A Guide to Accepted Best Practice in the Wholesale Markets in Sterling, Foreign Exchange and Bullion".

[36] Implied at common law and by reason of the Supply of Goods and Services Act 1982 s.13, except from 1 October 2015 in relation to consumer contracts, as which see the Consumer Rights Act 2015 s.49.

[37] See *Brandeis (Brokers) Ltd v Herbert Black* [2001] 2 Lloyd's Rep. 359 at [20] per Toulson J (considered further in para.15-051, below. See also *Rubenstein v HSBC Bank* [2011] EWHC 2304 (QB) (for a summary of the facts, see para.15-037, below), where HH Judge Havelock-Allan QC agreed with the general proposition that failing to comply with (the then applicable) FSA standards would ordinarily be regarded as negligent (although no point to the contrary appears to have been taken); *Rubenstein* was reversed on appeal [2012] EWCA Civ 1184), but on other grounds. In *Thomas v Triodos Bank NV* [2017] EWHC 314 (QB); [2018] 1 B.C.L.C. 530; [2017] 1 C.L.C. 536 at [59] et seq it was held that a bank that advertised to the claimants that it subscribed to the Banking Code (then an industry code) owed a duty to follow the best practice articulated in the Code (which it had "signed up to") and hence it owed more than a duty not to mislead or misstate. In *Adams v Options SIPP UK* [2020] EWHC 1229 (Ch) the court rejected an argument that a SIPP operator owed advisory duties in respect of the underlying SIPP investment under the COBS 2.1.1 duty to act in the client's best interests; such duty was inconsistent with the "execution only" terms of the retainer. In *Barness v Ingenious Media Ltd* [2019] EWHC 3299 (Ch); [2020] P.N.L.R. 10 the court struck out claims by investors in film-based tax schemes against the banks involved in those schemes; there was no basis to imply relevant duties owed to investors.

(iv) Duty of Care and Skill

Utility

Replace paragraph 15-024 (to incorporate new text after the fourth sentence after "to the claimant.") with:

15-024   In many cases the statutory cause of action for breach of a relevant regulatory rule may provide a more straightforward basis of claim to a private investor.[49] Reliance on breach of the contractual duty to exercise reasonable care and skill may then be superfluous. Usually a breach of a regulatory rule will also amount to a breach of that contractual duty. On the other hand, the statutory cause of action may not be available to the claimant.[50] But if the statutory claim does not extend to a particular claimant, the court will not undermine that limitation by implying the relevant rule into the claimant's contract so as to confer a breach of contact action.[50A] The common law duty of care and skill will then be an important basis of claim, including as an indirect means of invoking breaches of regulatory rules.[51] Moreover, it may not be possible to point to breach of a specific rule. Further, regulatory rules may have limited application or relevance to a claimant, as for example in relation to corporate investors in respect of sophisticated investments such as options, futures and contracts for differences or portfolio management.[52] In such circumstances it will be necessary to fall back on the common law, especially the duty of care and skill.

[49] See paras 14-080 to 14-082, above. See per Cooke J in *Basma Al Sulaiman v Credit Suisse Securities (Europe) Ltd* [2013] EWHC 400 (Comm); [2013] 1 All E.R. (Comm) 1105: the common law "adds little or nothing" to a s.150 (as it then was) claim.

[50] See para.14-081, above, as to whom the statutory right of action is available. The s.138D (previously s.150) claim may not be available as the claimant is not a "private person": *Diamantis Diamantides v JP Morgan Chase Bank* [2005] EWCA Civ 1612; *Titan Steel Wheels Ltd v Royal Bank of Scotland Plc* [2010] EWHC 211 (Comm); [2010] 2 Lloyd's Rep. 92; *Camerata Property Inc v Credit Suisse Securities (Europe) Ltd* [2012] EWHC 7 (Comm); *Nextia Properties Ltd v Royal Bank of Scotland* [2013] EWHC 3167 (QB); *Gestmin SGPS SA v Credit Suisse (UK) Ltd* [2013] EWHC 3560 (Comm); *Bailey v Barclays Bank Plc* [2014] EWHC 2882 (QB); *Thornbridge Ltd v Barclays Bank Plc* [2015] EWHC 3430 (QB); *London Executive Aviation Ltd v Royal Bank of Scotland Plc* [2018] EWHC 74 (Ch). See also *Gorham v British Telecommunications Plc* [2000] 1 W.L.R. 2129 (statutory duty not owed to claimant), considered further at para.15-041, below.

[50A] See *Flex-E-Vouchers Ltd v Royal Bank of Scotland Plc* [2016] EWHC 2604 (QB) (COB rules not implied where s.138D claim not available). And see *CGL Group Ltd, J v Royal Bank of Scotland Plc* [2017] EWCA Civ 1073; [2018] 1 W.L.R. 2137 (denial of s.135D claim where this would upset the architecture of FCA redress scheme (see para.14-131)).

[51] See para.15-021, above and *Gorham v British Telecommunications Plc* [2000] 1 W.L.R. 2129, considered further at para.15-041, below.

[52] *ANZ Banking Group Ltd v Cattan* unreported 21 August 2001, Morison J (see paras 15-055, 15-063, 15-060 and 15-081, below); *ED&F Man Commodity Advisers Ltd v Fluxo-Cane Overseas Ltd* [2010] EWHC 212; *Marex Financial Ltd v Fluxo-Cane Overseas Ltd* [2010] EWHC 2690 (Comm); *Redmayne Bentley Stockbrokers v Isaacs* [2010] EWHC 1504; *Wilson v MF Global UK Ltd* [2011] EWHC 138; *Bank Leumi (UK) Plc v Wachner* [2011] EWHC 656 (Comm); [2011] C.L.C. 454; *Nextia Properties Ltd v Royal Bank of Scotland* [2013] EWHC 3167 (QB); *Gestmin SGPS SA v Credit Suisse (UK) Ltd* [2013] EWHC 3560 (Comm).

(v) Agency

Common law agency principles

Replace footnote 55 with:

15-027   [55] See *Bowstead & Reynolds on Agency*, 21st edn (2019), art.27 at paras 3–021 onwards.

(f)   Tort-based Duties

(i)   *Deceit or Fraudulent Misrepresentation*

General

Replace footnote 59 with:

[59] See generally *Clerk & Lindsell on Torts*, 22nd edn (2017), paras 18-01 onwards.   **15-028**

(ii)   *Misfeasance in Public Office*

Replace footnote 70 with:

[70] For the (lack of) negligence liability, see para.15-046, below. For an unsuccessful claim, see *AAI*   **15-034**
Consulting Ltd v Financial Conduct Authority [2016] EWHC 2812 (Comm).

3.   BREACH OF DUTY

(b)   Misleading Promotion

(v)   *Dealing and Managing*

After paragraph 15-066, add new paragraph 15-066A:

In *Rocker v Full Circle Asset Management Ltd*[172A] the claimant substantially suc-   **15-066A**
ceeded in his claim for damages against the defendant asset management company
in respect of losses arising from a fall in capital value of a portfolio of investments
under management from an original investment of £1.5m in 2009 to £681,443 some
five years later. Morris J held that in certain periods, the actual risk profile of the
portfolio exceeded the agreed portfolio risk profile, and thus the defendant acted in
breach of its agreed mandate and client agreement. He also held that the defendant
was in breach of its contractual obligation to operate a stop loss policy by failing
to sell investments when losses exceeded 5%. However, the claimant's secondary
case was unsuccessful. The judge held that while the defendant may have been in
breach of provisions of COBS as to record keeping, they did not add to the breach
of contractual mandate or did not cause separate loss. Moreover, the defendant did
not act in breach of obligations under COBS relating to assessing suitability and
provision of information.

[172A]   [2017] EWHC 2999 (QB): see further para.15-087A below

4.   DEFENCES AND RELIEF

(c)   Restriction of Liability by Contract

Consumer Rights Act 2015 Pt 2

Replace footnote 200 with:

[200] See further *Chitty on Contracts*, 33rd edn, Ch.38   **15-073**

5.   REMEDIES INCLUDING DAMAGES

(c)   Remedies Available to Private Litigants

(iii)   Damages or Compensation

Measure of damages

After paragraph 15-087, add new paragraphs 15-087A and 15-087B:

15-087A   In *Rocker v Full Circle Asset Management Ltd*[233A] Morris J held that the claimant was entitled to damages for losses caused by breach of mandate and failure to operate a stop loss policy. As to losses caused by the breach of mandate, their calculation essentially entailed considering, in respect of each month where the medium risk band was exceeded, the overall profit earned, or the loss incurred, for the claimant's portfolio as a whole, and then reaching a cumulative total of those profits and losses. As to losses caused by failure to operate the stop loss policy, their calculation involved two stages. The first stage involved calculating the loss on all investments that were sold at a loss greater than 5% loss and subtracting from that total of losses the amount of loss on those investments, had they been sold at a point of 5% loss. The second stage involved an adjustment to avoid a possible element of "double-counting" in respect of the capital loss, arising from a claim both in respect of breach of mandate and in respect of stop loss.

[233A]   [2017] EWHC 2999 (QB): see also para.15-066A above.

15-087B   The judge rejected a claim for "opportunity loss", being the amount by which the claimant maintained that the value of the invested assets would have appreciated over the relevant period, had the defendant adhered to its instructions. The judge reasoned that the obligations which the defendant did not perform were to stay within risk mandate and to operate stop losses. Compensation for breach of those obligations involved assessing the position the claimant would have been in had breaches of those obligations not occurred. The relevant counterfactual was the defendant investing in such a way that the risk in portfolio stayed within the parameters of the medium risk profile and the defendant properly operated the stop loss policy as contractually required. The claimant was clearly aware of, and took, the risk that the investment, even if properly managed, might be ultimately unsuccessful. To award damages for opportunity loss would have the effect of removing any risk in his investment. The relevant comparator had to include the same level of portfolio risk and same strategy as agreed by the parties.

CHAPTER 16

INSURANCE BROKERS

1. GENERAL

(d) The Standard of Skill and Care

Expert evidence

Replace footnote 113 with:

16-040 [113] See, e.g. *Fanhaven Pty Ltd v Bain Dawes Northern Pty Ltd* [1982] 2 N.S.W.L.R. 57 at 63. In *Avondale Exhibitions Ltd v Arthur J Gallagher Insurance Brokers Ltd* [2018] EWHC 1311 (QB) (at [121]) HHJ Keyser QC regarded it as "striking and significant" that the claimant was asking the Court to find that the broker had fallen below the standard of reasonably careful and competent insurance brokers without adducing any expert evidence as to the standards in that profession. He stated that the lack of expert evidence significantly limited, but did not altogether exclude, the possibility of finding that the broker failed to act with reasonable skill and care.

2. LIABILITY FOR BREACH OF DUTY

The role of a broker

Replace footnote 124 with:

16-044 [124] See, e.g. the summaries of the roles and duties of a broker set out in *Dunlop Haywards (DHL) Ltd v Barbon Insurance Group Ltd* [2009] EWHC 2900 (Comm); [2010] Lloyd's Rep. I.R. 149 at [168] per Hamblen J; *Standard Life Assurance Ltd v Oak Dedicated Ltd* [2008] EWHC 222 (Comm); [2008] 2 All E.R. (Comm) 916 at [102] per Tomlinson J; and *Youell v Bland Welch & Co Ltd (No.2) (the Superhulls Cover case)* [1990] 2 Lloyd's Rep 431 at 445 per Phillips J. In *Dalamd Ltd v Butterworth Spengler Commercial Ltd* [2018] EWHC 2558 (Comm); [2019] Lloyd's Rep. I.R. 295 at [80] Butcher J stated that the duties of a broker were accurately stated in this paragraph.

(a) Failing Adequately to Assess the Client's Needs

After "reason to ask.", add new footnote 134A:

16-050 [134A] *Synergy Health (UK) Ltd v CGU Insurance Plc* [2010] EWHC 2583 (Comm); [2011] Lloyd's Rep. I.R. 500 in which Flaux J observed that the context in which brokers have been held to be under a duty to make enquiries and to elicit information is where the questions which should have been asked are ones which a competent broker might have been expected to ask in the circumstances.

(g) Liability Arising out of Material Non-disclosure

Broker's failure to disclose material facts

Replace paragraph 16-086 (to incorporate amendments to footnotes 229 and 231) with:

16-086 A broker owes his client a duty to take reasonable care to disclose any material facts of which he (the broker) is aware.[229] If a broker fails to disclose material facts, with the result that the insurers subsequently avoid the policy or exercise some other remedy,[230] then (subject to any defence of causation) the broker will be liable for the loss sustained.[231] There is a substantial body of case law on what constitutes a "material" fact, but a discussion of these authorities is outside the scope of this work. In brief, however, a fact is material if it was one which would have an effect (not necessarily decisive) on the mind of a prudent underwriter in deciding whether to accept the risk or the premium to be asked.

[229] *Synergy Health (UK) Ltd v CGU Insurance Plc* [2010] EWHC 2583 (Comm) at [204] per Flaux J. *Dalamd Ltd v Butterworth Spengler Commercial Ltd* [2018] EWHC 2558 (Comm); [2019] Lloyd's Rep. I.R. 295 at [81] per Butcher J.

[230] There may be a failure to disclose a material fact without negligence: see *Banque Keyser Ullmann SA v Skandia (UK) Insurance Co Ltd* [1990] 1 Q.B. 665 at 781; *Bank of Nova Scotia v Hellenic Mutual*

War Risks Assoc (Bermuda) Ltd, The "Good Luck" [1990] 1 Q.B. 818. However, a broker will find it difficult to establish that any non-disclosure of information known to him was not negligent.

[231] e.g. *Maydew v Forrester* (1814) 5 Taunt. 615. In *WE Acres Crabmeal Ltd v Brien's Insurance Agency Ltd* (1988) 90 N.B.R. (2d) 77 and 228 A.P.R. 77 New Brunswick Court of Queen's Bench, brokers failed to disclose the insured's claims history, entitling insurers to avoid the policy and rendering themselves liable. In *Akedian Co Ltd v Royal Insurance Australia Ltd* (1999) 1 V.R. 80, Supreme Court of Victoria, the brokers were found to have breached their duty to the client in failing to disclose to insurers the purchase price of machinery to be insured. In New Zealand, insurers would not be able to repudiate, if, as is customary, the broker receives commission from them, being fixed with the broker's knowledge of all matters material to the contract of insurance by s.10 of the Insurance Law Reform Act 1977: *Helicopter Equipment Ltd v Marine Insurance Co Ltd* [1986] 1 N.Z.L.R. 448; and *Gold Star Insurance Co Ltd v Gaunt* [1998] 3 N.Z.L.R. 80 NZCA. In *Roberts v Plaisted* [1989] 2 Lloyd's Rep. 341 at 345, col.1, Purchas LJ expressed dissatisfaction that in English law an insured who has made full disclosure to a broker could nevertheless find himself uninsured because his broker failed to make full disclosure to insurers. This statement was quoted with approval in *Avondale Exhibitions Ltd v Arthur J Gallagher Insurance Brokers Ltd* [2018] EWHC 1311 (QB) (HHJ Keyser QC) at [18].

Failure to advise the client regarding the duty of disclosure

Replace paragraph 16-091 (to incorporate amendments to footnotes 238 and 240) with:

The insurance broker should advise his client of the duty to disclose all **16-091** circumstances material to the insurance, and the consequences of failing to do so.[238] The broker owes a duty to take reasonable care to ensure that the client is aware of and understands the duty of disclosure.[239] The client may not appreciate which facts are "material" and the broker should indicate the sort of matters which ought to be disclosed as being material or at least arguably material.[240] It is part of the insurance broker's expertise to recognise matters which ought to be disclosed and he should make sure that they are disclosed to the insurers.[241] In *Akedian Co Ltd v Royal Insurance Australia Ltd*,[242] Byrne J described the broker's duty as follows:

> "The duty of a broker is to disclose material facts known to it and to have a knowledge and understanding of the requirements of the law relating to the duty to disclose and, in particular, as to the materiality of the given fact ... It is part of the function of a broker to advise its client as to what must be disclosed in this technical area [of Marine Insurance] as well as to communicate the fact or circumstance in question to the insurer so that the policy issued to the insured is not at risk."[243]

[238] *Nicholas G Jones v Environcom Ltd* [2010] EWHC 759 (Comm); [2010] Lloyd's Rep. I.R. 676 a [54], Steel J; *Dalamd Ltd v Butterworth Spengler Commercial Ltd* [2018] EWHC 2558 (Comm); [2019] Lloyd's Rep. I.R. 295 at [82], Butcher J. The guidance in ICOBS 5.1.4 states: "Ways of ensuring a customer knows what he must disclose include (1) explaining to a commercial customer the duty to disclose all circumstances material to a policy, what needs to be disclosed, and the consequences of any failure to make such disclosure; or (2) ensuring that the commercial customer is asked clear questions about any matter material to the insurance undertaking." Rule 4.3.2 of the ICOB sourcebook imposed an obligation on a broker to "explain to the customer his duty to disclose all circumstances material to the insurance and the consequences of any failure to make such disclosure, both before the non-investment contract commences and throughout the duration of the contract". Paragraph 3.7 of the General Insurance Standards Council Code for Private Customers (2000) stated: "We will explain your duty to give Insurers information before cover begins and during the policy, and what may happen if you do not." Paragraph 18 of the General Insurance Standards Council Commercial Code stated: "Members will explain to Commercial Customers their duty to disclose all circumstances material to the insurance and the consequences of any failure to make such disclosure, both before the insurance commences and during the policy."

[239] *Synergy Health (UK) Ltd v CGU Insurance Plc* [2010] EWHC 2583 (Comm) at [204] per Flaux J; *Involnert Management Inc v Aprilgrange Ltd* [2015] EWHC 2225 (Comm) at [318] per Leggatt J.

[240] *Nicholas G Jones v Environcom Ltd* [2010] EWHC 759 (Comm), Steel J (for the facts see para.16-159, below). However, when explaining the duty of disclosure a broker is not obliged to advise the client of specific matters which are material facts. That is because, unless all possible material facts are set out in the explanation of the duty of disclosure, specific mention of one or more facts is liable to be misleading and give a false impression that the duty is restricted to particular matters. Further, it is impos-

sible to set out all material facts. See *Avondale Exhibitions Ltd v Arthur J Gallagher Insurance Brokers Ltd* [2018] EWHC 1311 (QB) (HHJ Keyser QC) at [124].

[241] e.g. in *O&R Jewellers Ltd v Terry* [1999] Lloyd's Rep. I.R. 436, (Sir Godfrey le Quesne QC, sitting as a deputy High Court judge) the brokers conceded that they were under a duty to advise the claimant jewellers to disclose that the managing director of its parent company had convictions for burglary, if they were aware of that fact. The brokers were also found to be in breach of duty in failing to pass on to insurers information as to where the keys to the insured's safes were kept overnight, a failure which also led to avoidance of the policy.

[242] (1999) 1 V.R. 80 Supreme Court of Victoria. The brokers were found negligent in failing to disclose to insurers the purchase price of machinery which was to be insured, as required by s.24(1) of the Marine Insurance Act 1906.

[243] (1999) 1 V.R. 80 at 86–87.

Replace footnote 249 with:

16-094   [249] In *Nicholas G Jones v Environcom Ltd* [2010] EWHC 759 (Comm) (for the facts see para.16-141, below), Steel J found that the documents relied upon by the broker as satisfying its duty to explain the obligation of disclosure were inadequate for that purpose. He went on to indicate that he was not satisfied that it was sufficient for a broker simply to rely on written standard form explanations—a broker was obliged to satisfy itself that its client understood the position, which would usually require a specific oral or written exchange on the topic, both at the time of the original placement and at renewal. However, in *Synergy Health (UK) Ltd v CGU Insurance Plc* [2010] EWHC 2583 (Comm), Flaux J found that there was no immutable requirement on a broker to give oral advice as to the duty of disclosure, and that whether or not a failure to give oral advice amounted to a breach of duty would depend on all the circumstances (at [212]–[213]). Similarly, in *Avondale Exhibitions Ltd v Arthur J Gallagher Insurance Brokers Ltd* [2018] EWHC 1311 (QB) HHJ Keyser QC stated (at [18] and [122]) that there was no general obligation on a broker, applicable in every case, to give an oral explanation of material disclosure. The adequacy of any communication must be assessed on a case-by-case basis.

Duty to make enquiries

Replace footnote 251 with:

16-096   [251] In *Nicholas G Jones v Environcom Ltd* [2010] EWHC 759 (Comm), (for the facts see para.16-141, below) Steel J held that the broker "must take reasonable care to elicit matters which ought to be disclosed but which the client might not think it necessary to mention" (at [54]). See also *Synergy Health (UK) Ltd v CGU Insurance Plc* [2010] EWHC 2583 (Comm) at [204]. In that case, the insurers had imposed various risk improvement requirements following risk surveys during the currency of the policy. Flaux J held that the broker was in breach of duty in failing to check up and clarify with the insured prior to renewal the extent to which the insured had completed the risk improvement requirements (see [216]–[217]). See also *Dalamd Ltd v Butterworth Spengler Commercial Ltd* [2018] EWHC 2558 (Comm); [2019] Lloyd's Rep. I.R. 295 at [82], Butcher J.

Replace footnote 259 with:

16-097   [259] *Fanhaven Pty Ltd v Bain Dawes Northern Pty Ltd* [1982] 2 N.S.W.L.R. 57: the New South Wales Court of Appeal held that brokers were not negligent in these circumstances. The court also held that the brokers were not under a duty to advise the claimants generally as to their duty of disclosure. However, if the broker had notice of some questionable matter the position may be different: *Quinby Enterprises Ltd (In Liquidation) v General Accident Fire and Life Assurance Corp Public Ltd Co* [1995] 1 N.Z.L.R. 726 per Barker J. In *Avondale Exhibitions Ltd v Arthur J Gallagher Insurance Brokers Ltd* [2018] EWHC 1311 (QB) HHJ Keyser QC rejected a claim that the broker had acted negligently in failing to ask whether the insured's director had any convictions.

3.   DAMAGES

(a)   Causation

(i)   Loss Caused by the Claimant's Own Act or Omission

Failure to sue the insurer

Replace paragraph 16-143 (to incorporate replacement text at the end) with:

16-143   It is sometimes the case that, faced with a rejection of a claim by its insurer, an insured opts to issue proceedings solely against its broker. In such a case the broker may defend the claim on the basis that the true cause of the insured's loss was his own failure to sue the insurer. If the broker can show that the point taken by the insurer really was hopeless, then the broker will have a good defence. The defence succeeded in *Gaughan v McDonagh & Co Ltd*,[358] in which the insurer purported to avoid the policy when "there was no basis whatever" for the policy to be avoided. Not only was the insured's failure to challenge the insurer's wrongful avoidance the sole cause of the insured's loss, but also the broker could not reasonably be expected to foresee that the insurance company would take such a bad point or, that if such a bad point was taken, it would go unchallenged by the insured. In *Dalamd Ltd v Butterworth Spengler Commercial Ltd*[359] the insured brought proceedings against its broker alone, without having sued or settled with its insurer. The insured's case was that, in order to succeed in its claim against its broker, it did not need to prove that its claim against its insurer would have failed. It contended that it was sufficient to show that, as a result of its broker's negligence, its insurer had a reasonably arguable basis for declining an indemnity. That argument was rejected. Butcher J held[360] that, in order to succeed in its claim against the broker, the insured had to prove that its insurer was in fact entitled to refuse an indemnity. It was not sufficient for the insured to show that, as a result of the broker's negligence, the insurer had a reasonably arguable basis on which to refuse an indemnity. Consequently, if an insured contends that, as a result of its broker's negligence, it suffered loss in the form of the loss of the chance to receive an indemnity from its insurer, the insured must establish that it was not actually entitled to an indemnity. If it fails to do so then its claim will fail as a matter of causation: any negligence by the broker will not have caused the insured to lose the chance to receive an indemnity, and any loss will have been caused by the insured's failure to pursue a claim against its insurer. Butcher J recognised,[360A] however, that different considerations may apply if the broker's negligence has deprived the insured of the opportunity of having its claim against its insurer determined by a court.

[358] [2007] EWCA Civ 1115 (unreported).

[359] [2018] EWHC 2558 (Comm); [2019] Lloyd's Rep. I.R. 295; [2019] P.N.L.R. 6, Butcher J.

[360] At [130]–[135].

[360A] At [140].

(ii) The Claimant Would Not Have Received an Insurance Payment in any Event

After paragraph 16-148, add new paragraph 16-148A:

Policy would not have responded to the loss. If a broker is negligent in failing **16-148A** to arrange insurance on the claimant's behalf, then in order to show that such negligence has caused him any loss, the claimant will need to show that there was more than a speculative chance that the hypothetical insurance that would have been arranged by the broker would have provided him with an indemnity. In *Channon (t/a Channon and Co) v Ward (t/s Ward Associates)*[368A] the broker was negligent in failing to arrange professional indemnity insurance on behalf of the claimant, who was an accountant. It was common ground that, but for the broker's negligence, the claimant would have had the benefit of professional indemnity insurance cover with Aviva. The accountant was sued by third parties, and reached a settlement with them. He claimed damages from his broker on the basis that he had lost the chance to receive an indemnity from Aviva in respect of his liability to those third parties. His claim failed on the ground that there was no chance that he would have received an indemnity from Aviva, because his liability to the third parties fell outside the scope of cover afforded by the Aviva policy, and was also caught by exclusion clauses within that policy.

368A [2017] EWCA Civ 13.

Claimant would not have complied with a policy condition

To the end of the paragraph after "the defence failed.", add new footnote 370A:

16-149   370A For a further example see *RR Securities Ltd v Towergate Underwriting Group Ltd* [2016] EWHC 2653 (QB) (HH Judge Waksman QC) in which the judge rejected the broker's defence that, even if properly advised, the insured would not have complied with the insurer's minimum security requirements condition precedent in a policy of property insurance. The judge was satisfied that the insured would have complied with the clause if properly advised.

Insurance not available

Replace paragraph 16-153 (to incorporate new text following "of full recovery." at the end of the paragraph) with:

16-153   Where the availability of insurance is in doubt, the damage should be characterised as a loss of opportunity and damages assessed accordingly.[379] In *Cee Bee Marine Ltd v Lombard Insurance Co Ltd*,[380] the risk which was uninsured by reason of the broker's negligence was a fibreglass boat repair business carried on in a wooden building. This was not a risk likely to appeal to insurers. The New Zealand Court of Appeal held that the measure of damages was the loss of the chance to obtain insurance elsewhere. The award of damages should reflect the value of that chance. The court was satisfied that the client would not knowingly have carried on its business without insurance, so that there were four possibilities as to what might have occurred.[381] The court discounted the award of damages slightly to take account of these possibilities, including something for the sums which might have had to be expended on the premium and expenses in order to obtain cover. This approach was followed in *O&R Jewellers Ltd v Terry*.[382] The evidence in that case was that so long as a convicted burglar remained managing director of the claimant's parent company, the claimant was uninsurable. Even if cover had been obtained, there were further defences which underwriters could and would have raised, although they might not have succeeded. The judge followed *Cee Bee Marine* and awarded damages on the basis that the claimant would have tried to have the dishonest director removed and that, while underwriters would have raised other defences, they might have compromised a claim or lost at trial and, taking the matter broadly, awarded damages representing 30% of full recovery. More recently in *Pakeezah Meat Supplies Ltd v Total Insurance Solutions Ltd*[382A] Butcher J applied a reduction of 25% to the damages recoverable by the claimant from its broker to reflect the chance that, if the broker had acted with due skill and care, its client might not have been able to obtain any insurance cover for the loss which subsequently occurred.

379 In *Allied Maples Group Ltd v Simmons & Simmons* [1995] 1 W.L.R. 1602 (a solicitors' case), the Court of Appeal, holding that the claimants' claim was for loss of a chance, proceeded on the basis that the same principles applied to claims against solicitors as insurance brokers and relied upon *Dunbar v A&B Painters Ltd* [1986] 2 Lloyd's Rep. 38.

380 [1990] 2 N.Z.L.R. 1.

[381] The four most obvious possible outcomes were: (i) the client would have obtained insurance with a higher premium; (ii) the client would have obtained insurance conditional upon a change in the structure of the building; (iii) the insured would have moved its business elsewhere and obtained insurance; and (iv) it would have ceased to carry on its business so preserving the value of its stock.

[382] [1999] Lloyd's Rep. I.R. 436, Sir Godfrey le Quesne, sitting as a deputy High Court judge. In that case the judge followed the dictum of Lord Diplock in *Mallett v McMonagle* [1970] A.C. 166 at 176 which allows a court when deciding what the chance was that something would have happened (as opposed to deciding what did happen) to decide that the chance was more or less than 50% and award damages accordingly:

> "The role of the court in making an assessment of damages which depends upon its view as to what will be and what would have been is to be contrasted with its ordinary function in civil actions of determining what was. In determining what did happen in the past a court decides on the balance of probabilities. Anything that is more probable than not it treats as certain. But in assessing damages which depend upon its view as to what will happen in the future or would have happened in the future if something had not happened in the past, the court must make an estimate as to what are the chances that a particular thing will or would have happened and reflect those chances, whether they are more or less than even, in the amount of damages which it awards."

In *Markal Investments Ltd v Morley Shafron Agencies Ltd* (1990) 67 D.L.R. (4th) 422, the British Columbia Court of Appeal took a different view and held that a client whose broker had failed to obtain insurance had to show on the balance of probabilities that insurance would have been obtained. It is submitted that in the context of claims against brokers for failure to obtain cover, the approach taken in *Cee Bee Marine Ltd v Lombard Insurance Co Ltd* [1990] 2 N.Z.L.R. 1 is to be preferred.

[382A] [2018] EWHC 1141 (Comm) (at [22]).

Insurer entitled to reject the claim in any event

Replace paragraph 16-154 (to incorporate new footnote and text at the end of the paragraph) with:

16-154 In many cases there may be more than one basis upon which an insurer is entitled to reject a claim. For example, there may have been a material non-disclosure when the policy was effected, and also a breach of condition when the loss occurred. The insurer may reject the claim on the basis of the non-disclosure or the breach of condition, or both. It is also often the case that the broker is responsible for one, but not both, of the grounds upon which the insurer is entitled to reject the insured's claim. This may provide the broker with a good defence on causation.[382A] A distinction is drawn between cases in which the insured has reached a settlement with his insurer (addressed at para.16-168 below) and cases in which the insured has not reached a settlement with his insurer (addressed at para.16-155 onwards below).

[382A] Such a defence was advanced in *RR Securities Ltd v Towergate Underwriting Group Ltd* [2016] EWHC 2653 (QB) (HH Judge Waksman QC). The judge accepted that, if the insured were in breach of a reasonable precautions clause in a policy of property insurance, then its claim would fail due to lack of causation. However, the judge found that there was no such breach.

Replace paragraph 16-156 (to incorporate new text following the first sentence) with:

16-156 In such a case in order to succeed in a causation defence the broker must satisfy the court that the insurers would in fact have exercised their rights and declined to meet the claim.[383] The broker must also prove that the insurers were entitled to decline the claim as a matter of law (if and insofar as applicable) and on the balance of probabilities as regards any issues of fact.[383A] Only if this is established can it properly be said that no loss flows from the broker's breach of duty. Where this line of defence is put forward, evidence from the proposed insurers (or, if their identity is not known, from any representative insurers) is admissible to show whether or not they would have repudiated on the grounds suggested. In *Fraser v*

BN Furman (Productions) Ltd, Diplock LJ indicated that the absence of such evidence was one of the weaknesses of the broker's case.[384]

[383] In *Everett v Hogg Robinson and Gardner Mountain (Insurance) Ltd* [1973] 1 Lloyd's Rep. 217, it was held that the burden of proof was on the broker to show that the reinsurers would have repudiated liability in any event (for the facts, see para.16-166, below).

[383A] *Dalamd Ltd v Butterworth Spengler Commercial Ltd* [2018] EWHC 2558 (Comm); [2019] Lloyd's Rep. I.R. 295, Butcher J at [136].

[384] [1967] 1 W.L.R. 898 at 909. Diplock LJ held that the burden was on the brokers to show that the policy would not have covered their client's loss. In *Cee Bee Marine Ltd v Lombard Insurance Co Ltd* [1990] 2 N.Z.L.R. 1, the New Zealand Court of Appeal took the same view; but in *Toikan International Insurance Broking Pty Ltd v Plasteel Windows Australia Pty Ltd* (1988) 15 N.S.W.L.R. 641, the New South Wales Court of Appeal held that the onus was on the client.

Replace paragraph 16-157 (to incorporate amended text at the end of the paragraph) with:

16-157   Such a defence was successful in *Gunns v Par Insurance Brokers*.[385] There the brokers successfully argued that the claimant would not have recovered under the policy (which had been avoided for non-disclosure) because the insured was in breach of a condition that he should take all reasonable steps to avoid loss and damage and to safeguard the property insured from loss and damage. Such a defence was also successful in *Dalamd Ltd v Butterworth Spengler Commercial Ltd*.[386] In that case the broker was responsible for a non-disclosure which gave the insurer a good defence to the insured's claim. However, the broker established that the insured was in breach of a condition of the policy, for which the broker was not responsible and which meant that the insured was not entitled to an indemnity from its insurer in any event. Therefore the insured's claim against the broker failed as a matter of causation. If the insured is able to show that, notwithstanding its entitlement to decline the claim, there was a real chance that the insurer would have paid the claim or reached a settlement with the insurer, then the insured may recover damages on a "loss of a chance" basis.[386A]

[385] [1997] 1 Lloyd's Rep. 173, Sir Michael Ogden, sitting as a deputy High Court judge.

[386] [2018] EWHC 2558 (Comm); [2019] Lloyd's Rep. I.R. 295; [2019] P.N.L.R. 6, Butcher J.

[386A] *Dalamd Ltd v Butterworth Spengler Commercial Ltd* [2018] EWHC 2558 (Comm); [2019] Lloyd's Rep. I.R. 295, Butcher J at [129], [136], and [153].

(b)   Assessment of Damages

Loss of a chance

After paragraph 16-167, add new paragraph 16-167A:

16-167A   In *Dalamd Limited v Butterworth Spengler Commercial Ltd* [2018] EWHC 2558 (Comm) the court considered the proper approach to issues of causation and loss in cases where an insurer rejects an insured's insurance claim, and the insured commences proceedings against its broker. Butcher J held that, to succeed in such an action, the insured must show that its claim against its insurer would have failed as a result of the broker's negligence. Thus the Court had to decide, yes or no, whether the insured's claim against the insurer would have failed. If the Court concluded that the insured's claim against the insurer would have succeeded, then its action against its broker would fail. Similarly, if the broker defended the action against it on the basis that the insurer would have been entitled to reject the insured's claim in any event (i.e. even if the broker had not been in breach of duty), then the broker had to prove on the balance of probabilities that the insured's claim against its insurer would have failed even if the broker had acted with due skill and care.

Insured settling with its insurers

At the end of the paragraph, after "was unreasonably low.", add:

16-168   In order to succeed in his claim against the broker, it is not necessary for the insured to establish that the insurer's defence for which the broker was responsible was a good one.[416A]

[416A] *Dalamd Ltd v Butterworth Spengler Commercial Ltd* [2018] EWHC 2558 (Comm); [2019] Lloyd's Rep. I.R. 295, Butcher J at [133].

Credit for saved premium

Replace footnote 448 with:

16-178   [448] ibid. at [317]. Similarly in *Pakeezah Meat Supplies Ltd v Total Insurance Solutions Ltd* [2018] EWHC 1141 (Comm) Butcher J held (at [23]) that an assessment of the client's loss had to take into account the additional premium that would have been payable by the client.

After paragraph 16-179, add new paragraph 16-179A:

16-179A   **Insured with a limited interest**   In *Dalamd Ltd v Butterworth Spengler Commercial Ltd*[449A] the broker argued that the claimant insured had suffered no loss by reason of the absence of an indemnity from its insurer because the insured had no proprietary interest in the plant and machinery insured. Butcher J rejected that argument.[449B] He held that the insured as a bailee had an insurable interest in the property bailed. Therefore it was entitled to sue its broker for the full amount of indemnity payable under the policy, even if the insured would have had an obligation to account to the bailor for some or all of the indemnity that would have been payable under the policy. He held that the damages recoverable from the broker would be held on the same basis as the insurance proceeds would have been.

[449A] [2018] EWHC 2558 (Comm); [2019] Lloyd's Rep. I.R. 295; [2019] P.N.L.R. 6, Butcher J.
[449B] At [175].

CHAPTER 17

ACCOUNTANTS AND AUDITORS

2. DUTIES

(a) The Statutory Context

(i) Companies Legislation: the Company Audit

Appointment of auditors

To the end of paragraph 17-012 after "an audit committee.", add:

17-012   However, many of those provisions have been altered or repealed in respect of financial years beginning on or after 17 June 2017 by the Statutory Auditors and Third Country Auditors Regulations 2017 (SI 2017/516). There are also now provisions as to the maximum engagement as an auditor of a company for consecutive years: CA 2006 s.494ZA, which was added by the Statutory Auditors and Third Country Auditors Regulations 2017 (SI 2017/516).

Replace paragraph 17-013 (to incorporate amendments to footnotes 23 and 26) with:

17-013   The main aims of Pt 42 of the Companies Act 2006 are (i) to "secure that only persons who are properly supervised and appropriately qualified are appointed as statutory auditors" and (ii) "to secure that that audits by persons so appointed are carried out properly, with integrity and with a proper degree of independence".[23] A person may be appointed as a company auditor only if he is a member of a recognised supervisory body (RSB) and is eligible for the appointment under its rules.[24] The auditor must also comply with the statutory requirement of independence.[25] An organisation wishing to be recognised as an RSB must apply to the Secretary of State under the provisions of Sch.10 to the 2006 Act.[26] RSBs, their officers, employees and members of their governing body are exempt from liability arising (in broad terms) out of their supervisory and rule-making functions.[27]

[23] This closely tracks the wording under s.24(1) of the Companies Act 1989. Part 42 has been supplemented by the Statutory Auditors and Third Country Auditors Regulations (SI 2007/3494) which largely concern auditors' qualifications (including in relation to "third country" auditors); the Companies Act 2006 (Transfer of Audit Working Papers to Third Countries) Regulations (SI 2010/2537); the Statutory Auditors and Third Country Auditors Regulations (SI 2016/649); the Statutory Auditors and Third Country Auditors Regulations (SI 2017/516); the Financial Services and Markets Act 2000 (Markets in Financial Instruments) Regulations (SI 2017/701); the Statutory Auditors Regulations (SI 2017/1164); and the Data Protection Act 2018.

[24] CA 2006 s.1212. See paras 17-007, above and 17-091, below.

[25] CA 2006 s.1214. An auditor who ceases to be independent must resign (s.1215). See also the ICAEW Audit Firm Governance Code (first issued in January 2010, subsequently revised and published in July 2016) which for the time being applies to certain large auditors.

26 The organisation must demonstrate compliance of its rules with a number of requirements under Pt 2 of Sch.10, including procedures for maintaining competence, disciplinary procedures and the requirement that auditors must be "fit and proper persons". The requirements were further supplemented by the Statutory Auditors and Third Country Auditors Regulations (SI 2007/3494) and revised by the Statutory Auditors and Third Country Auditors Regulations (SI 2016/649); the Statutory Auditors and Third Country Auditors Regulations (SI 2017/516); and the Statutory Auditors Regulations (SI 2017/1164).

27 CA 2006 s.1218.

The preparation of accounts

Replace footnote 32 with:

32 CA 2006 ss.394, 396(1). In the case of a group, the directors of the parent company are under a duty **17-015** to prepare group accounts also unless the company is subject to the small companies regime (in which case it is optional): ss.381–384 and 399. See further para.17-081, below. See also the micro-entities regime (ss.384A–B). The requirement to prepare accounts for a financial year is subject to an exemption in respect of dormant subsidiary companies, where various conditions are met (ss.394A–394C). The provisions regarding group accounts have been substantially amended by the Companies, Partnerships and Groups (Accounts and Non-Financial Reporting) Regulations 2016 (SI 2016/1245). These changes apply to financial years beginning on or after 1 January 2017.

Accounting Standards

Replace footnote 38 with:

38 The IFRS requirement is for the accounts to "present fairly". Freshfields advised the Financial Report- **17-017** ing Review Panel on 22 June 2005 that references in any statute to "true and fair view" should be construed in relation to accounts prepared under IFRS as referring to the requirement to "present fairly", and that IFRS seeks to maintain the principle that the accounts show a true and fair view. The FRC obtained a further advice from Martin Moore QC in April 2008 to revisit the meaning of "true and fair" in light of the developments in accounting standards and the CA 2006. The Opinion concluded (inter alia) that the requirements of "true and fair" and "present fairly" are in substance synonymous (para.29). On 8 October 2013, Martin Moore QC wrote a further Opinion (in answer to an opposing view put forward by George Bompas QC) confirming that there was no tension between the duty under the CA 2006 to give a true and fair view and the duty under IAS1 to "present fairly". He also pointed out that the requirement of prudence did not require excessive caution where there was no uncertainty (see FRS18 paras 37 and 38). The Freshfields advice and the Opinions of Martin Moore QC are on the FRC website.

To the end of the paragraph after "breach of duty.", add:

Further amendments have been made to each of the FRSs subsequently. The FRC **17-021** website sets out the extant and historical publications, and the accounting periods to which the amendments apply.

Removal of auditors

Replace paragraph 17-027 (to incorporate amendments to footnotes 65 and 69) with:

An auditor may be removed from office at any time by a company by ordinary **17-027** resolution, notwithstanding anything in any agreement between them.[65] Special notice is required for a resolution at a general meeting of a company for the removal of an auditor.[66] The auditor proposed to be removed or the retiring auditor may make representations and provision is made for them to be circulated to members or to be read out at the general meeting, unless the court otherwise directs.[67] With effect to financial years beginning on or after 17 June 2016 the auditor of a "public interest company"[68] may be removed by order of the court following an application by a "competent authority" (i.e. the FRC) or a sufficient proportion of the members, so long as there are "proper grounds" for doing so.[69] An auditor removed by either of these mechanisms must nevertheless be notified of and may attend the general meeting at which his term of office would otherwise have expired.[70]

[65] CA 2006 s.510.

[66] CA 2006 s.511.

[67] CA 2006 s.511(3).

[68] Defined in CA 2006 s.519A(1).

[69] CA 2006 s.511A. "Proper grounds" are not defined, but divergence of opinions on accounting treatments or audit procedures are specifically stated not to be considered proper grounds (s.511A(6)). This provision was added to the Companies Act 2006 by the Statutory Auditors and Third Country Auditors Regulations (SI 2016/649).

[70] CA 2006 s.513.

Resignation of auditors

Replace footnote 72 with:

17-028   [72] CA 2006 s.516. Previously, the company was required to forward a copy of the auditor's resignation to the Registrar within 14 days of receipt, failing which the company and officers will be guilty of an offence: s.517. That provision was repealed by the Deregulation Act 2015 in relation to financial years beginning on or after 1 October 2015, subject to transitional provisions and savings.

(b)   Duties to Client

(iii)   Equitable Obligations

Confidentiality

Replace footnote 135 with:

17-046   [135] In some cases consent may be implied, e.g. a report to shareholders in a company audit or disclosure of assets to the Revenue in a tax return completed by an accountant for a client. In *Nam Tai Electronics Inc v Pricewaterhouse Coopers* [2008] 1 H.K.L.R.D. 666 (Hong Kong), NTE appointed PwC to conduct due diligence into Albatronics, a company which it was proposing to acquire. The acquisition went ahead. Albatronics then went into liquidation and there was a proposal to appoint a partner in PwC as liquidator. NTE objected, alleging a conflict of interests. PwC submitted a liquidation proposal to creditors summarising why there was no conflict. NTE then sued PwC for breach of confidence. The Hong Kong Court of Final Appeal was prepared to assume that PwC had a legitimate interest (i) in seeking appointment as liquidator and (ii) in countering the suggestion by the parent company that PwC lacked impartiality because it had previously conducted the due diligence review of the company now in liquidation. However, on the facts, that legitimate interest did not make it necessary for PwC to disclose that it had advised against acquisition of the company in question. The Court confirmed that an exception to the principle of confidentiality would be made where there was a legitimate self-interest to be protected, but only so far as proportionate to the protection of that interest. An accountant will not usually be under a duty to disclose confidential information about one client to another: *Harlequin Property (SVG) Ltd v Wilkins Kennedy (A Firm)* [2016] EWHC 3188 (TCC); [2017] 4 W.L.R. 30 at [494].

(c)   Duties to Third Parties

(i)   Overview

The different tests

Replace footnote 144 with:

17-050   [144] This test was adopted in *Caparo Industries Plc v Dickman* [1990] 2 A.C. 605, although it was observed in that case that proximity is "no more than a label which embraces not a definable concept but merely a description of circumstances from which, pragmatically, the courts conclude that a duty of care exists": [1990] 2 A.C. 605 at 633D per Lord Oliver; see also ibid. at 617B per Lord Bridge. However in *BCCI (No.2)* [1998] P.N.L.R. 564 the court said that the test was useful in focussing attention on the three essential questions of foreseeability, proximity and fairness. This test was also adopted in *Law Society v KPMG* [2000] 1 W.L.R. 1921. The courts in Canada have used element (iii) in a different fashion: they have continued to follow the wider pre-*Caparo* test set out in *Anns v Merton LBC* [1978] A.C. 728 at 751–752 but they have refused on policy grounds to allow claims where these would result in indeterminate liability: *Hercules Management Ltd v Ernst & Young* [1997] 146 D.L.R. 577 at 586 and 597.

In *Canadian Imperial Bank of Commerce v Deloitte & Touche* 2016 ONCA 922; (2016) 133 OR (3d) 561 Hoy A.C.J.O, with whom the other members of the Court of Appeal for Ontario agreed, referred to the decision of the Canadian Supreme Court in *Hercules Management Ltd v Ernst & Young* [1997] 146 D.L.R. 577 and said at [53]:

> "an auditor will owe a prima facie duty of care to a person if the auditor should foresee that the person will rely on its audit opinion and reliance would, in the particular circumstances of the case, be reasonable. However, as the Supreme Court of Canada explained, these criteria can be quite easily satisfied. In modern commercial society, auditors almost always should foresee that many different persons will rely on their reports for various reasons. Hence, the policy concern that auditors could be exposed to limitless or indeterminate liability arises: *Hercules*, at para. 32."

Where imposing a duty of care would result in an auditor having indeterminate liability, policy will tend to lead to the conclusion that no duty should be imposed. The position is different if the auditor knows of the particular purpose or transaction in relation to which his statement will be relied.

(iv)   Categories of Advisee

Bodies which are liable to compensate third parties

Replace footnote 244 with:

[244] ibid. at 1928–1930. The court suggested obiter (at 1930B) that a duty might not be owed to the Solicitors' Indemnity Fund, since this Fund is the solicitor's insurer and since the accountant's report is not prepared for its benefit. For criticism of this decision, see Powell [2001] P.N. 206. No duty of care is owed to clients of the firms subject to statutory or regulatory audits of their accounts, including client accounts: there is insufficient proximity between the clients, who will not see the audit reports, and the auditors: *Lavender v Miller Bernstein LLP* 2018 ONCA 729; (2018) 142 OR (3d) 401. **17-086**

(d)   The Standard of Skill and Care

(ii)   Auditing

Auditing standards

Replace footnote 268 with:

[268] The current ISAs (which are effective for audits of financial statements for periods commencing on or after 17 June 2016) and other documents referred to in this section are available on the FRC website. The previous standards, known as Statements of Auditing Standards (SASs), and historic versions of the ISAs are also available on that website. In this chapter the references are primarily to the ISAs. ISA 250 and ISA 330 were revised in 2017, and those revisions required other ISAs to be updated: ISQC 1, ISA 210, ISA 220, ISA 240, ISA 260, ISA 450, ISA 500 and ISA 505. Those revisions and updates will be effective for periods commencing on or after 15 December 2017. Further revisions and updates were made in 2019 and 2020 in respect of the Glossary of Terms, ISQC1, and ISAs 200, 220, 230, 240, 250, 260, 315, 500, 570, 580, 600, 620, 700, 701 and 720. They will be effective for engagements relating to financial periods commencing on or after 15 December 2019 and those revisions required other ISAs to be updated: ISQC 1, ISA 210, ISA 220, ISA 240, ISA 260, ISA 450, ISA 500 and ISA 505. Those revisions and updates will be effective for periods commencing on or after 15 December 2017. **17-091**

Replace footnote 277 with:

[277] ISA 540 paras 2–4 (nature of accounting estimates) provide that "accounting estimate" means an approximation of the amount of an item in the absence of a precise measurement, e.g. allowances to reduce stock and debtors to their estimated realisable value, depreciation, accrued revenue, profits or losses on construction contracts in progress and provision for deferred taxation, for losses from litigation, and for warranty claims. It is inherent in such estimates that they will be less conclusive than other evidence **17-093**

and that more judgment is required in order to decide whether the evidence is sufficient and appropriate. The equivalent description in the December 2018 revision of ISA 540 is at paras 2–3.

The detection of fraud

Replace footnote 291 with:

17-095 [291] This text is found both at ISA 240 para.12, and (in the version updated in January 2020) at ISA 200, para.5. Its repetition in the revised ISA 200 may indicate an intention to emphasise the point. See also "Professional sceptism: Establishing a common understanding and reaffirming its central role in delivering audit quality" published by the APB in March 2012 and which "sets out the APB's considered views on the nature of auditor scepticism and its role in the audit": *https://www.frc.org.uk/Our-Work/Publications/APB/Briefing-Paper-Professional-Scepticism.pdf.*

> "The auditor's risk assessment process should involve a critical appraisal of management's assertions, actively looking for risks of material misstatement. These may arise due to fraud or error and may reflect weaknesses in the design or the operation of management's system for controlling and reporting the entity's financial position and performance (such that relevant matters are not identified, or are not adequately controlled or reported, or that the design has not been implemented and operated effectively)."

In *Dairy Containers Ltd v NZI Bank Ltd* [1995] 2 N.Z.L.R. 30 at 54, Thomas J said that metaphors about dogs and detectives tended to obscure the basic duty to plan and carry out the audit cognisant of the possibility of fraud.

(f) Specific Defence to a Claim for Breach of Duty

(i) Illegality

Replace paragraph 17-101 (to incorporate amendments to footnotes 312 and 314) with:

17-101 The Supreme Court did so in *Patel v Mirza*,[312] holding that a claim will fail because of illegality if, allowing it to succeed "would produce inconsistency and disharmony in the law, and so cause damage to the integrity of the legal system".[313] This principle is not be applied mechanistically. It should not be applied without:

> "(a) considering the underlying purpose of the prohibition which has been transgressed, (b) considering conversely any other relevant public policies which may be rendered ineffective or less effective by denial of the claim, and (c) keeping in mind the possibility of overkill unless the law is applied with a due sense of proportionality."[314]

It is against this test that a potential defence of illegality by an accountant needs now to be considered.

[312] [2016] UKSC 42; [2017] A.C. 467.

[313] ibid. at [100] per Lord Toulson, with whom Lady Hale and Lords Kerr, Wilson and Hodge agreed. Lord Toulson referred to the judgment of McLachlin J in *Hall v Herbert* [1993] S.C.R. 159 at 175–176. See also *British Columbia v Zastowny* 2008 SCC 4; [2008] 1 S.C.R. 27.

[314] ibid. at [101]. For example, in *Khan v Hussain* [2019] CSOH 11; 2019 S.C. 322 the claimant had been sanctioned by the FSA for knowingly submitting a personal mortgage application containing false information. He sought to recover the resulting loss of earnings from the defendant accountant whom he alleged had created false payslips and advised that the claimant was entitled to draw on his company for the amounts shown on the application form. The claim was struck out on the grounds of illegality: it is not permissible to recover damages suffered as a result of a criminal act or sanctions applied by a regulator. However, in doing so Lord Ericht observed at [36] that there might be circumstances in which a claimant's ignorance that his acts were wrongful would lead to a different result.

Replace paragraph 17-105 (to incorporate amendments to footnotes 321 and 323) with:

17-105 This leaves open the question as to the availability of a defence of illegality to an auditor who is alleged to have negligently failed to detect a fraud being carried out through a "one-man" company or equivalent. If it does not "produce inconsistency and disharmony in the law, and so cause damage to the integrity of the legal system" to allow the liquidator to claim against the "one man",[320] why should allowing a claim by the liquidator against the auditor do so? In both cases the liquidator is placing equal reliance upon the company's participation in a fraud in order to make the claim.[321] Given the difficulty which a defence of illegality may now face on facts similar to those in *Stone & Rolls Ltd (In Liquidation) v Moore Stephens (A Firm)*[322] it may be that the more straightforward defence to such claims is one of causation: in the absence of any director or shareholder who was not privy to the fraud or dishonesty, how can the liquidator prove that any loss flowed from the allegedly negligent failure of the auditor to tell them what they already knew?[323]

[320] See para.17-101 above.

[321] In *Livent Inc v Deloitte & Touche* [2016] ONCA 11; (2016) 393 D.L.R. (4th) 1 at [112]-[1673] the Ontario Court of Appeal reviewed the relevant authorities and held that the defence of illegality did not apply so as to defeat a claim brought by a company whose main management (but not all directors and shareholders) had used it as a vehicle for fraud. The fraudulent managers would not benefit were the claim to succeed and would not avoid any sanction. On appeal, the Supreme Court of Canada held that the fraud of two directors should not be attributed to the claimant company, at least in the context of a claim against the company's auditors for failing to defect that fraud, while leaving for another occasion the position of a "one man company": [2017] SCC 63; (2017) 416 D.L.R. (4th) 32.

[322] [2009] A.C. 1391; [2009] UKHL 39.

[323] See paras 17-126 to 17-128 below. The decision of the Court of Appeal in *Singularis Holdings Ltd (In Liquidation) v Daiwa Capital Markets Europe Ltd* [2018] EWCA Civ 84; [2018] 1 W.L.R. 2777 provides some guidance as to how the courts approach a defence of illegality and the attribution of fraud in the context of companies all or some of whose managers and shareholders are involved in the fraud. But the Court emphasised that the specific context was important and that the duty owed to the company by the defendant bank was materially different from that owed by auditors to a company and its shareholders. In the context of the duty owed by the bank it was relevant that (i) the defendant had not proved that all of the company's directors were complicit in the fraud and (ii) that the company had a well-established, legitimate trading history. The decision is not authority for the proposition that the second factor is relevant in the context of a claim against auditors.

After paragraph 17-105, add new paragraph 17-105A:

A defence of illegality may be available in other circumstances. For example, in **17-105A** *English v O'Driscoll*[323A] a claim against accountants failed on the ground that, to the knowledge of the claimant, the transaction which formed the subject matter of the claim was designed to deceive the Revenue into granting the claimant capital allowances to which he was not entitled. The court took the point of its own motion.

[323A] [2016] IEHC 584; [2017] P.N.L.R. 9. The decision was overturned on appeal, on the basis that the fraud had not been alleged by the defendant or put to the claimant: [2019] IECA 153.

(ii) Statutory Relief

Replace footnote 327 with:

[327] *Dimond Manufacturing Co Ltd v Hamilton* [1969] N.Z.L.R. 609 NZCA. The court, while recognis- **17-106** ing that the section could be invoked even in the case of negligence, considered that there would not be many cases where a negligent auditor could be said to have acted reasonably. However, s.1157 clearly envisages that someone may have acted reasonably, even though they have been negligent: it follows that "reasonably" must have been intended to embrace wider considerations than those usually involved in determining whether someone has acted negligently *Manchester Building Society v Grant Thornton UK LLP* [2018] EWHC 963 (Comm); [2018] 1 P.N.L.R. 27, at [261] per Teare J.

3. LIABILITY FOR BREACH OF DUTY

(b) Other Breaches of Duty

Advice

Replace paragraph (to incorporate amendments to footnotes 425 and 427) with:

17-125   Accountants frequently give advice on tax,[423] insolvency[424] or business[425] matters. The principles to be applied are broadly the same as those which apply in the case of solicitors.[426] If the accountant assumes a responsibility for advising the client as to what investment policy he should adopt, he may find that he has crossed the line between "information" and "advice".[427]

[423] In *Dhillon v Siddiqui* [2008] EWHC 2020 (Ch), Livesey QC held that it was the duty of a tax adviser to advise his client of the pros and cons of the various options which were open to him on the facts known to the adviser, so that the client could make his own informed decision as to what to do. In *Midland Packaging Ltd v HW Accountants Ltd* [2011] P.N.L.R. 1; [2010] EWHC 1975 (Mercantile); HH Judge Brown QC held that the accountant had assumed a responsibility to advise on change of domicile. In *Integral Memory Plc v Haines Watts* [2012] EWHC 342 (Ch), Richard Sheldon QC held that an accountant's duty to advise on a change in the tax law was not a continuing duty; hence a claim brought more than six years after the date when advice allegedly should have been given was statute-barred.

[424] *Wade v Poppleton & Appleby* [2004] 1 B.C.L.C. 674, is an example of the duty of care owed by an insolvency practitioner to the company and its shareholders.

[425] In *Goldberg v Miltiadous* [2010] EWHC 450 (QB) at [138], Tugendhat J held that it was in the ordinary course of an accountant's business to advise on the risks associated with an investment. For example, in *Harlequin Property (SVG) Ltd v Wilkins Kennedy (A Firm)* [2016] EWHC 3188 (TCC); [2017] 4 W.L.R. 30 a firm of accountants was held to be in breach of duty for failing to advise its client to enter a particular contract.

[426] See Ch.11 (Solicitors) para.11-161.

[427] *South Australia Asset Management Co Ltd v York Montague Ltd* [1997] A.C. 191 (see para.17-129, below). e.g. see *Craig v Troy* (1997) 16 W.A.R. 96 Supreme Court of Western Australia, where an accountant was held liable for negligent advice as to the feasibility of a hotel development. In *Aneco Reinsurance Underwriting Ltd v Johnson & Higgins Ltd* [2002] P.N.L.R. 8, the House of Lords held by a majority that an insurance broker who wrongly advised an insurer that reinsurance was available was giving advice and not merely information. Although the House of Lords categorised this as an appeal which realised no point of principle, it might be seen as a retreat from *SAAMCO*. The distinction between information and advice has been clarified by the decision of the Supreme Court in *Hughes-Holland v BPE Solicitors* [2017] UKSC 21; [2018] A.C. 599. So, where, as was found in *Halsall v Champion Consulting Ltd* [2017] EWHC 1079 (QB); [2017] P.N.L.R. 32, a firm of accountants is guiding the whole decision-making process leading to a client deciding to enter a particular transaction, the firm will be liable on the advice basis, i.e. for all the consequences of entering the transaction, even though the decision to do so was taken by the client.

4. DAMAGES

(a) Remoteness

(i) Causation

Effective cause

At the end of the paragraph, after "from its auditors.", add:

17-128   So, where, had they received a non-negligent audit report, a company's shareholders would have exercised their power in general meeting to remove dishonest management, so preventing further losses caused by the dishonest management, those losses result from the auditor's negligent report.[439A]

[439A] *Assetco Plc v Grant Thornton UK LLP* [2020] EWCA Civ 1151, at [108] per David Richards LJ, with whom the other members of the Court of Appeal agreed.

Scope of duty

Replace footnote 446 with:

17-131

[446] See paras 3-003 to 3-008 above. The distinction between information and advice has been clarified by the decision of the Supreme Court in *Hughes-Holland v BPE Solicitors* [2017] UKSC 21; [2018] A.C. 599. So, where, as was found in *Halsall v Champion Consulting Ltd* [2017] EWHC 1079 (QB); [2017] P.N.L.R. 32, a firm of accountants is guiding the whole decision-making process leading to a client deciding to enter a particular transaction, the firm will be liable on the advice basis, i.e. for all the consequences of entering the transaction, even though the decision to do so was taken by the client.

After paragraph 17-132, add new paragraphs 17-132A and 17-132B:

17-132A

In every case where damages are claimed for the consequences of having entered a transaction in reliance on the advice of an accountant or auditor it is necessary to consider whether the case was an "advice" case or an "information" case, because the scope of the defendant's duty and the measure of damages for which it was liable were different in the two cases. In an "advice" case the defendant is given entire responsibility to determine what matters should be taken into account when deciding whether to enter a transaction and to make that decision or to guide the entire decision-making process. In an "advice" case the defendant would accordingly be liable for all the foreseeable financial consequences of the decision to enter the transaction. In an "information" case the defendant is only responsible for providing part of the information or advice upon which the claimant relied and, no matter how critical that information or advice is, the defendant is only liable for the foreseeable consequences of that information or advice being wrong.[450A] So, in *Manchester BS v Grant Thornton UK LLP*[450B] the defendant auditors had negligently advised that long-term interest swaps could be shown in the claimant's accounts on a "hedge accounting" basis, so as to reduce effects of the volatility of the swaps on the claimant's accounts. When, several years later, the claimant discovered that hedge accounting was not permissible, it closed out the swaps by exercising break clauses, incurring significant losses in the process ("the MTM losses"). The claimant would not have entered the long-term swaps but for the defendant's negligent advice. But that advice was only one of the factors leading to the claimant's decision to enter them: the Court of Appeal held that this was an "information" case. The consequence of the information provided by the defendant being wrong was that the claimant had to exercise the break clauses when it did. Had the information been correct, then the claimant could have continued to hold the swaps. So, to recover the MTM losses the claimant had to show that the MTM losses would not have been incurred had it continued to hold them. It could not do so: the value of the swaps depended on the market conditions at the time. The claimant had received market value when it exercised the break clauses. It failed to show that it would have achieved more had it continued to hold the swaps. This was a matter of proof of causation so the claim for the MTM losses failed. In any "information" case the claimant has to prove the consequences of the information being wrong. If as a result of the information being wrong the company's shareholders are not able to exercise the oversight over management which they would have done had there been a non-negligent audit report, it has been held by a majority of the Supreme Court of Canada that future trading losses which would have been avoided had the shareholders been able to exercise such supervision fell within the scope of the auditor's responsibility (and, it would seem, resulted from the audit report being wrong).[450C]

450A *Hughes-Holland v BPE Solicitors* [2017] UKSC 21; [2018] A.C. 599, at [38] and [44] per Lord Sumption, with whom the other members of the Supreme Court agreed.

450B [2019] EWCA Civ 40; [2019] 1 W.L.R. 4610.

450C *Deloitte & Touche (now continued as Deloitte LLP) v LIvent Inc* 2017 SCC 63; (2017) 416 DLR (4th) 32. However, in *Assetco Plc v Grant Thornton UK LLP* [2019] EWHC 592 (Comm); [2019] 1 Costs L.R. 197 at [955] Bryan J stated that this decision was "not of any real assistance in identifying the scope of the duty of an auditor under English law, or as to the circumstances in which legal causation will be established". Bryan J went on to find that the defendant auditor's negligence had deprived the claimant's shareholders of exercising their powers to call dishonest directors to book and to prevent the company being run dishonestly so that the losses resulted from trading in a particular way in reliance on the negligent audit.

17-132B   This approach is generally applicable to the liability of auditors, even though the audit report is not provided for the purposes of deciding whether to enter a specific transaction. In this context its purpose is to distinguish between a negligent audit which is merely the occasion for loss from a negligent audit which results in a liability to make good a loss.450D There are heads of loss to which the approach cannot be applied. An example is a claim for loss caused by payment of a dividend on the basis of inaccurate accounts and audit report.450E The dividend would have been paid had the information provided by the auditors been correct. But it does not follow that the amount paid cannot be recovered from the negligent auditors as damages, even though this would be an "information" case. That would be contrary to both intuition and established case law.450F On the other hand, where the auditor failed to detect the dishonest concealment of substantial losses and of the company's insolvency, the resulting failure to call the company's dishonest management to account and so to prevent the suffering of further losses over the next two years would be a consequence of the information being wrong and so recoverable.450G

450D *Assetco Plc v Grant Thornton LLP* [2020] EWCA Civ 1151, at [101] per David Richards LJ, with whom the other members of the Court of Appeal agreed.

450E See para.17-141 below.

450F *Assetco Plc v Grant Thornton LLP* [2020] EWCA Civ 1151, at [102] per David Richards LJ, with whom the other members of the Court of Appeal agreed. See also *BTI 2014 LLC v Pricewaterhouse-Coopers LLP* [2019] EWHC 3219 (Ch); [2020] P.N.L.R. 7, at [108]–[121].

450G Ibid at [108]–[110]. By way of contrast, the defendant auditors were not liable for the loss caused by a later fraud which was not of a type which they had failed to spot during their negligent audit: ibid. at [111].

(b)   Measure of Damages

Loss of a chance

Replace footnote 465 with:

17-137   465 See, e.g. *First Interstate Bank of California v Cohen Arnold* [1996] P.N.L.R. CA and *University of Keele v Price Waterhouse* [2003] EWHC 1595 (Ch); [2004] P.N.L.R. 8 (Hart J). The "lost chance" can include the chance to obtain a favourable decision from a court, although in some cases it may be appropriate to decide a point of law: *Altus Group (UK) Ltd v Baker Tilly Tax and Advisory Services LLP* [2015] EWHC 12 (Ch) (HH Judge Keyser sitting as a High Court Judge). In *Ryan Wealth Holdings Pty Ltd v Baumgartner* [2018] NSWSC 1502 damages were award for the loss of the chances (i) to bring a claim against a financial planning firm while it had professional indemnity insurance and (ii) to effect recoveries against persons liable to repay loans (including guarantors) at an earlier time when the prospects of recovery would have been greater. In *Assetco Plc v Grant Thornton LLP* [2020] EWCA Civ 1151 the Court of Appeal declined to overturn the assessment by the judge at trial that the relevant chance was 100%.

(d)   Avoidance of Double Recovery

Replace paragraph 17-147 with:

It is a long-established principle of company law that damages cannot be **17-147**
recovered by a shareholder in a company if the loss suffered was a reduction in the
value of their shareholding or in dividends paid by the company.[480] The scope and
rationale of the principle were less firmly established. They are now following the
decision of the Supreme Court in *Marex Financial Ltd v Sevilleja (All Party
Parliamentary Group on Fair Business Intervening).*[481] Following that decision the
following principles apply:

[480] *Prudential Assurance Co Ltd v Newman Industries Ltd (No.2)* [1982] Ch. 204; *Johnson v Gore Wood
& Co* [2002] 2 A.C. 1.

[481] [2020] UKSC 31; [2020] 3 W.L.R. 255.

1.   In many cases the cause of action (if any) will be vested in the company alone
     and not in its shareholders.[482] There may be other cases in which the cause of
     action (if any) is vested in the shareholders and not the company[483]: in those
     cases, the shareholders may sue for their own loss, measured by the diminu-
     tion in value of their shareholding. In neither of these two categories is there
     any problem of double recovery.
2.   However, there are cases in which duties are owed both to the company and
     to its shareholders, and in which both suffer loss. In such cases shareholders
     are not entitled to claim damages for a reduction in the value of their
     shareholding or in the dividends they received where such losses were caused
     by loss suffered by the company for which the company had a cause of
     action.[484]
3.   There are no exceptions in such circumstances, even where the wrongdoer has
     prevented the company from bringing its claim against him.[485]
4.   But this principle does not prevent a shareholder from claiming other losses.[486]
     In such cases the court will need to guard against double recovery, but it does
     so not by precluding a claim by the shareholder, but by a range of other
     means.[487]
5.   Nor does the principle extend to bar a claim by others, for example a creditor
     of the company, even though the company has a claim for substantially the
     same loss and whether the company did or did not bring a claim for its own
     loss.[488]

[482] *Caparo Industries Plc v Dickman* [1990] 2 A.C. 605; this principle was applied in *MAN
Nutzfahrzeuge AG v Freightliner Ltd* [2005] EWHC 2347 (Comm) at [324]–[327], Moore-Bick LJ.

[483] e.g. where the accountant has assumed a responsibility directly towards an investor. In *Dhillon v Siddiqui* [2008] EWHC 2020 (Ch), Livesey QC held that a claim by a shareholder was not barred where a
tax adviser owed a duty to the shareholder personally and owed no relevant duty to the company.

[484] *Marex Financial Ltd v Sevilleja (All Party Parliamentary Group on Fair Business Intervening)*
[2020] UKSC 31; [2020] 3 W.L.R. 255, approving the decision of the Court of Appeal in *Prudential
Assurance Co Ltd v Newman Industries Ltd (No.2)* [1982] Ch. 204 and the speech of Lord Bingham in
Johnson v Gore Wood & Co [2002] 2 A.C. 1, at 35–36. Lord Reed PSC, with whom Lord Hodge DPSC,
Lady Black and Lord Lloyd-Jones agreed, explained at [65]–[66] that in *Johnson v Gore Wood & Co*
the claim by the shareholder for loss caused by failure by the company to make payments into this pension fund was, in effect, a claim for a form of distribution of the company's profits and so the shareholder
could not recover damages for it.

[485] Ibid. at [69]–[71], overruling *Giles v Rhind* [2002] EWCA Civ 1428; [2003] Ch. 618 and *Perry v
Day* [2004] EWHC 3372 (Ch); [2004] 2 B.C.L.C. 405.

[486] Ibid. at [72]–[78], disapproving dicta of Lord Millett in *Johnson v Gore Wood & Co* [2002] 2 A.C.
1, at 62–67 and overruling *Gardner v Parker* [2004] EWCA Civ 781; [2004] 2 B.C.L.C. 554.

[487] See the judgment of Lord Reed PSC in *Marex Financial Ltd v Sevilleja (All Party Parliamentary Group on Fair Business Intervening)* [2020] UKSC 31; [2020] 3 W.L.R. 255, at [2]–[7].

[488] *Marex Financial Ltd v Sevilleja (All Party Parliamentary Group on Fair Business Intervening)* [2020] UKSC 31; [2020] 3 W.L.R. 255.

Replace paragraph 17-148 (to incorporate amendments to text) with:

17-148   In *Johnson v Gore Wood*,[489] the House of Lords held that the following heads of loss were arguably recoverable by the shareholder: sums invested in the company and lost; the cost of personal borrowings (in principle recoverable, provided that this was not a disguised claim for loss of dividend); loss of shares which were transferred to a lender as security for the personal borrowing; and additional tax liability of the shareholder. However a claim to diminution in the value of his pension was struck out, in so far as it related to payments which the company would have made into a pension fund for the shareholder, on the ground that this was merely a reflection of the company's loss, being, in substance, a claim for a reduction in a distribution by the company to the shareholder.

[489]   [2002] 2 A.C. 1.

(e)   Contributory Negligence and Contribution Proceedings

General

Replace paragraph 17-149 (to incorporate new text following "the accountant's retainer." at the end of the paragraph and an amendment to footnote 493) with:

17-149   Contributory negligence is a defence provided by statute[490] which enables the court to reduce the damages otherwise due from the defendant, based on the share of the claimant in the responsibility for the damage. The precise reduction will depend on the facts of the particular case. The defence is frequently advanced on behalf of accountants in claims against them.[491] It has been held that the defence is available, not merely where the contributory negligence prevented or hindered an auditor from carrying out his own duties, but also where the claimant failed generally to look after its own interests.[492] As in any professional negligence claim, the standard expected of the claimant will depend upon the factual matrix, in particular the claimant's level of experience and understanding, the accountant's reasonable perception of the same and the scope of the accountant's retainer.[493] When deciding what reduction to make to take account of the claimant's contributory negligence it is necessary to consider both the relative degrees of blameworthiness of the parties and the relative causative potency of their respective negligence for the losses for which damages are being awarded.[493A]

[490]   Law Reform (Contributory Negligence) Act 1945. See paras 5-172 to 5-179 above.

[491]   e.g. *De Meza v Apple* [1975] 1 Lloyd's Rep. 498 (damages reduced by 30%); *Slattery v Moore Stephens* [2004] P.N.L.R. 14; [2003] EWHC 1869 (Ch) (damages reduced by 50% for claimant's negligence in failing to query a tax refund which would have revealed his mistake in assuming that he was being receiving money offshore).

In the Australian case of *Pech v Tilgals* (1994) 28 A.T.R. 197, the claim against the defendant accountants for negligent failure to prepare and complete accurate income tax returns was reduced by 20% for contributory negligence on account of the claimant's failure to read the tax returns before signing them and to check their accuracy.

In the Australian case of *Daniels v Anderson* (1995) 16 A.C.S.R. 607 at 720–733, the CA of NSW held that the management of the company was negligent in disregarding advice it was given, in failing to set up or implement proper management and control structures and in failing to keep proper records, that the chief executive was negligent in failing to heed warnings about weaknesses in the system and that the board was negligent in failing to set policy to set up or implement a proper system of reporting to the board; nevertheless the auditor's negligence was of a higher order, in that he knew that there were no internal controls in existence, that the records were a shambles, and that no steps had been taken to rectify these defects; the court reduced the damages by one third for contributory negligence, but would have made a bigger reduction, but for the later breaches compounding the auditor's original negligence.

In the New Zealand case of *Dairy Containers v NZI Ltd* [1995] 2 N.Z.L.R. 30, Thomas J held that the directors had failed in their primary duty to monitor the business and management of the company and had thereby created an environment in which fraud could thrive; damages were reduced by 40% for contributory negligence.

In the Australian case of *Duke Group Ltd v Pilmer* (1999) 31 A.C.S.R. 213 S. Ct of S. Aus, Full Court at 326–336, the company, through its directors, was at fault, first in knowingly providing unreliable information to the accountant for the purpose of the valuation, even though it was the accountant's duty to check that information, and secondly in accepting a valuation when the directors, being sophisticated businessmen, must have known that it was wrong; damages were reduced by 35% for contributory negligence. (Reversed in part, but not on this point: [2001] 2 B.C.L.C. 773.)

See also *Mirage Entertainment Corp Ltd v Arthur Young* (1992) 6 N.Z.C.L.C. 68 at 213 (negligence by auditors in valuing assets: wrong accounting methodology; reduction of 40%). See also the following Canadian cases: *West Coast Finance Ltd v Gunderson, Stokes, Walton & Co* (1974) 44 D.L.R. (3d) 233 (50% reduction, but finding of liability reversed on appeal: (1975) 56 D.L.R. 461); *HE Kane Agencies Ltd v Coopers & Lybrand* (1983) 23 C.C.L.T. 233; (1985) 17 D.L.R. (4th) 695 (50% reduction); *Revelstoke Credit Union v Miller* (1984) 28 C.C.L.T. 17; (1984) 2 W.W.R. 297 (15% reduction); and *Bloor Italian Gifts Ltd v Dixon* (2000) 48 O.R. (3d) 760 (50% reduction).

[492] In other words, the contributory negligence does not need to be causally connected to the defendant's negligence; it is sufficient that it is a cause of the same damage: *Dairy Containers Ltd v NZI Bank Ltd* [1995] 2 N.Z.L.R. 30 at 74; see also *Platform Home Loans Ltd v Oyston Shipways Ltd* [2000] 2 A.C. 195 at 215 per Lord Millett (a valuer's case).

[493] Contrast *De Meza v Apple* [1975] 1 Lloyd's Rep. 498 (court reduced damages by 30% because client should have noticed an obvious arithmetical error) with *Walker v Hungerfords* (1987) 44 S.A.S.R. 532 at 553–554, Bollen J, upheld on appeal: 19 A.T.R. 745 at 747 Supreme Court of Southern Australia, Full Court (no reduction for arithmetical error made by clerk employed by company, since it was reasonable for him to assume that any errors would be checked by the accountant). See also *Craig v Troy* (1997) 16 W.A.R. 96 Supreme Court of Western Australia (no contributory negligence where accountant informed client of relevant facts but failed to explain their significance). See also *Cook v Green* [2009] Lloyds Rep. P.N. 5, HH Judge Pelling QC sitting as a High Court Judge. Even where the accountant/auditor gives highly technical advice it may be that the company's management will have been negligent in failing to spot flaws in that advice of which it should have been aware (*Manchester Building Society v Grant Thornton UK LLP* [2018] EWHC 963 (Comm); [2018] P.N.L.R. 27, at [251] per Teare J).

[493A] *Manchester Building Society v Grant Thornton UK LLP* [2018] EWHC 963 (Comm); [2018] P.N.L.R. 27, at [243] per Teare J. And even an unsophisticated client will have his damages reduced to take account of his imprudence, albeit the extent of that reduction might be limited by his reliance on the defendant accountant (*Cam & Bear Pty Ltd v McGoldrick* [2018] NSWCA 110; damages reduced by 10%).

Claims against auditors

Replace footnote 500 with:

[500] It was argued on behalf of the company that a special rule of attribution should be fashioned on the **17-151** ground that the auditors were "insiders", so that the Leeson's fraudulent representations were not attributed to the company. The judge rejected this argument both on the trial of a preliminary issue ([2002] P.N.L.R. 39; [2002] EWHC 461 Ch at [155]–[159]) and at the full hearing (at [718]–[719]).See the discussion of "victim or villain?" at para.17-100, above. However, in *Deloitte & Touche (now continued as Deloitte LLP) v Livent Inc* [2017] SCC 63; (2017) 416 D.L.R. (4th) 32 the majority of the Supreme Court of Canada held that damages should not be reduced by reason of the fraud of the claimant company's directors, it being the duty of the defendant auditors to have detected that fraud. To reduce damages on that basis "would undermine the very purpose of establishing a duty of care".

CHAPTER 20

INFORMATION TECHNOLOGY PROFESSIONALS

1. GENERAL

(b) Can Software be Characterised as Goods

Replace footnote 10 with:

20-005 [10] In *Southwark LBC v IBM UK Ltd* [2011] EWHC 459 (TCC) Akenhead J stated obiter that there was no reason in principle why software could not be goods at least where they were transferred on disk. In *Fern Computer Consultancy Ltd v Intergraph Cadworx & Analysis Solutions Inc* [2014] EWHC 2908 (Ch), Mann J expressed support, obiter, for the views of Akenhead J.

Replace footnote 13 with:

[13] In his decision at first instance in *The Software Incubator Ltd v Computer Associations UK Ltd* [2016] EWHC 1587 (QB); [2018] 2 All E.R. (Comm) 398 (later reversed in part by the Court of Appeal), HH Judge Waksman QC stated at [52] of the judgment that "there is no logic in making the status of software as goods (or not) turn on the medium by which they were delivered or installed".

After the fourth paragraph, add new paragraphs:

The case of *St Albans City and DC v International Computers Ltd* was considered by the Court of Appeal in *Computer Associates UK Ltd v Software Incubator Ltd.*[13A] The case concerned the correct interpretation of reg.17 of the Commercial Agents (Council Directive) Regulations 1993, and whether for the purposes of the Regulations "goods" could include software which had been supplied electronically.

[13A] [2018] EWCA Civ 518; [2018] 2 All E.R. (Comm) 398.

Reversing the decision at first instance on this issue, the Court of Appeal held that such software did not constitute "goods" within the meaning of the Regulations. In reaching that decision, giving the leading judgment, Gloster LJ surveyed relevant domestic, Commonwealth, and EU case law, and considered a number of leading academic texts.

Gloster LJ noted that it was difficult, as a matter of principle, to see why software should be treated differently depending on the mode of its delivery. She also expressed "sympathy" with the view that the failure to treat software and other intangibles as goods put the law out of step with recent technological developments.

However, the Court considered itself bound by precedent to interpret the Regulations to exclude software. In doing so, the Court stated that it was relevant that the Regulations were not aimed at consumers, but commercial parties, who were not in need of the protection which would be provided by adopting a more expansive interpretation of "goods".

2. DUTIES

(a) Duties to Client

(vi) The Importance of Co-operation Between the Parties

Replace footnote 71 with:

⁷¹ unreported 1 March 2000 QBD TCC, HH Judge Toulmin CMG QC. In *Triple Point Technology, Inc. v PTT Public Company Ltd* [2017] EWHC 2178 (TCC) the judge at first instance held that the findings in *Anglo Group* as to implied terms turned on the specific facts of *Anglo Group* and did not establish a general principle applicable to all software contracts. A further example of a court implying a duty to co-operate in the context of a contract to supply software and associated services is found in *Sanderson Ltd v Simton Food Products Ltd* [2019] EWHC 442 (TCC); [2019] B.L.R. 260.

20-031

To the end of the first sentence, after "time of delivery.", add new footnote 74A:

⁷⁴ᴬ In *Triple Point Technology, Inc. v PTT Public Company Ltd* [2017] EWHC 2178 (TCC) the judge at first instance distinguished the decision in *Anglo Group* on the basis that it concerned a standard system with no customisation to the purchaser's requirements which was not the same as the instant case. The judge further held that the scope of a duty to co-operate and whether there was any breach must be considered in the context of the specific contract and project.

20-034

(ix) User's Operation Manual

Replace paragraph 20-40 with:

Usually a computer or software supply contract will also be subject to an implied term that both a system specification (detailing the technical specification and capabilities of the system, and demonstrating how it meets the functional requirements) and a user manual will be supplied to the customer. Moreover the user manual should be in a form which the intended users will understand. The International Organisation for Standardization's ISO/IEC 26514:2008 titled "Systems and software engineering – Requirements for designers and developers of user documentation" contains recommendations for the preparation and content of user manuals and provides helpful guidance as to the likely extent of this obligation—both in relation to onscreen and printed documentation.

20-040

6. EXCLUSION AND LIMITATION OF LIABILITY

To the end of the second sentence after "in IT contracts.", add new footnote 180A:

¹⁸⁰ᴬ In *Persimmon Homes Ltd v Ove Arup and Partners Ltd* [2017] EWCA Civ 373; [2017] P.N.L.R. 29 the Court of Appeal recognised that exemption clauses were part of the contractual apparatus for distributing risk in major construction contracts and stated that the courts should not approach such clauses with horror and a mindset determined to cut them down. It seems likely that a similar approach will be adopted in relation to major IT contracts.

20-114

CHAPTER 21

PATENT ATTORNEYS AND TRADE MARK ATTORNEYS

1. GENERAL

Replace paragraph 21-001 with:

There are relatively few reported cases against patent attorneys or trade mark **21-001**
attorneys.[2] Reference should therefore be made to the general principles to be applied to professionals, set out in the first part of this work, and, given the analogous nature of much of their work, to the chapters on solicitors and barristers.[3] The relevant professional bodies in the UK are the Chartered Institute of Patent Attorneys and the Chartered Institute of Trade Mark Attorneys.[4]

[2] In part this is due to the small size of the profession. There are about 2,200 registered patent attorneys and 1,000 registered trade mark attorneys, with around 300 of these being dually qualified.

[3] See Chs 11 and 12. Birss J agreed with this analogy and cited para.21-001 of *Jackson & Powell* (7th edn) at [24] of his judgment in *Baillie v Bromhead & Co* [2014] EWHC 2149 (Ch); [2015] F.S.R. 16.

[4] The CIPA website, *http://www.CIPA.org.uk* [Accessed 4 October 2019] and the CITMA website, *http://www.CITMA.org.uk* [Accessed 4 October 2019], both contain useful reference material. Regard should also be had to the website of the Intellectual Property Regulation Board, *http://www.ipreg.org.uk* [Accessed 4 October 2019].

(b) The Function of a Trade Mark Attorney

Replace subsection title footnote 22 with: **21-006**

[22] For the law relating to trademarks, see *Kerly's Law of Trade Marks and Tradenames*, 16th edn (2017).

CHAPTER 22

ART PROFESSIONALS

1.   GENERAL

Professional regulation

After paragraph 22-006, add new paragraph 22-006A:

Auctioneers may also voluntarily join the National Association of Valuers and   **22-006A**
Auctioneers (NAVA), an organisation that aims to promote professionalism in the
auctioneering and valuation industry. In February 2017, NAVA combined with four
other associations (the Association of Residential Letting Agents (ARLA); the
National Association of Estate Agents (NAEA); the Institution of Commercial &
Business Agents (ICBA) and the Association of Professional Inventory Providers
(APIP)) to form "Propertymark". NAVA is now known as "NAVA Propertymark"
and auctioneer members are subject to Propertymark's Conduct and Membership
Rules and disciplinary procedures (see *http://www.propertymark.co.uk/media/
1045366/conduct-and-membership-rules.pdf* [Accessed 17 October 2017]). NAVA
Propertymark requires all members involved in conducting auctions where either

a consumer or a small business is involved to be registered with an appropriate Ombudsman scheme.

(a) Duties to Client

(i) Contractual Duties

Replace paragraph 22-008 (to incorporate amendments to footnotes 9 and 10) with:

22-008   Where property is offered for sale by auction, the terms on which the auction is to be conducted will be set out in the catalogue and should be on display to the public at the auction premises and reproduced on relevant documents.[4] The extent to which these standard terms may affect the statutory terms and conditions under which contracts of sale are made is now more complex following the coming into force of the Consumer Rights Act 2015. In general, Chapter 2 of the Act[5] applies where the goods are sold under a contract by a trader to supply goods to a consumer.[6] Both art dealers and auctioneers will be traders for these purposes. However, s.2(5) of the 2015 Act provides that, with certain limited exceptions, a person is not a consumer in relation to the purchase of second hand goods at public auction provided that individuals have the opportunity of attending the sale in person. The exceptions include, for example, s.11(4) under which information required by para.(a) of Sch.1 or Sch.2 to the Consumer Contracts (Information, Cancellation and Additional Charges) Regulations[7] (main characteristics of goods) is to be treated as a term of the contract.[8] Part 1 Chapter 4, of the Act, dealing with a contract for the supply of services, will apply where an art professional supplies services to a consumer. There are, however, no English cases dealing with a situation where an art professional simply supplies services for a fee. Finally, Pt 2 of the Act, which deals with Unfair Terms, will apply to contracts between a trader and a consumer, that is an individual acting "for purposes wholly or mainly outside the individual's trade, business, craft or profession".[9] It is not the function of this book to set out the laws on the sale of goods.[10] However, the terms and descriptions applied to such goods will affect the question as to whether a sale is one by description and, indeed, whether any description amounts to a condition of the contract.

[4] See the guidance at s.1.6 of the RICS Guidance Note referred to at para.22-006 above.

[5] Dealing with contracts for the sale of goods.

[6] See s.3 of the Consumer Rights Act 2015.

[7] SI 2013/3134.

[8] See also ss.12, 28 and 29 of the Act which are also applicable.

[9] See subs.2(5) where the definition of "consumer" is set out. Although this definition expressly applies to Pt 1 of the Act, it would appear also to apply to Pt 2 where the same word is used in the absence of a separate and competing definition. Generally, as to the Consumer Rights Act 2015 Pt 1 Chapter 4 ("Services") and Pt II ("Unfair Terms"), see paras 2-021 to 2-023, 3-028 and 5-025 to 5-029.

[10] For which purpose see *Benjamin's Sale of Goods*, 10th edn.

Replace footnote 14 with:

22-010   [14] For an example see *Hoos v Weber* (1974) 232 E.G. 1379. For facts see paras 22-020 and 22-028 below.

(b) Duties to Third Parties

Replace paragraph 22-014 with:

22-014   Given that auction particulars will almost invariably contain such a disclaimer, the real issue is likely to be as to whether such disclaimer is reasonable so as to satisfy the requirements of Pt 2 of the Consumer Rights Act 2015 where applicable.[23] It may also still be relevant to consider s.2(2) of the Unfair Contract Terms Act 1977 when dealing with a non-consumer where liability for misrepresentation is sought to be excluded.[24] The jurisprudence considering the Unfair Contract Terms Act is very limited. In *Morin v Bonhams & Brooks*,[25] the judge held that, had the relevant matter been governed by English law he would have found that a claimant who had brought a Ferrari from auctioneers in Monaco had overcome the fairly low hurdle of showing that that were reasonable prospects of success in a claim on the basis of a misdescription in auction particulars.

[23] This Act applies to contracts between a trader and a consumer. Although a person is not, in general, a consumer for the purposes of a sale of second-hand goods at public auction when considering Chapter 2 of the Act (dealing with goods), there is no such general exemption from Pt 2 of the Act dealing with Unfair Terms.

[24] This is because of the way in which Sch.4 to the 2015 Act amends s.3 of the Misrepresentation Act 1967.

[25] [2003] I.L.Pr 25 (Jonathan Hirst QC sitting as a Deputy High Court Judge).

(c)   The Standard of Care and Skill

(i)   Reasonable Standard

Replace footnote 34 with:

[34] See *Harlingdon Enterprises v C. Hull Fine Art* [1991] 1 Q.B. 564 at 577. In *Avrora Fine Arts Investment Ltd v Christie, Manson & Woods Ltd* [2012] P.N.L.R. 35, the placing of the artist's letters in capitals denoted that a warranty was being provided that the work was, in fact, by the artist concerned.   **22-018**

3.   DAMAGES

(b)   Measure of Damages

(ii)   Negligent Auction Description of Auction Property

Replace footnote 67 with:

[67] [1997] A.C. 191. The case is frequently referred to by the name of the parties in the first claim, *South Australia Asset Management Corp v York Montague Ltd* as abbreviated to "SAAMCO". See paras 3-003 and 3-003A above and references there to discussion of the case in other chapters.   **22-037**